Midnight in Sicily
Praise from the Australian press

'I loved this book. It left me in a sweet and sour mood of exultation, grief, despair and hope which lasted for many days.'

Peter Goldsworthy, *Australian Book Review*

'Peter Robb is the greatest discovery of the year. His book has the vivid detail of the very best writing . . . A debut as good as this must lead to a notable career.'

Robert Gray, *Sydney Morning Herald*

'I cannot recommend a better book to anyone interested in Italy . . . it is written from the inside, with a refined understanding of the psyche of Southern Italy . . . a triumph.'

Stefano de Pieri, *Adelaide Review*

'One of the most enjoyable books to be published this year.'
Jamie Grant, *Who Weekly*

'It leaves you with a portrait of Sicily so sharp and detailed that you feel as if you've made the trip and done the research and interviewing yourself . . . [Robb is] a master of the apt word and phrase . . . a new and original Australian writer.'
Peter Corris, *Sydney Morning Herald*

'Robb and I lived for four of the same years in Italy. His book showed me how much I had missed in not knowing him and I strongly recommend you not to miss it now.'

Duncan Campbell, former Australian ambassador to Italy, *Australian's Review of Books*

MIDNIGHT
IN SICILY

MIDNIGHT IN SICILY

On Art, Food, History, Travel,
and La Cosa Nostra

Peter Robb

FABER AND FABER, INC.
BOSTON · LONDON

First published in the United States in 1998 by
Faber and Faber, Inc., 53 Shore Road, Winchester, MA 01890.
Originally published in Australia in 1996 by Duffy & Snellgrove,
PO 177 Potts Point NSW 2011.

Copyright © 1996 by Peter Robb

Library of Congress Cataloging-in-Publication Data

Robb, Peter.
　　Midnight in Sicily / Peter Robb.
　　　p.　　cm.
　　Includes bibliographical references (p. 321)
　　ISBN 0-571-19932-1
　　　1. Political corruption—Italy—Sicily.　2. Sicily (Italy)—
Politics and government—1945–　3. Mafia—Italy—Sicily.
4. Political corruption—Italy.　5. Italy—Politics and
government—1976–1994.　6. Organized crime investigation
—Italy.　7. Andreotti, Giulio.　I. Title.
DG869.3.R63　1998
945'.8092—dc21　　　　　　　　　　　　　　97-41778
　　　　　　　　　　　　　　　　　　　　　　CIP

Jacket design by Adrian Morgan at Red Letter Design

Printed in the United States of America

I.M.

WANDA JAMROZIK

MANY PEOPLE helped in large and small ways with my visit to Italy in 1995. Some are named in the account that follows, others not. I'd particularly like to thank Letizia Battaglia, Angelo Benivegna, Pippo Bisso, Giorgio Bocca, Michael Burgoyne, Duncan Campbell, Gian Carlo Caselli, Maria Teresa Chialant, the staff of *Corriere della Sera*, Anna Maria Currao, Adrian Deamer, Claudio Fabio De Nardis, Michael Duffy, Enzuccia, the staff of *L'Espresso*, Renata La Rovere, Dora Lo Cascio, Guido Lo Forte, Marco Lucchi, Pasquale Marchese, Vincenzo Marchese, Marta Marzotto, Mara Mele, Ady Mineo, Saverio Montalbano, Leoluca Orlando, Lina Panetta, Tullio Pironti, Gordon Poole, Anna Puglisi, the staff of Libreria Feltrinelli Napoli [Regina, Luigi, Paolo, Carlo, Nino, Claudio, Gennaro, Pina], Clara Salvo, the friends of the Sant'Andrea [Bartolo, Dario, Emiliano, Nabil, Stefania, Totò], Umberto Santino, Roberto Scarpinato, Shobha, Alex Snellgrove, Max Suich, Rosario Würzburger. Since nobody was quite sure what I was up to, no one should feel implicated in the result and I hope no one will feel kindness has been compromised. Anyone whose name should figure above and doesn't I ask to forgive the omission.

PR

CONTENTS

History isn't
the devastating bulldozer they say it is.
It leaves underpasses, crypts, holes
and hiding places. There are survivors.
History's also benevolent: destroys
as much as it can: overdoing it, sure,
would be better, but history's short
of news, doesn't carry out all its vendettas.

History scrapes the bottom
like a drag net
with a few rips and more than one fish escapes.
Sometimes you meet the ectoplasm
of an escapee and he doesn't seem particularly happy.
He doesn't know he's outside, nobody told him.
The others, in the bag, think
they're freer than him.

Eugenio Montale, *Satura*

When it's night time in Italy
it's Wednesday over here.
When it's midnight in Sicily ...

The Everly Brothers, *Night Time in Italy*

COLA PESCE was always playing in the sea and one day his mother said in exasperation she hoped he'd turn into a fish. Which he practically did, and stayed under water for days at a time. Long distances he travelled in the belly of a big fish, cutting his way out with his knife when he reached his destination.

When the king wanted to know what the sea bed was like, Cola Pesce explored it and told the king there were gardens of coral, precious stones lying on the sand, and here and there heaps of treasure, weapons, people's skeletons, wrecked ships. He went down into the caves under the castel dell'Ovo in Naples and brought up fistfuls of jewels. The king asked how the island of Sicily stayed above the water, and Cola Pesce reported that it was held up by three huge pillars, one of which was broken.

One day the king wanted to know how far down Cola Pesce could go in the sea, and told him to bring up a cannonball shot from the lighthouse at Messina. Cola Pesce said he'd dive if the king insisted, though he thought he'd never come up again. The king insisted, and Cola Pesce dived after the cannonball as it sank, fast enough and deep enough to grab it finally. When he looked up, though, the water above him was now hard and still and closed like marble. He found he was in an empty waterless space and unable to swim and there he stayed forever.

Cola Pesce or Nick Fish has a long history. In Naples they said he was figured on the carved relief of the part man part fish from a Greek or Roman temple that was dredged up from the harbour in the late middle ages. In Sicily his memory receded to Norman times, recorded in the eleventh century by people who'd heard the story from people who'd personally known Cola Pesce himself. Whether he came from Messina or Palermo or Naples, Cola Pesce belonged to that southern part of Italy, hot, dry, sea-girt, wracked by earthquake and eruption, that Italians call the Mezzogiorno, that point in the Mediterranean where Europe is no longer entirely Europe but also Africa, Asia, America. The Mezzogiorno is the furthest part of Italy from Europe and the nearest to the rest of the world.

Cola Pesce had stayed in my mind for years and years, almost as long as Montale's poem about history's interstices and escape routes, with which, in the image of entrapment under water, it ended up coinciding. Cola Pesce was in my mind now, as I came back to Italy, drawn by curiosity and fear, came back to Naples and boarded the night boat for Palermo, preparing to dive into the past, to explore things once half glimpsed and half imagined, desiring knowledge but afraid of entrapment down there in a dire and lifeless mental world of power. I wanted to know how deep the sea was, and what was holding up Sicily. Ready to dive and hoping to surface again, or at least find a rip in the net.

I

A MARKET

I WOKE with a start about an hour after midnight. The boat was still throbbing doggedly through the dark but I couldn't breathe. The roof of the cabin was a few inches above my face and there was no oxygen in the damp salty fug that was gathered there. The passengers on the other three bunks made no sound in the darkness. Maybe they were dead. I sweated, pressed and paralyzed, buried alive. Deep regular breathing brought no calm. I scrambled down without the ladder, putting a foot on an unseen face. The dim corridor was hardly better. The fug was thick with ship's smell of engine oil and paint and stale brine. I found a companionway up to a deck where I waited till dawn among the lifeboats, still oppressed by the visible and palpable marine haze but breathing. All the oxygen seemed leached from the air on this fine and starless night.

Summer hadn't yet broken. The voyage south brought back other unbearable summer nights in the Mezzogiorno. The canopy of that heavy, airless dead stillness was over us like a fallen tent. In the morning, back in the cabin, I saw someone had screwed shut the cabin's ventilation duct. Everybody seemed to have had a bad crossing. As we eased up to the dock in Palermo smartly dressed passengers were pressing like desperate refugees or immigrants at the place the gangplank would reach. I tried to imagine the place the arriving Greeks and Phoenicians called Panormus, *all port*, three thousand years ago. A wheelchair with a slavering lolling-headed idiot was shoved into this edgy illtempered crowd, ready to be first off. A cluster of nuns was poised for flight.

The yellow taxis lined up on the dock were all gone when I disembarked. After a coffee, several coffees, near the waterfront, I trudged up toward the centre of Palermo, past a showroom with half a dozen new red Ferraris on display. A little further on the carabinieri had set up a road block. There were carabinieri and soldiers, a lot of them, and fretful. The little hotel on via Maqueda, the hotel opposite the *art nouveau* kiosk, was abandoned. The windows on the first floor were shuttered or glassless, and the peeling wooden door on the street swung open on ruins. Retracing my steps, I found another place, in a third floor warren back toward the harbour, reached in a rattling metal cage. The room was above a coffee wholesaler's, and full of the smell of roasting coffee. Down the road soldiers in camouflage were standing guard with legs wide apart at the entrance to a building of no evident interest. One of them caught my oblique glance as I passed and slipped the safety catch on his machine gun. Seven thousand troops had arrived in Sicily from *the continent* in the summer of 1992. Three years later the troops were still there. In a certain view, Operation Sicilian Vespers was yet another foreign occupation, and an oddly named one, since it recalled the bloody thirteenth-century uprising by the locals against the occupying Angevins from France, when thousands were massacred in days.

The new place was even closer to where I was headed, which was the *panelleria*. A lot of the best things in Sicily have lasted since Arab days, and fried slices of chick pea flour must have been around since the ninth century. I've never seen *panelle* outside of Palermo, and hardly ever outside the Vucciria market. The *panelleria* was down in a side alley of the tiny market square, a small bare room on the street with a table for cutting out the small rectangles of chick pea dough and a vat of hot oil to fry them in. The *panelle* were a cheap and austere food, but they were surrounded by abundance.

> As in certain sweet and savoury dishes that contain everything, where the savoury merges into the sweet and the sweet into the savoury, dishes that seem to realize a hungry man's dream, so the most abundant and overflowing markets, the richest and most festive and the most baroque, are those of the poor countries where the spectre of hunger is always hovering ... in Baghdad, Valencia or Palermo, a market is more than a market ... it's a vision, a dream, a mirage.

The market the Sicilian writer Leonardo Sciascia had in mind here was the Vucciria. It'd been like a dream when I first wandered into it at the end of an earlier summer years and years ago. Whenever I went back to Palermo, the market was the first place I headed for. It was a way of getting my bearings. That first time, twenty-one years earlier, I'd arrived in Palermo mapless from Enna, in the high parched bleak centre of the island, the poorest province in Italy, and strayed through the ruins of the old city. The old city centre of Palermo had been gutted by bombs in 1943, in the months before the allied armies invaded Sicily. A lot of its finest buildings, palazzi of the seventeenth and eighteenth centuries, the family homes of the Sicilian nobility, about a third of them, were destroyed.

Other European cities had been bombed in the forties, and many worse than Palermo. What was unique to Palermo was that the ruins of the old city were still ruins, thirty years, fifty years on. Staircases still led nowhere, sky shone out of the windows, clumps of weed lodged in the walls, wooden roof beams jutted toward the sky like the ribs of rotting carcasses. Slowly, even the parts that had survived were crumbling into rubble. There were more people living there in the early seventies, in the buildings that were still intact, or partly so, and it must've been a Monday because the washing was strung across the alleys like flags, whipping and billowing everywhere in the the powerful sun. It was a very hot day. When I stepped into the Vucciria from a narrow crooked alley, it was a move from the wings on to a stage set in mid-show. The noon sun fell vertically on the tiny space and the stallkeepers had winched out brown canvas awnings. The piazzetta of the Vucciria market was so small and deep that on one side you climbed a flight of stone steps to leave, and when the awnings were out on all sides the sky was covered and everyone was inside a kind of circus tent. The sun beating on the reddish canvas filled the space with a warm diffused light, and the canvas trapped and intensified the odours of the food that was steeply massed on display. It was the belly of Palermo and the heart too. The visual centre of the close and brilliant and almost claustrophobic indoor outdoor theatre was the big fish. On the table were the black eye and the silver rapier and the tail's arc of a swordfish whose body had been mostly sliced away, and blocks of blood red tuna.

The swordfish and tuna were flanked by many smaller fish, striped mackerel and fat sardines, and squid and prawns and octopus and cuttlefish. I don't remember seeing shellfish. I remember how the diffused red light of the market enhanced the translucent red of the big fishes' flesh and the silver glitter of the smaller ones' skins. The meat was bright red too, redder than usual in this hot muted light. The eye

17

passed more rapidly over the rows of flayed kids' heads with melancholy deep black eyes. There were coils of pearly intestines. There was horse flesh and beef and pork and veal and skinny Mediterranean kids and lambs. There were pale yellow chooks strung up by their bright yellow feet, red crest downmost, and batteries of eggs. The fruit and vegetables were summer things with the sun in their colours. Purple and black eggplant, light green and dark green zucchine, red and yellow peppers, boxes of eggshaped San Marzano tomatoes. Spiked Indian figs with a spreading blush, grapes, black, purple, yellow and white, long yellow honeydew melons, round furrowed canteloupes, slashed wedges of watermelon in red, white and green and studded with big black seeds, yellow peaches and *percocche*, purple figs and green figs, little freckled apricots. There were sprigs of leaves around the fruit.

It may have been too early for the oranges, but the lemons were there. There may have been only one kind of fig. *On that day*. There was bread, cheeses, sacks of chick peas, lentils, white beans and nuts, ranks of bottled oil and tinned tomatoes, big open tins of salted anchovies and tuna in oil, blocks of dried tuna roe, there were wine shops and coffee bars. Fat produce from the north, hams and salami, parmesans and gorgonzolas, was harder to find. The *odori* were in an alley just off the piazza, a bravura massing of thyme and oregano and marjoram and rosemary in dusty drying clumps, chilli bushes uprooted with their leaves still green and the fruit fat, larger chillies dried a dark laquered red and hanging like cords of horns against the evil eye, plaited ropes of garlic, papery white and tinged with purple, dried mud clinging to their root hairs, vats of olives, black and green, large and small, in brine and oil, spiced and not. The booth smelt like a hill in Sardinia at dawn in summer, a concentrate of fragrant Mediterranean scrub.

I list these things now because a lot of them were already gone by 1995. The Vucciria in the summer of 1995 was a slowly fading and diminished place, and words in any case seemed inadequate to recall the lost plenty. What you once found in the Vucciria, and all the markets of the south, were the dense, scarred, irregular and deeply coloured fruit of backbreaking labour. The meaning of this produce was in how it looked, and that was beyond semantics. It might have been caught in an image. Taste, texture, what each thing might become when cooked and combined, these were also matters for the eye. Flavour was form and colour. Freshness translated into the gleam in a fish's eye, the sheen on an eggplant, the resilience of a leaf, the moistness of a speck of manure still clinging to an egg.

There was no shouting at the Vucciria. We weren't in Naples. People in Sicily moved with quiet purpose, and the cadence when you heard it was reproachful, not protesting. The silence of buyers and sellers, housewives and growers and labourers, is enhanced now by the dreamlike patina of memory and the underwater feel of that heaped earthly plenty, and the sea's too, glowing under canvas. And high above the narrow alleys, the faded cottons whipping against the blinding sun. Years after wandering into this *hungry man's dream*, I learnt that this massed harvest was at that very same time being fixed in an image, though not in Palermo and not from life. It was taking form in the summer of 1974 as a painter's dream in the far north of Italy, and in writing the following winter about the sweet and savoury markets of the Mediterranean, Leonardo Sciascia was describing not the market itself, but this painting of *The Vucciria*, this dream, by Sciascia's friend the famous Sicilian painter Renato Guttuso, on the occasion of the first showing in Palermo of the painting that would thereafter be the icon of Palermo, the city's ideal image of itself. In the way of images, it represented, that dream of Mediterranean plenty and a people who gathered and consumed it, something that was no longer real. The market and the old city it fed were dwindling and fading as Guttuso painted them from miles away. If I hadn't seen the market for myself that first summer day when I was hungry, I'd've doubted now whether it ever existed.

Guttuso's name prompted a further twenty-year leap back in time, to 1954. In England 1954 wasn't a specially good year, half way down from coronation euphoria to the humiliation of Suez. But food rationing ended in 1954, and at the year's close Evelyn Waugh named Elizabeth David's *Italian Food* as one of the year's two books that had given him most pleasure. Elizabeth David was *stunned by the compliment*, coming as it did from *Mr Evelyn Waugh, a writer whose books have given me more pleasure than I have power to acknowledge*. She was particularly gratified because the book had given her a lot of trouble. *All that pasta. We've got enough stodge here already*, her English friends had said as she set off to garner material. First maddened by the preindustrial imprecision of Italian cooks, then stirred by *a fever to communicate*, finally returning home to be chilled by her publisher's indifference, she'd felt her two years' work was in vain. Then Renato Guttuso's promised illustrations, long awaited, started arriving one or two at a time from Rome.

> To have had for my book those magnificent drawings and the dazzling jacket picture ... I would have gone through the whole agony of writing it all over again.

What she liked was their unsentimentality. The cheap battered aluminium pans, the ravenous pasta eaters, the glistening fatty salame, the bunches of artichokes: everything was everyday,

> but by Guttuso invested with a quite dangerously blazing vitality,
> for this artist even the straw round the neck of a wine flask is unrav-
> elling itself in a manner positively threatening in its purpose and
> intensity.

Elizabeth David was as good a critic here of drawing as of cooking. Her
book matched its illustrations. *Italian Food* was a great hymn to the
intensity of everyday eating pleasures and a sustained denunciation of
Englishness in food, a denunciation whose fury seemed to intensify in
each new edition's revisions. Forty years after Elizabeth David's book
appeared, its author was lately dead and *Italian Food* was still in print and
still made an exhilarating read. The 1995 edition still included
Elizabeth David's passionate praise of Guttuso, but the object of her
praise was now gone. The new edition eliminated his illustrations.
Only the brilliant lemons remained, in colour on the Penguin cover.
The others had been replaced by plates from a sixteenth century cooking manual. Another tiny step had been taken in Guttuso's progress
toward oblivion. Twenty something years ago he'd been at the height
of his fame and painting *The Vucciria*.

That first blazing summer vision hadn't been my only sight of
Palermo before 1995. There'd been other visits in between. The second was five years after the first, at the end of the seventies, a wet winter's fag end when I started seeing the shadows in Palermo. By then I'd
been living in Naples for a couple of years, and Naples then was terminally decrepit but intact. The old capital of the Bourbon kingdom
belonged to the people who lived in it. By virtue, it had to be said,
largely of neglect. Naples was lived in, and densely, all through its centre. It was a city whose people possessed their streets, stayed out in
them until the early morning. It was a city whose days and weeks and
seasons were strongly marked for everyone by meal hours and holidays
and the sea. If it were March the nineteenth, for instance, it was San
Giuseppe and that meant *zeppole*, huge grooved shells of choux pastry
baked or fried, flattened in the centre by a splodge of yellow pastrycook's cream and a fleck of bitter cherry conserve and dusted with
icing sugar, would be on sale hot and fresh every few yards. It meant
that the street where I lived, a main street of the business centre, would
be given over, inexplicably, to an animal market, and full of goats, tur-
tles, ducklings, goldfish, puppies, monkeys.

I returned to Palermo at the end of the seventies with a certain feel
for the resources and shadings of city life in the Mezzogiorno, and by

comparison with Naples Palermo was desolate. The streets were closed and shuttered outside business hours, and empty of pedestrians. I saw for the first time the extent of the ruination in the centre, the rubble, the abandon, the places you couldn't see if they were lived in or not. Rain sharpened the sour smell of rotting masonry. Life after dark was silent files of cars along the main arteries. What spooked most was the newer area, the smart part of town I hadn't seen before, stacked with rows and rows of big apartment blocks along the via della Libertà, in place of the *art nouveau* villas and the parks of the *belle époque*. In the sinister quiet of Palermo, I realized, there was a lot of money, as there wasn't in Naples. Ingenuously, I asked a couple of people about the mafia. I remember the polite, puzzled blink, the inquiring gaze and the slightly cocked head before my interlocutor vanished. *Mafia?*

That first summer day in the Vucciria, everything above market stall level had been hidden by the lowered canvas awnings. It wasn't until a wet and miserable evening of the second visit when the canopies were furled that I saw that the building on one side of the little space had a kind of open verandah at first floor level, from which you could look out over the marketplace. This was the Shangai. It was an eating place reached through a poky door in a side alley and a narrow flight of stairs: you emerged into the kitchen space and thus to the verandah. The rudimentary and rather slovenly cooking there was done in an oven that was also out on the verandah. There was nothing Chinese about it except the name. I couldn't remember if the name came back from a distant port of call in the proprietor's seafaring days. I ate that rainy, gusty night on stuffed squid, the only customer on the dimly lit verandah, while the proprietor, who was whitehaired, exuberant and a tad intrusive, read aloud from his collected poems, which were written out in an exercise book. He had a loud voice and it rang out from the verandah over the dark and empty market square.

By the summer of 1995, heroin was now one of the more important commodities traded in the neighbourhood of the Vucciria. A lot more people had moved out. There was bad heroin on the streets of Palermo and junkies were dying like flies. There were killings in the Vucciria and raids every few days. A crowd the day before had rounded on a police patrol and roughed them up. It was lunchtime on a sunny day when I got there and the tables on the Shangai's verandah were taken by pink and grey couples from northern Europe. There was a TV crew from northern Italy. A couple of listless girls said their grandfather wasn't well. They knew nothing about the Shangai's name. They said I'd have to ask him. They didn't know when he'd be back. *And his poetry?* I asked. Was he still writing poems? *He was too busy drinking wine most of the time,* the poet's granddaughter said acidly, swiping at the laminex with a greasy dishcloth, *to think about writing poems.* It was the *panelle* I was really after, in any case, and the Shangai didn't have them. I went downstairs to the *panelleria* and filled my stomach.

THE SACK of Palermo sounded as remote as the Sicilian Vespers, but it happened in the fifties and sixties. Most of it happened in four years under two men. Salvo Lima and Vito Ciancimino were two who'd joined early and risen fast when conservative politicians formed the Christian Democracy party, *la Democrazia cristiana*, at the end of the war in Italy. From 1945 until everything fell apart in 1992, the Christian Democrats were never out of government. Outside Italy the DC had the overt and covert support of the United States, obsessed with stemming the communist tide, and inside Italy it had the support of a Vatican no less obsessed with routing communist atheism. The party's bedrock, though, was the Mezzogiorno and especially the *friends* in Sicily. People didn't talk about the mafia in Sicily but they talked a lot about friends. And through the postwar years the party's most powerful leader in Sicily was Salvo Lima, and Salvo Lima was more than a friend. He was a *made man*, a fully-inducted member of Cosa Nostra, bound by a lifelong vow to serve the interests of the mafia. As the most powerful politician in Sicily he was one of the more important people in Italy.

Salvo Lima was elected mayor of Palermo in 1958, which was when the sack of Palermo began, and after four years in office moved on to greater things. He later became a deputy minister in Rome and a member of the European parliament. Vito Ciancimino was in charge of public works under Lima and later mayor of Palermo himself. Lima and Ciancimino were an interesting pair. Ciancimino was a barber's son from Corleone who kept his close-clipped Sicilian barber's moustache and his country uncouthness long after he moved to Palermo at the end of the war and into politics. In 1984 he was the first public figure to be arrested, tried and eventually convicted as a mafioso. Twelve million dollars' worth of Ciancimino's personal assets were confiscated at that time. Lima on the other hand was almost too powerful to embarrass. Beyond a certain threshold, power erases embarrassment. He was a white-maned and silk-suited grandee, and when Salvo Lima walked into a Palermo restaurant, silence fell and people came to kiss his hand. The two worked well together in the interests of the friends and the transformation of Palermo in four years was concrete evidence of this.

In four years of early teamwork, these two released four thousand two hundred permits for new building in the city. Nearly three-quarters of these permits, over three thousand of them, were given to five obscure figures, illiterate or retired, who were fronts for mafia interests. The old centre's buildings, many of them stupendous palazzi of the seventeenth and eighteenth centuries, were encouraged to decay and their poorer inhabitants to leave for cheap mafia-built blocks on the city's outskirts. Those with money were urged into the flashier blocks sprung up over the ruins of splendid villas and parks along the more central artery of the via della Libertà. In the fifties, sixties and seventies, while the overall population of Palermo doubled, the old centre's population dropped by two thirds. By 1995 Lima and Ciancimino had both been removed from the scene. Their work remained. When you walked into the new parts of Palermo it was like walking into the mafia mind. The sightless concrete blocks had multiplied like cancer cells. The mafia mind was totalitarian and even on a summer day it chilled you. Italy for decades consumed more cement per capita than any other country in the world and in Sicily construction was in the hands of Cosa Nostra. Construction, property development, real estate had once been the main business for mafia firms. Now they were where the drug money went to the laundry.

Lima and Ciancimino had more in common than mafia. They were both Andreotti men. Giulio Andreotti was a Roman who'd had the most stunning rise of all in the DC after the war. Andreotti was a clever, scrawny little hunchbacked figure with heavy-lensed spectacles, thick black hair and triangular ears projecting batlike from his head. He was a *sacristy rat* who'd emerged from a war spent in the Vatican and catholic student organizations to rise in the shadow of the party's founder to become a cabinet minister in 1947 when he was only twenty-eight. Although he'd been a member of pretty well every Italian government thereafter, Andreotti had never, in the fifties and sixties, been prime minister. His faction in the DC was too narrowly based. He lacked a wide electoral base and so he lacked clout in the party and if he stayed that way he would never head the government. It was natural that a figure so wholly consumed by the hunger for power as the tiny ascetic Andreotti should want to enlarge his electoral base and it was natural that he should look to Sicily to do it.

So when Salvo Lima was elected to parliament in Rome in 1968, massively, Andreotti did a deal with him. Before their alliance was formalized, Lima advised Andreotti to check him out first with the Italian parliament's antimafia commission, in whose report he was later to figure so largely. *I knew I was talked about,* he said later, *and didn't want to cause him problems. Giulio asked and told me,* It's OK. And so, for years and years, it was, although the parliamentary commission shortly afterward identified Lima as a central element of the mafia power structure in Palermo. Lima's clout in Sicily secured Andreotti the first of his seven prime ministerships a little over three years later. Sicily, from then on, was Andreotti's power base. Lima was eleven years later elected, overwhelmingly again, to the European parliament, but he found little time to spend in Strasbourg. He was needed in Rome. He was needed in Sicily. Andreotti in those days was *the god Giulio* and Lima was Giulio Andreotti's proconsul in Sicily. He was for decades reckoned the most powerful man in Palermo.

It was as such that Salvo Lima spent the warm spring morning of 12 March 1992 in his claret coloured villa near the beach at Mondello. Lima was receiving allies and clients in the drawing room, which had a valuable sketch by Renato Guttuso on the wall, a preliminary for his painting of *The Vucciria*, that celebration of the market and its neighbourhood that Lima as mayor had bled almost to death. The sketch hung next to a photo of Lima with the Kennedy brothers, Jack and Bobby and Teddy. Lima that morning was discussing prospects for the Italian elections. They were due within three weeks and looking good. After heading the last two consecutive governments, Giulio Andreotti had decided to go to the polls.

There was an engagingly personal logic behind Andreotti's decision to go to the people, into which the people entered not at all. An ugly corruption scandal had broken out in Milan the month before and a determined magistrate called Di Pietro was pursuing it. The thing could only get bigger and uglier for the governing parties. It was a good moment for Andreotti to leave the fray for higher things. President Cossiga was about to cut short his increasingly bizarre term as head of state, to everyone's relief. Repository of a great many demochristian secrets, the president had lately been given over to bouts of redfaced public rage and the delivery of long and weirdly free-associating harangues that had his party colleagues on edge. They never knew what he was going to say next. Whether Cossiga was now jumping or being pushed, his retirement meant that the Italian prime ministership and the presidency were coming up for grabs at the same time. Bettino Craxi, the socialist who'd enjoyed two highly lucrative terms in office during the eighties, was anxious to try his hand as prime minister again. The highly public secret deal was that he could have it, the *quid pro quo* for the DC being Giulio Andreotti's final apotheosis as head of state. The president may have had less power day to day than the prime minister, but he made and unmade governments in a country that usually saw at least one new government a year. The Italian president had clout. This was the way things went in Italy and a normal margin of error in the popular vote would have changed nothing. A direct line to the president would be interesting, Lima doubtless thought.

At mid morning he left with two of his visitors for the Palace Hotel, where an electoral dinner with Giulio Andreotti was scheduled twelve days hence. Andreotti himself was due to arrive the next day to launch the Sicilian campaign. Lima and friends had hardly moved off when a Honda 600 XL motorbike with electronic fuel injection, straddled by two helmeted youths, overtook their car. Shots were fired from the bike. The car braked and stopped abruptly, and the three dignitaries scrambled out. Lima shrieked, *They're coming back!* and struggled out of his green loden overcoat and ran. They were his last words. His glove-soft leather pumps weren't made for speed, and it was an awful long time since those soft thighs had run anywhere at all. The next thing the other two noticed, from their hiding place behind a garbage skip, was the Hon. Lima lying face down and dead. He'd been neatly shot in the skull from close behind, at a slight angle. The killers ignored the other two DC potentates crouching behind the dumpster, one of whom was a professor of philosophy whose appointment Lima had been arranging to the board of the state railways, and leisurely left. *The friends no longer had any respect for him*, it was later explained by Gioacchino Pennino, a Palermo doctor, man of honour and DC politician who became the first political pentito. In the indictment of the Cosa Nostra leadership for the killing, the prosecutors described Lima as having been *Cosa Nostra's ambassador to Rome*. This was not said immediately. *Salvo*, said a close colleague, choosing his words of tribute carefully so soon after the actual shooting and exploiting Latinate abstraction to the full, *was a man of synthesis*. He didn't say of what.

Lima's standing within the DC was nevertheless undeniably such that certain people felt they had to come to Palermo for his funeral, however much they hated doing it, given the questions people were suddenly asking about the government's relations with the mafia. The president of Italy, still the demochristian Cossiga, at first said this was clearly a mafia crime, nothing to do with the state and that *he* wouldn't be coming to pay his last respects. Something or someone later

25

changed his mind, and he came. The secretary of the DC was there too. So was prime minister Andreotti, who'd perhaps had something to do with convincing the others to come. People were struck by the shrunken, terrorized and humiliated figure the prime minister cut when he came down for Lima's funeral. The minister of justice at that time, Claudio Martelli, remembered two years later how Andreotti looked after Lima's murder. *His face had an even waxier look than usual. He was terrified, either because he didn't understand, or maybe because he did.* Huddled in his heavy overcoat, Andreotti looked like an aged tortoise retracting into its shell. His nerves frayed by the media's constant linking of his own name with that of Cosa Nostra's latest hit victim, its most *distinguished corpse*, prime minister Andreotti snapped a few days later that it was *really absurd to divide even the dead into political factions.* The presidency was slipping from his grasp, the only thing he'd ever wanted and failed to get. He was made a Life Senator as a consolation prize, *for distinguished service to the Republic.* Not being president was anyhow no longer even the worst of it. Andreotti can't have failed to see that killing as a portent.

ONE OF the first to arrive on the scene of Lima's murder was Paolo Borsellino. He stood there looking at the corpse, the deputy chief from the Palermo prosecutors' office, leader of the Sicilian effort against the mafia, and shaking his head. Borsellino was shaking his head because while others were still wondering which politician in Rome had asked the friends to dispose of Lima in Palermo, he understood the mafia had just terminated its forty-five-year relationship with the DC. It was Borsellino's lifelong friend and antimafia colleague Giovanni Falcone who put the change into words. The crime hadn't been ordered by a politician. By the spring of 1992 the politicians were no longer in charge. *Now it's the mafia that wants to give the orders,* Falcone said. *And if the politicians don't obey, the mafia decides to act on its own.*

Falcone and Borsellino both had an acquaintance with Lima which went back well beyond the professional interest they'd developed over the previous decade, when they were the most formidable of the team of magistrates tracking the ever-more-fearsome Cosa Nostra in Palermo. Falcone and Borsellino had grown up in Lima's Palermo, a few streets apart in the old centre, the quarter known by its old Arab name as La Kalsa that lay between the Vucciria and the sea front. Falcone's family and Borsellino's had both been forced to leave their homes by *zoning regulations* in the fifties. Falcone and Borsellino were both sons of the embattled old petty bourgeoisie of the Mezzogiorno. Falcone's father used to boast that he'd never taken a coffee at a bar and the son was later scrupulous in avoiding those compromising social contacts that most people in Palermo found quite unavoidable. But the boys had grown up among inner-city mafiosi, been to school with them, knew them through and through, and it was this intimate knowledge of mafia culture, mafia values, the mafia mindset, that enabled judge Falcone and judge Borsellino to make human contact later with mafiosi in crisis, to win their respect and persuade them to turn.

There were mafiosi in personal crisis in the nineteen eighties because the organization itself was in crisis. Mafia values were in crisis. At the very time Cosa Nostra in Palermo was acquiring quite unprecedented wealth from the international traffic in heroin and cocaine, its old structures and friendships had been shattered by the rise of an unusually brutal and treacherous mafia clan from out of town, the family from Corleone and its chief Salvatore Riina, called Uncle Totò by the men of honour. When the mafiosi in crisis began to collaborate, they enabled Falcone and Borsellino to form for the first time in history a detailed understanding of the hitherto secret organization called Cosa Nostra, whose interested friends in government, the judiciary, the church and the media had insisted for decades didn't exist. The outcome of that collaboration was a monumental judicial defeat for the organization, a mass trial begun in the mid-eighties, which in all its phases of appeal had run for six years and which had received its final and almost unexpected sanction by the supreme court two months before the death of Salvo Lima.

Falcone and Borsellino had paid a high price for their success against Cosa Nostra. They'd disturbed too many interests. The Palermo maxitrial had convicted hundreds of leading mafiosi. It had ratified their thesis that Cosa Nostra was a single organization. But after the initial convictions in 1987 Falcone had been blocked by professional jealousy and obscure manoeuvres from heading the investigating magistrates' antimafia pool and continuing its work in the late eighties. The pool itself was dismantled and its efforts dispersed. Falcone had narrowly escaped death in a bomb attack engineered by *highly refined minds*, as Falcone put it, and highly placed informers. Borsellino transferred to the dire posting of Marsala, in an area of western Sicily that had an even higher density of mafia activity than Palermo itself and was the centre of the transatlantic heroin traffic.

Falcone had gone to Rome in April 1991 to head a new office in the justice ministry and Borsellino had ended up back in Palermo at the end of the year, in Falcone's old job.

Everyone had seen Falcone's move to Rome as a defeat or a surrender, both his colleagues and, it later turned out, Cosa Nostra. A former mafioso called Gaspare Mutolo explained later *The climate relaxed with the end of the antimafia pool ... and finally with the transfer of Falcone to Rome. He was now considered less dangerous to the organization ... we used to joke that he'd end up as ambassador to some south American country.* Soon after that, Cosa Nostra realized it'd made a mistake. New decrees started rattling out of Rome, where Falcone now had the ear of the minister Martelli. In less than a month there was a new law on recycling money and less than a month after that another law on mafia influence on local government. Six months after Falcone's arrival, the coordinating antimafia investigation police group was set up, and a month after that the national antimafia prosecutor's office. District antimafia pools were created, an antiracket law was passed, house arrest was ended for mafiosi appealing convictions. Measure by measure, Falcone was putting Italian justice into a condition to systematically pursue organized crime for the first time in history. *Gradually we began to understand that Doctor Falcone was becoming even more dangerous in Rome than he'd been in Palermo.*

The April elections that followed Lima's murder in 1992 were a disaster for the ruling parties. The DC got its lowest vote in history and the deal to make Andreotti president fell apart. Andreotti was now wearing Lima like an albatross. Craxi was mired in the corruption scandal. Voting for the president went on interminably. Falcone had been nominated to a new post as *superprosecutor* of all mafia cases, but this too got stuck in the general paralysis as government in Italy collapsed. On May 19 Falcone said in alarm *Cosa Nostra never forgets. The enemy's always there, waiting to strike ... we've got to act quickly to build the superprosecutor's office ... and we can't even agree on electing the president of the Republic.*

Four days later, on the Saturday afternoon of May 23, Falcone and his wife, the magistrate Francesca Morvillo, flew back to Palermo on a secret flight in a government plane. Falcone always went home to Palermo for the weekend. The plane landed around six in the evening and the Falcones were met by their three-car escort and seven bodyguards. Three of the guards went in the front car. Three more went in the last. In the middle car, Falcone took the wheel himself with Francesca Morvillo beside him, and got his driver to sit in the back. It was a small breach of procedures, a little indulgence. Before, a helicopter had always gone ahead to oversee the route into the city, but security had been cut back to save money, and the convoy set off fast along the freeway without aerial clearance.

Punta Raisi is one of the world's more dangerous airports. On the far western edge of Palermo, it takes up the last of the narrow strip between the cobalt sea and the mountainous teeth that encircle the city. The freeway to the city curves parallel to the coast, a little inland, affording glimpses of the sea on one side and olive groves under the rocky outcrops on the other, until both are obscured by houses and small factories closer to the city. It was where the freeway runs through Capaci, an outer suburb under mafia control, like all the suburbs of Palermo, that a skateboard had been used to manoeuvre five hundred kilos of plastic explosive into a drainage tunnel under the freeway a few days earlier. When the Falcone convoy passed on its way to Palermo that Saturday near dusk, a group of men of honour had been watching the freeway traffic for some time. They'd sawn off olive branches to get a better view, and littered the ground with the butts of the Merit cigarettes they'd smoked. As the first car passed over the drainage tunnel, the boss Giovanni Brusca detonated the explosive by remote control. *Hell opened up before us*, said a driver following the convoy. *A terrifying explosion ... a scene from the apocalypse ... screams of terror ... an unreal silence.* The explosion killed the three in the first car instantly. The guards in the last car were only slightly injured. In Falcone's car in the middle of the crater Francesca Morvillo was unconscious, eyes open, looking up at the sky. Falcone's face was *a mask of blood*, his head moving, his body trapped. Their driver in the back was injured but alive. Falcone died when they got him to hospital. Francesca Morvillo woke for a moment, asked *Where's Giovanni?*, fell unconscious again and died later that evening. *My account with Cosa Nostra remains open*, Falcone had said the year before. *I'll settle it with my death, natural or otherwise.*

Paolo Borsellino got to the emergency room in time to see him die. He came out and embraced his daughter, *his face lost, shaken, he'd aged visibly in just a few minutes.* He wept and his daughter wept and she was crying too because of what she'd heard him say a thousand times. *Giovanni's my shield against Cosa Nostra. They'll kill him first, then they'll kill me.* At the funeral Giorgio Bocca, a tough and sceptical journalist not easily moved to admiration, watched Paolo Borsellino place his hand on Giovanni Falcone's coffin, *in his black legal gown with the embroidered white shirt and for the first time he looked to me* bellissimo, *like an antique knight swearing fidelity before his fallen comrade.* Bocca also thought he saw something new, or something old renewed at this public moment.

It was years since I'd seen the faces of honest and brave Italians, not the grotesque and greasy masks of a corrupt and mediocre power, years since I'd seen people's pain and anger ... I saw the young people's faces, crowds of young people, as if they'd woken from a long sleep ...

Paolo Borsellino knew he had little time. Falcone had become a martyr in the Italian manner and now Borsellino found that *people seem to think I'm a saint*. The neofascists proposed him for president, the ministers for justice and the interior wanted him for the superprosecutor's job Falcone had been blocked from getting, and all Borsellino wanted was to find Falcone's murderers in the time he had left. New men of honour, shaken by the killings, wanted to tell him their stories and he listened and he tried to learn what he could. His newest witness told him Cosa Nostra was making so much money from drugs and government contracts it couldn't launder the money fast enough. It'd rented an apartment that was filled with banknotes, a cash warehouse. Borsellino had never worked so hard, harder even than for the maxi-trial. His family never saw him. He was gone when they rose in the morning and came home when they were asleep at night. *He seemed to have death in his eyes*, said a colleague. His assistant prosecutor said he was *a man in a tremendous hurry ... someone who knew that his hours were numbered ... he felt that time was running out on him.*

By the middle of July the press was announcing *the end of a regime*. The corruption being revealed in Milan was vaster than anybody could have imagined, and the governing class was going under. July 19 was a Sunday and before sunrise Borsellino wrote a letter to a school teacher, explaining his love of Sicily, his sense that he had a duty to work on its problems, his confidence in the growing awareness of its young people. He went out of town that summer Sunday with his wife, out in a boat with friends, then to lunch with other friends. Later in the afternoon he went back to Palermo with his escort of six. He wanted to see his mother, who was alone that day. Borsellino's weekend visits to his mother's place in via D'Amelio had become almost predictable, but he wouldn't give them up. There were cars parked around the entrance to the apartment block, despite an earlier request that it be cleared for security. The three cars pulled up, five agents, four men and a woman, surrounding Borsellino with their machine guns ready. When Borsellino pressed the bell at the gate, he was blown to pieces by a car bomb explosion that killed all five around him too, destroyed all the apartments facing the street to the fourth floor, though the building was thirty feet from the road, and shattered its windows as high as the eleventh floor. A few days later Antonino Caponnetto, the elderly founder of that Palermo magistrates' antimafia pool, to whose great maxitrial the events of 1992 were an epilogue, arrived from Florence to weep in the ruins of via D'Amelio. *It's all over*, the old man said. *It's all over*. But it wasn't.

FOURTEEN YEARS earlier, heading for south America in the late European summer, I'd stopped off for a return visit to the Mezzogiorno and ended up settling in Naples. In the spring of that year the former Italian prime minister Aldo Moro had been ambushed and kidnapped in Rome by terrorists of the Red Brigades. He'd been on his way to parliament for the swearing-in of yet another conservative DC government headed by Giulio Andreotti, a government for which Moro himself had most remarkably won the support of Italy's huge communist party, the PCI. After the murder of his driver and bodyguards, Moro was held prisoner for a couple of months in a secret place in the middle of Rome and then murdered. The events of Moro's long imprisonment, the government's total failure to find him or do anything to save his life, were extremely puzzling. The government had masked its inaction as intransigence, defending the state by not compromising with terrorism. Knowing the state of their state, Italians were sceptical about this. Still, the terrorist emergency wasn't a normal time. Learning the language, I followed the debate, and the deepening of a crisis that seemed entirely ideological, with interest and detachment

Then other things started happening. A year after Moro's murder, a journalist named Pecorelli was found shot in a Rome street. He'd been about to publish a piece on Moro's successor as prime minister, Giulio Andreotti. A new pope, intending to clear up the Vatican's tangled finances, had been found dead in bed in the papal apartments a month after his election. The next pope was shot and wounded in St Peter's square three years later. The Vatican bank was involved at the time in a huge financial collapse, and the government-appointed receiver of the Milan bank that caused it had been shot dead in the street. An Italian airliner flying from Genoa to Palermo with eighty-nine people aboard was shot down in the Mediterranean and the source of the missile attack was never identified. A bomb killed eighty-five people in Bologna station. A secret masonic lodge was discovered that had been plotting a coup d'état. Its members included dozens of leading politicians, magistrates, armed forces chiefs and secret service personnel, journalists and media owners. The general who'd eliminated left-wing terrorism was sent to Palermo and murdered there with his wife less than three months later. Hundreds and hundreds and hundreds of people died in a couple of years of shooting wars in Naples and Palermo. There was another and bigger banking crash in Milan, the world's worst since the war, and the man who caused it was found hanging under Blackfriars bridge in London. His mentor Michele Sindona, the architect of the earlier collapse, was himself found dead of strychnine poisoning in a top security prison. Another bomb killed eighteen people on the Naples - Milan express train. A lawyer's severed head was found in a parked car in Naples. And so on and so on and so on.

These events had a certain horrid fascination, and their unfolding enthralled, since nothing was ever explained or resolved. They seemed glimpses of the workings of something larger, something big and hideous that was working itself out in the dark. These constellations of mysteries were themselves constellated by other mysteries, not necessarily lesser, just more briefly or imperfectly glimpsed, or involving more obscure players, less spectacular events and therefore less able to compete for attention. A lot of the players in this endless turbid soap had entered the drama not as players at all but as observers, inquirers, searchers after truth. They were magistrates, journalists, police, lawyers, people trying to ascertain the facts who'd been sucked in and become part of the story itself and usually ended up as its stiffs. Others never went under. They appeared in episode after episode. Many of the episodes seemed unrelated, though you sensed hidden continuities. What you needed was an index, a key to all mythologies, a theorem, a Big Picture into which all the details would fit. Of course I never found one. In the nineteen-eighties Falcone and Borsellino had used the information provided by former mafiosi to elaborate a theorem for Cosa Nostra, the analysis that linked and explained the thousands of mysteries of organized crime in Sicily. What was needed now was something even larger, something that would take in the secret life of the Italian republic too, and the other orbiting mysteries of America and the Vatican and the east.

The most frequently recurring name in the linked and nested tales of the thousand and one nights of Italy was Giulio Andreotti's. He'd been around since the forties, a member of pretty well every government in the Italian republic. He'd been prime minister for a good part of the seventies. He was prime minister that disastrous spring of 1992 when everything fell apart. Until that spring of 1992, he was routinely called *the finest political mind in Europe*. He was a survivor, a winner. Of course his name would come up again and again. It came up too during that seething unstable interregnum after the collapse. Former men of honour started to speak about their former political friends. Most of all, about life senator Andreotti. Long and intricate stories were told about the secret history of crime and politics in Italy, and the magistrates who heard them found a deal of objective confirmation. As they wove the stories and the evidence into a thesis, all the old names and incidents of the eighties started coming together. The politician Moro and his death. The banker Sindona and his death. The journalist Pecorelli and his death. The general Dalla Chiesa and his death. And all the other mysteries of the living and the dead started falling into place around the tiny aging figure of the longest lived statesman in Europe. After fourteen years, after the massacres of 1992, I'd left Italy for good, yet I was drawn irresistibly back in 1995 because at the end of the summer Andreotti was going on trial. He was going on trial in Palermo for association with the mafia and a few weeks later he was going on trial in Perugia for murder.

I had some time in Palermo before the Andreotti trial started, and some inquiries to make. I went back to the Vucciria next day and up to the Shangai for lunch, and from the verandah I noticed a very thin young man examining a fish. He was inspecting it closely and speaking intensely with the stallholder. After a few minutes he moved on to another stall and looked rapidly over its wares. Then he moved on again. The fishmongers seemed to know him. He was young and thin and rather poorly dressed and haggling and the sellers were treating him with a certain respect. He was worth convincing, you could see they thought. He was in his early twenties and wearing an embroidered maghrebin cap. His chin had a few days' growth on it. I lazily observed his movements round the fish stalls of the little square, until someone banged down the *sarde alla beccafica*. These were fresh sardines splayed open and cooked wrapped around some fishy forcemeat. They must have been called that because they look like the little birds, figpeckers, long since gone like most birds from Italy, that Byron liked to eat.

When I got down the grubby staircase he was still there. He was so thin that at certain angles he nearly vanished from sight. He had made up his mind to buy, though not from a single seller, buying *sarago* from one stall, swordfish steaks from another and fresh sardines from a third. He headed off up a dogleg alley and I followed him. After a few yards he turned right into an even narrower lane and slipped into a doorway on the left. He entered a kitchen, and spoke with a cook about his own age, a fair bit more corpulent and wearing glasses and a serious look. Then its door swung shut. The lane, a little further on, opened to the left on a miniscule piazza before a derelict church. A couple of parked cars took up most of its space, but on the other side some heavy earthenware pots had been pulled out around two massive umbrellas of clean white canvas. A couple of tables and some empty chairs stood under them. A big stone step led to a closed glass door. The furnishings looked clean and new in the dirty piazzetta and yet apart from a large and grubby Persian cat sleeping on the step there was no sign of life. It looked like the restaurant whose kitchen was in the lane. Pushing on up a steep little lane, I arrived at piazza San Domenico. I thought I'd return to that piazzetta.

THE VILLA'S name, the one on the fax that had reached me in Sydney from Palermo, had a faint resonance. It wasn't till I got there weeks later that the distant memory took form.

> It wasn't yet fully dark and the road stretched ahead very white and boxed in between high walls. Just out of the Salina property on the left could be seen the half-ruined villa Falconeri, owned by Tancredi, his nephew and ward. A spendthrift father, married to the prince's sister, had squandered his entire wealth and then died. It was one of those total ruins in which they melt down even the silver thread in the epaulettes of the servants' liveries ... they drove past villa Falconeri, whose enormous bougainvillea cascaded over the gates its billows of episcopal silk and lent it an illicit air of opulence in the dark.

Rattling toward a sexual escapade in Palermo, the prince in Tomasi di Lampedusa's novel *The Leopard* is driven past a villa whose original is now nearly engulfed by the city, though still protected by its own grounds and the Favorita park and the great promontory of Monte Pellegrino. The villa Niscemi was instantly identifiable in the novel by those readers who remembered its blaze of bougainvillea. The real house never fell into ruin, and one of its last inhabitants, a child called Fulco who later became the last duke of Verdura, remembered a distant cousin who occasionally came to play and who when he grew up was to become the duke of Palma and prince of Lampedusa and write *a famous novel*, even if one the duke of Verdura judged to be *historically incorrect*. The duke remembered his cousin as *a fat, silent boy with big sleepy oriental eyes, who didn't like outdoor games and was shy with the animals.*

Nobody would ever have imagined, the duke noted tartly, *that in the distant future he would become the author of a masterpiece*. The duke wrote that Tancredi and Angelica, the glamorous characters played by Alain Delon and Claudia Cardinale in Visconti's film of *The Leopard*, were based on his maternal grandparents. *I noted a number of factual errors, but after all it is a novelist's privilege to alter the facts*. The duke didn't, in his childhood memoir that he published first in English with a title from Lewis Carroll, *The Happy Summer Days*, and only subsequently recast in the Italian version given me in Palermo, go into exactly what his quarrel was with his cousin's posthumous and fictional version of the family story, but he was sounding a note here that I found was to recur with some insistence over the time I spent in Palermo. The note was accusatory, and the issue was getting things right and getting them wrong. The problem was what made history, the status of fact, the weight of detail and the squaring of different versions of the same thing. It was the problem of interpretation, the question of meaning. The duke of Verdura alluded to matters of fact, a list of points to be corrected, in a tone that queried his cousin's whole way of being in the world. So, when the novel came out, did Leonardo Sciascia. The duke's quarrel with Lampedusa was over family and Sciascia's was over Sicily, and they both challenged the history.

Ways of perceiving the world were an issue in Palermo in 1995. Versions of history. The trial that was about to open, however it ended, and it wouldn't do that for years, was bound to revise a great deal of the known history of Italy since the war. In Naples just before I boarded the night ferry for Palermo, the publisher Tullio Pironti had given me a copy of his latest book. It was a wristbreaking large format volume of nine hundred and seventy-three pages, printed on good white paper, and it must have weighed a couple of kilos. Its cover was plain blue, with an outline map of the Italian peninsula and the islands in white. The title, printed at the top in small sober yellow letters, was *The True History of Italy*. A subtitle read *Interrogations, testimony, evidence, analysis. Gian Carlo Caselli and his assistants reconstruct the last twenty years of Italian history*. This massive book consisted of an edited version of the main testimony that prosecutors had gathered against Andreotti. I'd taken it dutifully, this monster collection of legal depositions. I'd opened it and been transfixed. By the time I disembarked in Sicily *The True History of Italy* had become a talisman. *History was on trial*. The years I'd lived in southern Italy, from the later seventies to the early nineties, when Andreotti's power was greatest, were also exactly the years, from 1978 to 1992, that in the words of the prosecutors' preliminary findings, set out on page 9 of *The True History of Italy*,

> relations between Sen. Andreotti and Cosa Nostra were established
> – in a form not contingent or occasional – at least from 1978 and
> maintained until 1992, such as to materially confirm the charge of
> membership of a mafia organization.

A few questions were in order in Palermo in 1995, about what made
history, and who made it, and how things were.

The last duke of Verdura was long since dead. He'd in any case left
Italy many years before. The happy childhood over, he served as an
army officer in the first war, and before the second came around he was
settled in Hollywood, later New York. He'd turned out to be artistic,
and to have social gifts that eluded his shy and awkward cousin. Soon
he was designing splendid jewels and in charge of bijoux for Coco
Chanel. He became the jeweller to the Beautiful People in America and
Europe, and a Beautiful Person *ante litteram* himself, among whose
clients and friends were the duchess of Windsor, Salvador Dalì, Rita
Hayworth and Marlene Dietrich. He came back to Europe to write his
memoir and die and take the the the family crypt's last remaining place in
Palermo cathedral. The princesses who inherited villa Niscemi also
lived in America, and in 1987 they sold it to the city of Palermo. Even
the bougainvillea that briefly flared in the dark in the opening pages of
The Leopard was gone when I arrived at the gates of the villa Niscemi
and crunched down its deep gravel drive under the midday sun.
Leoluca Orlando, the mayor of Palermo, had invited me to lunch.

IT'D BE less official, less portentous, but not the first visit Orlando
had received from an Australian. A few years earlier the Australian
ambassador to Rome had decided to visit, during his tour of duty, all
those places in Italy from which people had emigrated to Australia. His
itinerary naturally got denser and more complex as he moved south
into the Mezzogiorno, the territories of the old Bourbon Kingdom of
the Two Sicilies. It was these poor and prolific regions with a difficult
past that had contributed so largely to Europe's populating of the
Americas and Australia. The ambassador covered the region of
Campania around Naples, the kingdom's old capital, a couple of hours'
drive south of Rome, he visited Apulia in the eastern heel of the Italian
boot, Calabria in the peninsula's far southern toe, poor and tiny
Lucania, hemmed in by these other three. Finally he arrived on the

island of Sicily. Its capital Palermo, the other great city of the old Bourbon kingdom, is almost as close to Africa as to the nearest extremity of what Sicilians call *the continent*, and a lot closer to Tunis than it is to Rome.

It was in Calabria that the ambassador struck trouble. All of these regions, with the exceptions of Lucania and until very recently Apulia, had a long history of organized crime. That history had been part of a long and dire history of foreign occupation, exploitation and neglect. The Spanish Bourbons, who'd lasted until the time of Garibaldi and Italian unification a little over a century earlier, were merely the most recent of a succession of invaders that went back to the ancient Greeks and Phoenicians nearly three thousand years earlier. From the point of view of the locals, the national government in Rome was not a great improvement. For Rome, the south had always been *the problem of the Mezzogiorno*.

The criminal activities and organizations developed differently in each region. The volatile urban criminality of the Neapolitan camorra was very different from the old rural mafia's activities in the Sicilian hinterland, and the Calabrian 'ndrangheta another thing again. But in each case a parasitic criminal class had inserted itself in the interstices between rulers and the ruled, exploiting both. Crime, like any successful industry, moved with the times, and these organizations became urban and multinational, vastly rich and powerful conglomerates. The Sicilian mafia, Cosa Nostra, dominated European crime and a piece of the European economy. The others were allies operating under a kind of regional franchise agreement. The mafia most active in Australia was the Calabrian 'ndrangheta, and the 'ndrangheta happened in Calabria to work out of the most impenetrable terrain in Italy. In the mountainous and densely wooded range of the Aspromonte that ran like a backbone down the middle of the region, the 'ndrangheta still ran a kidnap and ransom business. Prisoners could be held securely for months and years in the Aspromonte, while their families drummed up the tens of millions of dollars required to buy their release. The jailers had little to fear from the carabinieri's military search operations. From time to time a once-sleek industrialist, now almost forgotten, with a wispy grey beard to his waist and haunted eyes, would totter out of the mountains to the appalled embrace of his loved ones, after years of living in a hut, chained like a dog, fed from tins.

Since the earnings from these kidnappings were invested in the marijuana plantations of New South Wales, and since the profits from these, running at around sixty million dollars a year when they were disturbed in the late seventies, in turn flowed back into Calabria, it was the 'ndrangheta that particularly had a bone to pick with Australian authorities. Calabrian criminality was, in the words of the parliamentary antimafia commission chairman, a *traditional presence in Australia ... along with honest immigrants*. The ambassador was perfectly aware of this when he set out, but he was startled to find that the Italian government refused to guarantee his safe conduct over large tracts of Calabrian territory. It was under the control of the 'ndrangheta and the government in Rome politely forbade the ambassador to extend his goodwill tour into those parts. He hadn't expected that in western Europe at the close of the twentieth century. It was a time, in fact, the end of the eighties, when the man recently appointed antimafia high commissioner had had to report that the Italian state was indeed no longer in control of all of the national territory. *In many parts of Sicily, Calabria and Campania the domination of the territory by organized crime groups is absolute*, he'd said.

The mayor of Palermo, Leoluca Orlando, said Cosa Nostra was *buying the Italian state piece by piece*. It was a time when the governor of the Bank of Italy reported that organized crime was *contaminating the entire national economic mechanism*. It was a time when the national governing body of Italian magistrates, whose head was the president of Italy, reported that justice in Sicily was *impossible*, and a magistrate in the antimafia pool in Palermo said Cosa Nostra had *capillary control over every quarter of Palermo*. The ambassador did make it to Sicily and was officially received by Orlando. Cosa Nostra had no specific quarrel with the government of Australia and the visit of its representative passed unnoticed. Cosa Nostra did, however, have a quarrel with Leoluca Orlando, and the ambassador might have felt even less easy about government control of the territory if he'd been shown the twenty-eight bullet-proof vests neatly stacked in the mayoral wardrobe, ready to be donned by staff and visitors in case of attack. The mayor of Palermo, the dissident demochristian and antimafia Leoluca Orlando, had been condemned to death.

At a mafia summit in 1987 the head of Cosa Nostra, Salvatore Riina, had handed down three death sentences. Those who were to die were Giovanni Falcone, Paolo Borsellino and Leoluca Orlando. Six months later Riina's assistant, Baldassare Di Maggio, took delivery of two bazookas, two kalashnikovs, one of them fitted with a grenade launcher, and two containers of plastic explosive. He was instructed that these were *to carry out the killing of Falcone, Borsellino and Orlando*. The weaponry was concealed in a tomb in the cemetery of San Giuseppe Jato, not far from Palermo. The family of San Giuseppe, headed by Bernardo

Brusca and his son Giovanni, were the oldest and closest allies of Riina's group from Corleone that now controlled Cosa Nostra. Falcone and Borsellino were to be killed for the maxitrial. Orlando's offence was political. *He was speaking out too much against the mafia family.*

Getting rid of them was easier said than done. The designated victims knew a lot about the ways of their intending killers. There was no hurry, however. When the moment came the three would be removed. The moment very nearly came for Falcone in the early summer of 1989. He'd rented a house on the rocks by the sea at Addaura, and one day in June, just before his *top secret* movements took him there on his second visit that year, his security escort noticed a skindiver's Adidas bag left negligently on the rocks in front of the house. When they looked into it they found fifty-eight sticks of plastic explosive and a remote-controlled detonator. Nobody was supposed to know Falcone was just about to arrive, or that he was bringing some visitors for a swim and lunch, some Swiss magistrates who were opening up Cosa Nostra's bank accounts.

It was mafia procedure to isolate and discredit a representative of the state before removing him. It made him easier to pick off, and it minimized reprisals. Falcone was an isolated and vulnerable figure at that time, lately the slandered victim of a jealous colleague's anonymous letter campaign, attacked openly and covertly by interested parties in the judiciary and the government. The attempt on his life, some whispered when it failed, hadn't been serious, or he'd planned it himself, for sympathy. Falcone did however receive one striking expression of solidarity, and it was the first to arrive, an early-morning phone call from the Hon. Giulio Andreotti to congratulate him on his narrow escape. Falcone wasn't at all reassured. The next day he told a couple of friends, fellow judges, about it *in a somewhat agitated manner.* Falcone had never met Andreotti or had any dealings with him. As a Sicilian and student of mafia culture, Falcone was greatly disturbed by his phone call. On page 150 of Tullio Pironti's *True History of Italy*, I found that one of the judges Falcone confided in later testified that

> He told me that when he was killed we would have to find out who had sent the first wreath of flowers to be placed on his coffin. He explained that this was a widespread custom in mafia crimes ... He took the Hon. Andreotti's phone call as underlining the isolation in which he found himself ... Giovanni told me that to save his life he would have to really get to know his political enemies ...

The other added that

after that, among us three any mention of the Hon. Andreotti's phone call became a kind of coded signal to indicate who had ordered a crime or some other disempowering strategy.

Cosa Nostra killed Falcone in the end, and Borsellino, but their murders had many and curious consequences. One of them was the arrest eleven months later of Salvatore Riina, who turned out to have been living comfortably in Palermo while he was *on the run*, so to speak, for twenty-four years. *Who are you?* was Riina's first question when he was flung to the ground in a Palermo street. His first thought was a leadership coup inside Cosa Nostra. It didn't enter his mind that these people might, after all these years, be police. He breathed a sigh of relief. The man who led the undercover police commando to Riina was the one who'd taken Riina's orders five years earlier to kill the three. Baldassare Di Maggio had realized that Riina was about to kill him too. Riina was like that, with people close to him.

LEOLUCA ORLANDO was still alive and ready to talk and ready to lunch at villa Niscemi on a hot September day in 1995. The functionaries fussed around like family servants at the villa's entrance, and for a moment I expected a derisive child in a sailor suit to appear with the family dogs and a fretful Irish governess. Up the early eighteenth century staircase they led me, past a row of glowering kings of Sicily to a smaller room which must have been the child Fulco's *telephone room*, the one he'd described as the focus of family life. After a wait on balding red velvet I was summoned to the library. Orlando charged in wearing a dark grey suit and looking small and dark. He'd lost a lot of weight. Five years earlier he'd been a worried bearlike man in a crumpled suit, with a clump of dark hair that kept flopping over his face. Orlando's undapperness, in that Italian context of ruling party power brokers in shiny silk suits, gossamer stockings and glossy black dancing pumps, was deeply sympathetic. So was the way he ignored the insults being heaped on him by president Cossiga.

Another potentate of the ruling party with a submerged and secret past, Cossiga wonderfully embodied the senile arrogance of a *fin de régime*, as well as that clerical shiftiness that had always characterized the church's party, and was now lost in cloudy dreams of resurrection. Orlando had a lot of trouble with his fellow demochristians in those days, apart from the head of state. As the son of an establishment lawyer in Palermo, a clever boy who'd also studied in Heidelberg, he'd gone naturally into politics and inevitably joined the DC. As a stubborn man of principle, he soon ran into trouble, but fought back. In 1990 Orlando resigned as mayor of Palermo. Claire Sterling described him then after his first years in office:

> The effort had transformed him from a hopeful young believer to a weary, harrowed, and sadly battle-scarred figure in just four years. He was the first reformer in a century to last that long in office ...

She was writing him off too early. Orlando came out fighting again. He broke with Italy's ruling party because in Sicily it was the party of the mafia and beyond reform. In 1991 he formed La Rete, the network, an antimafia association that was to be the nucleus of a new politcal party. Since the DC had southern Italy politically locked up, Orlando's was a brave act. There was no intimation then that a small corruption inquiry in Milan would bring down the regime. Neither could Orlando have foreseen how the murders of Falcone and Borsellino would rouse people to fight Cosa Nostra. In the 1990 elections, the prime minister Andreotti had urged Sicilians not to vote for Orlando in Palermo, although he was the number one candidate of Andreotti's own party. Andreotti's word at that time was still law in the DC, though something was starting to change. *People understood the message, and everybody voted for me*, Orlando told me now. Orlando for his part had refused in 1989 to head a DC ticket for the European parliament if it included Salvo Lima, because Lima was mafioso. Forced to choose, the DC chose Lima.

Everybody knew that Andreotti was the protector of Lima, said Orlando now. *And everybody knew that Lima was the political voice of the mafia. Lima was the link between Andreotti and Riina, between the political mind of the mafia and the killers, the bosses.* Everyone knew that in Sicily the mafia organized the votes at election time, neighbourhood by neighbourhood, for the candidate who best represented mafia interests. The candidate was almost invariably demochristian. There was a long-gathered inevitability about Orlando's final break with the ruling party. *When no one dared speak against Andreotti, I spoke against Andreotti.* He was theatrically simplifying a little, but not much. Orlando's oddity in the eighties had been to be a demochristian who was both a Christian and a democrat. After first Falcone and then Borsellino were killed in 1992, Orlando was urged to leave Sicily for a while for his own safety. He said, *If I'm killed I'd like people to know it wasn't only the mafia* ... He was referring to *the friends of the friends*, the politicians nobody else was yet mentioning in connection with that year's massacres. He stayed in

Palermo and slept in a carabinieri barracks. When he stood again for mayor of Palermo in 1993, he won more than three-quarters of the first-round vote. By the time I called two years later his hopes of building La Rete into a national party had faded, as had his popularity. Not that he seemed depressed. He plonked himself in a sofa now and started talking about the last duke of Verdura, the jeweller to the stars. He became expansive. It was the setting, the villa and the garden. When he left the city administration behind and came out of town to the villa Niscemi, Orlando said, he moved into a more reflective mode. He loved coming here. Orlando was flamboyantly pessimistic about the Andreotti trial. *I'll be there of course, on the first day. Calling for a conviction in the name of the people of Palermo.* The city administration had declared itself an *interested party*, and would be represented at the trial.

This trial's a defeat, Orlando proclaimed nevertheless. *It's like Nuremberg. Victor's justice.* There was something to be said for Nuremberg, I thought, with all its faults. You had to offer an accounting to history. You had to assign responsibilities, however imperfectly. *It's a political defeat*, he insisted. *Andreotti should've been dealt with when he was still in power. So should Hitler.* It was hard to disagree with that. And sunk in a sofa among the duke's family's incunabula, Leoluca Orlando, who was once the youngest professor of law in the history of Palermo university, gave me a lesson on mafia and politics in postwar Italy. He was saying the trial would never have happened if the Berlin wall hadn't come down, if the Soviet Union hadn't disintegrated. I tried to demur, to qualify, to question– *When Andreotti talks about an international conspiracy against him*, interrupted Orlando, *he's right in a way. He no longer enjoys international protection that he had for all those years of the cold war. The Americans don't need need him now the fear of communism's gone.*

There was no point trying to make this thing a dialogue. Orlando was no longer even looking at me. He seemed to have forgotten my presence. His eyes were fixed on some distant imaginary point beyond the library wall. *The mafia isn't just a criminal organization. It isn't just people with guns. It's a system of power, and it became the formal, legal political system in Sicily at the end of the war. The Americans brought it. It all goes back to 1943 ...* The sun was just past its zenith outside and a blinding white light enveloped the jagged promontory and the green gardens at its foot. The air was quite still. Professor Orlando raised his voice still further, weighted his cadences and gestured somewhere over my shoulder. He was no longer speaking to me. I slumped forgotten on the low divan. Orlando was speaking to History.

II

A SECRET KISS

AROUND MIDNIGHT in Sicily they started coming ashore. It was the night between the ninth and the tenth of July, summer on the southern coast between Licata and Gela. It was 1943, a year before the Normandy invasion. The allied armies were making their first European landing. Nine days later Rome was bombed for the first time and five days after that the fascist government fell. Two months after the Sicily landings the new Italian government signed an armistice with the allies and a month later declared war on Germany. As partisans fought the retreating nazis and the fascist rump regime in the north, behind allied lines the political parties of the coming republic took form. In Sicily a rather particular state of affairs prevailed.

Disembarking on the southern coast between Licata and Gela, the US seventh army went through central and western Sicily with curious ease. It took the American troops seven days to secure the mountainous German-occupied island, a little under half the size of Tasmania with ten times the population. Casualties were negligible. General Patton exulted that it was *the fastest blitzkrieg in history*. The unparalleled speed and painlessness of the American operation didn't pass without comment, especially when people compared it with the five-week slog up the east coast of Sicily by the British and Canadian forces under Montgomery, who suffered thousands of losses.

Leoluca Orlando reminded me now of the old story about the allied invasion. The vanguard of the invading Americans, he said, carried flags and foulards of yellow silk, embroidered with the letter *L*. One had been dropped by a lowflying US reconnaissance plane on the hill town of Villalba, at the doorstep of the local priest, brother of don Calogero Vizzini. Don Calò was about to be made an honorary colonel in the US Army. He was already *capo di tutti i capi*, boss of bosses of the Sicilian mafia and had thirty-nine murders, six attempted murders, thirty-six robberies, thirty-seven thefts, sixty-three extortions on his personal charge sheet. He was heavily into black market business when the kerchief fell from the sky. As the Americans moved toward Palermo, two thirds of the defending Italian troops deserted. The *L* had stood for Lucky Luciano, born Salvatore Lucania in Lercara Friddi, a few miles west of Villalba. At the beginning of 1943, Luciano had been serving a thirty-to-fifty-year sentence in a US penitentiary and was considered the *capo di tutti i capi* of the American Cosa Nostra.

Five months before the allied invasion of Sicily he'd appealed for a reduction of his sentence in return *for services rendered to the nation*. He was said to have been aboard the plane that dropped the foulard. He was certainly released and deported to Italy in 1946. An elderly lawyer once recounted to me his horror and indignation when many years earlier he'd found himself at the next table from Luciano in one of the smartest restaurants in Naples, where Luciano set up residence after the war and where he eventually died in 1962. Luciano was living off contraband in drugs and cigarettes, and a Naples police report of 1954 described how his *attitude of insolent self-assurance and lack of visible income* were *a cause for scandal among decent people*. That same lawyer, a Neapolitan with the hunched and stunted figure of one who'd lacked essential foods in the period of growth, not unlike Andreotti's, bright wily eyes and a nose and chin that went a considerable way toward meeting at some ideal point in front of his hooked and deeply smiling mouth, knew something at first hand about the deals done by these returning native sons on the backs of starving Neapolitans and Palermitans. The lawyer had himself spent much time at the war's end skulking around the Naples waterfront with American tinned foods secreted inside a heavy overcoat that was far too big for his malnourished frame. Sixty per cent of the food unloaded by the allies on the Naples docks went not to the starving people but directly on to the black market, with help from a lot of the military.

Gore Vidal remarked once that Sicily had been liberated by Lucky Luciano, Vito Genovese *and the American army*. It was certainly a matter of record that Genovese, Luciano's man in New York and a major drug trafficker of the day, also ended up in Italy at this time, as official interpreter and advisor to the US military governor in Naples. Colonel Charles Poletti was already, in Luciano's words, *a good friend*. For some reason Genovese was bundled back to the States in the summer of 1944, after less than a year of rendering services to the nation, though not before he had set up the vigorous black market operation which was then taken over by Luciano. These star turns among the returning native sons were backed up by a heavy representation among the foot soldiers. Fifteen per cent of the invading US forces were Sicilian born or of Sicilian descent.

All of them carried a slim booklet signed by General Eisenhower outlining the island's *long and unhappy history*, its *primitive and underdeveloped condition*, the lack of running water and sanitation in most of the houses, the illiteracy of nearly half the population, the special risks presented by typhus, dysentery, malaria and *the mafia, a secret society*. It may have been among these lower ranks of the occupying forces that the indigenous mafia found its closest and most useful friends. The American records are still secret that would make clear the role of the American Cosa Nostra in smoothing the allied invasion of Sicily. *There is no proof ... of a plot*, Sicily's modern historian has written of this time, and Orlando's story of Luciano's yellow silk foulard might have been a myth. What happened during the military occupation wasn't. As they handed over the administration of the island to the locals, the military authorities found that those established figures whose records were most convincingly antifascist were, whether the allied military knew it or not, the local mafia bosses. The repression by Mussolini's egregious *iron prefect* Mori had forced them for twenty years to lie low, if not in jail. In that wartime context they looked impeccably antifascist. So with a certain rapid plausibility don Calò Vizzini was installed as mayor of Villalba, and so were the heads of many other mafia families made the administrators of their localities throughout central and western Sicily. It wasn't necessarily planned, but it set the pattern.

The British military governor wrote later that *many of my officers fell into the trap ... of following the advice of their interpreters*. Who were, he added, mafiosi. A US Army captain, in a worried report of October 1943 on the black market in food supplies, found that the mafia was not merely a criminal organization but also *a social system, a way of life, a profession*. It was an acute remark, and it echoed the Tuscan observer Leopoldo Franchetti's brilliant report on the Sicilian society of seventy-odd years before. That *underdeveloped* in the soldiers' guide to Sicily had been an understatement. If the foot soldiers of the liberating army had had time and resources for more extensive and more analytical reading, they might have learnt that although feudalism had been legally abolished in Sicily in 1812, the territory through which they were passing with such suspect ease still largely consisted, despite a history of peasant agitation and uprising that had occurred regularly at least once in every generation since, of vast hereditary estates.

These feudal estates hadn't much changed in a couple of millennia, since the days when Greek-speaking Sicily became a Roman province two hundred years BCE, and its latifundia the *Republic's granary*, as Cato wrote, *the nurse at whose breast the Roman people is fed*. The island then was a freshly-deforested and ruthlessly exploited domain of endless wheat-growing estates worked by slaves. Most of the following two millennia were also spent under foreign rule, and the people who worked the land lived hardly better than in slavery. *It is impossible to calculate*, wrote the late Moses Finley in his history of ancient Sicily, *how much produce and money have been taken out of Sicily in rents, taxes and plain looting in the past two thousand years*. Speaking of the damage done, Finley added

> not to all the people ... for the traditional way of ruling Sicily has been through the agency of local magnates ... who shared rather handsomely in the profits in return for their services in exercising the administrative and police powers.

For centuries the *latifondi* had been owned by aristocratic families who were seen less and less on their land. They disported in Palermo, Naples, Rome or Paris, while their estates, guarded by armed *campieri*,were controlled by the tenant farmers who managed them, the hated *gabellotti*. These let them out in turn to sharecroppers, and the land was worked for the sharecroppers by day labourers subsisting on bread, pasta and beans in conditions of poverty and precariousness that the demure phrases of General Eisenhower's *Sicily Soldier's Guide* barely hinted at.

One of the few extant images from the American invasion of Sicily is Robert Capa's photo of a trimly uniformed American soldier hunkered down on muscular haunches in some dusty road of the Sicilian interior, taking directions from a bandy-legged and white-bearded old peasant with a kerchief on his head, who's pointing the way with a knobbly stick that looks like an extension of his own limbs. The photo's clearly posed, fake as hell and freighted with propagandistic intent. *We know*, said Sciascia, *that he's showing him the right road*. But nothing could fake the story of the two physiques. The old Sicilian, as upright as he's able to stand, is no taller than the squatting young soldier. You could imagine variants of the image for every invasion of

Sicily back through the millennia. The allied landing of 1943, said Sciascia,

> took place in almost identical conditions to the landing of the Arabs on 16 June 827, with the Germans' Goering division in the place of the Byzantine garrison ... the island as ever without defences, crushed by a greedy and corrupt administration, terrified of the present and uncertain of the future.

Through legal chicanery, political temporizing and a lot of down-home intimidation, Sicily's tiny group of hereditary landowning families had in fact added to their estates in the hundred and thirty years between the formal end of feudalism and the allied invasion. Common lands, assigned in law to the peasant farmers, had been absorbed by the big estates, which took up more than three quarters of Sicily's cultivated land. Garibaldi's liberation brought none of the promised land reform. Sicilian peasants, the mass of the people, were worse off in unified Italy than they'd been in the eighteenth century. In huge numbers Sicilians were forced by hunger to emigrate to the Americas. By the time fascism arrived that escape route was closed off, and by the time fascism collapsed Sicilians were desperate. The key to the landowners' continuing grip was the down-home intimidation. Which was where the mafia came in.

FOLKLORISTS AND etymologists played with unanswerable questions about the origins of an enigmatic word. Was mafia an Arabic word for a place of refuge, as Norman Lewis suggested? I couldn't trace a source for this, though Italian etymologists last century proposed *mahjas*, the Arabic for boasting. An Arabic origin for a word whose use was first recorded late last century, some eight hundred years after the Arabs had left Sicily, seemed improbable. That it was the cry *ma fille!* of a mother whose daughter's rape by French soldiery provoked the uprising of the Sicilian Vespers, almost as long ago, was fanciful. Was it a political acronym from the time of Italy's unification? Someone else suggested a link with *guappo*, the figure of the young Neapolitan gangster, and that came from the Spanish. That was stretching it too. Praising a man, or a horse, or a woman, as *mafiuso* meant the animal was elegant, proud, vital, spirited, and a *mafiuso* late last century was like his Neapolitan counterpart the *guappo*, an elegant thug.

The word mafia was first formally recorded by the prefect of Palermo in 1865, after the unification of Italy. It wasn't included in the

Italian penal code until 1982. The mafia until the end of the war was mainly that criminal element in rural Sicily that the landowners, and the state too, found useful in maintaining property and power. The *Oxford English Dictionary* was still insisting in the nineteen seventies that the mafia was

> often erroneously supposed to constitute an organized secret society existing for criminal purposes.

When the *New Shorter* came out in 1993 it got its definition by removing the first five words from the phrase.

The mafiosi were closely allied with the *gabellotti*, whose own name derived from the Arabic and meant tax collectors, and who administered the estates. They were often the same people. The mafia afforded a form of social control through its extortion and intimidation of the peasant families. It also, in the towns, became a fast if dangerous way of acquiring wealth and power. Even in its origins, the mafia was a parasitic presence that grew in the space between the state and the people. The mafia was outlaw but tolerated, secret but recognizable, criminal but upholding of order. It protected and ripped off the owners of the great estates, protected and ripped off the sharecroppers who worked the estates, protected and ripped off the peasants who slaved on them. The mafia ripped off everyone as it protected everyone, in the historian Paul Ginsborg's words, *above all against itself*.

The mafia soon diversified and citified. It was too good an idea to languish in the backblocks, and not long after the war had radically transformed and internationalized itself, but the essential qualities were there from the start. There were a lot of ways of making money if you were prepared to kill for it. The rural mafia had offered a social order based on violence and terror. It insinuated itself where ordinary human trust and solidarity had been worn away by poverty and exploitation. It was strong in proportion to the weakness of the state. Conservative by nature and opportunistic in its procedures, mafia criminality had always been parasitic of established political power. Its political parasitism was another face of its economic parasitism. The essence of the mafia, its criminal genius, had always been to know how to make itself needed. The mafia had always known how to cosy up to those in power.

————

A LOT of people uncertainly in power felt they needed the mafia in the mid nineteen-forties. The landowners of Sicily and their allies were anxious about the uprisings of hungry Sicilians that were going on all over the island. Crowds were demanding food in the cities and peasants were demanding land in the country. There were confrontations and deaths. In Palermo in 1944 the army fired into a hungry crowd, killing forty-four and wounding many more. The allied military government, ~Italy~ as Ginsborg remarked, *ensured the southern rural élites a painless transition from fascism* and maintained *a status quo based ... on the most ruthless exploitation of the rural poor.* A hunger-driven surge of activism was now filling the political vacuum after the collapse of fascism. The landowners were also looking with alarm at what was going on across the water on the continent. The communist party was out of hiding and entering mainstream politics. It was formidably organized and active, reaping the political rewards of its long fight against fascism. A communist minister of agriculture in the provisional government was issuing radical decrees on land reform. The new conservative catholic party, the Democrazia Cristiana, despite the furious backing of the Vatican, didn't yet look particularly convincing to the landowners of Sicily. Democracy was in the air, and the Sicilian élite, which had managed the transition from reaction to fascism to allied occupation smoothly enough, was now greatly disturbed. It looked around for friends.

American wealth and modernity had been glimpsed in the occupation, the nearness of it felt after a century when America was that dreamt-of distant land where poor Sicilian emigrants had become rich. America was the source of those monthly dollar remittances that had kept alive whole families who'd sometimes kept a framed dollar note among the icons on the hovel wall. Agitation for land in Sicily, reform in Italy, the pull of American wealth and power, historic distrust of the continent, all fed into the curious and short-lived Sicilian separatist episode at the end of the war. In 1944 there were half a million members of the separatist movement, five times as many as all the other parties together. It was not exactly independence the movement was after. Voltaire had described Sicilians a couple of centuries earlier as *hating their masters and rebelling against them, but not making any real effort worthy of freedom,* and separatism ran true to form. While the peasants of Sicily wanted to be owners of the land they worked, the separatists wanted new masters, not freedom. The separatist movement lurched toward extremism when the allies handed over Sicily's administration to the new Italian government. A secret army was formed to lead a separatist uprising. The mafia, gravitating as it always does to real power, became the separatists' close ally. Sicily would become the forty-ninth state.

Sicily would be part of America. Big, rich, powerful America, where Sicilians had so many friends.

Mixed up with the mafia and the separatists were the bandits. In September 1943, a young peasant from Montelepre, Salvatore Giuliano, not quite twenty-one years old, was stopped by a patrol of carabinieri. He had a horse with a load of contraband grain. Compulsory grain stockpiles were a wildly hated measure that barely hindered the busy mafia black market and badly hurt the desperate poor of the interior. Giuliano pulled a revolver and killed a carabiniere. Caught up in a police raid near Montelepre four months later, he killed another with a machine gun. A few weeks later he organized a prison breakout whose escapees became the core of a bandit group that took to the hills behind Montelepre in January 1944. Second in command to Giuliano was his cousin Gaspare Pisciotta. This daring news commenced his wild and oddly long career.

Giuliano's bandit gang was one of forty or so bandit groups loose in poor and lawless western Sicily by the end of 1943. As the mafia reassumed its powers under the allies most were quickly eliminated. Giuliano's was notable for the charm and sense of theatre shown by the people's bandit, the king of Montelepre: the florid pronouncements and the shows of populist justice, and the diamond ring he wore after removing it himself from the duchess of Pratameno's finger in her Palermo home. And for the impunity the gang enjoyed, the uses to which this impunity was put, and the nature of his end. As a much-photographed celebrity bandit, Giuliano was sought out and visited by the national and international press and Vito Genovese, the New York mafia boss and US army advisor, and had less well-documented contacts with politicians and carabinieri. He had a little romance with a Swedish photoreporter. He also met with the chief prosecutor of Palermo. *The only people unable to find him*, wrote the judges of Viterbo grimly a long time later of Giuliano's seven-year career, *were the police*. Some found him, however. Giuliano celebrated Christmas eve of 1949 with *panettone* and liqueurs brought by an inspector-general of police.

Everyone in this uncertain time was playing a double or a multiple game and there were informers everywhere. Giuliano had plants among the police, and they had informers in his band. It wasn't clear whether Genovese, when he met Giuliano, was calling as advisor to colonel Charles Poletti of the US Army or in a less formal capacity. Around this time the honorary US colonel don Calò Vizzini was also getting to see a lot of colonel Poletti. Giuliano was asked by the separatists, now including don Calò Vizzini, to be one of their military leaders. The mafia, typically, was playing it both ways here. Its leaders were also joining the newly formed DC in case the separatist adventure failed. Giuliano's separatist convictions, his suspicions of Rome and the communists, whom he called the *vile reds*, were deeper than his resentment of the mafia and the landowners, and he took the rank of lieutenant colonel in the ragtag separatist army. He expected to rise soon to general. He probably also expected American military support. After a year of sporadic armed clashes, in one of which Giuliano's allies murdered eight ambushed carabinieri, and in which the insurrectionary leader was not always clearly distinguishable from the Giuliano following a parallel criminal career as king of Montelepre, the Sicilian insurrection fizzled. For once, an initiative from Rome headed off disaster.

In early 1946, even before the constitution of the new Italian republic had been approved, Italy's provisional government responded to the alarm in Sicily by backing its decrees on land reform with a radical regional constitution. It granted Sicily a great autonomy and an elected parliament. A flow of funds began to arrive from Rome that would continue for thirty years. These billions of dollars were under Sicilian control. There were no strings. The landless farmers of Sicily suddenly found parliamentary politics more persuasive. The activity of trade unionists, socialists and communists was reinforced by the radical decrees coming from Rome, and made land reform through collective action seem possible. For a moment, Sicily had broken out of the archaic cycle of social distrust, political resignation and periodic violence.

It took courage to be an activist in Sicily then. Party sections and union offices were attacked and burnt by Giuliano's bandits, and in the ten years from 1945 the mafia assassinated some fifty trade unionists and political organizers in Sicily. Don Calò had already shown reformers what to expect. As the reforms were being debated in Rome, an eloquent communist leader and a local socialist took the struggle to Villalba in September 1944, where don Calò's brother was the priest and his nephew alternated with him as mayor and secretary of the newly-opened DC branch. Don Calò allowed a meeting in the piazza, *as long as neither the mafia nor land reform were discussed and no peasant took part*. It was a matter of showing *respect for the hospitality they were offered*. The meeting went ahead. Drawn by the arguments, peasants started appearing at windows overlooking the piazza and at corners of the cordoned-off streets. As the communist started to talk about the land, the mafia and the local big estate, they joined the discussion. The priest started ringing the church bells to drown the voices. Don Calò shouted *It's all lies*. Then the mafia started shooting and throwing bombs into the crowd. Fourteen people were wounded, one of them the communist speaker. The socialist slung the speaker over his shoulder and carried him to safety.

Though demochristian opposition hobbled the land reforms, and though the communist party leaders were more interested in power manoeuvres in Rome than the struggles of southern peasants, the labourers and their families continued to occupy the untilled land that was now legally theirs. The legal challenges by the peasant cooperatives went ahead in the courts of Sicily's hinterland. In April 1947, in the first elections for the new Sicilian parliament, the reforming left won. The DC went into a tailspin and separatist support withered. It was an evanescent and local triumph, however, in a world that was hardening into cold war blocs. The Truman Doctrine was a month old, and Harry Truman, who'd been the possibly rather startled recipient of a letter from the barely literate bandit Salvatore Giuliano on the need *to stem the communist tide in Sicily*, made special reference to Italy. Italy was in the front line of the fight against world communism. On May 1 the US secretary of state George Marshall wrote to the American ambassador in Rome urging that the communists be excluded from the Italian government.

That same day, happy at the left's success in the Sicilian elections ten days earlier, fifteen hundred people from several nearby towns gathered in family groups to celebrate May Day on a rolling open piece of country at Portella della Ginestra, overlooked by a stony crag called *la Pizzuta*. It'd been an annual thing for a couple of decades, interrupted by fascism, and the place was near Piana degli Albanesi, in that high country just south of Palermo and not far from Montelepre. They arrived on foot or in those brightly painted wooden carts Sicilian peasants still used then, drawn by mules and horses, bringing their food and wine. The noise, as the speeches began, was taken for celebratory fireworks and raised a festive cheer. *Then we saw a horse fall*, said a survivor. *Then we heard people screaming. People ran and tried to hide.* Only of course there was nowhere to hide. Machine guns were firing from the rocks of la Pizzuta. Hand grenades were hurled into the crowd. *They were Giuliano's men. They were all wearing white raincoats, so they all looked alike.* The shooting continued for fifteen minutes and left eleven dead, some of them children, and sixty-five wounded. *The bodies lay on the ground for hours, with the wounded, who were groaning until a truck arrived.* There'd been another death before the massacre began. A *campiere* who'd noticed the bandits preparing the attack was seized and killed and thrown down an eighty-metre well.

THE ONLY sure thing about Portella della Ginestra on 1 May 1947 was the number of dead and wounded. That it had been Giuliano's bandits who carried out the massacre was also soon agreed. Beyond that, nothing was clear. Twenty-five years later, an Italian parliamentary commission that had spent ten years examining the revival of the mafia in Sicily after the war, concluded that

> the reasons why Giuliano ordered the massacre of Portella della Ginestra will long, perhaps forever, remain cloaked in mystery. After a long and thorough investigation such as the commission has conducted, it is absolutely impossible to attribute responsibility either directly or morally to this or that party or politician ...

The commission stated that the origin and content of a mysterious letter delivered to Giuliano, read and burnt just before he told his men *the hour of our liberation has come* and ordered the killings, and

> his relations with journalists and military personnel from other countries and with Italian politicians, remain obscure pages of an extremely confused and tormented period in the history of our country.

This was intended in 1972 as a summary of a disturbed unhappy time now more than twenty years past. It sounds now like a judgement on the last half century. There was a trial for Portella della Ginestra. It was held years later and miles away in Viterbo, on the continent. Looking back in 1995 on the long complicities of Italian justice, another Palermo judge who'd worked with Falcone in the antimafia pool described this trial's findings as *the first grey page* in the postwar history of Italian law. The trial was bound to fail because the principal accused wasn't there. Giuliano was dead. He'd been shot in his sleep by his cousin and lieutenant Pisciotta on 4 July 1950.

The world learnt that Giuliano had been killed in a shootout at Montelepre with the men of the Banditry Suppression Taskforce Command, a body lately and hastily created, as its name suggested, by an embarrassed government. After Pisciotta had or hadn't killed Giuliano, as he later accused himself of doing, the carabinieri, on whose behalf the mafia had in any case arranged Giuliano's death, dragged the body from its bed to a courtyard and shot it up, setting the scene of the fatal showdown. The summoned press who raced to the scene, and photos of that day show a crowd of them, was first awed, then suspicious, and finally derisive. The scenario fell apart. The blood, for one thing, was flowing uphill from the body. One began his report for an Italian weekly, *The only thing for sure is, he's dead* ... The leader of the Banditry Suppression Taskforce Command was promoted. The shootout scenario collapsed totally.

Giuliano before he died had already felt used and entrapped by his friends. He'd wanted out and would have taken an amnesty in Italy or a passage to the United States or Brazil. To his former friends in the new republic the Giuliano outlaw gang was a growing embarrassment, a primitive anachronism. Politically, Giuliano was now what Italians liked to call a *mina vagante*, a floating mine of deeply compromising knowledge that might at any moment blow up in the face of respectable conservatives. Not to mention the police, carabinieri, magistrates. There were obscure manoeuvres. Giuliano's brother-in-law, one of the gang's leaders, slipped away to the United States, where he was arrested and returned to Sicily. Another leader of the gang, who was also a police informer, was killed while under arrest in a carabinieri barracks. It was a police inspector friend he used to meet regularly who'd warned Giuliano to *watch out for your cousin*. Giuliano had said more than once in his last days that he knew Scelba wanted him dead, and he'd had his suspicions about Pisciotta.

Scelba was the minister for the interior, a Sicilian and a demochristian who was to become notorious for the savagery with which he put down union struggles in the newly-industrialized Italy. There'd been a letter from Scelba promising an amnesty for Giuliano. Somebody said it was forged. When Pisciotta announced during the trial at Viterbo that he and not the carabinieri had killed Giuliano, he told the court he'd killed at Scelba's request. He said Scelba, and a group of separatist and monarchist politicians in Sicily, had ordered the massacre at Portella della Ginestra. The mafia had commissioned the crime for the politicians and the mafia had arranged Giuliano's removal three years later, just as it was picking off individual communists, socialists, trade unionists. Another dozen were killed that same year of 1947, by the mafia directly or through the agency of the bandits. The mafia was making itself useful to its new political protectors by dispatching its enemies, establishing a pattern that was to continue for decades, until Cosa Nostra decided in the nineteen eighties that it was no longer taking orders from anyone. The court in Viterbo refused to look into this, because a second trial was to be held in Palermo of those politically responsible. Its findings, however, were such that the Palermo court later found itself unable to determine whose, if anyone's, the political responsibility was. This was what was meant by *grey*. In the middle of a trial that was memorable for equivocation and contradiction on the part of the state's witnesses and general incredulity and derision among the public, Pisciotta shouted, *Bandits, police, state, they're all one body, like father, son and holy ghost!* Years later, that was all people remembered.

Pisciotta had announced at the trial that he was going to *reveal all* about the politicians behind the massacre and the Giuliano gang's other activities. He'd say who'd ordered the shooting and firebombing attacks on left-wing party offices and carabinieri barracks. Pisciotta was taken back to the Ucciardone prison in Palermo. The Ucciardone had always functioned as a mafia nerve centre, the place where its politics, wars, plots, alliances and eliminations were decided. Pisciotta had hardly arrived when someone put strychnine in his coffee. After several days of agony he died. No charges were ever laid. That same day, 8 January 1954, Scelba was sworn in as prime minister of Italy.

A FLURRY of aides outside the library door roused me from my trance. The door opened a crack and a hesitant personal assistant whispered that all was ready. Behind him, against the light, I saw the fuzzy outlines of figures in wine coloured jackets carrying silver trays. Orlando seemed oblivious. Orlando was now quoting Goethe in German. And saying he'd been the first Italian politician who named names when he talked about the mafia, shocking the demochristians by *naming the sinners as well as the sins*, and describing himself as a Lutheran catholic or a catholic Lutheran. *Southern Italy's problem is that it lacks the ethic of individual responsibility. We had the counterreformation in the south without having had the reformation*, said the man who went to university in Heidelberg.

Finally it looked as though we might be going to eat. Orlando had suddenly remembered that he had to race off to a conference of European police. He was pushing for greater integration of police activity internationally against organized crime. He was also concerned that arms were gaining on drugs as a mafia business, and that other governments were being drawn into collusion with the mafia. We'd come full circle. At the end of our long talk and the start of a new age, the cold war over, the problem was still crime and politics. He was still talking enthusiastically about the buzz of heavy Sicilian dialect you heard now in business class on flights to Moscow and how convenient enriched plutonium was to handle, even better than refined heroin, when we walked across the hall and into another room. It was the ante-room to a vast canopied terrace, which I could see through a fluttering muslin curtain, and its sole furnishing was a long table covered by white cloth and a spread for maybe a hundred people. We seemed to be the sole partakers. The table was manned by white-gloved waiters wielding outsize silver spoons and forks in one hand and empty plates in the other. I was hungry now, and looking forward to a real Sicilian meal. Tuna, swordfish, sardines. Nearing the table, though, I found much blander fare. There were plates of salmon and ham and cold turkey. Russian salad and a big paella and lettuce and much else beside that failed to lodge itself in the memory. Everything was pastel coloured. With a tiny sigh I prepared to hoe in nonetheless, hoping the insipid international cuisine wasn't a concession to my presumed taste. It was therefore with some dismay that I noticed Orlando was taking almost none of it. He was following a new regime. He'd been serious-ly ill twice in the previous year. He'd found he had cancer, and had nearly died of pneumonia, and the double assault had shocked him into change.

Out of respect for his crisis I joined him in abstinence. At least I knew why he now seemed so slight. Even the chilled bottle of Regaleali, a delicious Sicilian white wine, that I'd noticed earlier gath-ering dewy beads of moisture had now vanished unopened, like a mirage in the shimmering heat. I held out my glass for a little more tepid mineral water. Orlando had a sweet tooth, however, and the police chiefs of Europe waited elsewhere as he forked up a confection of chocolate and whipped cream out on the terrace. We took our cof-fee and he was off with his guards and assistants, in the back of an armoured Alfa Romeo with tinted windows. Its wheels spun in the deep gravel, found purchase and the car powered down the drive. Someone called me a taxi, and as I waited in the vestibule I imagined the cleaners, gardeners, waiters, handymen, gatekeepers and kitchen-hands upstairs, all descending on the laden board we'd left. A scene, I thought, Lampedusa might have used for *The Leopard*.

ALL THAT afternoon I pondered The Kiss. I went back to the rabbit warren hotel and lay on my back in a darkened room, breathing in the smell of roasting coffee and raking over memories of body language in the Mezzogiorno. *It is not a crime to kiss the boss of Cosa Nostra*, Orlando had said that morning. *Very bad taste, yes, but not a crime. Ça manque de bon ton*. Orlando was merely correcting an emphasis. He knew very well it was no ordinary kiss. He knew as well as anyone how much more was involved. Like most of the rest of the story, the kiss was a men's affair. It was exchanged, if at all, in 1987. Eight years later it was occupying the finest and most highly paid legal minds in Italy. A moment of physical intimacy was witnessed, recalled, denied, hypothesized, contextualized, theorized, reconstructed and deconstructed. It had led the legal minds to call on others, anthropologists, psychologists, historians, students of the ways of power and affection. The aim was always the same, to establish in principle, after the manner of Italian intellectuals, that it could or could not ever have taken place. And thus that it did or did not take place in 1987. A lot of history hung on this kiss.

In 1987, in the heat of another Palermo September, the Sicilian DC had held that year's annual Friendship Festival. It was a sort of regional fair of the ruling party that ran for a week from the nineteenth to the twenty-seventh. It'd been well known for months before that the Hon. Andreotti would be coming to Palermo to take part and he was awaited with excitement. For nearly twenty years the alliance with Salvo Lima had made Palermo the heartland of Andreotti's power. On the second day of the festival, in fact, he was scheduled to speak twice. At ten-thirty in the morning he would be speaking on *Europe, Sicily and the Countries of the Mediterranean Basin*. After lunch, at three in the afternoon, he would speak on *Overcoming Ideological Thinking and the Risk of Mere Pragmatism in Political Alignments*. This second speaking engagement was later put off until six in the evening. The dog days of the Sicilian summer were barely over, and someone may have suggested to the organizers that the theme was a little heavy to handle straight after lunch.

Andreotti duly flew to Palermo on September 20, and duly spoke at the party festival that morning. Then he went to the Villa Igiea, his usual hotel when he came to Palermo, a temple of *art nouveau* built on the water and that day crowded with demochristian politicians. At lunch time Andreotti dismissed his police security escort, and arranged to meet them later in the afternoon. He didn't in fact join his fellow politicians for lunch in the hotel restaurant, and his absence was noted. Nobody saw him again until he reappeared in the late afternoon and met up again with his escort. Andreotti had left the Villa Igiea at half past two in the afternoon. In another part of Palermo at exactly the same time, Salvatore Riina's driver Baldassare Di Maggio was collecting the head of Cosa Nostra as instructed from a prearranged address. Di Maggio arrived smartly dressed, as Riina had told him to. He drove

Riina in a white VW Golf turbo to the gracious home of Ignazio Salvo in No 3, piazza Vittorio Veneto.

Ignazio Salvo and his cousin and business partner Nino Salvo, who'd died of a brain tumour in a Swiss clinic a year earlier, had been for decades two of the richest businessmen and most powerful demochristians in Sicily. Ignazio Salvo was at home that day in 1987 because he was under house arrest, awaiting sentence in the maxitrial. Di Maggio couldn't remember, when he spoke about it in 1993, the exact day in September 1987 he drove Riina to Salvo's house, but he remembered everything else. He described with precision the concealed side entrance to the basement garage of No 3, and the private lift that ran from the garage directly to the Salvo apartment. He identified the man of honour called Rabito, Salvo's personal driver and assistant, who'd met them at the garage gate and taken them up to the house. He described walking down a hall and being shown into a room on the right at the end of it. He and Riina had entered a sitting room suite with a parquet floor and a big carpet. On the left had been a large bookcase and a desk in dark wood. There'd been a sofa in front of the desk and another at right angles to it, and an armchair. On the other side he'd seen a table and chairs. The room had led out on to a large terrace and he'd seen a lot of plants growing there. The walls had been hung with paintings, he couldn't remember of what, or their styles, which given his background as a car mechanic and killer wasn't all that surprizing, and the windows with long heavy curtains. Sitting on the sofa he'd seen Ignazio Salvo. He'd seen the Hon. Salvo Lima and the Hon. Giulio Andreotti, *whom I recognized without a shadow of doubt.* They'd all stood up when Riina entered.

> I shook hands with the parliamentarians and kissed Ignazio Salvo ... Riina, on the other hand, kissed all three persons, Andreotti, Lima and Salvo.

This was The Kiss. Di Maggio had then gone back down the passage to wait with Rabito in another room. After three hours, perhaps three and a half, Ignazio Salvo had called him back to the sitting room, where he'd shaken hands again with Andreotti and Lima and left with Riina. On the way back in the car, Riina had made no mention as they chatted of what had passed between himself and Andreotti, but Di Maggio had had his own strong reasons for believing they'd talked about the maxitrial. He couldn't really imagine the subject having been anything else, and he'd interpreted the kiss between Riina and Andreotti as *a sign of respect ... for as long as things went well.* Back at the Friendship Festival, the Hon. Andreotti arrived with his security escort barely in time to address the faithful at six on *the risk of mere pragmatism* in politics.

I tried to imagine the scene Di Maggio described to the magistrates. The luxurious drawing room on a hot Sicilian summer afternoon. The small, hunched and fragile figure of the minister for foreign affairs rising from the sofa as the stocky and uncouth mass murderer entered the room. What'd passed through that subtle mind as they'd embraced? Andreotti had never been known for physical effusiveness. He was already sixty-eight then, but he'd little changed over the years. The long lipless downward curving mouth, the *moneybox mouth* hardly seemed made for kissing. He'd said once that he never recalled his widowed mother kissing him as a child, and the ways of affection are learnt. There was no trace in Andreotti of affection or carnality, no intimation of closeness. A friend of mine as an exuberant young woman in the early seventies once had the job of tottering across an exhibition hall in swimming costume and high heels and proffering to prime minister Andreotti a satin cushion bearing the ceremonial scissors he'd use to cut a ribbon and open an international trade fair. She's never quite got over the lemonsucking narrow-eyed glare of disapproval the head of government shot her as he reached for the instrument. Andreotti's voice was dry and small. Utterance was concise, formal, throwaway, deprecatory, minimalist. It was deliberately flat, clerical, ordinary, except for the intermittent verbal echoes and elaborations of the little flashes of malice and cynicism that glinted behind the lenses. These had earned him a reputation for irony.

He was a politician grown in the shelter of the Vatican, a government minister since his twenties who'd never had to ingratiate himself with the people he served. He'd never had to press the public flesh with those *diaphanous* hands. By the nineteen seventies, after sealing his alliance with Salvo Lima, he'd eliminated all challengers to the power he held, even if the party game and the parliamentary ritual had required a certain rotation of posts. He'd perfected a system that revolved around himself. He'd provoked admiration rather than affection in his followers, but this was never a minus. The famously sentimental Italians had always nursed a deeper feeling for the sly and heartless, for the diabolically clever. His admirers, at the height of his power, called him *the god Giulio*. Others called him *Beelzebub*, which of course was a more colourful name for Satan. Former men of honour said they'd known him as *Uncle Giulio*.

The person you had to imagine Andreotti embracing was eleven years younger and also short, formerly known indeed to his colleagues as *Shorty*, though stocky and a lot more robust. *He'll be even shorter when we're through with him*, they'd said in Palermo once, but they'd been wrong and very soon they were dead. He was a country person, a peasant from Corleone without formal education, who spoke limited Italian and hardly wrote at all. He'd used figures scribbled in a little notebook to run a multinational business with an annual turnover of many billions of dollars His wife had studied Machiavelli at school, which might've helped hone the family management skills. A jovial figure and an expert cook, Uncle Totò Riina was said to have shown the strength of a bull when he throttled his guests after banquets. In his ten year rise to total power in Cosa Nostra, he'd killed or had killed eight hundred men of honour. In Cosa Nostra they'd stopped calling him *Shorty* and started calling him *The Beast*. He'd eliminated all challengers to the power he held and perfected a system that revolved around himself. What'd passed through that subtle mind as the two embraced?

On page 761 of *The True History of Italy* I found a section of seven pages on the *meanings of the rituality of the greeting between Riina and Andreotti*. It turned out to be a tiny sketch of Cosa Nostra and its relations with the Italian state. Unscrewing a plastic lampshade that fell into two pieces in my hand, in the full glare of the light shed by the fifteen watt bulb of the hotel reading lamp, I studied it. *The kiss*, Andreotti's defence had submitted, was *a hypothesis sailing through the rarefied atmosphere of the absurd*. And since the kiss had become the image of the case against Andreotti, symbolic and concrete, *The True History* had to demonstrate that the notion of the vastly powerful man with the fine political mind kissing the illiterate peasant killer, *Italy's most wanted criminal*, wasn't at all absurd. That it was, in the circumstances, inevitable. First you had to acknowledge Cosa Nostra's existence. The hardly trammeled growth of Cosa Nostra from the end of the war until the eighties had been enabled, the prosecutors said, by the state's refusal to believe that the mafia existed as an organization, a refusal reflected in the attitudes and practices of criminal investigators and trial judges in mafia cases.

That a coherent overall picture of Cosa Nostra had never been articulated was no accident. Interested parties in the media, the judiciary, the church and in parliament had always been ready to muddy the waters, to dismiss the mafia as a literary chimera or communist propaganda or an insult against Sicily. Police practice and judicial practice, the very articles of the law, reflected a belief that Cosa Nostra didn't exist. Nobody even knew its name until Tommaso Buscetta revealed it in 1984. And the police and magistrates who'd had open eyes and the wit to make sense of what they found had soon been identified as dangers and soon removed. Cesare Terranova, for instance, had known. When the Sicilian judge Leonardo Sciascia called *an acute and implacable enemy of the mafia* had returned from parliament in Rome in 1979 to head the investigative office in Palermo, he was murdered before he could start, shot in his car as he left home for work.

His tough and determined successor as chief prosecutor, Rocco Chinnici, had known too. He'd encouraged Falcone's early investigations of the heroin traffic between the Asian golden triangle and Sicily, when a ship was seized in the Suez canal carrying two hundred and thirty-three kilos of refined heroin to Sicily. Chinnici spoke out against the mafia in schools and piazzas at a time when nobody else mentioned the word, and was blown up by a car bomb with two of his escort and a bystander in 1983. A few months earlier Ciaccio Montalto, another judge who'd known, had been shot in Trapani. The season of *distinguished corpses* was beginning in those first years of the eighties.

These murders were partly a sign of the growing strength of Riina's brutal Corleonesi, though if Cosa Nostra had never killed magistrates before, it really hadn't needed to. Chinnici had left a private diary when he died, that named names, recording his private suspicions and fears and accusing many of his colleagues in the Palermo justice building of complicity with Cosa Nostra. When this became known its contents were assimilated with hints that Chinnici had become paranoid. After the murders of these vigorous and intelligent magistrates, it seemed the final defeat for antimafia activism when a frail elderly magistrate on the verge of retirement called Antonino Caponnetto came down from Tuscany to replace his two murdered predecessors in Palermo, remarking that *at sixty-three one should be used to living with the idea of death,* Yet Caponnetto formed the antimafia pool with Falcone and Borsellino and the others, and the maxitrial verdict was the pool's work, the final recognition in law that Cosa Nostra was a single body. All those magistrates had been murdered to prevent that.

The prosecutors of Andreotti underlined Cosa Nostra's permanent aim of eliminating the *historic memory* built up by those few who'd understood that Cosa Nostra was *a state within the state.* Cosa Nostra, *The True History* reminded you, was a state organized territorially, divided into clans, governed by a central commission known as the Cupola at the apex of its pyramid and served by thousands of members at its base, who were controlled through rules and sanctions. It wasn't *an indistinct galaxy of criminal gangs, often at war among themselves and without a unified organization and leadership.* Cosa Nostra was a state that maintained relations with professional, political and judicial representatives of that other state, the Italian republic.

> This state within the state murdered the president of the regional government, the leader of the main opposition party, the provincial secretary of the main governing party, the prefect of Palermo, two chief state prosecutors, an advisory judge, two heads of the investigative police, two commanders of the carabinieri, the director general of the ministry of justice, a deputy prosecutor. It has also killed dozens of other citizens loyal to the state's institutions, doctors, businessmen, magistrates, law enforcement officers and hundreds of ordinary people.

The anti-state of Cosa Nostra had featured

> ... in the darkest pages of the history of the republic from the end of the war to the present: the massacre of Portella della Ginestra, the BORGHESE coup d'etat attempt, the MORO kidnapping, the P2 affair, the CALVI case, the SINDONA case, etc.

When Totò Riina had entered the Salvo drawing room that summer afternoon, he'd entered as a head of that other state, and it was as such that the past and future leader of the Italian government had greeted him. It was a summit. They were Kennedy and Krushchev, Nixon and Mao, and thus the two leaders greeted each other.

At the time of The Kiss, the maxitrial had been going for a year and a half, and it had only three months more to run. As the trial moved inexorably to its conclusion, the leaders of Cosa Nostra were becoming more and more perturbed. Two legal attempts to derail proceedings had failed. They'd challenged the presiding judge in April 1986, accusing him of partiality and misconduct two months into the trial. This had failed in the appeal court. Six months later defence lawyers had tried a kind of filibuster, requesting that all the documents on the case be read out in full in court. Since the prosecution's case alone ran to nearly nine thousand pages, this would have prolonged the trial beyond the legal limit for preventive custody, and freed the hundreds of the accused mafiosi before the verdict was reached. In early 1987 the Italian parliament quickly passed a new law to prevent this happening. The DC, to the great anger of Cosa Nostra, had done nothing to stop this law being passed. At one point Cosa Nostra had decided to express their dissatisfaction with the feeble performance of their defence lawyers by waxing a few of them, *pour encourager les autres*, but the project stalled over which barristers to eliminate. Cosa Nostra was unhappiest of all with the demochristians who seemed to be doing nothing to impede or compromise the maxitrial. They hadn't been given votes to do nothing. It was this that Giulio Andreotti had to answer for to Totò Riina that afternoon of The Kiss. Cosa Nostra wanted reassuring.

To teach the DC a lesson, Cosa Nostra had ordered a switch in votes in the 1987 elections, away from the DC. All the candidates supported by Cosa Nostra had been elected, and while the DC vote had increased in the rest of Italy, it'd fallen sharply in Palermo, in some central Palermo electorates dropping by more than half. It'd been a nasty little taste of a possible future for Andreotti, whose electoral strength in Sicily, assembled and mediated by Salvo Lima, was the source of his power. Lima himself, the man of honour who'd gone on from being mayor of Palermo to be Andreotti's undersecretary of the budget in Rome, was in a delicate position by 1987, now that the Corleonesi had taken over Cosa Nostra. Lima had always dealt with the old guard, civilized mafiosi who'd understood the ways of mediation. He wasn't known or trusted by the new bosses. The new Cosa Nostra did business differently and their dissatisfaction over the maxitrial had left Lima dangerously exposed. They'd been less flexible, less gracious than the mafiosi they'd eliminated. *Stick to the agreement or we'll kill you and your family*, the new Cosa Nostra had told him. This was an overriding reason for Andreotti to respond to Riina's request for a summit.

Italy's most wanted criminal came without the slightest fear of arrest or entrapment. When he kissed Andreotti, a kiss the prosecutors described Andreotti as having *undergone*, Riina was taking the initiative and sending a complex message. It was a reassurance offered on Cosa Nostra's own territory in a moment of crisis, prelude to a new understanding between the states. It must have been a relief. When he'd come down secretly to Palermo seven years earlier, to get an explanation for Cosa Nostra's murder in 1980 of Piersanti Mattarella, president of the Sicilian regional government, Andreotti had been shouted at by the Palermo boss Stefano Bontate.

> In Sicily we give the orders. And if you don't want to wipe out the DC completely you do what we say. Otherwise we'll take away your vote. Not only in Sicily but also in Reggio Calabria and all through southern Italy. You'll only be able to count on the vote up north, and up there they all vote communist anyway. You can make do with that.

Riina was now more quietly reminding Andreotti of his commitments. Politically, Andreotti had less room for manoeuvre than before. Vito Ciancimino, the former mayor of Palermo, and the Salvo cousins, his link with Cosa Nostra, had all been charged as mafiosi. A dossier on

Salvo Lima had been tabled in the European parliament in Strasbourg. The maxitrial was being followed closely.

Riina suspected that Andreotti now wanted to slither out of his undertakings to the mafia without losing the electoral power base Cosa Nostra guaranteed. It was another instance of the Andreotti *double game*. So Riina had to remind him. He had to remind Andreotti that he couldn't *distance himself*, that Riina and Andreotti, like Lima and Salvo and the others in the room, were *the same thing*. Cosa Nostra is *our thing* and a man of honour identifies another as *la stessa cosa*, the same thing, and the four powerful figures present that afternoon were all the same thing and were in it all together. It made little difference, *The True History* said, whether or not Andreotti had been formally sworn in. Whether Andreotti's finger had been pricked by a senior man of honour in the presence of other men of honour, whether he had dropped blood on to a sacred image and held it burning in his hands as he prayed *that my flesh may burn like this holy image if ever I betray my vow*. This, said the Palermo prosecutors, didn't matter.

> The one thing that mattered, and what [Riina] wanted to remind [Andreotti] once again, is that whoever had made a pact of mutual loyalty and assistance with Cosa Nostra had got to understand that there could be no grounds for withdrawing from that pact for the rest of his life. And to keep that clearly in mind.

At such a meeting, the kiss wasn't *absurd* at all. The kiss and the embrace were inescapable.

BALDASSARE DI MAGGIO, the witness of The Kiss in 1987 and the man of honour who'd led the police to Riina in 1993, had started adult life as a mechanic. He was the son of a mafioso shepherd in the old mafia town of San Giuseppe Jato, thirty kilometres inland from Palermo, and three years older than Giovanni Brusca, son of the district boss. He'd been approached in his twenties and done his first killing in 1981 with the Brusca son. He'd had no idea who he was killing or why and knew not to ask. Then he was taken to a country property nearby and met Totò Riina and his wife and four children. The house had been made available to the Riinas by a Palermo doctor. After takeaway roast chicken, the boys told Riina they'd been impressed by Di Maggio's grace under pressure. He'd returned the fire of a carabiniere. Four months later Di Maggio was initiated by Brusca senior. Over the next five years, Di Maggio had killed, for Riina and

Brusca, twenty-three people in a variety of ways. He'd torched a number of houses, including an ex-mayor of Palermo's, and dealt in drugs and public works. He'd become a particular favourite of Riina's, who often said *Baldo's in my heart* and made Di Maggio his driver. Thus, when Brusca senior was in jail and Brusca junior exiled to a remote island, Di Maggio was made boss of their *cosca*, their mafia family. He'd built a million-dollar villa, with swimming pools and pillars and *original art work* on the walls.

It turned bad when he lost interest in his wife and fell for a girl that Brusca junior also wanted. It turned nasty when Brusca came home and wanted to take command as well. In early 1992 a conference was called with Totò Riina, to make the peace. At the end of the discussion Riina confirmed his trust in Di Maggio, and kissed him. *Baldo's not some old orange to chuck away.* Di Maggio, however, knew his boss's ways. He'd seen too many scenes like that not to realize Riina's was a Judas kiss. He realized he was about to be killed. Uncle Totò had Baldo *in his heart* and was going to kill him. He was choosing the Bruscas. It was like that with Riina. Di Maggio fled with his heavily pregnant girlfriend to Canada. Unable to get a visa, they returned to Italy, going north to Novara where Di Maggio had a friend. The police knew this, knew about the quarrel, and arrested him in the first days of 1993, just after the birth of Di Maggio's child. The violence of Riina's Cosa Nostra in 1992 had plunged a lot of men of honour into crisis. *Profoundly shaken by the terrible atrocities committed against judges Falcone and Borsellino*, the leading man of honour and Riina intimate Gaspare Mutolo had decided to talk three months earlier. *Cosa Nostra has undertaken an irreversible strategy of death*, he said. It was the thought of being sent to Palermo, of being surrounded by men at Riina's orders in the Ucciardone that now turned Di Maggio. *I'm a dead man*, he said. *But I'm a man of honour. I can take you to Riina.* And he did. And when Riina was taken, Di Maggio, Mutolo, Buscetta, Mannoia, all the pentiti who knew the most overcame their last inhibitions. Unknown to each other, in their secret safe houses in Italy and America, in 1993 the men of honour all started talking for the first time about Giulio Andreotti.

———

THE STRUGGLE to hold *The True History of Italy* up to the naked fifteen watt bulb taxed the wrists. It was a weighty history. By now the weak daylight that reached into the room had quite gone and beyond this tiny glow all was dark. Descending in the clattering old iron cage of a lift, I found the Palermo evening stroll outside at the height of its frenzied saunter. The streets were full of people purposefully going nowhere in particular. After a poke around Flaccovio's bookshop, I walked around the expensive part of Palermo and observed the short sleek people who were doing their window shopping. Roney's bar was full of decaying aristocrats, monied nullities and sinister, purposeful people. The shop windows were full of expensive things to buy. Apart from the inevitable and endless boutiques with laden racks of designer clothes and accessories, among them a lot more furriers selling ankle length minks than the Sicilian climate would seem to warrant, there were a lot of jewellers, a lot of watchmakers. Authorized dealers in Rolex and IWC Schauffhausen. And there were even more of those shops you saw all over southern Italy, that specialized in wedding presents. Heavy things in silver, in crystal, in porcelain, in gilt, and in horrid taste. Weddings were still big in the Mezzogiorno. Even the humblest were dynastic affairs. The trousseau mattered, the wedding dress, the reception. The wedding gift.

It was now past closing time. Lights were going off, keys being turned in locks, shutters slammed down, alarm systems activated. The streets were suddenly empty. Where people went I couldn't see, and never would later, however attentively I studied them on nights to come. They just vanished, moving with the same nonchalant and preoccupied directionless speed with which they'd earlier thronged the footpaths. They were, it occurred to me, in training. There'd been a thousand or so violent deaths in the crowded streets of Palermo over the last fifteen years, and very few witnesses. This was a population with some experience in melting away and always aware that the need might return. The streets at night were terribly empty. The streets were empty at night all through the south now. Nobody wanted to be a witness. You might as well be the victim. Having lunched on a mirage, I decided to go back to the little restaurant I'd found between the Vucciria and piazza San Domenico, into whose kitchen I'd seen the fish marketer disappear and where a grubby Persian cat had been sleeping on the doorstep.

III

A CASE OF KNIVES

LIGHTS WERE on and people were sitting now under the umbrellas at the bottom of the dogleg lane that dropped precipitously to the restaurant and then twisted into the dark. It wasn't a place you'd have felt like going down to at night without those lights in the window. The Persian cat was watching the outside diners like a jailer. I went inside to the corner of a clean uncluttered room where centuries of plaster had been scraped away, baring stone and beams. Some young people were drifting around in loose clothes. They looked like art students, and one of them was. The whole outfit was run by family and friends. One or two drifted over amiably with a vague look of inquiry, and soon a saucer of green olives and anchovies was sitting on the table, and some bread, and some mineral water. A small woman with dark hair and dark eyes and precise features whirled up like a woodland bird. She perched lightly at the table and rattled off a long list of antipasti, first courses and seconds, and every single one of them came out of the sea. This was Palermo in summer for you. She thought spaghetti with sea urchins, and the steaks of some larger sea fish with a kind of sweet and sour onion and vinegar sauce, would be *a very brave choice*. I hoped it wouldn't take bravery to eat them and she said, *oh no*. She hadn't meant that.

The spaghetti with sea urchins were excellent, the urchin eggs still raw and moist, flung into a pan with a little oil and garlic at the instant the spaghetti were flung in too and briefly tossed. This was a nearly ideal way of dealing with sea urchins. The warmth of the pasta and oil charged the flavour of the roe without killing it by cooking, and the pasta's bulk prolonged without weakening the sensation. Sea urchins and I went a long way back, to a dinghy anchored off Sardinia. A friend's son dived for them and we sat in the boat, cutting them open with a knife and scooping out the cruciform lines of golden eggs with the blade. The son also brought up huge oysters like plates from the sea bed, but these were for later, back at the house. At Trani in Apulia, on the Adriatic coast, men used to sell sea urchins on street corners on Sunday mornings, freshly cut in half and laid out on sheets of newspaper, a dozen half shells to the sheet.

All the shellfish were wonderful in Trani. The fishing port on the Adriatic coast had been another bastion of the Normans and the Angevins and the Swabians in the Mezzogiorno, and the golden Norman cathedral standing on the water made you weak at the knees. You couldn't buy fresh fish there though. Big refrigerated lorries carried off the entire catch every morning before dawn. Shellfish, however, abounded. They were for the locals. There were glossy mussels, sleek brown *datteri di mare*, sea dates, who lived inside narrow holes they burrowed in the soft yellow tufa below the waterline, *cannelicchi*, which were Chinaman's fingernails, pipis, *taratufoli*, *vongole*, others whose names eluded me, though not the memory of their shape and flavour, the smooth mottled shells and the dark grooved ones. The mussels were excellent in Trani, and clean, and so were Apulian tomatoes, oil and pasta, so the Sunday urchins were naturally followed by *spaghetti con le cozze*, brilliant black shells, golden oil and unequalled intensity of red in the tomatoes. With chili, unless locals were coming to lunch.

An elderly publisher in Bari showed me a trattoria in a dark and narrow street that as a prelude to its grilled fish and crustaceans from the Adriatic did a pasta dish of *spaghettini* with a little fresh San Marzano tomato flesh and a variety of shellfish and crustaceans, shrimps, clams, Chinaman's fingernails. In Apulia they habitually used a finer strand of spaghetti than is usual elsewhere. It seems hairlike, almost Asian, and well suited to these almost souplike seafood dishes. It also took a lot less time to cook.

The seafood there was why the place was frequented by *malavitosi* who even as one ate must have been plotting the birth of the Holy United Crown. Until the eighties, Apulia was unique in the south in having no organized crime, but mafiosi from Sicily and camorristi from Naples who were jailed there soon fixed that. The Apulians copied their initiation rites and soon the Pugliesi were taking lessons from nobody. A few years later the beautiful Petruzzelli theatre in Bari was torched and an age of placid decency went up in smoke.

The grey-haired man who now brought over a bottle of white wine from nearby Alcamo was Pippo, the husband of the dove-like Anna Maria. Two of the staff were their sons. Emiliano had a Van Dyke beard and short hair and moved like a footballer and studied politics. The younger, with long, long straight hair and a Palestinian *kefiah*, was Dario, who studied art. A longhaired friend called Stefania was doing sociology. Pippo worked during the day for telecom and the Sant'Andrea, called after the piazzetta, was new. New in this form, newly theirs. Pippo and I were still talking several hours later, long after the last diners had left. The staff had gathered around the largest table to eat, and when the cooks emerged from the kitchen I recognized them from the first morning at the Vucciria. The plump bespectacled figure was Totò, the head cook, who came in lifting off his toque and dabbing at his beaded forehead. The knifeblade silhouette from the market was Nabil's. He was a Tunisian, a fisherman's son from just across the water, which explained his expertise with fish. He was wearing another embroidered cap.

A bottle of brandy came out and friends drifted in. It was about two in the morning. Most of the arrivals were students. Vincenzo was an architecture student living in the Vucciria. He talked eagerly about Glen Murcutt. He said he would have given anything to work with Murcutt in Australia. I told him quite gently Murcutt had no assistants, that he always worked alone. Vincenzo was the son of a friend Pippo had been talking about. This friend had withdrawn a few years earlier from regular work and life in society to live in an old mill with a few thousand books. He'd known Guttuso and Sciascia, and knew a lot too about the history of Italy since the war and the artistic life of Palermo. They were all going to the mill on Sunday, to make a barbecue and have a day in the country, and asked me along.

A couple of days later Pippo and Anna Maria and Dario and I set off in their knocked-around old Fiat on Sunday morning and headed for the mill. The others were travelling separately. The Fiat was loaded with food to barbecue at our destination. Fresh baby mackerel, ropes of Sicilian sausage, lambs' intestines knotted up with fresh rosemary and chickens to roast in the mill's oven. Palermo faces north-east, looking out over the sea to the continent and over its shoulder, as it were, to the new world and Africa. The town's settled into the fertile curve of the Conca d'Oro, a rim of richly orcharded lowland, the sweet ground of orange and lemon trees, almonds and olives, lying between the

Mediterranean and the other world of the Sicilian interior, mountainous, arid, closed, inaccessible. If it weren't for the sea's perpetual promise of escape, you'd feel trapped in Palermo, menaced by the jagged teeth of the encircling rocky hills. Getting out of the city and out of the Conca d'Oro, the coastal golden bowl, and heading inland meant climbing steeply. Leaving from the Vucciria, we headed south-west and within minutes the battered Fiat was high above the city, winding up a dry precipitous hillside. We went through a mountain pass and into a windswept desert landscape of dead grass and dirt and huge white boulders. The remote scattering of these giant stones generated a sense of ancient violence. It was utterly bleak and sterile. The blue sea of the gulf and the dark green sea of citrus trees and the busy life of the city had vanished. The air was suddenly colder. We fell silent. Always in the high country of Sicily you sensed exhaustion and abandonment. It was like walking into a deserted house. Anna Maria, who had been working until three in the morning, was now asleep. Dario was hunched over *Il Manifesto*, maybe the last daily in Europe to proclaim itself communist.

A road sign woke me from my daze. A black on yellow notice, as we curved over the shoulder of a hill, announced Montelepre. Montelepre had been the home of the bandit Giuliano. The hills of western Sicily, the wild and remote interior, were just above Palermo. Half an hour's drive from the city centre. Dario remarked, pulling up his *kefiah* and lighting a cigarette, the roads were worse in those days, and bandits harder to chase, but the nearness lent a new weight to that judge's sardonic words about the bandits being inaccessible *only to the police*. We passed the grim, closed town huddled on the hill and spun downhill through land that was looking green again. Soon we were at the mill, which stood high in a valley that swept down to the rich and mafioso town of Partinico and the sea. Montelepre stayed just in sight behind us, a bleaker reminder higher up, a cluster of walls and roofs you saw when you looked back over your shoulder at the barren hills. Dogs and cats came cartwheeling out to greet us. Pasquale was less excited by the invasion of city life. He was working at something over the kitchen table, half moon glasses jammed on his nose.

The mill had stood there since the middle ages. The building had accreted over centuries into two high storeys and three big wings. It'd milled the grain of Sicily until sugar cane arrived from Egypt in the eleventh century, the time of Arab Sicily, when it was made over to process sugar. When Columbus discovered the Americas four hundred years later, he'd taken cane plants with him, and sugar went west, to the

Azores, the Indies, Brazil, and Sicily's sugar cane plantations were superseded by the slave estates beyond the Atlantic. Sicily and the mill reverted to grain. The rusted machinery of Pasquale's mill had stood unused for years, and the little torrent that had powered the wheel no longer flowed under the rambling mill building. Part of the stream still flowed down the steep and stony hill outside, watering the large neglected gardens around the mill and the overgrown fruit orchard.

Vincenzo went off to fill the demijohns with yellow wine, which was getting low, and Pippo built up a big fire in the courtyard from sticks and twigs we gathered. We sat round drinking the yellow wine and eating fresh bread and arranging the baby mackerel and the lambs' intestines and the rope of sausage on a gridiron. The dogs and cats looked on attentively. Yellowing leaves were coming down in the wind from the vines that grew on the walls. The mill felt a lot closer to Montelepre than it did to fat coastal Partinico, and summer was over. We could see scuds of rain coming down on the hills near Montelepre. The dead leaves eddied in little unseen vortices, the column of smoke blew across the courtyard and a few drops fell. I wandered off to the disused wheelhouse, and poked around the great rusted wheels inside the gloomy dusty cavern that had once been the throbbing heart of the place. It too was now used, like most of the other dark corners in this vast place, as a repository of printed matter. Great piles of old reviews were stacked here, spiders racing lightly over them as they toppled into dust. Pasquale took me upstairs.

On a wall near a window hung a black and white photograph in a frame. Pasquale took it down and held it to the light. It showed three young men standing by some big rocks. They looked Sicilian, and so did the rocks. The men were smartly dressed in country gear and the one in the middle was grinning. It was Salvatore Giuliano the bandit, with his cousin Gaspare Pisciotta and his brother-in-law Pasquale Sciorino. The photo was taken outside the mill fifty years ago. We went downstairs and Pasquale showed me a door that Giuliano's men had hacked into the back wall of the mill. If they saw carabinieri coming up from Partinico, they had quick and unseen access to the hills. Giuliano photographed well. He was goodlooking, dark and not yet twenty-one when he'd shot the first carabiniere and taken to the hills behind us. He posed willingly with his guns and his gold belt buckles for the Italian and foreign journalists. The glamour of the Giuliano myth was such that when Francesco Rosi made his starkly late neorealist film *Salvatore Giuliano* in the early sixties, the people of Montelepre threw eggs at the screen in protest during its brief season in that town, or so the composer Stravinsky was told when he visited Sicily just after the film's release. Leonardo Sciascia saw the film among an audience of Sicilian peasants who shouted with laughter during the most harrowing death scene, because they'd never seen themselves in a film before.

The mill was a maze of discontinuous rooms, alcoves, passages, landings on different levels. There were iron beds in some of the rooms and little other furniture, apart from roughly fashioned bookshelves everywhere. He'd made it liveable piecemeal over the years. There were books and papers everywhere. They seemed to be in total disorder, but every time he wanted to check some obscure detail, he found it instantly. Pasquale was a person of eclectic interests. He'd published a bibliography of Italian fascist writings and an extremely learned history of the fork and its use at the dining table, its evolution from the ancient Greeks, almost but not quite down to modern wielders of plastic forks and eaters of junk food. In Pasquale's hands, the fork became an index of civilization.

————————

TABLE FORKS, he reminded me, hadn't always been with us. The instrument used daily by billions was a fairly recent invention and not at all inevitable. The Chinese had created a plurimillennial civilization that bypassed the fork entirely. There were no forks used at the Homeric beach barbecues with which the epos of western dining began. *They put their hands on the food*, said Homer again and again, when a banquet began in the *Odyssey*. And so people ate for many centuries. The knife had been the fork's ancestor, as its use extended from cutting meat or cheese or fruit at table to spearing portions. The appearance of the fork, specifically designed for spearing food and delivering it to the mouth, was hard to pin down in time. When did this separate instrument appear, to be held in the other hand and used in conjunction with the cutting knife? The moment would have marked a qualitative leap in refinement and luxury, not to say personal hygiene. At Plato's *Symposium*, guests were eating with their hands and most people went on doing so for the next millennium.

Ovid, in his *Art of Love,* implied an absence of cutlery in Roman high society by advising women, in Peter Green's translation, *Take your food with dainty fingers ... Don't besmear your whole face with a greasy paw.* Protoforks however were very much in use by Nero's time at Trimalchio's lavish and hugely vulgar dinner party in the *Satyricon*, though cutlery still hadn't made the great split of spearing from cutting functions. *Arbiter elegantiae*, Petronius would have remarked on it. What happened to the fork after that was inseparable from the decline and fall of the Roman empire and the rise of Christianity. As the Goths and Huns and Ostrogoths descended on Rome, Roman civilization had decamped to the new capital in the east, and the proto-table fork and table manners had gone sailing to Byzantium with it. The Huns, when they ate their raw meat after tenderizing it under their saddles for a few days, ate it with their hands.

The first person in recorded history to use what was indisputably a modern table fork was, Pasquale said, a Byzantine princess called Maria who arrived in Venice toward the end of the tenth century to marry the doge. Saint Pier Damiani, who probably didn't himself get to see her do it, because Princess Maria died of the plague in 1005 when the future saint was seventeen, wrote that she didn't touch her food with her own hands, but had it cut up into bite-sized pieces by her eunuchs. The princess then raised these morsels to her mouth *fuscinulis aureis bidentibus, with little gold two-pronged forks*. The detail would've been noticed because the church regarded the use of the fork as sinful. Pier Damiani was making a point. He was himself more given to fasting and flagellation than to eating and drinking. Dante noted his abstinence in the *Comedy*. The table fork was a sign of that oriental decadence the fathers of the western church were casting their anathemas against, and the saint was convinced the Byzantine princess's use of the table fork had been one of the luxurious habits which caused the outbreak of plague that killed her and her husband the doge.

In Sicily the Arab courts were as opulent as Byzantium, and when the Normans arrived at the beginning of the eleventh century, Palermo and Naples became the centre of civilized Europe. The crusades, said Pasquale, which started as a convulsion of religious fanaticism, ended up as a civilizing experience of cultural exchange for the Mediterranean area. The table fork made great inroads at this time around its western shores, in all those cities that were in touch with Byzantium and the east. By this time life had improved in the west, and the church of Rome was now busy denouncing the luxury at home. In the Abbess of Hohenbur's twelfth-century codex *Hortus Deliciarium*, a miniature showed a dinner table in the garden of delights laid with very conspicuous forks. Saint Bernard stormed out of the convent at Cluny around this time, in protest against its *cuisine gourmet*, and in the following century Saint Bonaventura wrote a treatise *De Disciplina Circa Comestionem*, *on discipline in eating*, which condemned luxury and greed and harped back monotonously to the *just punishment* suffered by the unfortunate

Byzantine princess and her husband the doge to whom she introduced the table fork.

All the theologians of the day agreed that the table fork was a *tool of the devil* and anathematized the *instrumentum diaboli* as a sinful luxury. By now, however, the tide was beginning to turn in favour of the fork, and pointed remarks began to be heard from the laity that it was about time the clergy learnt some table manners. Some of them evidently did. In 1298, an archpriest in Pisa made a will leaving to various relatives his silver knives with coral handles, two silver spoons, four table knives with ivory and jade handles *and four silver table forks*. And yet, and yet. *Did Dante eat with a table fork?* Pasquale insisted. *Or Boccaccio?* There was no sign any of their characters knew of it. Twelfth-century notes on etiquette by a Milanese, Bonvesin de la Riva, offered advice on gracious eating that strongly implied an absence of forks.

> Do not upset the common eating dish when fishing with the fingers for a large morsel. Do not spit. Do not touch cats and dogs while eating. Do not lick your fingers or stick them up your nose. Do not comment when you find dead flies or live cockroaches in the eating dish.

A counsellor on seduction techniques, Francesco Barberino, was advising at the same time in his *Documents of Love* that men at table should avoid staring into a woman's face when she was eating, or looking at her hands, as it tended to cause embarrassment.

Pasquale took off his half-moon reading glasses. He pushed his papers back and got up from the kitchen table. He poured us each a tumbler of yellow wine and led me out into the courtyard. The fire was blazing now. Rain the night before had wet the wood, and some of the branches were green, and dense smoke twisted around the space enclosed by the three sides of the mill. The kittens had their eye on a gridiron packed with tigerstriped mackerel. Pippo was wrestling with the fire and the dogs were watching the length of sausage Nabil was coiling on another gridiron. Pasquale led me across the paved yard to the low parapet that ran along the fourth side. From the parapet we looked down the green valley of citrus trees on to Partinico and the sea. *The Arabs*, said Pasquale, *did all that.*

> *A thousand years ago they cultivated the rich land along the coast. The Conca d'Oro – behind the hills over there – and all this fertile coastal land below us, down to Marsala. It was the Arabs made it the flourishing garden it still is, really. They made dykes against the sea, they built navigable canals, they irrigated with further waterways, they planted the palms and citrus crops and sugar cane and cereals.*

There were a lot of old fruit trees just below the mill and a lot more on the hill around the side. They were bedraggled now, sagging and covered with lichen. Peaches were rotting on the ground. Pasquale flung his arm in a triumphant arc, sloshing his wine on the wall. A dog moved smartly out of reach. After two centuries of Arab rule, the Normans had driven out the emirs by 1061. But there was no ethnic cleansing when the Normans arrived. There was synthesis and continuity, the best of both worlds. Under the liberal Norman regime the Arab settlers stayed on in Sicily, mixing and living with Greeks and Latins and Sicilians. And the great growth of Sicilian agriculture was the work of these Arabs. All round the western edge of Sicily, from Marsala to Palermo and further still toward the Italian peninsula, skilled farmers from Mesopotamia had settled.

An Arab writer called Abu Abdallah Muhammad ibn Idris wrote a great work of geography at this time for the Norman emperor Roger II, who wore Arab dress in his court, spoke Arabic and cultivated Arabic arts and sciences. It was entitled *The Delight of One who Loves Travelling Around the World*, also known as *King Roger's Book*. It was a remarkable confluence of Christian and Islamic cultures. Idris wrote of Sicily in the twelfth century as

> the pearl of the century for abundance and beauty, the first country in the world for its nature, its buildings and its antiquity. Travellers come from everywhere, merchants and dealers from every city and metropolis, and all agree in praising it, and praise its splendid beauty, speak of its happy circumstances, its various advantages and the good things Sicily attracts from every other country of the world.

Palermo was described in detail,

> the huge and beautiful city, the greatest and most splendid place to stay, the vastest and finest city in the world ... It lies on the sea in the western part of the island. High mountains surround it, and yet its shore is joyous, sunny, smiling. Palermo has such beautiful buildings that travellers come to admire the architecture, the exquisite workmanship, the art ... All around the city are streams and perpetual springs. Inside the town are many gardens, beautiful houses and canals of fresh running water, brought from the mountains that surround its plain. Outside the southern side runs the ever-flowing Abbas [Oreto] river, which has enough mills built along it to fully satisfy all the city's needs.

Sicily's beauty and plenty were in the Arab poetry too, I thought. Years earlier in Naples I'd bought a book of verse by the Arab poets of Sicily, done into Italian and Sicilian in versions by modern poets. Much of it was about the beauty of Sicily, some of it aching with nostalgia from poets forced into exile. Around 1100, 'Abd ar-Rahman of Trapani, a little further down the coast to the south, had written

> Oranges ripening in the island are fire on chrysolite branches
> Lemons are like a lover's pallor after painful nights away
> Palms are like loyal lovers on guard against their enemies ...
> O palms of Palermo's two seas, be watered by rains of abundance ...
> In your shade may love be inviolate ...

Pasquale broke in, bored with poetry. *They didn't just produce*, he said. *They processed food too. The Arabs invented spaghetti.* I looked around for the demijohn. Vincenzo poured us more wine. Being without preservatives, it was delicious. Was I going to hear some new version of the old story about Marco Polo bringing pasta back from China? *No, no*, said Pasquale the bibliographer eagerly.

> *That came from a bad translation. Remember that the original manuscript's been lost. The one Marco Polo dictated in prison in Genoa in 1298. What we've got are manuscript copies and translations into Latin, French, Tuscan, Venetian and so on. There are at least a hundred and thirty of them and some are far from reliable.*

The story of Marco Polo's Chinese pasta had come from a late and wildly inaccurate Latin version. The best versions, such as the Tuscan, had Marco Polo describing the kingdom of Fansur in Chapter 166, and saying that the people there had no grain but ate plenty of rice. He noted *a great wonder*, which was that in Fansur *they have big thin-barked trees that are full of a kind of flour inside*. They made much pasta from it, which Marco Polo said he'd often eaten. The Latin version had elaborated this freely into *lasagna and other dishes* eaten with sauce, whence the story of Marco Polo's discovering spaghetti in China. Later I looked this up. From the notes to a critical edition of the thirteenth-century Tuscan version I found that *the kingdom of Fansur* was *in the region of Baros on the south-eastern coast of Sumatra* and that *Fansur was the Arab transcription of the Malay toponym Pancur*. This seemed to be the largish island of Bangka, separated from south-east Sumatra by the Bangka Strait. Marco Polo said it had *the best camphor in the world, which is sold there for its weight in gold*. The Arabic for camphor transcribes as *al-kafur al-fansuri*. The pasta that legend transformed via lasagna into spaghetti was sago. Marco Polo had been describing sago and the sago palm.

In any case, resumed Pasquale, *every version of Marco Polo makes it clear the Chinese had no grain or any cereal crops other than rice*. This was the point about Sicily, *the type of cereal*. Before the Arabs invented spaghetti, pasta in Italy was mostly eaten in the form of gnocchi-like dumplings. Whatever form the pasta was worked into, it was *pasta fresca* and was eaten straight after it was prepared. *Pasta fresca*, often with egg added to become *pasta all'uovo*, has to be eaten fresh. It's made with tender grain flour and doesn't keep. *Pasta asciutta*, dry pasta, which kept for months and even years before being cooked and eaten, and so could be stock-piled and exported anywhere, was the Arabs' innovation in food technology. *Pasta asciutta* can only be made from a paste that contains mostly the hard-seeded, gluten-rich durum wheat, *triticum durum*, and in those days durum wheat was grown only in Sicily and other hot countries around the Mediterranean. The Arabs developed a way of working the paste made from this grain into forms thin enough to dry out completely, by working it into little strings, *spaghetti*, or into even thinner little worms, *vermicelli*, or into any of the hollow tube-like forms of macaroni that let the pasta dry out on both sides. It was the geographer Idris who left the first recorded mention of spaghetti in his *Delight*, proof that in the first part of the twelfth century Sicilians knew not only how to work pasta but how to dry it, preserving it for long sea voyages to cities on the European and north African coasts of the Mediterranean, as well as across the strait of Messina to Calabria.

The technique soon spread, but for centuries dry macaroni were still known as *maccaroni siciliani*. A cookery book published around 1450, Maestro Martino's *Libro de Arte Coquinaria* called both macaroni and vermicelli *siciliani*. Another recipe of a few years later for *minestra siciliana*, in Platina's *Honest Pleasure, De honesta voluptate*, explained how to prepare hollow macaroni. *Dry them in the sun and they'll last you two or three years, especially if made by the August moon*. For even longer, when regional insults were being exchanged, Sicilians were called *macaroni eaters* by other Italians. Neapolitans were leaf eaters. What it all had to do with the invention of the fork was that you couldn't eat spaghetti with a knife or a spoon. You could eat it with your bare hands, holding a bunch above your face and lowering the strands into your mouth as you chewed and swallowed. The street people of Naples ate like this, and tourists and smart Neapolitans gathered to watch the *lazzaroni* eat. They'd never have stared if they'd eaten like that at home, Pasquale argued, so they must have had forks.

AN OBJECT from the days of 1943 and 1944 was a large shallow oblong wooden case about two square feet in area. Vincenzo brought it out after lunch. It was a plain varnished case with hinges at the back and a clasp at the front, of peasant manufacture: not finely finished but solid and strong. Covering most of the lid's surface, carved elaborately into it, was a fierce American eagle, wings outspread, eye glaring and beak hooked. Near the clasp the letters *U S A* were carved in big capitals into the wood, among the painstakingly rendered wing feathers. When it was made the wooden box had represented food. It was something to sell an American soldier. Something for him to take home to the States. Something that might get its Sicilian carver some of the allied currency then circulating, the notes with Roosevelt's four freedoms printed in English on the back. *Freedom of speech. Freedom of religion. Freedom from want. Freedom from fear.* It was a paleotourist souvenir, whose maker hadn't thought, hadn't been able to think, of what token of Sicily a stranger might've wanted to take away. The maker's mind was filled with the imagery of the invading power, the symbol of the liberating wealth he too desired. As a crude reminder of that time of need, the box was desperately touching. The saddest thing about it was that it must have remained unsold, and never left the place where it was carved. The box was a knife case. When Vincenzo opened it I saw a collection of rusting peasant knives, they too largely homemade, with wooden handles and blades of various shapes, determined as much by what was available in the way of iron and steel as by any specific job they were designed to do. This was the Sicilian component. These knives were the real souvenir. They looked murderous. Some of them had curved blades, almost hooked. I thought of their probable uses. Sheep and goats and pigs. Cutting throats. Docking tails. Gutting. Skinning. Castrating.

The writer Dacia Maraini recently published a memoir of going back to Bagheria as a girl at the end of the war. Bagheria was once a beautiful town on the sea a few miles east of Palermo, now a cluster of crumbling noble villas overwhelmed by a cancerous mafia-built slum. Maraini's memoir made much, in the manner of such memoirs, of the aristocratic eccentricity in the author's forebears, and its tone was rigorously bittersweet. Except, that is, when she recalled a woman who'd worked for the family and the stories she'd told. Innocenza was the child's one link with the surrounding peasant world, and for an instant the memoir opened a door on a different life.

It was she who told me about the boy of eleven who'd seen something he shouldn't have seen. They'd taken him one morning, tied him up and blinded him with a knife used for gutting pigs and sent him home tied up like a salame, gushing blood. And about Don

Peppinuzzu, known as *sciacquatunazzu*, which means handsome in Sicilian. He'd said something he shouldn't have said. So they killed him with a shotgun blast and cut his balls off and stuffed them in his mouth. Which is how his mother found him when she went off to work in the fields one morning, under a mulberry tree.

This was revenge, punishment and warning in the archaic peasant world. It expressed the rural poverty and violence that had surrounded and sustained Sicily's islands of art and privilege, such as Bagheria was. Those expressions of violence were rustic antecedents of the culture that now made Bagheria an horrendous unplanned aggregate of apartment blocks built with the profits of heroin sales, and a place of terrible violence. They announced the warnings, deaths and insults of 1995. Kalashnikovs and car bombs came out of the world evoked by those rusty knives in their handcarved case. Cutting a man's throat, in that world and this, was little more than cutting a sheep's. Death in the world of the rural mafia survived in that form of murder by strangulation known as *incaprettamento*. The victim's hands and feet were tied behind his back with a rope then passed in a noose around his neck, so that he slowly strangled as his muscles yielded. A kid, or *capretto*, was tied in this way when taken to market. The country art survived in the world of the industrial mafia because it left the human body, as rigor mortis set in, conveniently shaped for transportation in the boot of a car. The oddly intimate link between the mafia's rural past and its industrial present had tightened since the Corleonesi came to power.

THE APPROACH to Corleone is deceptive. You potter at first in the blue AST bus through the benign and opulent coastal Sicily of the orchards, taking rather longer than the fifty or sixty kilometre distance from Palermo would seem to warrant because the blue bus takes its time, and when it does start climbing into the hills to that particular promontory five or six hundred metres above the sea where Corleone squats, the roads become narrow and winding. You meet little traffic. The odd farm vehicle, the odd speeding BMW. The day I went to Corleone the blue bus took an inordinate time because the driver had forgotten to drop a suitcase belonging to a carabiniere in Palermo, and pulled off the road at a country intersection to rendezvous with another bus on another route, whose driver would collect the carabiniere's suitcase and take it to the city. It was a pleasant sunny morning and I sat dreaming in trancelike travel mode, trying to follow the driver's interminable monologue on his cellular phone. He was talking a lot about the *picciotti*, praising them. The Sicilian *picciotto* was like the Neapolitan *guaglione*, a boy or lad, embodied male values and loomed large in the cultural landscape of the south. Admiring the *picciotto* and the *guaglione*, their youth, energy, grace and daring was one of the ways people recognized that the married man was a diminished and limited figure, unsexed, subordinate to wife and family as the woman came into her own as the fertile mother. The patriarch idea never really caught on in the Mezzogiorno. Southern society being what it was, the *picciotto* inevitably became invested with the values of the *mafiuso* and his grace and daring expressed in the activities of the mafia. The organization depended greatly on the qualities of its foot soldiers, and each mafia family needed to recruit the boldest and quickest, the smartest and strongest from the rising males of the neighbourhood. A mafia without prestige, a mafia whose values were not those of the society's young males, would die. To talk about *picciotti* was a conservative way of speaking, a rural way and a mafia way, and I sat there in the sun trying to catch the nuance of the driver's amiable talk. I was in no hurry.

Others were. Something about the carabiniere's suitcase made our immobility less than easily bearable, and a small wave of restiveness blew through the bus. A woman who looked like a schoolteacher said sharply she had to be at Corleone by half past midday. The driver shrugged her off and called his small daughter on his cellular phone. Riina's wife, I remembered, had been a schoolteacher. The carabiniere's suitcase, you felt, wasn't for these passengers a neutral cargo, but a vaguely charged and dangerous object. A meeting at a country crossroad was a very mafia situation. Nasty things had happened at country crossroads. People grew edgy, and when the other bus at length arrived, and the carabiniere's suitcase was offloaded without incident and we were away again, there was a gust of relief.

An amazing moment came when the bus got away from the coast and started serious climbing. The arid hills we were heading into, the universal terrain of the interior, were suddenly covered by a dense green forest of oaks, quite vast, over four thousand hectares I later found, such as I'd never seen anywhere in the poor stripped Mezzogiorno. For the minutes it took the bus to pass a part of the perimeter of the forest of Ficuzza, where the Bourbons used to hunt wild boar and the mafia hid stolen cattle, I could imagine, as I'd often tried and failed to do, the Sicily that antedated the Roman deforestation, the bush-covered island of Theocritus. For a nanosecond I thought I saw now an interior Sicily of poetry and sex, pipes and panic, light and shade that lingered in a few old poems.

> Galatea, why do you treat your lover harshly?
> You are whiter than ricotta, gentler than a lamb,
> Livelier than a calf, firmer than an unripe grape ...

I was merely daydreaming though, and so, probably, was Theocritus. Pastoral art and its staying power in western culture said a lot about the seductive resilience of dreams of simplicity, dreams of escape. History suggested they were always dreams, a dream even when Sicily was wooded and Theocritus was first giving elegant speech to herdsmen. Theocritus wrote his *Idylls* in the third century BCE, and Peter Green had written in his recent history of the Hellenistic age that

> The sheer record of atrocities during the fourth and third centuries, in Sicily particularly, is worse than for almost any other period of ancient history: a grisly chronicle of mass executions, public torture ... rape, pillage and enslavement, with the Romans as the worst, but by no means the only, habitual offenders.

Green thought Theocritus might even have been driven into exile by the banditry and unrest in Sicily during his lifetime, which would have made his country *Idylls* exercises in nostalgia for a Sicily that might never have quite existed, perhaps like the poems of Sicily's exiled Arabs thirteen hundred years later. Nevertheless, one of Theocritus's poems, the possibly spurious twentieth *Idyll*, in which a city girl was repelled by the uncouthness and smell of a country herdsman, had something peripheral to say about the world of Corleone, though sex wasn't directly the issue.

Corleone might've chilled me less if the bus hadn't got in at lunch time. A sense of movement through the windows as we pulled into the narrow piazza had reduced itself, by the time I actually got off, to a single child running home from primary school with a fluorescent knapsack on its back, running in some alarm because the others had already disappeared, like the lame girl after the pied piper. The place was quite deserted. I set off along a narrow street like a ravine, heading uphill from the piazza. A few metres along the empty street I saw another figure coming toward me, on foot but fast. It was a Capuchin friar in a hooded brown habit with a rope around it. He was young, bearded and barefoot and running for his life. He came flying past me with terror in his eyes, his white feet silently pounding the stones. Nobody followed him. I pushed on, sometimes glimpsing a female figure in black from the corner of my eye, choosing between unappetizing alleys as the main road disintegrated. The houses were poor, mean, crumbling, though some had had a lot of money spent on the inside. I knew the signs from Naples. The place seemed dead but I knew there were people behind the shutters. Corleone got poorer and more decrepit the closer you got to the river.

The river was a milky trickle at the bottom of a deep ravine that the poorest extremity of Corleone seemed about to fall into. Some things already had. A lounge suite, a fridge, a smashed TV set were sitting in the foul white water, by the green slime. Above the ravine and the teetering houses loomed a monolith with what'd been the town jail for three centuries built on top of it. I walked back to the main piazza and went to the bar and there were some people inside. When I opened my mouth half a dozen heads stiffened on their necks then slowly, slowly turned to take an oblique look. The murmured conversations died. I walked out and noticed how conveniently central the cemetery was in Corleone, just a little below the piazza. To make it even more convenient to reach, a little curved road, lined with cypress trees and beautifully paved with white marble, had been lately cut through the patch of waste land that stood between the piazza and the cemetery gates. Corleone's frequent hearses arrived at the the liveliest and most colourful place in town. The cemetery was immaculately kept and populated by bustling groups of women in black and children, who hurried knowledgeably up and down its avenues with bunches of gladdies.

Perhaps in an impressionable state after my stroll through the rest of town, I found the Corleone *campo santo* quite festive. The prominent notice at the entrance that it was *forbidden for reasons of hygiene to remove material from the cemetery* gave pause. One knew about extra bodies secretly buried in family vaults, and weaponry stored there too, but why anyone would want to remove *material* was far from clear. I wandered up and down, looking for the tomb of Luciano Liggio, latterly landscape painter, Totò Riina's mentor and predecessor as *capo di tutti i capi* and the man who might be said to have made Corleone famous. I failed to identify the dead for sure among the same direly familiar names that appeared over and over in the neat flowered rows, but I soon had a brush with the living. It was later, up in the other end of town, where the extensive new building was, the hideous blocks of flats, that a very new and powerful black Alfa Romeo cruised slowly down the hill toward me and rolled past at walking speed. It was driven by a redfaced youth wearing a black leisure suit with green and purple panels and a mean look on his meaty face. I knew the face. I'd seen it in the papers. I'd just been brushed by Totò Riina's son.

The face would come back to me seven months later. It looked out of *Repubblica*'s front page announcing Riina junior's first arrest. He was seized in June of 1996, in his grandmother's house in Corleone, where he was living with his mother and two sisters and *spending all day in the fields*, according to his tearful elder sister, *leaving home early in the morning to work the land and coming home at sundown, and in the evening, when he wasn't too dog tired, going to the bar with friends or out to eat a pizza. Nice friends. The mayor of Corleone could bear witness.* In the police version, at barely twenty the young Riina was already a made man. He'd first killed at nineteen, his victim a young mafioso who'd offended his uncle Leoluca Bagarella.

The arrest concerned the strangling of a thirteen-year-old child, who'd been kidnapped at eleven and held prisoner for over two years before being murdered. The boy was the son of one of Falcone's killers, a boss who'd later turned. The young Riina and Giovanni Brusca had ordered the child's death. *He opposed no resistance*, reported the boy's strangler, *his strength being already exhausted.* The child was killed because his father had been one of the men who'd laid the explosive that killed Falcone and the others, and then turned, in remorse and horror at the Riina apocalypse. The killers of his child said among themselves that if the murder became known *it'd cause more trouble than Falcone's killing at Capaci*, acknowledging in their own way that they'd passed a new threshold of infamy. *If you talk*, they warned their weakest link, who later did, *we'll drink your blood.* When young Riina was arrested, his sister recalled their crowded life as children in hiding. *Like little chickens, we used to help each other*, she said. *I know Giovanni and his goodness.* His anxious mother called out to the carabinieri who were bundling young Riina into their car, *Make sure you treat him well. He's only a boy.*

The young Riina, normally adorned with gold chain, gold crucifix, gold bracelet and gold ring, may have been only a boy, but he'd been causing people some worry for a while. A barman in Palermo whose fried snacks the young Riina hadn't liked was nearly dusted for it. Journalists at Liggio's funeral had been chased and insulted by the teenage Riina. *Born on the run*, as the papers liked to say, and brought up in hiding for a long period in that poetic and pastoral grove of oaks at Ficuzza, he'd plunged his fingers into a jar of gel while the police squad was searching his grandmother's home and pomaded his hair, ready for the photographers on arrival at the Ucciardone. Like the silk shirts Brusca had packed for jail, it was a sign of the times. The old mafia chiefs had been discreet, austere, even, some of them, personally poor. They'd been more concerned with power than luxury. The idea of young Riina's working the land from dawn to dusk showed a touching loyalty on his sister's part, and a sense of culture, of dynastic continuity. *Working the land* was how it'd all started half a century earlier, and the family's return to Corleone two days after their father's arrest in 1993 was a reminder of just how *country* the Corleonesi had always been. Young Riina's first act back in Corleone was to pray on the tomb of his father's father, who'd died fifty years earlier, a peasant labourer blown up in 1943 when he was trying to defuse an allied bomb, a person already noted by the carabinieri as *harmful to the person and property of others*. Among the Palermo families, the ones they'd basically exterminated, the Corleonesi had always been known as *i viddani*, which is *the villains* in the old Shakespearean sense, shading from *country people* into vile peasants and killers. Even when it described people running a huge multinational business, the word stayed exact. Not even the child murder, when you came to think about it, was new.

IN THE wild days of hunger and banditry at the end of the war, a zealous young captain of carabinieri from northern Italy was posted to Sicily and put in command of one of the antibanditry patrols. His name was Carlo Alberto Dalla Chiesa, a name that would loom large in *The True History of Italy*, because many years later his path would intersect fatally with Giulio Andreotti's. The young captain Dalla Chiesa filed acute and detailed reports on the unremarkable town of Corleone where he was stationed, in which he recorded the birth of that barbaric new mafia that years and years later would kill him. His first reports from the forties described the twilight of the old feudal mafia of the big landowners, and

> a decadent society preyed on by those profiteers ... still known as *gabellotti* and *campieri*. The first are almost always camouflaged ambiguously as estate *administrators*. The second are hired for their unscrupulousness and their reputation for violence to guard property from thieves and neighbours. Both are key elements on a vast mafia network.

The youngest-ever *campiere* was Luciano Liggio, who after arrests in his teens for carrying illegal weapons and stealing grain, got the job after the unexplained murder of the *campiere* whose place Liggio took. Liggio, his real name Leggio thus wrongly spelt in an early police report, was a year younger than Vito Ciancimino, who around this time gave up helping in his father's Corleone barbershop and moved with his parents down to Palermo, ready to begin his notable career in business and politics. This was the time when the mafia reconstructed itself in Sicily with the help of the American friends, and Corleone made an interesting paradigm of the forces in play. It was a time when the modest town of Corleone saw sixty-odd homicides between the arrival of the Americans in 1943 and the elections of 1948, so closely followed ˙ from the US embassy on the via Veneto in Rome and in Washington.

Two Corleonesi who'd fled to America during the fascist repression in the twenties now came home. One was known as Mr Vincent, who'd become *close* in New York to Frank *Three Fingers* Coppola, on whose account he now arrived in town. The other was captain De Carlo of the US marines, who'd arranged the trouble-free liberation of Corleone for the Americans. Before he entered the military, captain De Carlo too had been a made man of the American Cosa Nostra. A vicious struggle for power followed between Mr Vincent and captain De Carlo. The latter won, in the person of his cousin, Dr Navarra. Michele Navarra was, after the unexplained murder of his predecessor, Corleone's chief medical officer, director of the local hospital, head of the local DC and for years afterward Corleone's undisputed mafia boss. Mr Vincent bought a butchery and was relegated to the lower part of the town as its underboss.

I thought of Dr Navarra when I read about that later child murder, and remembered another boy's death in the Corleone of 1948, in the days when the left was organizing itself as well as the mafia and the peasants were claiming the untilled land of the big estates. He was a shepherd boy, that other thirteen-year-old, out with his animals on the hill above the town on a warm March evening. He came running down into town, sick with terror. In the dark he'd seen a dreadful thing. He'd seen two men take another and hang him on a tree. The boy was in a state of shock as he babbled out his story in the street, but he'd recognized Liggio and among the bystanders were friends concerned enough by what they heard to take the boy to the hospital to be treated and sedated. Dr Navarra attended personally to the minor emergency and injected a calmative. Whereupon the boy died.

That the child's night vision hadn't been induced by loneliness and impressionable youth was suggested by the disappearance earlier that evening of a very well known member of the Corleone community. He was a young Corleonese called Placido Rizzotto, a socialist who was the secretary of the local trade union council and an organizer for the farm labourers, the activist behind their claim to take over the unfarmed land of a big local estate. He'd had remarkable success in patiently overcoming centuries of fear and distrust among the rural poor. He'd last been seen at nine that evening walking toward the edge of town in the company of a *gabellotto* from the estate in question, and the young *campiere* Luciano Liggio. Mr Vincent had been waiting on the hill for the young trade unionist when Liggio walked him out of town with a gun in his back. Two years later pieces of the unionist's decomposed remains were retrieved from one of the deep, almost bottomless crevasses with which the bleak eroded hill above Corleone was riven. Everyone had seen in the crowded main street, everyone had known, no one had spoken. It was a chance not taken, a moment that marked Corleone's history, Sicily's and Italy's, for decades. *He was our hero,* said one who'd been on the street that night, *and we let him go. All we had to do, every one of us, was pick up a stone from the street and we'd have been too many.*

Captain Dalla Chiesa described Dr Navarra, the capomafia of Corleone, in his reports as

cunning, cultivated, a fluent but careful speaker ... uninterested in personal profit ... careless in his dress, corpulent and florid, a keen card player and enthusiastic hunter, he succeeded in creating an air of considerateness that particularly among the poorer people earned him *respect* and gratitude.

Dr Navarra was better-educated than most, but otherwise the very image of the old mafia boss. Cards, hunting and the DC were far from his only interests outside medicine. His cousin captain De Carlo got him US army authorization to commandeer abandoned military vehicles, and he used these to found the still-flourishing bus company, the AST, whose blue bus had brought me to Corleone. He was also heavily into petrol distribution and hospital management and medical insurance. The Corleonesi called Dr Navarra *Our Father,* and when they mentioned his name made the sign of the cross.

Liggio and Mr Vincent murdered the unionist at the orders of Dr Navarra and Dr Navarra was acting in the interests of the landowners, as were his peers all round western Sicily. From 1946 to 1948 was the time of the great political massacre. Even one brave demochristian mayor died for trying to stop the mafia joining his local DC. Liggio was a cruel and arrogant and hugely ambitious youth, but Dr Navarra needed him and his band, however dangerous they were, because Mr Vincent still nursed secret hopes of taking over Corleone. When Liggio and Mr Vincent were eventually tried for the unionist's murder, long after the event, some witnesses retracted their stories and others disappeared and the two were acquitted. Identifying Liggio as the killer, Dalla Chiesa also charged Navarra in his report with murdering the shepherd boy. Navarra was tried in Palermo, sentenced to five years' exile in Calabria and through the agency of his friends in the DC was welcomed back to Corleone by the town band in the space of a few months.

The young Totò Riina meanwhile at the age of nineteen had killed a friend during a game of bowls in Corleone and been imprisoned. It was the same age at which his son would commit his first murder in 1995, and I wondered whether Giovanni Riina had been impelled by Oedipal haste to match his father. Totò Riina reappeared out of jail in 1955, after only six years, and went to work for Liggio, butchering stolen cattle for sale in Palermo. The stolen animals were hidden in the magical wood at Ficuzza. Liggio was quietly forming the nucleus of his own *cosca*, spurred on by his uncle, who'd told him he couldn't go on being a *picciotto* all his life. *Cosca*, the more exact Sicilian word for a mafia family, I was told derived from *artichoke*, as indicating how the members of the family were equal, overlapping, close together around the centre, like the artichoke's leaves, but I could find no confirmation of this etymology.

The slowly building enmity between Dr Navarra and Liggio was also a conflict between the values of power and money. Liggio's prime value was money, whereas the doctor was a power man. Even captain De Carlo now found his cousin too old fashioned in this way. The ex-marine had moved to Palermo, made political friendships and seen how the new city mafia was growing with the DC. It was time to get into construction, public works and the huge bureaucracy of autonomous Sicily. The crisis came in 1958 when Liggio and Riina were ambushed and shot at while riding their horses at dawn to their secret abbattoir. Liggio escaped with a flesh wound. By saving Liggio's life, Riina strengthened his status as second in command. He was *in Liggio's heart*. Dalla Chiesa's carabinieri reported the attack as Navarra's, but a retired man of honour later claimed it was organized by Liggio's uncle and the captain, and intended to provoke a war with Navarra.

It did that. A month later Navarra and another doctor were ambushed in their car and pulped by machine gun fire. It was the start of a war in Corleone that lasted five years and cost a hundred and forty ascertained killings and uncounted disappearances. Riina, who went into hiding, was identified as Liggio's main killer. By 1963 Liggio had won the war of extermination, but that year an intensive police action against the mafia throughout Sicily, after the death of seven carabinieri in a car bomb explosion, sent thousands of leading mafiosi to jail. The Cupola governing Cosa Nostra and all the families were dissolved until the trouble passed. At the end of the year Riina was arrested at a road block and five months later Liggio joined him in the Ucciardone. Liggio now had Pott's disease, and spent his time in jail reading Kant's *Critique of Pure Reason* and Freud's *Interpretation of Dreams*. Riina played chequers and his opponents made sure he always won.

When Liggio and Riina finally went on trial in Bari with sixty-odd others for the killings in the five year war in Corleone, judges and jury were well softened up with ominous messages and all were acquitted in 1969. But when Riina returned to Corleone he was arrested again and exiled to a small town near Bologna in the north. Instead of going, Riina disappeared. He would be on the run for the next twenty-four years and spend nearly all of that time in Palermo. The Cosa Nostra commission was formed again at the end of 1970 as a temporary triumvirate of two Palermo bosses, Gaetano Badalamenti and Stefano Bontate, and Liggio, representing Corleone and the other families of the interior. Liggio wasn't a man to share power. Five months later he and Riina assassinated the Palermo chief prosecutor because Liggio felt he was *favouring Badalamenti*. It was the first assassination of a judge since the war, the first distinguished corpse, a challenge at once to the state and to the Palermo mafia. Three years later Riina married Ninetta Bagarella, the sister of another rising man of honour from Corleone. The priest who married them in secret was a man of honour. The four children were born in rapid succession thereafter.

Hunted for the killing of the judge and convalescent after being operated on by the Italian president's surgeon in a private clinic in Rome, Liggio now retired to a safe house in the country. Riina's rival as heir apparent was Bernardo Provenzano, who was admired as a killing machine but little else. He lacked peasant cunning. *Shoots like an angel but he's got the brains of a chicken*, decided Liggio, and kept Provenzano as company in the country, sending Riina to Palermo as his stand-in. Liggio was a fussy and querulous invalid. Riina meanwhile, whose fault Liggio saw as *biting off more than he could chew*, was cultivating a smiling affable manner. People had always found Riina a killer utterly without charisma, but he was working on it. *I never saw him angry*, said the pentito Mutolo, *sometimes a little flushed but never aggressive or rude*. Buscetta also found that *he looks like a peasant, true, but he's got a very diplomatic manner and God only knows how much diplomacy matters in Cosa Nostra. He was a great persuader and he knew how to work people up when he needed to*. The pentito Calderone remarked that Riina had *cunning and ferocity, a rare*

At this time, the start of the seventies, the Corleonesi were badly short of money. Several big trials, with huge costs in lawyers' fees and bribes, had precipitated a crisis. Riina's mission in Palermo was to make money fast and he did it by kidnapping. This was a great financial success for the Corleonesi, but the wealthy objects of the kidnappings were all people with ties to the demochristian political establishment and the Palermo mafia families, who had such richly nuanced relationships with that establishment. Bontate and Badalamenti were ropable that all the old understandings were threatened, but they were impotent because both happened to be in the Ucciardone at the time. Liggio, Riina and Provenzano pissed themselves laughing at the memory of the two enraged bosses, *like a couple of throttled chooks*, though formally Liggio promised to rein in Shorty Riina. *He'll be even shorter when we've finished with him*, said Badalamenti. Liggio resumed his place in the Cosa Nostra triumvirate. The Palermo provincial commission was reconstituted and its first act was to forbid kidnapping in Sicily. Kidnapping put valuable friendships at risk. In 1972 Liggio moved to Milan, and got involved in kidnapping on the continent. One job was the Getty boy, taken by the Calabresi of the 'ndrangheta and held in the Aspromonte. The old tightwad Paul Getty had to be sent a piece of his grandson's ear before he paid up.

When the regional Cupola of Cosa Nostra was properly reconstituted in 1975 with six members, one representative for each mafia province, it solemnly confirmed the ban on kidnapping. Riina's response was to kidnap the *potentissimo* Nino Salvo's father-in-law, one of the richest men in Sicily, who was seventy and died of a heart attack. The Salvos were very close indeed to Bontate and Badalamenti, and the Palermo bosses, as the pentito Antonio Calderone later put it, *were made to look like shit to Nino because they couldn't even get the body back*. This had been the whole point. Riina was telling the Salvos where the power centre now lay. The huge income from the ransoms had given him new clout, and by sharing it around Riina made new allies. The first was the family of San Giuseppe Jato headed by Bernardo Brusca, and it was an alliance that lasted. When Brusca Sr and Riina Sr were long in jail, the sons Giovanni of each were killing together until their own arrests in 1996.

One by one other families entered the Corleone orbit. Palermo, Trapani, San Giuseppe, Partinico, Mazara del Vallo. Riina joined forces with the camorra in Naples. He organized country lunches and barbecues for the boys, and turned out to be a great cook and a specialist in game. Once he made an exquisite casserole of fox, but didn't tell them what it was until they'd eaten. When Liggio, who'd always terrified people, was seized in 1974 in Milan and jailed for good, Cosa Nostra was collectively relieved to be dealing now with the *almost human* Riina. Provenzano was astutely sidelined and a couple of plans to rescue Liggio were squelched or sabotaged by Riina. The astutest move of all, however, was to persuade the Cupola that each family, each territory, should put a couple of boys directly at Riina's own service. Pleading his special needs as a boss on the run, he thus built up a private army of killers loyal only to him. It broke every principle in the history of Cosa Nostra, gave Riina spies and allies in every family, but the bosses bought it and were undone.

All were soon disturbed by Riina's rise, but even the bosses who'd always loathed and distrusted him continued to underestimate the danger. Through the middle seventies the rest of the commission held secret meetings, and always they split between those for killing Riina and those for managing him. At these discussions Riina had a spy, the boss Michele Greco, jealous of the other Palermo bosses' power, won over with promises by Riina. Knowing what each thought, Riina used his knowledge to create suspicions and rivalries and pick them off one by one. Badalamenti was accused of permitting the murder of another boss, a killing fomented by Riina, was expelled from the commission and fled to Brazil. Greco took his place. Riina then won permission to punish the boss who'd done the killing. Riina organized the killing of another boss, and when it was done made a moving oration in the Cupola that reduced one man of honour to tears. Stefano Bontate knew what was going on and responded by killing two bosses linked to Riina and then going for Riina himself.

In early 1979 Riina went underground and simultaneously ordered a series of *excellent* killings without consulting the Cupola. The head of the DC for Palermo province, Michele Reina, was killed for getting in the way of Vito Ciancimino's construction friends. Boris Giuliano, deputy police chief of Palermo, was killed for getting too close to the drug traffic and discovering a hideout of Riina's brother-in-law Bagarella. Judge Terranova, arriving to take over the Palermo prosecutor's office, was killed with a police officer. In the new year of 1980 the president of the Sicilian region, Piersanti Mattarella, was killed. He too had been getting in the way of Vito Ciancimino and Riina. Four months later the carabiniere captain Basile was killed, for looking into the affairs of a *cosca* allied to Riina. Nothing like this campaign of murder had ever happened before. It was Riina's way of showing who was in command.

Now even Bontate's own brother had become a spy for Riina, who always knew of the moves against him and so survived a Bontate assassination attempt. The boss Salvatore Inzerillo then had the Palermo chief prosecutor Gaetano Costa killed while he was browsing at a book stall. This too was done without informing the Cupola, as an answer to Riina's arrogation of power. As all the old rules broke down, Bontate called in Tommaso Buscetta, a man of honour who enjoyed a singular reputation for intelligence and independence, in a last attempt to mediate the crisis in Cosa Nostra. It was a failure. After celebrating the new year of 1981 at the Salvos' Hotel Zagarella, Buscetta left for Brazil.

It was a good moment to leave. Riina and the Corleonesi were preparing the final assault. In April, driving home from a champagne celebration of his forty-third birthday, Stefano Bontate stopped at a traffic light in his bright red Alfa Romeo and was cut down by a kalashnikov. Inzerillo knew he was next and planned a preventive killing of Riina, who was forewarned by his men in the Inzerillo *cosca*. Inzerillo had ordered an armour-plated Alfa Romeo at great cost and was about to step into it the day after its delivery when he too, three weeks after Bontate, was riddled by bullets from the same kalashnikov. Riina and the *picciotti* ate *cannoli*, a Sicilian delicacy of pastry, ricotta and candied fruit, and toasted with Moët & Chandon. The authors of *The True History of Italy* later wrote of these two killings,

> These homicides marked a turning point in the history of Cosa Nostra, and affected the entire future of the organization and its strategies, down to the most recent tragic events [of 1992]. They represented the change from a situation of hidden conflict inside a pluralistic organization still formally governed by democratic rules, to a strategy for the conquest of absolute power by Riina's Corleonesi, who would transform Cosa Nostra into a dictatorship, no longer founded on consensus but on terror alone, both within the organization and toward society and the state.

MAFIA WAR, it was called at the time. It was really the Riina terror. *There was no mafia war in Palermo*, said Gaspare Mutolo after he turned collaborator. *There was a massacre.* In 1981 and 1982 there were two hundred bodies on the streets of Palermo. There were at least three hundred other disappearances. The *white shotgun* it was called, a touch of rural nostalgia in the age of kalashnikov, when the body wasn't found. *Una mattanza*, said Guido Lo Forte, one of the Palermo prose-cutors who reconstructed its history. He was using the Sicilian word for the annual tuna killing, when the schools of great fish migrating past the island are corralled into traps of nets and harpooned en masse from open boats and the sea turns red. It was a killing of the losers and the losers' families and the losers' friends, a hunting down of real and potential and imaginary enemies. There were meetings, stranglings, goat ropings. Bodies burnt, bodies dissolved in acid, bodies buried in lime, bodies thrown in the sea and down crevasses and set in concrete. Inzerillo's sixteen-year-old son, who'd sworn to avenge his father, had his right arm cut off *so you won't go shooting Totò Riina* before he was killed. The first year ended with the bungled Christmas massacre, when a group of mafia losers were pursued on foot and then killed with passers-by in the crowded streets of Bagheria. After he turned, Buscetta remembered Riina thus:

> He lived Cosa Nostra twenty-four hours a day. Always talking and discussing. Got information on everything. Followed every family's internal affairs. Got news from his spies. Cold and attentive to the smallest detail ... [he had] the memory of an elephant. If you'd told him something ten years earlier, you could be sure he wouldn't forget it ever. He'd remind you of it ten or twenty years later, with the same words. He never tired of making suggestions, giving orders, handing out death sentences.

By then Riina had eliminated all Inzerillo's and Bontate's men, filled the Cupola with his own men and halved its members. The immediate threat removed, he was now at that point reached by every megalomaniac who achieves total power, of looking round for potential enemies, and seeing them everywhere. Phase two of the terror now began. Many of his allies now looked insufficiently loyal. *Waiting for my body to come floating down the river*, said Riina. First there were two more distinguished corpses. Pio La Torre had just returned to head the communists in Sicily. He was an anti-Riina, a son of poor peasants who'd been a labour organizer in Corleone when Riina was starting out as a killer. La Torre had been on the parliamentary antimafia commission and had proposed a law to confiscate mafia property, and for this he was killed with his driver in April 1982. The day of La Torre's funeral in Palermo another nemesis returned. Carlo Alberto Dalla Chiesa, now a general of the carabinieri and national hero of the antiterrorism campaign, arrived for his third posting in Sicily as prefect of Palermo, to lead the fight against the mafia. He'd been in Palermo a hundred days when he and his wife and his driver were ambushed and killed with the same kalshanikov used on Bontate and Inzerillo. Buscetta and Badalamenti were hiding out on Buscetta's vast property near Belém in Brazil when they saw the news on TV. *Some politician's used the mafia to get rid of him*, the former boss told Buscetta enigmatically.

Cosa Nostra's festive season comes earlier than most people's. The mafia year ends on November 30, and when the boss Rosario Riccobono was invited to lunch with Riina and Brusca at the Brusca villa in San Giuseppe Jato for that day in 1982, he dressed up in his smartest suit and so did all his *picciotti*. Riccobono was a powerful boss of a big and rich mafia territory, and he'd sided with the Corleonesi, betraying former friends to their death. The invitation to the annual festivity was natural, as it was that all his *picciotti* should have been invited to the larger barbecue party for sixty-odd guests that same day on the boss Michele Greco's gracious country estate not far away, the estate where all the Cupola meetings were now held. Riccobono was in fact powerful enough to be conceived as a danger to Riina, if you were Riina, and his vast territory was badly needed by Riina to pay off closer allies with ambitions of their own. Riccobono didn't think of this, however, as he dressed up for the annual party and set off in the rain. To be disarmed was *de rigueur* on these festive occasions of friendship and trust. When Riccobono arrived around eleven that morning from Palermo, he was greeted by the elder Brusca, who kissed him and took his arm and led him in to where Riina was already sitting at the head of the table. The whole Brusca clan was there, and Pino *The Shoe* Greco, who'd cut the arm off the Inzerillo boy. Riina was particularly jovial that day. *Welcome among us, Saru. Today we'll banish ill thoughts and think only about filling our bellies*, he said expansively as he embraced the guest.

Riccobono's personal bodyguard of three ate in another room with Giovanni Brusca and Baldassare Di Maggio. The meal went on for ever, there were so many different courses, so many wines. At the end of it all Riccobono was slumped in a digestive doze. It was then that Greco and the elder Brusca grabbed him while Totò Riina went for his throat. He throttled the guest in barely three minutes as the others held him down. Alerted by a whistle at the same time, young Brusca and Di Maggio, who'd eaten little and drunk less, jumped the bodyguards and strangled them with cords. The bodies took forever to dissolve in their drums of acid, maybe because of the rain that day. Then all that afternoon and evening, over at the Greco country place, Riccobono's men went down. It happened so fast that none of them realized what was happening. Some were strangled while strolling the paths of the extensive gardens, others were shot in the house. They were buried with quicklime or dissolved in acid. The few remaining Riccobono boys who'd missed the party were picked off over the next couple of days in Palermo. Then they were all gone.

Everything was now his. Only the Corleonesi and their oldest, closest allies were left. Michele Greco, *the Pope*, was left as a puppet to head the Cupola, who were all Riina's men. And yet things were still not quite perfect, power not quite total. It was time to look at the Corleonesi themselves. Who among them might one day challenge his supremacy? So began phase three. It was summarized by the Palermo prosecutors.

> This work of selection, which would lead in time to the formation of a highly restricted and utterly compact nucleus, totally subject to Riina's will, was brought about with great *political* intelligence, cleverly exploiting the differences that inevitably emerged in the group's relations ...

He started removing the successful, the assured, the charismatic killers who'd served him well. People like Pino *The Shoe* Greco, who'd personally killed over a hundred victims and was getting cocky. Then the people close to those people had to go. Even so, a rebellion flared up in 1989 and its leader had to have his head smashed in with a cast iron frying pan as he slept in his cell in the Ucciardone. It was done by the brother of Bagarella's wife, a relative by marriage, who thus killed his own boss for Riina. By now Riina had killed and had killed rather more than eight hundred men of honour in the course of his rise to power. This simple fact was behind the phenomenon of the pentiti. Everything they'd lived for had been destroyed, materially and morally. They had nothing left to lose and endless anger at the man who'd destroyed their world.

Riina's internal transformation of Cosa Nostra also transformed Cosa Nostra's relations with the outside world. Until the early eighties each family had run its own businesses and its own relations with government and industry. All that now went. Everything was centralized in Riina's Cosa Nostra, and he now wanted control in his relations with business and politics. After killing Bontate, who'd been the old mafia's great mediator with the politicians, Riina told the Salvo cousins, *Tell your friend Lima that from now on he deals only with me*. After that, said Mutolo, *the normal circuit for Cosa Nostra's interests, when they needed the help of decisions or actions in Rome, was Ignazio Salvo, Salvo Lima and senator Giulio Andreotti*. On really serious matters, even this was too indirect.

Totò Riina spoke directly to Giulio Andreotti. Andreotti was interested in power too, and an historian's remark around that time hinted at a parallel between Riina's rise among the families of Cosa Nostra and Andreotti's among the factions of the DC. The historian Gianni Bazet Bozzo wrote that

> Andreotti was the first to understand that real power is transverse, in the sense that the powerful one is he who holds power in all the other powers ... Andreotti is a silent component of all the demochristian policies and all the histories.

It was a relief to get back to sweet coastal Sicily at the end of my grim expedition to Corleone, though nothing now felt quite the same. I was reminded of Leopoldo Franchetti's words, in his acute and still pertinent report on *Political and Administrative Conditions in Sicily*, written after a visit the young Tuscan had made with two friends to the crime-ridden island over a century earlier, a few years after Italy became a nation. After being struck by the florid beauty of Palermo and its gardens, and the courtesy and hospitality of those he'd met, he'd started hearing about what was going on. They were mafia murders mostly. Retailing a few true stories in the opening pages of the report he made for the Italian parliament in 1877, a report that identified that class of *middle-class thugs* that was still much in evidence in Sicilian business and politics over a century later, Franchetti remarked that

> After a certain number of stories like that, all that perfume of orange blossom and lemon blossom starts to smell of corpses.

IV

A THIN MAN AND
A FAT MAN

ROBERT WAS an archeologist from Oxford preparing a dissertation on the carved panels from the temple at Selinunte, the time-worn scenes from the myths that were now in the archeological museum at Palermo. Maybe we were the only people in the city that wet Easter of 1980 who were unaware of the terrible mafia violence that was about to engulf Palermo, because we seemed to be the only people around. We kept meeting in the museum or over cheap meals at the Horse Shoe or walking the deserted streets. Robert was the son of a Harvard entymologist and had spent a large part of his childhood following his father in pursuit of butterflies through the Amazon rainforest. He dragged me along to a midnight Easter service in Greek in a Byzantine church and I'm fairly sure it was his idea too that we spend a pleasant afternoon in the Capuchin catacombs. Robert was into this kind of thing. I'd've preferred butterflies in the rainforest.

A bearded and faintly sinister monk in a coarse brown habit sold us tickets and asked where I was from. When I told him Australia he stared hard and mentioned that he'd been a prisoner of the Australians during the war. There was no sign the memory was a happy one. Then we were sent underground to the company of eight thousand mummified corpses. Some of these were concealed in coffins or stretched out in horizontal niches cut in the walls, but these weren't the ones that seized your attention. The ones you noticed were the crowds stretching along corridor after corridor, propped upright in their smartest clothes. The best clothes, the velvets, the silks, the lace, the taffetas, were often no longer more than faded accretions of dust, and even the best-preserved outfits had been gnawed by mice and nibbled by insects. The wearers likewise were no longer at their best, but lolling-headed, hollow-eyed, pigeon-toed, baring their teeth in the cosmic rictus. The odd skull or limb had dropped away and clattered to the ground over the years, but loving hands had reattached the bones with wire. Inaugurated at the end of the sixteenth century for dead monks, the catacombs were later extended and opened on payment to the general public of the dead. They reached the height of popularity in the last century, and were busy until 1880 when the catacombs' last guests checked in. When families of the deceased fell behind in their annual rental payments, the mummies were evicted to make space for new big spenders. Death was no leveller down in the catacombs. Earthly power, sex, religion and professional status were even more rigidly distinguished than in the world of the living. Apart from the religious division, there were separate corridors for men, women and children. Within the women's department was a special first class section for virgins. The aristocracy and the upper bourgeoisie of the nineteenth century were vastly present down there. The entire casts of Tolstoy's, Balzac's and Dickens's novels seemed to have been dried out and stacked away vertically in their disintegrating dress uniforms, their rotting ball gowns, their dusty frock coats, rows and rows of the upper strata of nineteenth-century society, rigorously grouped in their Darwinian or Marxist categories. Married couples were sometimes together for eternity, grinning toothily at the privilege, heads sagging on to spouses' shoulders.

The Sleeping Beauty in the children's alcove was in some respects a cheat, because she'd been let in forty years after closing time and her perfect preservation was due to twentieth-century science and not, like that of all the others, to the local properties of earth and air. She was embalmed with secret-formula injections in 1920, her long golden hair was combed out and she was placed on display shortly after her death at the age of two in a nauseating mise en scène reminiscent of an old Myer Emporium Christmas window in Melbourne and featured, with special glass and lighting, as the catacomb's main attraction, a necro-pedophile delirium. Monks had an evil reputation as child stealers when Leonardo Sciascia was little, were known to often carry guns under their habits. Children were told to keep away from them.

Sciascia remembered a monk's warning visit to a shopkeeper. The shopkeeper was behind on his protection payments and when the monk called his little daughter was playing in the shop. The monk caressed her head, remarking on the child's beauty and saying, by way of warning, that *she seemed almost alive*. In the fifties a monastery full of Capuchins in central Sicily had run an extortion and murder racket for which they were eventually jailed. I looked up from the Sleeping Beauty and noticed that the catacombs were now deserted except for Robert and me, that through the little grilles the daylight was fading. I remembered the sinister monk guarding the entrance and a fear came over me of being buried alive. Enough was enough of that particular manifestation of Palermo's intimacy with the dead. We hurried to the surface. The monk was gone and the door still open. I never felt the need to return. Later I heard the mummies had been imprisoned behind metal grilles and no longer mingled with the living on such free and equal, not to say promiscuous, terms.

ONE NIGHT not long after that, I set out to eat *pasta con le sarde* and *involtini di pesce spada* and drink white Rapitalà wine at the Charleston. The smartest and most expensive restaurant in Palermo, and the best, many said, required some effort to smarten up. I scrubbed and changed and peered at the minimal improvement in the spotted oval on the sagging wardrobe door. I'd got very wet trying in vain to get into the oratory of San Lorenzo. I wanted to see the late Caravaggio painting of *The Adoration of the Shepherds with Saints Francis and Lawrence* that was supposed to be inside. Frustration and discomfort had earned a treat. I might've felt this even more if I'd known then that Caravaggio's painting had been stolen from the oratory ten years earlier, and that the prevailing theory on its fate was that it'd never left Palermo and secretly adorned the home of a mafia boss. *Pasta con le sarde* is a quintessentially Palermo dish and oddly little known outside the city, let alone outside Sicily. It's a fairly simple dish. It also sounds a little odd to anyone who doesn't actually know it. The possibly mythological Ada Boni, in her *Talisman of Happiness*, a robust and practical kitchen classic that isn't particularly alive to regional subtleties, remarks before listing the dish's very heterogeneous ingredients that

> ... these apparent dissonances come together to make a first-rate harmony. *Pasta con le sarde* is a kind of mosaic in which each little piece finds its reason for being there in the final result. It would

thus be an error for anyone to want, as many do, to make personal modifications out of a taste for simplification or variation without first having tried the true recipe.

That *true* is interesting. All the more so in that la Boni's recipe turns out to be for a *timballo*, that is pasta baked into a drum-like form deriving from the shape of the oven dish. I never encountered *pasta con le sarde* as other than a spaghetti dish, or some similar form of long pasta. In Sicilian matters I was coming across the words *true* and *truth* more and more often, and starting to interpret them as expressions of a fervent longing rather than objectively established fact. Never as in Sicily was *the truth* invoked so often, never had it seemed so chimerical. In any case, the flesh of the fresh sardines is mixed and sauteed with already sauteed chopped onions and a little salted anchovy. The crucial additional ingredient is wild fennel, boiled and chopped and added to the sardines along with pine nuts, raisins and saffron. The late Waverley Root wrote once of encountering almonds, for which he may have mistaken the pine nuts, which he didn't mention, unless the almonds were a substitute, and other unconvincing additions like beaten egg that suggested the prudence of sticking with Boni. Fennel seeds are also sometimes used as a substitute when there is no wild plant growing nearby.

What nobody mentioned was that this was surely an Arab dish. You only had to look at the ingredients. The tomatoes would have been added five hundred years after the Arabs invented this way of presenting their newly-invented long thin strands of *pasta asciutta*, when Columbus brought the fruit back from the Americas to transform southern Italy's cooking. Elizabeth David offered a perfunctory second-hand version of *pasta con le sarde* in two lines. She wrote of *salted* sardines, which would've been a disaster, and adding tomatoes, admitting she'd never eaten the dish in loco. She did cite a 1935 description of the dish as *discordant but exhilarating*. Since the *Talisman* was first published in 1932, this sounded like a reply to Boni, who insisted on its *harmony* at greater length than the above quotation shows. The Charleston's pasta was good, as it should have been, and so were the swordfish involtini and so was the straw-coloured Rapitalà. The place however had the fatal air of an hotel dining room. Diners all seemed engrossed in their own sotto voce discussions. What the subject was of these intensely murmured conversations might have intrigued me more if I'd known then that a few months earlier, in the summer of 1979, Michele Sindona had been dining often at the Charleston.

MICHELE SINDONA at that time was being pursued by the police of two continents, but this was the least of his worries. Michele Sindona had lately lost billions of dollars of other people's money and a lot of it was mafia money and he was in Palermo as a *guest* of Cosa Nostra. Sindona's was an exemplary story of Italy in the seventies. A few years earlier, he'd been a whisker from total dominance of Italian finance and control of the biggest financial group in Europe. He'd been Cosa Nostra's financier when heroin was first multiplying its income madly. He'd been the Vatican's financier. He was called a financial wizard. When it all fell apart, Sindona caused the worst crash in American banking history and the worst in Italian history. By the time the government receiver of his Italian bank was assassinated in a Milan street in July 1979, most people understood what kind of man the financier Sindona was and where his money had come from. What people didn't understand was why the prime minister, Giulio Andreotti, was still in extremis trying so hard to salvage the disgraced Sindona's financial empire.

Sindona was born sixty years before these disasters, a florist's son from Patti, a town on the north coast of Sicily, not far from Messina and the continent. His father specialized in funeral wreaths and floral decorations for tombs. The adolescent Sindona, after a wholly undistinguished school career, at the age of seventeen suddenly discovered an ability to solve complex equations in his head and fairly early decided to turn his gift to the service of a quick buck. He met the allied liberator Vito Genovese at the end of the war and did some deals in black-market lemons and wheat. The young Sindona also caught his bishop's eye, and he set off for Milan in 1945 with letters of recommendation from both. He set up there as a small-time speculator, tax lawyer, real estate developer. He did people favours and got favours in return. He cultivated secrecy in the operations of his clever financial mind, and secrecy about his friends. He wanted to be a banker. Banks stood for power. *Companies are bought and sold, banks are bought and held,* he used to say. It took him fifteen years. By 1961 he was majority partner in the Banca Privata Finanziaria, in which four years later Hambros of London and the Continental Illinois of Cicero, Illinois took a forty per cent holding. By 1973 Sindona had bought them out and become sole owner of a much bigger bank. He'd bought another bank in partnership with the Vatican bank, the IOR, and three of Italy's biggest banks were his clients. His network of partnerships and operations was international. He was a friend and partner of Nixon's treasury secretary, his banks a conduit for CIA funds to the Greek colonels at the time of their

1968 coup and four years later for eleven million dollars of secret electoral support to twenty-one anticommunist politicians in Italy. By the end of the sixties *Business Week* was calling Sindona *the most successful Italian financier* and *Fortune* went further and called him *one of the world's most brilliant businessmen*.

Sindona was also one of four people named in a letter sent in November 1967 from the head of Interpol in Washington to the Italian police in Rome. The letter said he was involved in drug trafficking between Italy and the US and in Europe. The American and Italian governments might have saved themselves many billions of dollars if either had responded to this warning. Neither did. At the start of the seventies Sindona was running a mafia finance corporation which defrauded Sicilian emigrants from the Agrigento province of millions of dollars in savings. He was buying up real estate corporations, insurance companies, industrial concerns, hotel chains and ever more banks. As ever, his success in making money stifled people's suspicions about the origins of the funds he multiplied. Sindona did financial magic. He had in those days some prestigious partners. He'd made a strategic friend of Pope Paul VI in the sixties when the future holy father was archbishop of Milan. In 1969 he bought the Vatican's property development company for three hundred and fifty million dollars, billions today. The agreement was signed personally by Sindona and His Holiness in an unrecorded meeting late at night on the third floor of the papal apartments. He'd displaced the Vatican's traditional advisors, and at a moment when the Vatican bank's new head, archbishop Marcinkus, formerly of Cicero, Illinois, and now a prelate close to Paul VI, was shifting the Vatican's huge investments from Italy to the international market. As the Vatican's financial advisor, Sindona used his new prestige to intensify his own international operations. By now he controlled at least five banks and more than a hundred and twenty-five public companies in eleven countries.

In 1971 Sindona was poised now for his biggest coup of all. He wanted control of Italy's two biggest holding companies, the bastions of old money in Italy. He wanted to merge them and simultaneously take over one of Italy's biggest banks. The governor of the Bank of Italy later remarked that if Sindona's *programme had been realized, it would have created ... perhaps the biggest financial group in Europe*. It would have given Sindona, the friends' banker, total dominance of the creaky Italian financial system. In August 1971 he won control of the first holding company, the Centrale. The august figures of Italian capitalism were immediately shunted off the board and replaced with Sindona's men, one of them the still obscure Roberto Calvi, the banker who would shortly outdo even his mentor Sindona and end his life hanging under Blackfriars bridge in London. At the eleventh hour, the alarmed Italian financial establishment, after years of connivance with Sindona, blocked his bid for control. The Bank of Italy blocked his takeover bids for Bastogi, the second holding company, and for the national agricultural bank and ordered an inspection of the other Sindona banks. Sindona was days from making a public offer for the second holding company, with the approval of the entire financial media, when the Bank of Italy blocked that takeover too and thus Sindona's grand design.

Yet when his inspectors found huge illegalities in Sindona's banks and urged that their administrators be sacked, the governor of the Bank of Italy did nothing. Sindona was a very powerful man. He had major international banks on side, he had the support of the DC and the Vatican. He was stronger than the Bank of Italy. *The decision not to take disciplinary measures derived ... from a political judgement about the Bank of Italy's capacity to administer the coup de grace to Sindona*, decided a parliamentary committee many years later. And he'd just bought in 1972 the eighteenth-biggest bank in the USA, the very profitable Franklin National Bank, with money, it turned out later, not his own, and gone to live in New York. The Bank of Italy vaguely hoped his absence might improve the behaviour of his Italian banks. Other banks began to sniff danger, though. Hambros precipitately severed its links with Sindona and others followed.

As Sindona's establishment allies began to abandon him, he speculated ever more wildly on the financial markets and at the same time strengthened his ties with the DC in Italy. In April 1973 he took three hundred and fifty million dollars out of his banks in Milan to finance new expansion. By the end of July the two banks were insolvent. He speculated heavily and secretly against the lira. Having made all the money he could from this, he *helped and advised* the Bank of Italy and the Italian government to recover from the mysterious run on the lira. In December of that year Giulio Andreotti, the prime minister, ignored the warnings of the Italian ambassador in Washington and spoke at a gala banquet offered by the generically identified Italo-American community in New York and hailed Sindona publicly as *the saviour of the lira*.

Sindona was buying support from the DC with huge gifts and loans to the party. He gave two and a half million dollars to Fanfani, another past and future DC prime minister with a powerful base in Sicily. Meanwhile he made a series of blunders on the stock exchange and the currency and commodities markets. In the summer of 1974, Sindona's financial crisis became Italy's. Germany was in alarm. *ITALY MANOEUVRES ON THE EDGE OF THE ABYSS*, headlined the *Frankfurter Zeitung*. *DANCING ON THE BRINK*, said *Die Welt*, and *FIVE MINUTES TO MIDNIGHT*. So was France. *ITALY ON THE VERGE OF BANKRUPTCY*, said *Le Monde*, and *Le Figaro* conducted an *AUTOPSY OF BANKRUPTCY ITALIAN STYLE*. Sindona merged his two Milan banks as the Banca Privata Italiana. The Franklin National Bank was now in trouble in America, and two German banks tied to Sindona went under. When the Italian treasury minister put a veto on further recapitalization of the holding company Sindona had created to save his fortunes, it was more or less the end. A few days apart in October 1974, both the Banca Privata Italiana and the Franklin National were declared bankrupt. Days before the Franklin collapse the federal reserve bank had lent Sindona one point seven billion dollars to save it. It was the biggest bank failure in American history. Two arrest warrants were issued in Milan for fraud. Sindona fled to Hong Kong and then Taiwan. On the advice of David Kennedy, Nixon's treasury secretary, he returned to the United States, where he was arrested and released on three million dollars bail. He withdrew to his vast suite in the Pierre Hotel, ever the optimist, to plan his comeback.

As a bankrupt facing criminal charges on two continents, Sindona was now something of a pariah in the world of international finance, and a grave embarrassment to his former political friends. The main thing he had going for him at this point, he realized, was his capacity to be an even worse embarrassment. On one frantic summer day in Rome just before the crash, a yellow envelope containing Sindona's *list of five hundred*, the names of Italy's most distinguished secret capital exporters, had been passed around like a hot potato among the heads of the Bank of Italy and the Bank of Rome. Nobody dared open it, fearing it would have revealed the entire Italian business establishment as lawbreakers, and it disappeared again. It'd been a foretaste. Sindona had cost Italy something near four billion US dollars, in 1995 money.

He'd also cost the Vatican a lot of money. Most importantly of all, from his own immediate point of view, he'd lost his friends in Sicily an awful lot of money, proceeds of their heroin sales in the US. The late Claire Sterling wrote that by 1979 Cosa Nostra's people *were sending somewhere around a billion dollars yearly from America to Palermo by way of Switzerland, Liechtenstein, London, Caracas and the Cayman Islands*. The drug money was now gone, billions of dollars of it. Sindona believed in 1979 that if he could get back into business, through one political-financial salvage plan or another, have another throw of the dice, he could conjure back the lost billions.

He'd also lost money for Licio Gelli, an extremely shadowy figure with thirty-nine listings in the index of *The True History*, a person who'd begun adult life in the fascist secret services and gone on to involvement with right-wing terrorism, international arms trafficking, the mafia and the Vatican. Gelli would be arrested in 1981 as leader of a secret masonic lodge called the P2. The members of the P2 included a large piece of the Italian judicial, political, military and secret service establishment, and it was believed to be planning a military coup in Italy. Sindona had been Gelli's financial advisor as well as Cosa Nostra's. *Sindona ... was an intimate of the impenetrably mysterious Licio Gelli. The two of them juggled astronomical sums together*, wrote Claire Sterling, who didn't usually let a little international criminal intrigue get the better of her.

In all these quarters, only the hope of recovering lost money was restraining vengeful anger. And all Sindona had now to help him recover was his secrets. It was time for blackmail.

IN ITALY, the government had appointed a receiver to wind up the affairs of Sindona's bank. This was a thankless task, given Sindona's deviousness. There'd been, for instance, parallel accounts kept, and Sindona's people had managed to remove or shred most of the real accounts. The receiver, Giorgio Ambrosoli, was an energetic, meticulous and stubborn man, however. The job was a challenge. The lack of enthusiasm for clearing up the Sindona mystery on the part of certain public officials was worrying, and the isolation in which Ambrosoli increasingly worked, the lack of support, almost fearsome, but the receiver treated these too as challenges of another kind. Soon he was flying around Europe, from bank to bank in the Sindona constellation. Geneva, Zurich, Basle, Hamburg, Luxembourg, Paris. He found that though the money which flowed from Sindona's Italian banks to these was registered as deposits, and therefore assets of the banks in Italy, in fact it flowed on, in the name of these foreign banks, into a series of companies set up in tax havens around the world, all of which turned out to belong to Sindona. Ambrosoli's great coup was to get his hands, in a lightning action in October 1975, on the shares of a Sindona company called Fasco A.G., whose head office was in Liechtenstein. Fasco was the mother company, the Russian doll that contained three hundred other companies, which in their turn contained companies that contained companies ... In exile Sindona was enraged by the Fasco discovery. There was a flurry of legal actions and press interviews. He sent a message to Ambrosoli from his suite in the Hotel Pierre. *Vengeance is sweeter when it comes from afar.*

Though in disgrace with fortune and men's eyes, Sindona was not yet quite all alone. Giulio Andreotti still found time among the pressures of affairs of state to think of a friend in need. On page 427 of *The True History of Italy* I found that in November 1973, a year before the crash, Sindona's son-in-law, who was also the director of his banks, had written to prime minister Andreotti about *the strategy our group wishes to pursue in Italy* and *permitting himself* to call the prime minister *a sincere friend and a formidable expert with whom to agree on ... the most important decisions.* On the same page of *The True History* I saw that in late 1976, *in the most difficult moment of my life*, Sindona himself had written to the *Illustrious and dear prime minister*, as Andreotti was again by then, to thank him for his *renewed expression of esteem* and the *interest you have shown in my affairs.* Coming from a bankrupt awaiting criminal trial in the United States and Italy to a head of government, this was a little startling. The letter became even odder further on, as Sindona explained how he would defend himself *legally and politically.* He wrote, *I shall be forced against my will to present ... the real reasons for the arrest warrant ... with appropriate documentation ...* It sounded almost threatening. Andreotti was already doing a lot to help Sindona. A month after becoming prime minister again in August 1976 he'd had a visit from two types later linked to the mafia and the P2, a lawyer and an ex-priest turned businessman, members, as they described themselves, of the Italo-American community. They wanted Andreotti's help in preventing or delaying Sindona's extradition to Italy. The prime minister spoke privately with them for nearly an hour and the members of the Italo-American community emerged delighted and told Sindona's lawyer on the way back to the hotel that Andreotti had promised *his total attention.* Then they went straight to call on Licio Gelli. Gelli blamed the communists for Sindona's misfortunes. *The communists hate Michele Sindona because he's anticommunist and has always supported free enterprise ...*

The first concrete sign of Andreotti's *total attention* for Sindona's problems was a salvage attempt soon after the visit from the two Italo-Americans. It was followed by another more ambitious effort in 1978. Both heavily involved Licio Gelli and the P2. Beyond that there were glimpses. Andreotti's factotum, the deputy minister Franco Evangelisti, met at least once with Sindona when he was on the run, a *chance meet-*

ing, when he was buying toy soldiers at F.A.O. Schwarz, just near the Hotel Pierre. The prime minister himself met Sindona in New York in 1976 and 1977, according to the FBI. Andreotti denied it. Nevertheless, in the months of national trauma when the DC president and former prime minister Aldo Moro was kidnapped and murdered, Andreotti was amazingly accessible to Sindona's people. Between 1978 and 1980 there were at least a dozen meetings recorded between Andreotti and Sindona's lawyer in the prime minister's office. Moro in his days awaiting death found time to think and write about Andreotti's relations with Sindona, how he'd insisted on appearing as Sindona's guest of honour at the New York banquet, despite the appalled urgings of the Italian ambassador and Moro himself. The salvage effort promoted by Andreotti in 1978 failed in the end because it was resisted by the leading banks and above all by Italy's most powerful financier, the wily old Enrico Cuccia, and the stubborn and incorruptible Giorgio Ambrosoli, who was determined to trace the sources of Sindona's money.

In the very last days of 1978, Giorgio Ambrosoli began to receive threatening phone calls, a dozen in as many days. *Could be a madman*, Ambrosoli noted at first in his diary. The anonymous caller persisted. He sounded well informed. He said Ambrosoli *hadn't told the truth* about Sindona. Ambrosoli recorded the conversations.

> UNKNOWN CALLER: They're pointing the finger at you. I'm in Rome and they're pointing the finger, because you're not cooperating ...
> AMBROSOLI: But who are they?
> UNKNOWN CALLER: The Big Boss.
> AMBROSOLI: Who's the Big Boss?
> UNKNOWN CALLER: You understand me. The Big Boss and the little boss, everyone is blaming you ... You're a nice guy, I'd be sorry ... The Big One, you understand? Yes or no?
> AMBROSOLI: I imagine the big one is Sindona.
> UNKNOWN CALLER: No, it's Andreotti!
> AMBROSOLI: Who? Andreotti!
> UNKNOWN CALLER: Right. He called and said he had everything taken care of, but it's all your fault ... so watch out ...

On January 12 Ambrosoli received his last call.

> UNKNOWN CALLER: Good morning. Tried to be smart the other day? You recorded the call.
> AMBROSOLI: Who told you that?
> UNKNOWN CALLER: It's my business who told me. I wanted to

save you but from now on I'm not saving you any longer.
AMBROSOLI: Not saving me any longer?
UNKNOWN CALLER: I'm not saving you any longer because
you only deserve to die shot down like a fuckwit. You're a fuckwit
and a bastard!

One night Ambrosoli's youngest son Betò, aged seven, woke and heard
his father come home from work at almost one in the morning. The
child heard his parents listening to a recording of a voice shouting *We'll
kill you like a dog! We'll kill you like a bastard!* When Ambrosoli realized
his son knew of the threat, he explained soothingly as he put the child
to bed, *They'll never do it because we know who they are* ... The financier
Cuccia too, the other obstacle to a Sindona salvage, was receiving
threats. His house had been attacked, his children followed. Trusting
nobody, he refused to speak. Then Ambrosoli found Sindona had got
hold of a copy of the highly secret and devastating confidential report
he'd just made, detailing his findings on the operations of Sindona's
bank.

Ninety-nine criminal charges of fraud, perjury and misappropria-
tion of funds were filed against Sindona in the US over the collapse of
the Franklin National Bank. The March day in 1979 that Sindona was
charged in New York, the journalist Mino Pecorelli was murdered in
Rome, just after being persuaded not to print an article on Andreotti's
role in another financial scandal. Four days later the director of the
Bank of Italy who'd most vigorously opposed Sindona's rehabilitation
effort was arrested and the bank's governor was presented with a sub
poena. The Bank of Italy was the one Italian institution people still
respected. And three and a half months later, in July 1979, the fearless
and determined Giorgio Ambrosoli was shot dead one night in front of
his home in Milan by the *UNKNOWN CALLER*, an American
mafioso. The man who ordered the killing was Michele Sindona. The
governor of the Bank of Italy came to Ambrosoli's funeral, and a few
judges and magistrates, but from the government which had appointed and abandoned him, and the state in whose service he'd been murdered, there was no one.

On the second of August, three weeks after Ambrosoli's assassination, Michele Sindona skipped his three million dollar bail and disappeared. He walked out of the Hotel Pierre in an improbable chicken-
skin mask, wig, shades and false beard and his secretary received a call
from *communist terrorist kidnappers*. Sindona was actually on his way to
Palermo. The chicken skin started lifting at the airport, due to heavy
sweating in the summer heat, but Sindona got to Sicily nevertheless

with the friends from the New York Gambino family who'd organized the trip. The friends never left his side. They were joined by people from Gelli's P2, though not, it seemed, from the third of Sindona's big losers, the Vatican. The Vatican's IOR had covered a loan of nearly one and a half billion dollars of nineteen-seventies money which, Claire Sterling wrote, had simply disappeared *after passing through Panamanian banks owned by Sindona, Licio Gelli and the Vatican itself.* Sindona spent seventy days in Sicily, living in a mafia villa outside Palermo, conferring for hours and hours with the bosses, moving around without too much trouble in John Gambino's black Mercedes. It was with Gambino, who'd flown over from New York, that Sindona had dined at the Charleston. What they talked about over their own *pasta con le sarde* and their own *involtini di pesce spada* was presumably the purpose of Sindona's visit.

The purpose was expressed in faked kidnappers' threats to extort from Sindona the list of five hundred capital exporters and their foreign bank accounts, the names of Sindona's foreign companies whose funds were available to the DC and the socialists, the records of Sindona's payments to politicians and his irregular operations for such clients as the Vatican and the Agnellis of Fiat. Messages went out to those concerned and a meeting was arranged in Vienna to *negotiate Sindona's release*. Then a banal case of service as usual by the Italian post office had consequences that would be, for Cosa Nostra and Italy, really quite unimaginable. It opened up Giovanni Falcone's very first mafia investigation, revealing what he'd later describe as *an enormous new reality to decipher*, a dazzling glimpse of the connections between drugs and real estate, Italy and America, mafia and politics. A letter of instructions posted in Milan failed to reach Sindona's lawyer in Rome in time for the meeting in Vienna. The lawyer was told by phone that a courier was coming with a copy of the instructions. The phone was tapped and the courier intercepted. The whole thing aborted. Sindona and Gambino flew back to New York and Sindona told the FBI the kidnappers had let him go.

The courier's identity let Falcone get his toe in the door. It was Vincenzo Spatola, brother of Rosario Spatola, who'd started his working life as a milkman and was twenty years later Palermo's richest building contractor and property developer, the fifth biggest taxpayer in Italy. Rosario Spatola, apart from an early arrest in the fifties for watering down his milk, was an unblemished member of the business community. He'd lately offered a campaign dinner for the reelection of the DC minister Ruffini. *Tell your friends, and the friends of the friends,* he'd said, *that they must support this man of integrity and honour*. And the friends all had. But Rosario Spatola turned out to be the cousin of John Gambino and to have done extensive business with him across the Atlantic. Falcone was up and running. The identity of the message-bearer Vincenzo Spatola made clear that Sindona's financial activities and his Italian political alliances built their foundation on Cosa Nostra's transasian and transatlantic drug trafficking. Sindona had been Cosa Nostra's financier as well as the Vatican's, and Andreotti had been his political protector.

1979 WAS the year the magistrate Giovanni Falcone transferred from the bankruptcy court to work with his boyhood friend Paolo Borsellino in criminal investigations. And Falcone's very first criminal investigation was into the affairs of the Spatolas, the Inzerillos, the Di Maggios and the Gambinos, four families linked on both sides of the Atlantic by a dense pattern of dynastic marriages. 1979 was the year *distinguished corpses* began to fall. The head of the investigative police in Palermo, Boris Giuliano, was murdered that summer for looking into the transatlantic traffic in drugs and dollars. On the luggage carousel at Palermo's Pùnta Raisi airport he'd found a suitcase with half a million dollars in small denomination notes. Two weeks later he'd found four kilos of freshly refined heroin in a Palermo house and a week later he was shot in the back as he took a cappuccino in a city bar. At summer's end judge Cesare Terranova returned from Rome to investigate the drug traffic and two days after coming home to Palermo he was shot with a kalashnikov after breakfast. *What'll people think?* went through his wife's mind as she flew down after hearing the machine gun and the pistol shots of the coup de grace. *A woman in her nightie. They'll think I'm mad*. The chief prosecutor Costa was shot dead the next summer. Uncooperative politicians were going down too. That spring, Michele Reina, head of the DC in Palermo had been assassinated, and the following winter Piersanto Mattarella, DC president of the Sicilian region, was murdered. It was apropos of Mattarella's killing that Salvo Lima remarked to Andreotti's factotum, the deputy minister Franco Evangelisti, *when pacts are made they've got to be respected*, not imagining, probably, that twelve years later he too would be slain for not playing by Cosa Nostra's rules. Four months later Emanuele Basile, the captain of carabinieri who'd taken up Giuliano's investigation into the drug traffic, was shot as he left a religious festival with his wife and child, falling dead over his unharmed small daughter.

As for Michele Sindona, it all ended badly. In New York he got twenty-five years for the Franklin crash. In Italy he got fifteen more for the Banca Privata Italiana crash plus life for ordering the murder of Giorgio Ambrosoli. Andreotti had the roughest ride of his long career during the parliamentary enquiry into the Sindona affair. He was foreign minister by then, and parliament was about to vote to sack him. The communists saved him by abstaining. Sindona appeared demented toward the end, *like a scrawny plucked chook* someone said. He never talked, though. He never revealed any of his formidable secrets. His life sentence for murder became definitive in 1986, and Sindona was taken to the high-tech maximum security prison at Voghera, where he was watched twenty-four hours a day by live guards and closed-cricuit television. Two days later he drank an espresso laced with strychnine in his cell. Death was instantaneous. The finding was suicide. The next day *La Repubblica* printed a cartoon showing Sindona in jail being offered a tiny steaming espresso. The offerer was seen in silhouette. A tiny hunchbacked figure with triangular batlike ears and heavy black-framed glasses was extending the cup and enquiring *One sugar or two?*

WAS THIS the very table where Sindona and Gambino had sat? I sipped a second marsala and looked gloomily around and thought *zero ambience* and got a creepy but quite undefined feeling from the new Palermo. But ghosts from the past persisted. I noticed a small brass rectangle screwed into the wall just behind my head. The plate was engraved with a statement to the effect that in the cafe which had previously occupied the premises where the Charleston now stood, Giuseppe Tomasi, duke of Palma and prince of Lampedusa, had written *The Leopard*. Sindona faded fast. Here the aged aristocrat, last of his line, the great but unknown writer, had sat in the Caffè Mazzara composing his single slender masterpiece, the distillation of an age, a class, a vanished Sicilian culture.

The aged aristocrat in his overcoat, actually not yet sixty, wrote a *summum* of his dynasty which reads now as if composed among the dying magnificence it celebrated, but it was all in the prince's mind. What Tomasi di Lampedusa was doing, sitting here in the ugly Caffè Mazzara day after day in the last two and three quarter years of his life, with an exercise book and a ballpoint pen, was *amusing himself.* He told his wife this, Alessandra Wolff, the Freudian psychonanalyst, a Latvian baron's daughter driven from her Baltic castle by the war. She read the first chapter and said it showed talent. He said the same thing to his uncle, who was also his wife's stepfather, the former ambassador to St Petersburg and London. He was playing it down.

It was his cousin Lucio's doing, really. The greatest modern Italian poet Eugenio Montale had received by mail in early 1954 a handful of barely legibly printed lyrics in an envelope with insufficient stamps on it from an unknown Sicilian. The great poet usually ignored unsolicited material, but he looked at these to see whether they were worth the hundred and eighty lire he'd had to fork out in extra postage. He found he was reading the work of a real poet. That summer Montale was invited to a literary conference near Milan where he and other prominent writers would each introduce a young unknown. Montale decided that his unknown would be the Sicilian poet. Like everyone else who'd gathered to meet the youthful revelation, Montale was stunned when his young protegé Lucio Piccolo turned out to be an intensely shy Sicilian baron as old as himself, formidably erudite, astronomer, mathematician and musician as well as poet, learned among other languages in Greek and Persian, a distinguished but taciturn presence dressed in a dark formal suit at the height of summer. Lucio Piccolo was awarded a prize at the conference for his *9 Lyrics*. Montale later remembered that he *came and went without saying a word*.

The poet had been accompanied by his cousin the prince of Lampedusa, even less forthcoming than himself and more heavily dressed, wearing that summer a hat and a buttoned overcoat and using a heavy stick; and by *a bronzed and sturdy servant* who attended the two cousins everywhere. The novelist Giorgio Bassani remembered that he too, remained silent throughout the conference, and when introduced would bow without saying a word. The two were silent because they'd had little contact with others, even at home in Sicily. Together in Palermo or on Piccolo's family estate at Capo d'Orlando, they spoke torrentially. The prince too had read vastly in history and the literatures of five languages. Lampedusa and his cousin kept up a flow of discussion, quotation, improvisation, allusion and absurd jokes that amazed visitors who heard it. When Piccolo sent off his handful of poems to Montale, with a covering letter that was actually written by Lampedusa, it was their first opening to the larger world.

This was the origin of *The Leopard*, in Lampedusa'a own account. The silent observer at the summer conference was not overwhelmed by the famous writers he found there, and he later wrote to a friend in Brazil that if his cousin Lucio could win a prize, ... *certain I was no more foolish, I sat down and wrote a novel.* The real origin and impulse behind Lampedusa's one and incomparable book are inaccessible. The fat, silent boy who didn't like outdoor games contemptuously remembered by his cousin Fulco di Verdura had grown into a bulky, pale and silent man who'd spent an entire life reading. Passing from a dominating aristocratic mother to a formidable aristocratic wife, he hardly impinged at all on the society in which he moved. After his death at sixty and his amazing posthumous fame, the little world of the Palermo aristocracy struggled to account for what the book revealed and could remember only the prince's silence, his bulk, his pallor. *He usually had lunch at the Pizzeria Bellini ... he would catch the bus home in the afternoon ... he spent his evenings reading while his wife worked on her cases.* Lampedusa eluded his biographers and his book largely eluded his critics.

Twenty years before he started writing he'd contemplated some kind of book centred on the figure of his great-grandfather and set in the time of Garibaldi and the unification of Italy. It'd come to nothing. His widow vaguely suggested later that he'd been too busy, with *the war ... finding a new house,* to act on this for several years. Fortunately he didn't have to look after a family, or earn a living. Even his war, as wars went, went well. Palermo became uncomfortable as the bombing raids began, but Lampedusa spent a lot of time visiting his cousins at Capo d'Orlando and in early 1943 moved there for the rest of the war. In 1942, while most of Europe starved, or nearly, and armies died at Tobruk and Stalingrad, he wrote to his wife of a lunch of lasagne, vol au vent with lobster, crumbed cutlets with potatoes, peas and ham and a tart from Escoffier with cream and candied cherries, *all in their usual quantities.* A later letter mentions tender and tasty steaks two inches thick and a slice of fresh tuna *as large as a car tyre.* Later still, a light summer lunch consisted of fettucine with butter and parmesan, a huge fish with several sauces, and a *pâté de lapin made according to the rules of the old game pâtés: liver purée, black truffles and pistacchios and consommé jelly.* This was followed by meringues with chocolate ice cream.

AMERICAN SUPERFORTRESSES flew over Palermo on 5 April 1943. It was the bombing raid that destroyed a good third of the old city centre, a prelude to the coming invasion. The palazzo Lampedusa received a direct hit and Lampedusa's material link to the world of childhood, family and the past was gone. After Lampedusa saw the ruins, he walked twenty kilometres to the prince of Mirto's house by

113

the sea near Bagheria, at Santa Flavia, where the Salvo cousins would later build their pharaonic Hotel Zagarella. Lampedusa arrived filthy with dust and unrecognizable, and according to count Sarzana, who was there, sat three days without speaking a word. Although Lampedusa mourned its destruction for the rest of his life, the physical loss of his family palace, like the sale twenty years earlier of the palace at Santa Margherita di Belice, where he'd spent his childhood summers, were the necessary events that freed his imagination. The lost palace at Santa Margherita, sold to a hostile family to pay the debts of his socialist uncle, was transformed into the Donnafugata of the novel Lampedusa was to write. The death of his mother, the dominating dowager princess, in 1947 may have been equally liberating.

Without this violent loss, without this clearing of the ground, his imagination might never have been so deeply engaged. Lampedusa would never have written anything as fatuously chipper as his cousin Fulco di Verdura's little memoir, or anything that so astutely blended nostalgia and indignation as Dacia Maraini's short book about Bagheria. But without the loss that drove him into the caverns of the imagination, Lampedusa might have written nothing at all. Oddly, having started at the end of 1954, the year of his cousin's success in poetry, on the work that would in his biographer David Gilmour's words provide *an escape from the years of disappointment and an opportunity to redeem what he recognized had been a largely wasted life*, Lampedusa interrupted it six months later to write a memoir of *the places of my early childhood*, which he intended at the time to be the beginning of an autobiography. His widow suggested later that the memoir had been her idea, a way to neutralize his nostalgia and get over the loss of his family homes. Alessandra Wolff wasn't for nothing Italy's first woman psychoanalyst. Whether her advice was necessary we can't know, but if it was, it worked brilliantly. After thirty pages or so he returned to the novel, and the novel he wrote never gave way to the yearning pull of the lost world of the past. The more sensuously the vanished past was evoked, the more implacably his intelligence resisted, heightening the tension in the language until the novel transformed itself into an examination of life and death in Sicily, one that closed in a mood of sublime and unSicilian levity. Lampedusa like Proust made sensuous recall the means to understanding and not to consolation. Like Proust, he had a formidable intellect. A group of student friends had been drawn to the pale and taciturn prince, who was described around this time as looking like a retired general. Realizing they *knew nothing*, as he put it, he'd also delved into his life's reading and written a series of lectures on English and French writers they read together in the evenings. The man who was old in his fifties, remembered by Bassani for *the bitter twist to his lips*, opened out to these young people. One of them he adopted, perpetuating his titles, and made *The Leopard*'s quick, ironic and ambitious Tancredi in his likeness.

Tancredi is the penniless young aristocrat who rises through his wit and a strategic marriage to the beautiful daughter of a newly-rich mafioso. He's the nephew of don Fabrizio, the prince the novel revolves around, a tall fair idealized alter ego of its writer. The novel's action pivots on the historical moment of Garibaldi's unification of Italy. Nothing much happens in *The Leopard*. The big events are anticipated or looked back on or heard of from afar. Small domestic things refract an image of the big world outside. The prince's family move to their country estate for summer. They hold a dinner party for the locals. The prince goes rabbit shooting. Tancredi and his fiancée Angelica wander through the deserted rooms of the palace. Don Fabrizio turns down an invitation to join the Italian senate. There is a ball in Palermo. The prince's chaplain goes home to his family village. The air of suppressed erotic expectancy that hangs heavy over Angelica and Tancredi in the first part finds no sequel. It elides into the information, thrown as it were over the novel's shoulder years later, that theirs was not a successful marriage.

> Those were the best days in Tancredi's and Angelica's lives, lives that would be so variegated and wayward against the inevitable backdrop of pain. But they didn't know it then and pursued a future they reckoned would be more substantial, though it later turned out to be made only of smoke and wind. When they'd become old and uselessly wise their thoughts returned to those days with insistent regret. They'd been the days of a desire that was always present because it was always overcome ...

> Those days were the preparation for a marriage that even erotically turned out badly. But it was a preparation that seemed a self-sufficient whole, exquisite and brief, like those overtures that survive forgotten operas and contain, merely touched on, their playfulness modestly veiled, all the tunes that were to be developed without skill in the opera itself, and fail.

The Angelica glimpsed at the end as a corpulent widow with stumpy legs and varicose veins makes her entrance as an incomparable seventeen-year-old at the first dinner at Donnafugata. The food served at this dinner is given some attention. It matters because the local notables have heard ominous stories of French *haute cuisine* and are afraid they'll be offered an insipid first course of soup. So when the three liveried and powdered lackeys enter each holding a huge silver dish with a towering *timballo di maccheroni* on it, a collective Sicilian sigh of relief and anticipation goes round the table.

> The burnished gold of the outside and the fragrance exuded of sugar and cinnamon were only preludes to the sensation of delight released from the interior when the knife slit the crust; aroma-charged steam burst out first, then chicken livers, little hard boiled eggs, fillets of ham, chicken and truffles could all be seen imbedded in the mass of hot and glistening short macaroni, that the meat juice gave an exquisite soft brown tinge.

The diners then reveal something of themselves in their way of tackling the divine pasta. The antithesis of this sturdy and exquisite native food is the *monotonous opulence* of the dishes spread on the buffet tables at the Ponteleone ball toward the end of the book.

> Coral pink the lobsters boiled alive, waxy and rubbery the *chaud-froids* of veal, steel-glinting the fish immersed in soft sauces, the turkeys gilded by the ovens' heat, the boned woodcocks reclining on mounds of amber toast decorated with their own chopped guts, the *pâtés de foie gras* rosy under their gelatine armour, the dawn-coloured galantines and a dozen other cruel coloured delights ...

Under don Fabrizio's unhungry gaze, the delicacies exude a hint of baroque horror. His survey of the even more gorgeous desserts ends in a vision of Saint Agatha's *hacked-off breasts*. I was reminded of the mirage lunch with Orlando at the villa Niscemi. Belatedly I understood that certain traditions were being kept up and a certain notion of quality was staying alive that had little to do with appetite. I'd have been one of those sighing with pleasure at the sight of the *timballo di maccheroni*.

In *The Leopard*'s richly emblematic moments and a series of contrasting dialogues, mainly between the fatalistic prince and various less radically disabused interlocutors, Lampedusa wrote a spare and lucid account of Sicily and its place in history. The book's dialectical intelligence is the hard and bony structure that articulates its yielding flesh. Without this toughness of mind it might have been like Visconti's film, whose director had a more formidable aristocratic lineage than Lampedusa and the mind of a window dresser. It might have been more like a novel too. Lampedusa learnt so much from Tolstoy and Stendhal that his book creates the illusion of being a nineteenth century novel. It's really closer to Plato's *Symposium*, a series of conversations, contrasting theories, views and voices on the past, present and future of Sicily. *Every word is weighted,* he wrote to his friend in Brazil, *and every episode has a hidden sense.* The original time span of twenty-four hours would have made this clearer, but the story burst its bounds. An illusion of life and movement is created out of stasis and death. *The Leopard* seems to be a novel, has always been taken for a novel, but is really a great baroque meditation on death.

The Leopard in its first version was finished in March 1956 and two more chapters were added a year later. It'd been sent to Mondadori, Italy's biggest publisher, when it was still unfinished. It was rejected *with intense regret* at the end of the year. Seven months later Lampedusa was dead at sixty of lung cancer. Another copy of the typescript had been sent off anonymously not long after the first. It lay unread and ignored for over a year until someone sent it on to the novelist Giorgio Bassani, who found it the work of *a real writer ... a real poet,* and wanted to publish it immediately. Bassani had no idea at first that the author was the Sicilian prince he'd met four years earlier. He went to Palermo and pieced together a version incorporating some further parts of the manuscript he found in the care of Lampedusa's young friends. *The Leopard* was published by Feltrinelli in November 1958. In just over a year fifty-two further editions followed.

The little world of letters in late fifties Italy wasn't pleased at all that the country's first-ever international bestseller should be such an unfashionable work, even though its author was already dead. Cardinal Ruffini, uncle of that DC minister elected by the friends, said *The Leopard* was one of three things that dishonoured Sicily. The other two were Danilo Dolci, the reformer and writer who was drawing the world's attention to Sicilian poverty, and people who said the mafia existed. In the ideology-ridden culture of those cold war days, however, the people who most disliked it were the progressives, and what they most disliked was distilled in don Fabrizio's great denunciation of hopes for change. When the liberal functionary Chevalley comes from the north to ask him to join the Italian senate, the prince refuses.

In Sicily doing well or doing badly doesn't matter. The sin we Sicilians never forgive is simply that of 'doing'. We're old, Chevalley, terribly old. For at least twenty-five centuries we've been carrying magnificent and heterogeneous civilizations on our backs, all of them coming fully perfected from outside, none sprouted from ourselves, none that we've made our own ... for two thousand five hundred years we've been a colony. I'm not complaining when I say it. Most of it's our fault. But we're worn out and exhausted all the same ... Sleep, my dear Chevalley, sleep is what Sicilians want, and they will always hate anyone who wants to wake them ...

Among the many who found this defeatist and retrogade, the apologia of a failed ruling class, was Leonardo Sciascia, who was then starting out as a writer. When *The Leopard* came out Sciascia's own first novel and biggest success, *The Day of the Owl*, was a couple of years off. Assimilating the prince in the novel to the prince who wrote the novel, as most of the book's critics did, Sciascia charged him in a 1959 review with making a *climatic-geographical abstraction* of Sicily and assuming an aristocratic detachment from its realities. He was still saying this twenty years later. In 1978 he repeated

> It's always seemed to me that the Sicily described by Lampedusa in *The Leopard* is nothing other than a geographic and climatic abstraction removed from time and history. Maybe that Sicily inhabited by sceptics and aristocrats afforded Lampedusa a way of writing a fine book, but if Stendhal had had the time to make that journey to Sicily he so much wanted to, he could have written that book a century earlier.

Sciascia claimed in the sixties that in *The Day of the Owl* of 1961 he'd been the first Sicilian writer to deal with the mafia in a work of imagination. *Nobody had underlined this problem in a work of fiction for the mass market. I did*, he said firmly in 1965. What, I wondered, could have made him forget the vivid and crucial part that don Calogero Sedàra plays in *The Leopard*?

THE CARAVAN of carriages moves through the parched heat of central Sicily in summer and reaches the perimeter of the family estates. Things are noticed in the landscape that are far from aristocratic and not at all abstract. For instance, the well:

> ... it served as a swimming pool, drinking trough, prison, cemetery. It slaked thirst, spread typhus, guarded the kidnapped and concealed the carcasses of beasts and men until they were reduced to smooth anonymous skeletons.

A lot of rural Sicilian life and death is condensed into that informed glance. Those carcasses are recalled not only in the stories of kidnappings and dismemberments with which Tancredi later teases the northerner Chevalley, but quite soon in the figure of Tancredi's future father-in-law, Angelica's father don Calogero. Arriving in his palace, the prince learns from his estate manager that don Calogero Sedàra, the local mayor, has been buying up land to the extent that his income from it is drawing level with the prince's own, *and that around here is the least of his properties*. Sedàra's political influence has grown too. He's *vaguely understood to have been very busy at the time of the liberation* and now leads the local liberals, the new political force, and is sure to be a member of the new national parliament.

Sedàra can barely speak Italian. He's small, mean, avid, less than clean shaven, highly intelligent and already very rich. He has a beautiful uncouth wife kept under wraps. The prince learns from his hunting companion that her father, *so filthy and foul tempered everyone called him Peppe Shit. Excuse the word, Excellency*, was found dead on a country path two years after her marriage to don Calogero. *Peppe Shit* had twelve shotgun blasts in his back. *Always lucky, don Calogero. That fellow was getting greedy and overbearing.* Out hunting, the prince learns not only that the woman his nephew Tancredi, prince of Falconeri, wants to marry is the granddaughter of the rural mafia hit victim *Peppe Shit*. He also discovers that her father the mayor rigged the local vote in the referendum on the unification of Italy. The vote had been announced as a hundred per cent in favour. The prince remembers.

> Italy was born that frowning evening at Donnafugata, born right there in that forgotten town just as much as it was in the lethargy of Palermo or the agitation of Naples ... it was born and one had to hope it would survive in this form. Any other would have been worse. Agreed. Yet this persistent unease had to mean something. He felt it during the too-dry announcement of the figures, the too-emphatic speeches. Something or someone was dead in God knew what hidden corner of the country or fold of the people's consciousness.

Now he understands what it was.

> What had been strangled at Donnafugata and a hundred other places during that night of filthy wind was the newborn good faith ... Don Ciccio's negative vote, fifty similar votes at Donnafugata, a hundred thousand NOs throughout the kingdom would have changed nothing in the result. Rather, they'd have made it more meaningful and the twisting of minds would have been avoided.

Tancredi wants to fuck Angelica simply because she's so desirable, but he wants to marry her to recover his family's lost wealth and restore that abandoned villa with the bougainvillea. The prince his uncle understands this strategic necessity, and ends up himself recommending don Calogero Sedàra as a senator instead of himself. Even lifted here from the body of the story, this didn't look to me like an abstraction out of time and history. Spare and barely suggested, it's the most succinct representation in fiction of that original Sicilian confluence of business, crime and politics in modern Italy, the germ of everything that was to come. There's a sly unspoken analogy running through the story of don Calogero and his political rise through the liberation of Sicily in 1860. It's with the later American liberation of 1943 and those local elements who were rising through Christian Democracy when Lampedusa wrote. *The Leopard*'s don Calogero Sedàra shares more than his first name and his shabby appearance with don Calogero Vizzini, the *capo di tutti i capi* who welcomed the American armies when they arrived with Lucky Luciano's yellow silk foulard. Don Calogero also bears a strong and quite ahistorical resemblance to Totò Riina, the scruffy nondescript illiterate who ran a multinational with a turnover in billions from pencilled sums in a dog-eared notebook. Lampedusa doesn't talk of mafia here, but he shows its essential presence. The well, the corpses, the sudden wealth, the prince's armed *campieri*, the estate guards whose shotguns were *not always innocuous*. There is a direct glance at rural men of honour in a later episode, Father Pirrone's descent to the netherworld of his home village. The Jesuit priest returns for a family visit and becomes involved in a brutal episode of feuding, seduction and inheritance, which he resolves by arranging a strategic marriage of interests that parallels Tancredi's and Angelica's.

If we want everything to stay the same, everything's got to change, says Tancredi early in the novel, as he eagerly explains to his uncle why he's joining Garibaldi. It's an acute summation of the way the Sicilian ruling class has always sought accommodation with the island's new invaders; and having found the accommodation, gone on to bend the outsiders' will to their local interests. It's not quite true that everything stays the same, as the prince knows and the novel shows. History showed it too. What was to stay the same, through the shifting alliances at the top, was the lives of the Sicilian poor.

Glimpsed in the livid light of half past five in the morning, Donnafugata was deserted and looked despairing. In front of every habitation the rubbish from wretched tables piled up along the leprous walls. Shivering dogs rifled through it, their eagerness always disappointed. The odd door was already open and the stench of the huddled sleepers spread through the street. By the flicker of oil lamps mothers examined their children's trachoma-inflamed eyelids. They were almost all dressed in mourning and quite a few had been the wives of those scarecrow corpses one stumbles over at the bends in the country tracks. The men had grabbed their hoes and were leaving to look for anyone who might, God willing, give them work. Stupefied silence or exasperated screeching hysterical voices

...

Just before he wrote *The Leopard*, Lampedusa in 1955 had made his first-ever visit to Palma di Montechiaro, the town near Agrigento of which he was duke, a town founded by his ancestor in 1637 as a *New Jerusalem*. Some of the details in *The Leopard* were clearly derived from what Lampedusa found at Palma, for instance the closed convent where the prince's ancestress had withdrawn, in life and in the novel, and where another forebear had spent his last years sleeping in a coffin. The year after *The Leopard* was published, in 1959, a young doctor from Bologna, a parasitologist, spent several months in Palma studying conditions of life in Sicily. He found a town where over half the people were illiterate and child mortality ran at fifty per cent. Farm animals, mules, horses, goats, cattle, pigs lived with their owners in their houses. Only a third of the houses had running water, in any case polluted, and twenty council cleaners, who hadn't been paid for seven months, carried off the nightsoil in open mule carts. Sewers ran open in the streets, flies swarmed and the stench was overpowering. Apart from a rich fauna of intestinal parasites, malaria, typhus and trachoma were rampant, and other more obscure viruses thought not to exist in Europe. The children worked in the lime quarry and almost nobody ate meat. The prince's town in 1959 was the town of a hundred years earlier, and to describe Sicilian wretchedness in his *historical* novel, in those lines about the town at daybreak, Lampedusa had merely to record what he found on his visit. Nothing had changed.

FROM MARSALA, after landing in 1860 and liberating Palermo and the island, Garibaldi fought his way north with relative ease. The *picciotti* fought with him in Sicily, as Sciascia reminded Andreotti one of the few times they met, because they'd been sent by their bosses, and in Naples the *guaglioni* of the camorra were transformed temporarily into a national guard to keep order, and thrown into jail when the liberator passed. The Bourbon monarchy was swiftly defeated and the Mezzogiorno soon incorporated into the united Italy that was now ruled by the Savoy monarchy from Piedmont in the north. It was a shift in Italy's economic and political centre of gravity from which the south never recovered. Naples went into an irreversible decline. All its embryonic heavy industry was carted off to fuel the growth of the north, where the industrial heart of Italy remained. Protectionist tax concessions were granted to the companies of that industrial triangle whose apices were Turin, Genoa and Milan. By the beginning of the twentieth century the economy of the industrialized north had taken off. Turin, the old capital of the house of Savoy, became the headquarters of the Fiat motor company, one of the biggest industrial groups in Europe. In the same years, the southern economy plunged into crisis as the prices of oil, wine and wool dived, setting off the huge turn-of-the-century peasant emigration to the Americas. Through all this, and though it was poorer, the Mezzogiorno was still paying higher taxes and getting less back in public expenditure and capital investment than Italy's northern regions. The savings of the south, and the money sent home by emigrants, were sucked toward the north and the gulf widened between developed and underdeveloped Italy. In the modern state of united Italy the Mezzogiorno remained what pope Leon X had called it, *the tail of Italy*. The southern ruling class, with its reactionary and parasitic representatives and its criminal allies, was the political expression of these realities. Everything, as *The Leopard*'s bright-eyed young Tancredi had foreseen, had changed, and everything had remained the same.

There were older causes too. A political scientist from Harvard called Putnam has found the paths of northern and southern Italy were already diverging nearly a thousand years ago. The feudal kingdom founded in the south by the Norman mercenaries was, like the Byzantine and Arab states before it, a centralized and absolutist state. Administratively, economically, socially the southern regime was very advanced. Its constitution in 1230 included Europe's first codification of administrative law in seven hundred years. It founded Europe's first state university in Naples in 1224. It was a multicultural society *ante litteram*, tolerant in religion, in which Greek, Arabic, Jewish, Latin and Italian vernacular arts flourished together. But wealth in the south came from land, not commerce, and the regime's efficiency of rule reinforced the social hierarchy. Its very strengths inhibited change, while in the north by the twelfth century Florence, Venice, Bologna, Genoa, Milan had already evolved into a network of communal republics. They were city states with an active citizenry and a professional public administration. They made their money in finance, trade and commerce and the institutions of modern capitalism had their origins there. For Putnam, the split between the hierarchical, autocratic and bureaucratic south and the democratic, entrepreneurial and outward-looking north was formed then. By the end of the seventeenth century, aristocratic power was already eroding in the north, while the Bourbons in the south ruled the biggest and worst-administered Italian state. In 1791, when it was twice as big as Rome and three times the size of Milan, its capital Naples was

> a grotesque parasite, many of whose inhabitants were royal employees, priests, domestic servants and beggars ... [living] on the back of a desperately overworked, desperately poor peasantry who were given no civic rights.

After unification it was the south that overwhelmingly filled the emigrant ships to the new world. From the Mezzogiorno, nearly one and three-quarter million immigrants entered the United States between 1901 and 1910. From the north in the same time came a third of a million. Colonies and communities formed beyond the ocean. In the early nineteen twenties the quota acts in the United States reduced the flood of immigrants to a trickle, and Italy was closed off by fascism and another world war. Twenty years later the Italian economy was in ruins and most of the south was starving. When the war ended many young southern men migrated north, strangers in their own country, to be the cannon fodder of Italy's postwar reconstruction and the coming economic boom. Some, mostly single men, went further north, to Switzerland and Germany and the mines of Belgium. In 1977 Manlio Rossi-Doria, the great student of southern agricultural society, wrote that

> Of all the changes brought about in the Mezzogiorno in the last thirty years, the emigration to the northern regions of Italy and Europe of nearly five million southerners has certainly been the greatest, the most painful and the most distressing ... It is impossible to calculate the enormous cost of emigration for those who took part in it ...

Some still looked overseas. In the eleven years after the war, between 1946 and 1957, Italy's emigrants outnumbered the homecomers by well over a million and nearly three-quarters of them came from the south. After Argentina, sixty per cent of whose people were of Italian origin and where most still went, Australia was one of the few foreign destinations left. It was terribly distant but more or less promising. Many stayed away for ever. Between 1951 and 1971, even counting those returning home, the Mezzogiorno lost over four million people out of a total population of little over eighteen million. *It was a phenomenon of colossal dimensions.* The poor farming communities of the interior, Rossi-Doria's *naked south* of grain and pasture, a third of the Mezzogiorno's population, lost half their inhabitants. The gap between the two Italies got wider and wider.

V

A PRISONER

IN 1971, Leonardo Sciascia published a short book rather different from any of his earlier novels, which had all treated their Sicilian themes in a straightforwardly realistic manner. *Il Contesto*, however, or *The Context*, which later became known in English as *Equal Danger*, was subtitled *una parodia*, and was a detective story, or a parody of one, set in a context of political intrigue in an unnamed country very like Sicily. A literary detective called Inspector Rogas, who as his Latin name hints is a patently literary creation as well as a detective who knows his Voltaire, investigates the serial murders of a string of distinguished judges. He soon finds his own line of thinking, which is that the murders are revenge killings by an unjustly convicted man, is in conflict with the one his superiors would like him to pursue, which would lead Rogas to discover political killings by left-wing groups. In Sciascia's story, however, the logical processes of detection, clarification and resolution are reversed, and what seems at first a reasonably straightforward problem, susceptible to rational solution, starts spiralling down into a murky vortex of hidden powers, obscure relationships and concealed motives. At the end of the story Rogas himself is murdered. Rogas has confided his suspicions to a writer friend the day before, but the reader never learns quite what these suspicions are. By the end of the story, the reader knows nothing. Yet in trying to make sense of the abruptly concluded novella, the reader is forced into trying to relate the incidents into a series of gut-clenching hypotheses. Sciascia vanishes and a faint sense of nausea descends. My own queasiness was enhanced by a French critic who wrote that *it was possible, though difficult*, to reconstruct the dynamic of the killings in the art gallery at the end. I'd tried and failed, and felt now I'd missed the point.

The effect of reading *The Context* is of a concentrated hit of the daily papers in Italy during the period of *The True History*. Hideous deaths, disturbing coincidences, plenty of detail, enveloping menace and no real knowledge at all. Inspector Rogas, *like every self-respecting investigator, that is, one who has that respect for himself that he wants to win from his readers*, lives alone, with a vague memory of having once been married. Toward the end of the story, he goes to his Thursday restaurant to think things over at lunch. Rogas also knows his food and eats at a different restaurant for every day of the week, so that each of the seven *considered him a good customer but not so trusting and regular that they could treat him badly*. After carefully choosing food and wine, he eats distractedly, his mind on the problem.

> Within the problem of a series of crimes that it was his duty and his profession to solve and hand their author over to the law, if not to justice, another problem had arisen. It was highly criminal in nature, a crime contemplated in the fundamental principles of the State. But it had to be solved outside his professional duty, against his duty. It was a question in fact of defending the state against those who represented it, those who held it in their power. The State was held prisoner and needed setting free. But he too was a prisoner. All he could do was try to open a crack in the wall.

To reread *The Context* after an immersion in *The True History of Italy* is to be struck by how early and how acutely Sciascia sensed what was going on in Italy. The quotation above could stand as an epigraph to *The True History*. Italy's history in the seventies and eighties is foreseen in *The Context*. Rogas happens on his secret meeting of the chief justice, heads of the police and armed services and members of the government ten years before the P2 conspiracy was revealed. *The Context*'s judges and politicians are assassinated years before the Red Brigades and the mafia began killing them in life. The equivocal behaviour of the left opposition party at the story's conclusion greatly disconcerted the communist party when the book appeared. And when Rogas observes a state limousine discreetly leaving the chief justice's house after the secret meeting, and sees inside *shrinking so far into one corner ... that it seemed empty, the minister for foreign affairs*, I made an instant reality check, only to find that Giulio Andreotti was still a year or so from becoming prime minister and over a decade from becoming minister for foreign affairs. He did spend the greater part of the sixties as minister for defence.

Having a feel for the subterranean movements in Italian society, and a particular sensitivity to those tremors that started in Sicily and later hit the mainland, Sciascia condensed tendencies into images and acts with such precision that reality followed where his imagination led. Evidently, he had the feeling as he wrote that he was being overtaken by events, even as his story moved away from its starting point in reality. He wrote in an afterword to *The Context* in 1971 that having begun his story as a joke,

> ... the story shifted to a quite imaginary country; a country where ideas were no longer current, where principles, though still proclaimed and acclaimed, were daily mocked, where ideologies in politics were reduced to mere names in the power play, where power for its own sake was all that counted. An imaginary country, I repeat. Italy and Sicily might also come to mind, but only in the sense my friend Guttuso intends when he says, *Even if I paint an apple, it's Sicily*. The light. The colour. And the worm eating it inside? The worm, in my parody, is quite imaginary. The light and the colour, if there are any, may be Sicilian and Italian, the incidents, the details. But the substance, if there is any, is meant as a reflection on power in the world, on the way power degenerates into the impenetrable form of a chain of connections that we can roughly call mafioso.

He'd kept the parody in a drawer for two years after writing it. It was, he said, perhaps because he'd started it as an entertainment and when he got to the end it no longer amused him at all.

Not that Sciascia, even in his lightest moments, is ever a laugh a minute man. His next book, *Todo Modo*, later translated as *One Way or Another*, was published in 1974 and set in a place of *spiritual retreat* for a group of very worldly demochristian politicians and power brokers. The retreat is held in a luxury hotel built over an old hermitage by the entrepreneurial priest who leads the spiritual exercises. A famous chef's brought in so that the politicians can *dedicate themselves for a whole week to spiritual gymnastics without mortifying the flesh*. During the networking and sex, a series of murders takes place, and as in the earlier novel solutions to the deaths are implied but never revealed. The first murder victim is a former senator, a man with *an acute, foxy face ... far from ill informed in matters of patristic and scholastic theology*. The former senator is shot dead during the evening recitation of the rosary, and a few days later the investigating magistrate receives a mountain of photocopies of cheques signed by the victim. They've been *drawn on special or secret funds he had access to.*

> *– Are there any cheques made out to someone here?*
> *– Someone? Everyone. There's not one person here who hasn't had his share.*

The time lag was shortening here between Sciascia's premonitory imaginings and the reality that followed them. *Todo Modo* was only two or three years ahead of the Italcasse scandal. This huge and complicated matter was seething away underground in the late seventies and is extensively described in *The True History of Italy*. It was so complex and the efforts to suppress it were so far reaching and effective that only twenty years later were the details coming to light. Italcasse was an Italian government-owned bank, controlled in effect by the DC, and *The President's Cheques* were the subject of a very celebrated article, written about five years after *Todo Modo*, about cheques drawn by Giulio Andreotti *on funds he had access to* and made out to some very dubious people indeed. Nobody's ever read *The President's Cheques* because the article disappeared before publication and its author was shot dead. A film made of *Todo Modo* a year or so after the novel came out made the book's outlined characters readily identifiable as real DC potentates, and another of the characters was easily recognizable as Aldo Moro.

Moro was the prime minister before Andreotti in the later seventies, the consummate catholic ideologue and the patient, tireless *great weaver* of that new understanding with the communists that the communist leader Enrico Berlinguer called the historic compromise and Moro called *the inevitable convergence of parallel lines*. It would be another exploit of Italian transformism, when the establishment swallowed the opposition and assimilated it. *Everything would change so that everything could remain the same.* The left had been growing stronger. The communists wanted to govern and were already moving hopefully to the right to show how responsible they were. Some were unhappy about this, especially the Red Brigades, who'd killed fifteen in the previous two years in their *strategy of annihilation* against the Italian ruling class and were determined to wreck all understandings. So were the plotters and terrorists on the right, and maybe the great and powerful friends. When Moro had tried to explain *the inevitable convergence of parallel lines*, in Washington, Henry Kissinger had shouted and threatened him in a rage. Yet the demochristian snake had patiently, quietly hypnotized the communist bunny and was ready now to devour it.

MORO WAS heading for parliament for the swallowing on the morning of March the sixteenth in 1978. The day was already a success for the president of the DC. A new government was being sworn in, headed by Giulio Andreotti. It was actually the third consecutive government headed by Andreotti, his fifth that decade, but this new one would have the support of the communists. The *great weaver* Moro had won the support of the communists without having had to give them any power, and who better now to swallow and transform the communist challenge than the archdemochristian Giulio Andreotti? *Power wears out those who don't have it* was his personal motto. He'd promised to consult. The communists would be *in the area of government* and they were thrilled. Moro, in his lugubrious way, was satisfied.

He'd hardly left home that morning when he and his security escort were ambushed in the middle of Rome. A BR commando blocked their cars in via Fani, killed Moro's driver and his four bodyguards and hustled Moro into another car and disappeared. Except by his BR jailers, and in the polaroids they issued from the *people's prison*, Moro was never seen alive again.

For fifty-five days the BR held Moro prisoner in Rome while the Italian police and security forces tried with marvellous inefficiency to find him. A series of BR communiqués and letters from Moro punctuated the drama. Nobody seemed to know what to do. Nobody seemed to expect the police or security forces to save Moro as he was tried in hiding by a *people's tribunal*. There was a strong whiff of hidden secret service agendas. The socialists wanted to open negotiations with the BR for Moro's release. The communists, now so close to respectability and yet still so far from real power, had a peculiar horror of acquiring guilt by association with this nightmare left fringe and urged that the state not deal with the kidnappers. The DC leaders already thought this but the communists were the firmest of all. No deal with the BR. Aldo Moro was condemned to death.

Not simply and quickly however. Fifty-five days was a long time and the arguments went back and forth on what to do. Moro sent out letters to his closest DC friends begging them to negotiate, offering reasons for saving his life, using his years of intimacy to second guess their thinking and their moves. The communists were closed and frozen, but in the DC Moro's colleagues read the communiqués about interrogation and trials with growing alarm. Moro knew all the DC secrets and a lot of them were deeply compromising. Some DC leaders were more gravely compromised than others and would've felt unease at Moro's telling all. A year earlier, defending his colleagues caught in the Lockheed scandal, Moro had said ringingly

> There must be no scapegoats, no human sacrifices ... The DC
> stands firm in defence of its men ... You won't judge us in the piaz-
> zas, we won't let ourselves be put on trial.

His old friends and allies failed to reciprocate this loyalty. They found
they shared the communist concern to save at all costs The State,
which the demochristians had always tended to identify with the DC,
when they thought of it at all. As the weeks passed, some of those who
thought saving a life was worth some compromise, and that a deal
needn't necessarily mean the end of the world, or the state, began to
wonder at the DC's readiness to wrap itself in the national flag, began
to wonder about individual motives. But hearts hardened as Moro's
letters grew more desperate and bitter, and prime minister Andreotti
had no trouble keeping his troops in line. There was no deal and on
May the ninth Moro's body was found in the back of a red or purple
Renault 4 parked contemptuously in via Caetani in the centre of Rome,
exactly midway between the DC's headquarters and the PCI's.

The fifty-five days of Moro's imprisonment had transfixed Italy,
including, it turned out, the Antistate of Cosa Nostra. The very first
pages of *The True History of Italy* contain a recollection of the Moro kidnapping as the Cosa Nostra commission lived it. In the summer of
1991 the mafia pentito Francesco Marino Mannoia recalled those days
to magistrates from Rome and Palermo who were interrogating him in
New York. Cosa Nostra's leaders had split over Moro, Mannoia said.
The boss Stefano Bontate, a *convinced demochristian* with many political
ties, had wanted to mount a mafia operation to free Moro. He argued
strongly for this in a commission meeting held a couple of weeks after
the kidnapping. He was opposed by the boss Pippo Calò, who was
based in Rome. Calò skirted the issue for a while, posed logistical problems and finally turned on Bontate and said, *You still haven't got it,
Stefano. Leaders in his own party don't want him free.* This split over Moro
was an early sign of the coming war of extermination that was already
looming over Cosa Nostra. Calò had allied himelf to Riina and the
Corleonesi, who mistrusted politics and hated politicians. Bontate was
eliminated three years later.

I found another recollection of those days of 1978 on page 225 of
The True History, from the prosecutors' third volume. Claudio Martelli
was the socialist party's young deputy leader and later minister of justice in the last Andreotti government. It was he who'd become
Falcone's ally in Rome at the beginning of the nineties and enabled

Falcone's battery of antimafia measures to become law, for which Riina had added Martelli's name to Falcone's and Borsellino's on the death list. Recalling the Moro kidnapping to the prosecutors, Martelli compared the Andreotti government's intransigence over Moro with the DC's behaviour during BR kidnappings a couple of years later, when the government had gone to quite embarrassing lengths to meet the BR's demands and save the prisoners. It had shut down a prison to save a judge, and enlisted the Neapolitan camorra to release Ciro Cirillo, a close political associate of Andreotti's man in Naples, Antonio Gava. Martelli told the prosecutors about

> the suspicions aroused in us socialists about the way the Moro kidnapping was handled ... then as now I was convinced that there was some obscure motivation behind the flaming shield of intransigence [of which] Andreotti was the main proponent ... we socialists were struck humanly and politically by Moro's letters and his not accepting to be sacrificed to reasons of state. Andreotti maintained that the letters weren't his, that they couldn't have been written by him ...

ONE PERSON who'd followed the events of those fifty-five days with peculiar horror was Leonardo Sciascia. That summer, a couple of months after Moro's murder, he wrote a pamphlet on the whole affair that came out in October. It was elegantly and austerely printed for the Palermo publisher Sellerio, a little over a hundred pages, small rectangles of type surrounded by vast creamy margins and a good deal of the text taken from Aldo Moro's own letters. It arrived bound in a fine white paper cover and finished in a *rétro* French manner with a striking engraving by the metaphysical artist Fabrizio Clerici on the front cover. The cover was covered itself in turn by a dustjacket of semi-transparent glassine paper. A special run of a hundred and twenty copies, presumably *hors commerce* and numbered from 1 to 100 and I to XX was printed on hand-made paper and issued each with a hand-pulled copy of Clerici's engraving and signed by the author.

The trade edition's wide creamy pages were uncut, and gaining access to the text by means of a knife, a process that both distracted and concentrated the attention, imposed reflective pauses and prolonged and intensified your involvement with what Moro and Sciascia had to say. This pamphlet was altogether a physical experience. It arrived with a downbeat warning printed on a bookmark insert, written surely by Sciascia himself, ... *the book is not fascinating, not moving, has no literary quality and is only a hard and naked search for a hard and naked truth.* It was about how the politicians condemned Moro to die. Sciascia used public pronouncements and Moro's published private letters to trace the story of how the government decided not to deal with the BR, how it justified its decision to the public, and how the decision led down to its inevitable consequence, the assassination of Moro. The pamphlet was an exercise in reading the language of Moro's letters, what they said and what they didn't say. In his two months in the *people's prison*, Moro has written and the BR delivered some fifty to seventy letters to colleagues and family.

Sciascia started his pamphlet by remembering an old friend, a writer, now dead, who'd had a polemical vein to more than match his own. Pier Paolo Pasolini, the poet and film maker who was murdered in November 1975, had often denounced the DC regime in the last years of his life. *I know*, Pasolini had written on the front page of Italy's most influential and widely read newspaper, the *Corriere della Sera*, a year before his death.

> I know the names of those responsible for the slaughter ...
> I know the names of those responsible for the slaughters ...
> I know the names of the summit that manipulated ...
> I know the names of those who ran ...
> I know the names of the powerful group who ...
> I know the names of those who, between one mass and the next, made provision and guaranteed political protection ...
> I know the names of the important and serious figures who are behind the ridiculous figures who ...
> I know the names of the important and serious figures behind the tragic kids who ...
> I know all these names and all the acts (the slaughters, the attacks on institutions) they have been guilty of ...

Pasolini followed this with a disarming admission. *I know. But I don't have the proof. I don't even have clues.* Instead he claimed the artist's prerogative of an *imaginative* statement of political reality. The court room wasn't the only place where truth was decided. The court room was often the last place to look for it. Pasolini went on:

> I know because I am a writer and an intellectual who tries to follow what goes on, to imagine what is known and what is kept quiet, who pieces together the disorganized fragments of a whole and coherent political picture, who restores logic where arbitrariness, mystery and madness seem to prevail.

Two months before his murder, Pasolini narrowed his aim. In the *Corriere della Sera* he demanded simply that the DC be put on trial for

unworthiness, contempt for citizens, manipulation of public money, intrigue with the oil companies, with industrialists, bankers, connivance with the mafia, high treason in favour of a foreign country, collaboration with the CIA, illicit use of organisms like the SID [secret services], responsibility in the massacres of Milan, Brescia, Bologna ... destruction of Italy's urban and rural environment ... responsibility for the *fearful*, as they say, state of schools, hospitals and every basic public service ...

By now his polemics had become a wild, desperate joke. Twenty years later it was hard to recall the mad daring of Pasolini's provocation in the autumn of 1975, on the front page of Italy's leading paper. The accuracy of it all, however, still quickened the pulse.

Let the image of Andreotti or Fanfani, Gava or Restivo, handcuffed between the carabinieri, be a metaphoric image. Let their trial be a metaphor. To make what I say comic as well as sublime ... and above all much clearer.

A month before his murder he was writing another litany of things *Italians want to know*. Among others:

Italian citizens want to know why ... the division between northern Italy and southern Italy has become even deeper, making southerners ever more second class citizens ... Italians want to know how far the mafia has taken part in the decisions of the government in Rome or collaborated with it ...

Pasolini had earlier that year described Moro as

the one ... who seems the least implicated of all in the horrible things that have been organized in this country from 1969 until now, in the attempt, at least formally successful, to hold on to power.

Wading through the press clippings of the previous spring, Sciascia seized now on the way the other politicians started speaking of Moro, a few days after his kidnapping, first as *a statesman*, and then as *a great statesman*. Moro, said Sciascia, had never been a statesman, let alone a great one, the DC never having had any sense of the state. Moro was a first-rate politician who continued to be one during his imprisonment. The *statesman*-talk was a way of sharply distinguishing the earlier Moro from the author of the letters now arriving from the prison, which urgently argued for negotiating his release. The letters, said his old DC colleagues, were if not dictated by terrorists then written under pressure of physical or psychological torture. Moro had written first in the hope of being rescued, playing for time and probably trying to convey, in his habitually oblique and contorted language, useful information. At a certain point in his *well fed* isolation Moro must have realized the rescuers weren't coming. No commando squad was going to kick down the door of the people's prison. After twenty days, Moro had sent a vigorously argued letter to the DC leaders pointing out, truthfully, that he'd always been in favour of negotiating to save lives in cases like his own, and reminding the communists what they owed him. Unable to suppress their president's letter, the DC leaders had issued a note saying it had been written under duress *and could not morally be attributed to [Moro]*.

From there on Moro's letters had become more personal, more desperate and more acutely argued. Sciascia described the sequence as a tragic breaking down. The mask, the character, gave way to the man, and the man to the creature, the bare forked animal, and it was when Moro shed his political mask, dropped his political voice and started to sound in his letters really and deeply human, that the DC, the communists and the Italian press repudiated him. One DC leader, challenged by Moro, had replied that he *wasn't going to debate with the BR*. The communist Antonello Trombadori had cried in the corridors of the Italian parliament, *Moro is dead!* A famous conservative commentator had published a *Requiem for Moro*. All this was while Moro was alive and hoping to live. The culminating touch had been a public statement put out by a group describing themselves as friends of Moro, which had announced that *the Moro who speaks from the 'people's prison' is not the Moro we have known*. The fifty-odd signatories had described themselves as old friends who'd shared with the earlier Moro a *common cultural formation, Christian spirituality and political vision*. The Moro who still hoped to negotiate his release was *not the man we know, with his spiritual, political and judicial vision that inspired the contribution to the drawing up of the republic's very constitution*. The *great statesman* was dead, they were saying, dismissing the lucid and intelligent living writer of the letters being received as the voice of the Red Brigades.

Moro had then realized his party had condemned him to death. *I wouldn't have believed it possible*, he had written. The closing words of a long letter in which he foresaw his death and his funeral were a portent, or a curse:

This bloodbath will not go well ... neither for Andreotti, nor for the

DC, nor for the country: each will bear his responsibility.

~~I do not want, I repeat, men of power around me. I want those~~ who have really loved me to be near me ... If all this has been decided, let God's will be done. But let none of those responsible hide behind a pretended duty. Things will be made clear, they will soon be clear.

Sciascia ended with a paragraph from a story by the Argentinian metaphysical writer Jorge Luis Borges. A narrator describes a mystery story whose plot he's forgotten. He remembers though that a final paragraph contains a sentence which makes the reader realize that the story's solution to the mystery is wrong. *The unquiet reader re-reads the pertinent chapters and finds another solution, the true one.* Sciascia was implying Moro had left an oblique message about the state's complicity in terrorism in one of his last letters. But the lines from Borges also bore on Sciascia's belief that Moro was loyal to the end to *his* DC and never revealed compromising secrets to his captors. *Maybe 'findings' will come to light*, Sciascia wrote, *but it will be too late not to suspect an expert set-up ...* Years after Sciascia wrote this, 'findings' did come to light. And though Sciascia had reason to be sceptical of anything emerging from the riven, nightmare world of the Italian secret services, the discovery of these 'findings' had consequences that were powerful reasons for believing the 'findings' to be authentic. In his terrible abandonment Moro had revealed more than Sciascia imagined. The *unquiet reader* has to go back now and reread some more chapters of *The True History of Italy*. On an essential matter of fact, Sciascia got it wrong.

THE FINDINGS made their first appearance less than five months after Moro's body had been dumped in the boot of the red or purple Renault 4. On the first of October 1978 a group of the antiterrorist carabinieri who were working under general Dalla Chiesa raided an apartment in via Monte Nevoso in Milan. They surprized nine members of the Red Brigades at work typing out documents of Moro's. There were unsent letters, various notes and his lengthy replies to BR interrogators on Italian politics.

The documents had hardly been discovered before they vanished. The originals disappeared at any rate, and questions about them were being asked within days. The journalist Giorgio Bocca wrote in *La Repubblica* five days later that political and military figures had gone through the Moro papers before they reached the magistrates. The BR members who were arrested themselves insisted that a part of the material disappeared on its way to the judiciary. A radically incomplete forty-nine page version was later released to the press. It contained a series of charges against the DC and especially Andreotti. Moro accused Andreotti over his relations with the mafia banker Sindona; over the Italcasse financial scandal which involved both Andreotti and elements of Cosa Nostra; and over the state's complicity in the 1969 terrorist bombing of a bank in piazza Fontana in Milan, which had killed sixteen people.

None of it was really new, and the edited version of the Moro papers added little to what was already known, though there was some piquancy in the accusations' now coming from inside the DC. Later that October a curious piece on the Moro papers appeared in a little-known magazine called *Osservatorio Politico*, and known as *OP*. This paper was a one-man outfit in the person of Mino Pecorelli, who had come to journalism from the very murky background of the Italian secret services. *OP* was a kind of newsletter that presented insider knowledge in an oblique and intimidatory way, and its purposes were often closer to blackmail than information. It was assumed that Pecorelli was still at least close to his previous employers.

OP's article contained some very brief extracts from the Moro papers that weren't in the version given to the press. The accompanying text remarked *Giulio Andreotti is a very lucky man, but his path has been smoothed by a series of only partly fortuitous circumstances ...* The article was a warning that Pecorelli knew what was in the complete original. Apart from this dangled bait, it was twelve years before the contents of the unmutilated Moro papers became known to more than three or four people. In October 1990 some workmen doing alterations to the same Milan apartment where the earlier papers had been seized in 1978 found a copy of a more complete set of documents hidden behind a plaster wall panel. Whether or not these Moro papers were the same as those found in 1978, which seemed to have disappeared without trace, this new version contained a great deal more than had been let out before. Moro here revealed that a secret and illegal anticommunist military network set up in Italy at the end of the war and linked to NATO was still in existence. He confirmed that the DC was financed in part by the CIA, something the left had been saying for years. He spoke about the state's involvement in the right-wing terrorist *strategy of tension* in the seventies, and on many other matters. These parts had clearly been censored in 1978 as state secrets.

So had a lot of material that concerned Andreotti alone. Andreotti, the newly-found papers said, had lately won a power struggle for control of the secret services and so was privy to all state secrets. Moro described Andreotti as vastly powerful both inside and out of Italy, and went on to make a solemn denunciation of the man the law had given so much power. He described Andreotti as *cold, impenetrable, devoid of human feelings ... given over to the conquest of power in order to do evil, as he has always done in life.* A very dangerous man, Moro warned, to have in charge. In a striking phrase, Moro evoked an Andreotti *livid, absent, closed in his dream of glory.*

Unlike the earlier published version, these Moro papers contained information about Andreotti's dealings with Sindona and a fairly detailed account of Andreotti's part in the Italcasse scandal. This was a complex and deeply compromising matter. Andreotti had used loans from the Italcasse bank, which was owned by the Italian government and controlled by the DC, to help business friends of his who were in trouble. The transactions involved money launderers working for the Cosa Nostra boss Pippo Calò, the one who'd argued against rescuing Moro. The publication of what Moro knew about this would likely have destroyed Andreotti's political career. Somebody had got hold of the signed cheques that proved Andreotti's involvement with mafia interests. The damage done to Andreotti when these these raw facts were known would be compounded by questions they'd now raise about why Andreotti had refused to negotiate for Moro's release. And the compounded damage would be compounded still further by the discovery that prime minister Andreotti had suppressed those parts of the Moro papers that told the story. And a flameout was the last thing prime minister Andreotti had in mind in 1978.

In October 1978, the *OP* article on the Moro papers had come at a time of frantic activity in some quarters. At two o'clock in the morning Franco Evangelisti, the deputy minister who was Andreotti's factotum, had an unexpected home visit from general Dalla Chiesa, who asked him to read a typescript of about fifty pages. The general said it came from Moro and that he was going to give it to Andreotti the next day. Evangelisti said he never found out later whether he did or not. The mother of Dalla Chiesa's wife also said she remembered her daughter telling her about the Moro papers at this time. She told her mother Andreotti had asked the general for them. She said Dalla Chiesa had given a part to the magistrates, a part but not all to Andreotti and that he'd kept a photocopy of the papers for himself. Andreotti's memory of this period was quite different, and minimal. He said he knew nothing of Dalla Chiesa's night call on his assistant, that he'd merely run a distracted prime ministerial eye over the Moro documents when they were passed to him. He added that before he was charged in 1993 he'd refused to read the Moro papers, because *he didn't want to trouble the memory* he had of his murdered colleague.

People who worked closely with Dalla Chiesa and Pecorelli remembered that the general of the antiterrorist force and the muckraking journalist met quite often over the six months from September 1978. This improbable couple, the model of military rectitude and the sleazebag journo with the dubious past, seem to have had one thing only in common. They were the only two, apart from Andreotti and maybe the ineffable Licio Gelli and one or two of Gelli's people in the secret services, who knew what was in the Moro papers. Pino Arlacchi, an informed writer on the mafia and in 1995 deputy head of the parliamentary antimafia commission, gave an interesting take on Pecorelli at this time. Pecorelli had lately broken with Licio Gelli and the secret right-wing P2 lodge, and as Pecorelli and Dalla Chiesa got to know each other, they became allies, helping and protecting each other in their search, drawn together by a shared sense of acute danger.

> [Pecorelli] ended up taking seriously what was initially his 'cover' as a journalist. Before that, his magazine had simply been a weapon used by a faction of the secret services, but after May 1978 its financiers had increasingly lost control of their mouthpiece. *OP*'s exposés of the regime's misdeeds and its attacks on very powerful figures continued ...

A third person was present at one of the secret night-time meetings of Dalla Chiesa and Pecorelli in the last days of 1978 or the first of 1979, inside the general's white Alfa Romeo. A little further on in *The True History*, on page 554, in the prosecutors' sixth volume, I found the testimony of Angelo Incandela. He was a senior prison officer who was a close and trusted ally of Dalla Chiesa's. It was Incandela who convinced the BR's Patrizio Peci to collaborate with Dalla Chiesa, and this was the state's breakthrough against left-wing terrrorism. In the prison at Cuneo where Incandela was working, there were a number of brigatisti and mafiosi of note among the prisoners. Dalla Chiesa was hunting for a packet of documents on Andreotti that he believed had been smuggled into the prison, and Pecorelli, whom Incandela only identified later from a photograph, was there to explain how and where the packet of documents, rolled up and tightly bound in plastic tape *like a salame*, had arrived. Incandela recalled

> Three days later the general ... repeated that I absolutely had to

find those papers from the Moro kidnapping ...

General Dalla Chiesa was very anxious to have information about the Hon. Andreotti.

Often over the years he asked me insistently to pass on information learnt from the inmates about the Hon. Andreotti.

He was utterly convinced that the Hon. Andreotti was an extremely dangerous person ...

In Milan once he said to me, to get me to make a secret report on what he thought I knew about Andreotti, *But don't you understand that this is the only way I and you and others like us can hope to save our lives?*

The papers had reached the prison. Incandela found the packet and handed it unopened to Dalla Chiesa. This meeting had a sequel in the summer of 1981, another secret meeting between Dalla Chiesa and Incandela, in which the general tried very hard to get the officer to hide a big envelope containing a document, about forty pages Incandela thought, behind a lavatory cistern off the prisoners' recreation room. The envelope would then be discovered during a prison search. Incandela angered Dalla Chiesa by refusing, but only because there was no way he could hide the envelope unseen by the guards. *His tone changed suddenly and he stared into my eyes,* Incandela remembered. *Are you an officer with balls?* Dalla Chiesa had said. *We're writing history ... For the Fatherland, men who've got balls sometimes have to take risks.*

One of the men of honour imprisoned at Cuneo then was Tommaso Buscetta. As a senior mafioso Buscetta expected privileges in jail, and when he failed to get them he told Incandela one day, *You know that in Rome we can count even on Andreotti? We could have saved Moro, only they didn't want it.* Cosa Nostra had ordered Buscetta to make contact with the BR in prison during the first weeks of Moro's imprisonment. This was when Cosa Nostra still thought saving Moro would be a favour to the friends in the DC. When they realized the real favour would be to let Moro die, Buscetta's orders were countermanded.

Dalla Chiesa's idea of the envelope behind the lavatory cistern, which seems to have been an attempt to get the Moro papers back into circulation without the general's being linked to their reappearance, showed that Dalla Chiesa, even in the middle of the war against terrorism, still had the Moro documents very much on his mind nearly three years after they were first found. Pecorelli's interest in what the Moro papers revealed didn't last as long as the general's, but it was very intense while it did. *It's a bombshell! Italcasse isn't over it's hardly started – who took the cheques will come out in the new year,* he jotted among his notes. He'd discovered Cosa Nostra's involvement in Andreotti's Italcasse loans to Andreotti's business friends.

At the end of January 1979, Pecorelli was invited to a dinner. The dinner was held in the restaurant of the Famija Piemonteisa club in Rome and it was organized and attended by the club's director, Walter Bonino. This dinner takes a lot of space in *The True History of Italy*, which gives much attention, for instance, to the seating arrangement, which was intimate enough for two of the diners not to be able to carry on a private conversation unheard by the others. *The True History* also gives the information that at the end of the meal the diners moved to an adjoining room where coffee was sipped. It doesn't tell the reader what was eaten. Was it something typical from Piedmont, in keeping with the club's name, a truffle dish maybe? The fragrant white Alba truffles would have been barely out of season. Served *alla piemontese* they would have been thinly sliced and placed in a covered pan in alternating layers with equally thin slices of parmesan cheese and a hint of salt, pepper and olive oil. They cook in ten minutes. Or given the very hardbitten and experienced old capital hands who were gathered there that evening, something more characteristically Roman like *fingerburning* barbecued ribs of baby lamb? Either dish would've been apt, though it was too early in the year for one of that spring's tender sucking lambs. Maybe none of the diners remembered what they ate on what sounds like a far from convivial occasion.

Apart from Pecorelli and Bonino, three others were present at the dinner. They were Claudio Vitalone, Adriano Testi and Donato Lo Prete. The first two were magistrates and the third a general in the Guardia di Finanza, the Italian financial police. All three were *closely tied* to Andreotti, especially Vitalone. Vitalone worked in the Rome prosecutor's office and was Andreotti's *legal advisor*, a bitter rival of Evangelisti's in aspiring to be Andreotti's closest confidant of all. He was elected senator later that year for the DC and later became a deputy minister and finally a minister in 1992, in the last months of the last Andreotti government. Testi was a member of the Italian magistrates' governing body and was later given charge of an important department of the justice ministry, a position he still holds. Lo Prete was facing corruption charges in an oil scandal, for which he was later convicted, and had been attacked, as Vitalone had, in *OP*.

For fifteen years little or nothing was known about this dinner. When Bonino, Vitalone and Testi were asked about it the following year, they all denied that anything of importance had been talked about over whatever it was they ate. They all denied it again in 1994 when the magistrates who were looking into some new claims by Tommaso Buscetta asked them again what they'd talked about with Pecorelli. The reason the dinner was ever of interest at all was that a few weeks after it took place Mino Pecorelli was dead. He was shot in the head outside the office of OP in Rome. It happened in the evening of 20 March 1979, the same day Andreotti presented his new government and became prime minister of Italy for the fifth time. Somehow the original investigation into Pecorelli's murder, conducted by the Rome prosecutor's office where Vitalone worked while Andreotti was head of the government, never got very far in the face of the distinguished guests' denials of rumours that money, or OP or Andreotti had been discussed at dinner. Nor indeed did it go far in any other direction. The investigation died and Pecorelli's death remained a mystery. The magistrates from Perugia who reopened the case in 1994, however, charged the group with perjury when they repeated their story of *a normal occasion*, and one of the dinner party cracked. Walter Bonino, whose presence had in any case been coincidental, admitted he'd lied about the evening. He said he'd organized the dinner because Vitalone had said he wanted to meet Pecorelli. Bonino had the clear impression it was to do with Andreotti.

On the Tuesday evening of the dinner, things had started with some low-key bickering between Vitalone and Pecorelli over a passport and proceeded to an ugly personal confrontation between Pecorelli and Lo Prete, who showed *great animosity*. Tension around the table increased when Vitalone discovered to his great surprise and anger that not only did Pecorelli know well Franco Evangelisti, Andreotti's aide and Vitalone's rival, but that Evangelisti had made a series of payments to Pecorelli and OP. Then Pecorelli told them about the next issue of OP. It was coming out at the end of that week with the cover story on *The President's Cheques*. Since the Italian prime minister was formally known as the president of the council of ministers, the *president* was Andreotti. It was an exposé of Andreotti's role in the Italcasse affair.

Everyone froze. The table fell silent. Vitalone spoke first, asking about the content of the article. Then he asked Pecorelli whether he couldn't suspend publication while Vitalone spoke about it with *a highly placed person*. Pecorelli told him he had until Saturday. Three days later Pecorelli told Bonino that Evangelisti had telephoned the day after the dinner and Pecorelli had met him in his deputy minister's office. Evangelisti had made a series of offers of money, help with printing, publicity and distribution of OP, asking after each new offer, *Is that OK for you?* The article on *The President's Cheques* never appeared and it's never since been found, neither the original typescript nor the proofs. Two days after receiving Evangelisti's promises of money and help, Pecorelli took the cover, with its menacing headline over a colour photo of Andreotti's thinly featured face staring blankly out through heavy blackframed glasses, to Evangelisti. Andreotti was meanwhile showing himself extremely solicitous toward Pecorelli, whom he'd never met. More than twenty-five years later, Pecorelli's sister was to recall their surprise at a telephone call of condolences from the Hon. Andreotti for the death of their mother. And learning that Pecorelli suffered from migraines, Andreotti, who also did, sent round a packet of migraine remedy with a little note to the journalist he'd never met, remarking on their common problem and offering the cure. Bonino remembered that at a later dinner Pecorelli made jokes and *even vulgar wisecracks* about it, because *the medicament was in the form of suppositories, and Pecorelli didn't fail to be ironical about the Hon. Andreotti's intentions and allusions.* The day after Evangelisti delivered the promised cash in person, Pecorelli was shot dead in the street. The same day in 1979, March the twentieth, Giulio Andreotti was busy forming his new government of Italy. At seven-thirty the following morning, twelve hours after the murder, the delivery man brought a telegram of condolence from prime minister Andreotti to Pecorelli's house. It was the first message the family received after the murder and they were amazed.

In 1995 Andreotti and Vitalone went on trial together for the murder of Mino Pecorelli. The prosecutors in Perugia charged that Andreotti had communicated his wish to be rid of the troublesome journalist to Vitalone, who'd communicated it to the Salvo cousins in Palermo, who'd told the Cupola of Cosa Nostra, who'd passed it on to the Cupola's man in Rome, the boss Pippo Calò, who'd arranged the physical execution of the mandate in association with a Rome criminal gang. The murder charge, like the Palermo mafia charge against Andreotti, had as its premise the existence of a chain of communication and command that linked the prime minister to Cosa Nostra through a series of trusted intermediaries in the overlapping worlds of politics and crime. In the murder case, the prosecutors offered to illustrate this with a great deal of circumstantial evidence of meetings between politicians and criminals. Andreotti's factotum Vitalone looked in it up to his neck.

TOMMASO BUSCETTA told the Palermo magistrates fourteen years after the event that in 1979, the year Pecorelli died, when Buscetta was still a man of honour in jail in Cuneo, he received another message from outside asking him for a second time to make contact with members of the BR in the prison. This time a personal emissary from Stefano Bontate asked Buscetta to find out whether the BR would agree to claim responsibility for the murder if Cosa Nostra were to get rid of general Dalla Chiesa. The general had been the BR's prime target for years, but Buscetta had no idea why Cosa Nostra might've wanted to eliminate him. In 1979 Dalla Chiesa was entirely taken up with the antiterrorist campaign and was no trouble at all to the mafia. Buscetta duly made contact and passed on the request, only to be told that the BR's condition was that one of their militants take part in the killing. When this answer was passed outside, the plan was cancelled. Cosa Nostra didn't do joint venture assassinations.

General Dalla Chiesa became a national hero at the beginning of the eighties. Following the historic pentito Peci, other BR militants had turned against armed struggle and political assassination. Dalla Chiesa swiftly took advantage of their defections to destroy the BR. By 1981 Italy's terrorist emergency had moved to the mopping up stage. The state was intact, and so was that demochristian regime with which the state was more and more closely identified. *In this country*, Dalla Chiesa himself was to remark bitterly some time later, *party membership counts more than the State*. In April 1982, with much fanfare, Dalla Chiesa was posted to Palermo as prefect. It would be his third posting to Sicily. The first had been his time in Corleone as a young captain in the days when Liggio and Riina were starting their rise. From 1966 until 1973 he'd commanded the Palermo carabinieri, a posting that'd given him responsibility for law enforcement over a large part of Sicily. During those recent years as a colonel in Palermo he'd developed considerable understanding of the ways of Sicilian politics and administration, and its penetration by Cosa Nostra. Dalla Chiesa knew the major players in Palermo. He knew Andreotti's man in Sicily, Salvo Lima, and the dominant demochristian's closeness to Cosa Nostra. He knew that other former demochristian mayor, Vito Ciancimino from Corleone, and his closeness to Cosa Nostra.

Before he left for Palermo, Dalla Chiesa told the prime minister and the interior minister about his worries. He was now returning to Palermo for the third time with tremendous prestige but in the heartland of Cosa Nostra he needed more real power. They promised that he would be invested with special powers as high commissioner in the fight against the mafia. He had, he was told, the government's full support. In a letter to the prime minister, Dalla Chiesa referred to sinister messages sent through the press by *the place's most polluted 'political family'* and foresaw that he would face *operations of subtle or brutal local resistance if not rejection*. The polluted family was Andreotti's faction in the DC. Three days earlier, before the new appointment had been announced and while special powers were being discussed by the government, the mayor of Palermo, an Andreotti man, had given a newspaper interview. The mayor said that talk about the mafia *was branding a whole people as criminals, as well as that political power that was the democratic expression of the people*. Proof that the state was fighting crime in Sicily, he added, was that among *the many slaughtered Palermitans* were a number of distinguished corpses and he listed the many names of murdered police chiefs, judges, politicians. Dalla Chiesa knew Sicily and he knew the mafia and he got the message. *That*, he said, showing the interview to his son, *is a warning*.

The general kept a private diary. Each evening he wrote up the events of the day in the form of an intimate letter to his late wife Doretta. On April 5, two days after the general's new appointment was announced, Andreotti, who wasn't then in the government, asked the general for a meeting and the next evening Dalla Chiesa wrote it up in his diary. Andreotti, he wrote to his dead wife, had wanted to know about his intentions in Palermo. *I told him I'd show no consideration for that part of the electorate his great supporters draw on*. There was no need to tell Doretta who that part of the electorate was. He told his son that on hearing this *Andreotti went white in the face*. In the diary he added that Andreotti, speaking about the Sindona affair, had mentioned a *mafioso killed in America and sent home in a coffin to Sicily with a ten dollar note in his mouth*.

Four years later Andreotti denied all this, saying under oath that he was *naturally pale*, that he hadn't sought Dalla Chiesa out and implying that it was all, as the magistrates of *The True History* put it, a *nocturnal fantasy* of the general's. Andreotti ascribed it to *the very nature of the diary, which had the form of an imaginary conversation with his dead wife ...* It wasn't the only insinuation that general Dalla Chiesa had lost his marbles. Andreotti, discreetly conveying fastidious revulsion to the judges, also strongly denied having brought up the subject of the mafioso sent home from America with a ten dollar note in his mouth. He'd never even heard of the corpse in question, he said. It had in fact belonged to Pietro Inzerillo, the brother of Salvatore, boss of one of the main mafia families of Palermo. Salvatore Inzerillo had been murdered the year before, two weeks after his ally Stefano Bontate had been cut down by the same kalashnikov. Inzerillo's sixteen-year-old son swore to avenge his father, and for this had his right arm hacked off before he was shot. Inzerillo's brother went to meet the Corleonesi with a propitiatory suitcase of money and was never seen again. Inzerillo's uncle walked out of his house in New Jersey and was never seen again. Bontate's clan was wiped out. Pietro Inzerillo had fled to New York. When he was found, in a Cadillac belonging to the Gambino family, the dollars were stuffed in the mouth of a head that had been severed from his handcuffed body. Dollars were also stuffed in the groin. The American police had put the pieces in a sealed coffin and sent them home. At issue were ten million dollars in drug money Riina claimed the Inzerillos owed. Was it delicacy or ignorance that elided these further circumstances? The statesman Andreotti was later greatly concerned that people shouldn't get the impression he'd been aware of details like this.

On the last day of April 1982, as Dalla Chiesa was making his farewells in the north, the PCI's leader in Sicily and his driver were ambushed and murdered in Palermo. Pio La Torre had been a young labour organizer in Corleone after the war, when Dalla Chiesa was a young captain of carabinieri there and Totò Riina a young killer. He'd lately been in parliament at Rome and a member of the antimafia commission, but the year before he'd asked to return to Palermo. He'd led the opposition in Sicily to the American missile base at Comiso, in part because it would intensify the criminal traffic between Sicily and the United States. He'd also studied the new mafia and the new wealth gained from government contracts, building speculation and drugs. He'd drawn up a proposal for a complex and radical new law that would for the first time make membership alone of Cosa Nostra a serious crime. It would deny banking secrecy when suspect assets were investigated. It would let the government seize assets gained by criminal violence. The three elements were premised on the understanding that Cosa Nostra existed as a criminal organization, a fact hitherto unrecognized in Italian law. As a law, the La Torre proposal would make a real onslaught on the mafia possible for the first time. It was still only a proposal when La Torre was killed.

So general Dalla Chiesa arrived in Sicily earlier than planned. When news arrived of the La Torre assassination, he had to rush south from a military parade in the Milanese drizzle, the signing off from his military career, to show the flag in Palermo. He stopped off for a brief and frantic meeting in Rome with the prime minister and plummeted, as he described it to Doretta, into *superheated* Palermo. He arrived without warning in a civilian suit and dark glasses and caught a taxi from the airport. Nobody was expecting him when he turned up at the prefect's office. Dalla Chiesa now had the responsibility of national coordinator of the struggle against the mafia. He didn't have the powers. *I suddenly find myself away from home*, he wrote that night to Doretta's shade, *in an environment that on the one hand expects miracles from your Carlo and on the other curses my destination and my arrival.*

Pio La Torre's funeral was held on May Day. Enrico Berlinguer, the leader of the PCI, came, and Pippo from the Sant'Andrea restaurant, still just a trade union militant, was part of his bodyguard, as he always was when Berlinguer came to Palermo. President Pertini and prime minister Spadolini came too, and sat ashen and immobile on the dais in the piazza as the young communists ruined the protocol of mourning. *You'll pay dearly!* the kids stood in the piazza and shouted at the demochristians on the platform. *You'll pay for everything!* A party of Dutch tourists trooping through the centre in sandals and grey woollen socks stopped openmouthed and took out their cameras as the farm labourers and steelworkers raised their fists.

> *Governo DC*
> *la mafia sta lì,*

the kids chanted. *The mafia was there, inside the DC government.*

> *Lima! D'Acquisto! Ciancimino!*
> *Chi di voi è l'assassino?*

Which of you is the killer? The young people of Palermo turned out in the following weeks to be Dalla Chiesa's most visible supporters, along with other ordinary people who had little voice and no clout. The obstruction, hostility and undermining he'd foreseen from the political establishment in Palermo was palpable from the start. The promised support from the government never came, as he'd foreseen.

While writing to Doretta, Dalla Chiesa had been courting a striking woman much younger than himself, the beautiful Emanuela Setti Carraro, another northerner. In his isolation and despite his fears for her, the general let her join him in Palermo where, as Claire Sterling describes in *Octopus*,

> They were married in a setting of nightmare violence. The bloodletting was then at its height in Palermo. Killers roamed the streets on big motorbikes at high noon, firing almost casually. Beheaded corpses were left in cars at the railroad station, dead men were burned on downtown streets, bodies were dumped at the door of police headquarters. *The atmosphere was pitiless, terrible in its arrogance*, wrote the presiding judge in Palermo's maxitrial.

It was the time of Riina's terror. In Naples that year the same thing was happening, for reasons that were not unrelated to events in Palermo. In Naples there were even more bodies on the ground. For the Mezzogiorno, 1982 was zero year. I escaped to Brazil that summer, and it was in Rio, on the beach at Copacabana that I opened the *Jornal do Brasil* one morning in early September and read of the ambush and murder in the streets of central Palermo of general Dalla Chiesa and his wife Emanuela Setti Carraro and their driver.

He'd seen it all coming, in total lucidity and utter helplessness, as the vacuum was created around him. In early August he'd spoken to Giorgio Bocca of the danger, in a long interview that was published in *La Repubblica*. The general told Bocca

> I believe I've understood the new rule of the game. The powerful man is killed when this fatal combination is brought about: he has become too dangerous but he can be killed because he's isolated ... The mafia is cautious, slow, it takes your measure, it listens, it makes sure about you from a distance ...

I'm up to my neck in this, he told his son the same month. *This* was the quicksand of Andreotti's DC. While the mafia was taking his measure, subtly isolating and discrediting him, Dalla Chiesa was spending his last month vainly trying to meet the national leader of the DC, vainly asking the interior minister for greater powers. He was still asking on the morning of his murder. His last throw of the dice, an act even more eloquent than the general's own words in the diary to Doretta, was to make a secret visit on the last day of his life to the United States consul in Palermo, to ask him to put pressure on the Italian prime minister, to get Dalla Chiesa the support he needed against Cosa Nostra and its political allies. About the sovereignty of the Italian state in the postwar half century, this secret visit of general Dalla Chiesa's says everything. In his moment of greatest need, one of that state's most loyal, intelligent, scrupulous and effective servants turned to the Americans.

The consul, whose name was Jones, later recalled the meeting for the *Wall Street Journal*, from which Sterling quotes an anecdote Dalla Chiesa recounted. It was about his days as commander of the Palermo carabinieri in the seventies. The captain of carabinieri posted to Palma di Montechiaro, Tomasi di Lampedusa's Palma, the town described in *The Leopard*, had called Palermo to tell his commander of threats received from the local boss. Colonel Dalla Chiesa had gone to Palma and at the time of the Mezzogiorno's ritual evening stroll had walked slowly up and down the main drag, arm in arm with the captain.

147

They'd paused for a while outside the boss's house, and then walked on. Recalling his little demonstration of solidarity, Dalla Chiesa told the consul, *All I'm asking is for somebody to take my arm and walk with me.*

Emanuela Setti Carraro called at the prefect's office that night to take the general home in her mini. It was already dark. Dalla Chiesa set store by inconspicuousness, mobility, unpredictable times and itineraries rather than armour and guards. A single escort, Domenico Russo, followed in another car. They were overtaken by eight men in via Carini, four on two powerful bikes, four in a BMW. Dalla Chiesa threw himself across his wife, but she was shot first. They were killed by the same kalashnikov used to dispatch Bontate and Inzerillo. Somebody got out of the BMW and delivered the final shots. Russo died later of his wounds.

When he arrived in Palermo a hundred and twenty-seven days earlier, the general had confided to Doretta's shade

> I'm perfectly aware that it would be suicide not to face my new task not so much with guards and escort but with the intelligence it demands and a little imagination. I'm nevertheless sure my Doretta will protect me, so that I can still do a little good for this society that too many people have really betrayed.

Intelligence and imagination hadn't been enough. The general was betrayed along with the society. *Here lie the hopes of all honest Palermitans*, said a note on a wreath placed at the scene of the massacre. In the finest Italian style, a wave of feeling now swept the nation and gave in death what the general had been denied in life. The post of antimafia high commissioner with overarching powers such as Dalla Chiesa had pleaded for was immediately created. And the Italian parliament passed without debate the bill Pio La Torre had proposed two years earlier. It now became the *La Torre law*. The new high commissioners appointed were such ineffectual bureaucrats that nobody minded when the post was abolished not long after. The La Torre law changed everything. For the first time ever the words mafia and mafioso appeared in the Italian penal code. The soon-to-be-famous *Articolo 416 bis* achieved Pio La Torre's aim of incriminating the organization Cosa Nostra, and the camorra and the 'ndrangheta, and not just the individual crimes of its thousands of component members. The law made a global strategy possible against Cosa Nostra. Without *Articolo 416 bis*, Falcone's maxi-trial would never have taken place, or Cosa Nostra's terrible revenge in 1992. Without *Articolo 416 bis* the statesman Giulio Andreotti would never have gone on trial in Palermo in the summer of 1995.

While I was staring at the *Jornal do Brasil* in Rio de Janeiro that fourth of September, near Belém on the mouth of the Amazon, two thousand kilometres away in the north of Brazil, Tommaso Buscetta was learning the same news on TV. Buscetta was in the company of Gaetano Badalamenti. Badalamenti had been the first of the Palermo bosses Riina had defeated. He'd seen the writing on the wall in time and got out before the slaughter and was doing good business running drugs in north and south America. Buscetta too, after seeing that mediation between the Palermo families and the Corleonesi was hopeless, had returned to Brazil to his own drug business and his wife and family. Commenting expertly on the circumstances of the killing and who must have ordered it, Riina's Corleonesi, and who'd carried it out, the Catania mafia of Nitto Santapaola, the former boss remarked to Buscetta,

> *Masino, some politician's used the mafia to get rid of the general. He'd become too awkward a presence ... They sent him to Palermo to get him out of the way. He hadn't done anything yet in Sicily that could justify that great hatred of him.*

A little later, Badalamenti got to speaking of the murder of Pecorelli, and he confirmed exactly something that Buscetta had already been told two years earlier by Stefano Bontate. Which was that *the Pecorelli killing was a political crime carried out by Cosa Nostra, at the request of the Salvo cousins, who'd been asked in turn by the Hon. Andreotti.* Buscetta's evidence went on

> General Dalla Chiesa had to be killed because he was in possession of secrets – I don't know if they were information, documents, papers or what – connected with the Moro case and liable to give Andreotti serious trouble. The same secrets Mino Pecorelli had, the journalist ... It was Badalamenti who told me that *Pecorelli and Dalla Chiesa are two things intertwined together* ...
>
> The general's posting to Palermo was merely a way of making his elimination easier – above all more logical, more justifiable. It had already been decided some time earlier, and for reasons other than the antimafia policy.

Ever the gent, the old-style mafioso Buscetta added

> His wife was killed too, and not because the mafia had lost its ancient respect for women and innocents, but because Dalla Chiesa might have revealed those secrets to her, or given her dangerous papers.

In 1993 Vito Ciancimino reminisced to the investigating magistrates of

The True History about the *collective psychosis* of that summer in Palermo when Dalla Chiesa arrived, and how the general ended up isolated and powerless. Soon after the assassination, the former mayor and mafioso found himself chatting, naturally enough, with the former mayor and mafioso Salvo Lima and the mafioso multimillionaire Nino Salvo. He asked them why, if Dalla Chiesa was *already washed up at every level, and even the stones knew it, why kill him?*

> Lima, his eyes reddening with hatred and losing his normal self-control, said, *For certain Romans he was more dangerous shoved aside with a pension than as Prefect with special powers.* Lima went on to say, *The ones who are going to take it up the ass are going to be us and who knows how long it'll go on.*

He meant, explained Ciancimino, *us Sicilians. And Nino Salvo nodded agreement, looking very upset.* Andreotti's viceroy in Sicily was furious that Andreotti had put the friends to all that trouble, and exposed them to the incalculable damage that Article 416B would do to Cosa Nostra, in order to cancel the memory of his own past, to cover his own tracks. Lima was soon mollified, when Andreotti came south in late 1982 to counter the negative fallout from the assassination and hold a rally with Lima and Ciancimino. *You Sicilian demochristians are strong, that's why people attack you*, Andreotti told the crowd. *We reject the false moralism of critics who foam at the mouth while you get stronger and stronger at every election.* By now Lima was beaming again.

In November that year His Holiness John Paul II also visited Palermo, apparently recovered from the bullet wounds received in the attack by an agent of the Turkish mafia in St Peter's square the year before. The investigation of this seeming assassination attempt was being directed toward Bulgaria, and many people supposed the attack was linked to the holy father's activism in support of the anticommunist Solidarity movement in his native Poland. Others would later say the attack had been ordered within the Vatican itself and had only been intended as a warning. In Palermo the Pope spoke to a hundred and fifty thousand people in the central piazza of Palermo at the end of that terrible year. He didn't mention the mafia.

VI

A BAD HABIT

THE SUGAR always goes in first. The sugar goes in when the tiny cup is fished from the standing tray of boiling water. Before the coffee oozes from the nozzle. Only that way can the slow, hot, thick drip, soon rising dangerously, unless the operator acts fast, as he does when he whisks the cup from the boiling water with his fingers, to a hotter, thinner, faster, weaker falling trickle of newly expressed coffee, meld with the white powder that fills most of the tiny white cup. Only thus do you get a wholly caramelized double hit of caffeine and glucose. The intrusion of a spoon would compromise the process. At this point. So, at home, the sugar is placed in the upper part of the faceted aluminium coffee pot before it ejaculates, lightly stirred in as heat still rises from the flame.

Only in Naples does the sugar go in first. You have to intercept the barman as he makes his first move if you want little or none. If it is a high turnover bar he may code your little cup with a speck of coffee on the rim to mark the difference. You will mark yourself too, indelibly, as slightly bizarre if you refuse sugar. I went back last year to the Bar Messico after three years away. The Bar Messico is near the station, and the barmen there make thousands of coffees a day every day of the year except Sundays. There was a new barman up my end of the bar. The older barman up the other end went through the elaborate pantomime that Neapolitans always do go through if you disappear and reappear after a long absence, a performance which consists of not betraying any awareness that you have ever been away. It's a way of reclaiming you. You've never really left. Without in any way acknowledging my presence, as I hadn't yet spoken first, the older barman muttered to the younger, *That's a no sugar down on the end there.*

Later I went back to the tiny Bar Nilo, so called because it stands opposite, in the very heart of Naples, the tiny piazzetta Nilo which has an ancient marble statue of the reclining river god of the Nile. It was put up a couple of millennia ago by immigrants from Alexandria, who brought the worship of the Nile with them to Naples. Over the centuries Neapolitans have got to know it more familiarly as *'o cuorpo 'e Napule*, and consider that it represents the body of the city itself. A newspaper seller used to work from a trestle table in front of the statue, and strung porno magazines around its plinth. When Naples cleaned up for president Clinton and the promised return of the tourists in 1994, the newspaper seller was forced round the corner, which was where I found him when I went back. Day by day, he was inching his news stand back to the body of Naples. The statue and the bar are on Spaccanapoli, the straight and narrow street that splits the city and was marked out by the founding Greeks two and a half thousand years ago. When I went back there too, after years away, the walleyed barman's first words were, *Sempre amaro, professò? Still no sugar?* The Bar Nilo won a prize once, for the best coffee in Naples. That would make it the best coffee in the world. I think the Messico is better, but there are days when I vacillate. The Nilo is one of the best. And when I went back too to a little bar in the Spanish quarters, where I used to breakfast in 1978 and hadn't been since, the barman, who was the same, remembered. *So you've been making money*, they used to say when you reappeared in Naples after an absence. It was understood that money was only made elsewhere, and that making money was the only reason anyone would leave.

Every transaction in Naples, every social act, requires a complex and at times exhausting social trafficking, a subtle and insidious play whereby the socially weaker player contrives to ingratiate himself and at the same time take the piss out of the stronger, to catch the other wrong-footed, but delicately, imperceptibly, to introduce some subliminal sense of social unease that may then be used as leverage. To create if possible a sense of obligation, of gratitude, even dependency. There isn't necessarily any malice in this. It's an old art of creating strength out of weakness and Neapolitan amiability itself is part of it. In Naples it has always been a necessary art of survival. If *respect* is the crucial concept in social relations in Sicily, the Neapolitan counterpart is its opposite, *disrespect*. Naples is infinitely more labile, more difficult a world. The dour Sicilian Sciascia noticed the Neapolitan way of charging so simple an act as making a coffee with hidden pleas, taunts, complicity, when in his first novel, the 1961 *The Day of the Owl*, the carabiniere captain

> drank a boiling coffee, a coffee that the carabiniere-barman made in a special way for him, in the special amount of coffee and the skill in making it that a Neapolitan, as the carabiniere-barman was, could deploy to obtain the special esteem of a superior.

The bar opposite the San Carlo where I went some evenings had changed entirely. I drank rum there after dinner and played the juke-box a long time ago. It was the only bar I knew in Naples that had a jukebox. Kids from the Pallonetto, Santa Lucia's little promontory warren of contrabbandieri, used to hang around the bar at night. One night the owner of the bar asked me if I wanted to join him in an orgy at his villa. *These kids*, he said, *will do anything I want*. He used to sing in the opera chorus at the San Carlo over the road, and I told him once I'd recognized him on stage in a production of Rossini's *L'Italiana in Algeri* that had just concluded its season, singing in the eunuchs' chorus. His face darkened when he heard this. *I was in the chorus of Algerian nobles*, he said. A couple of years later he was murdered in his villa.

Why coffee should have become such a particular obsession in Naples, of all places in Europe, I don't know. In Milan they go in for aperitivi, which are unknown in Naples. The aperitif implies both an alcoholic relaxation of attention and the promise of a stomach-filling meal to come. The meal to come in Naples is historically in doubt. Which is also why Naples has given the world the classic quick cheap stomach fillers, the original fast food, like pizza and pasta and all their variants. A Neapolitan coffee packs the kick of a mule. It keeps you going, and at minimal cost.

Italian coffee gets worse fast as you move north of Naples. In Rome it is often undrinkable. Southward, standards are generally maintained. The coffee in Palermo is excellent. *Maybe the ideal espresso for Sicilians*, the journalist Giorgio Bocca decided after calling on the magistrates of the antimafia pool in Palermo's justice building, *is a black drop containing a superconcentration of all the caffeine in the world*. There is no guarantee, though, even in Naples, that coffee will be good. A bar needs well maintained machines and a high turnover as well as good coffee. A coffee in Naples may be quite as thin and sour and bitter as anything to be found in Sydney. This happens in a bar whose owner has put himself in hock to the suppliers to pay for refurbishing his premises. The thousands and thousands of tiny bars in Naples are always competitively redecorating. An overextended coffee bar owner is tied in perpetuity to that supplier, who is thus free to dump inferior coffee on him forever. Coffee is the Neapolitan drug. Apart from a little wine with meals, Neapolitans rarely drink, at most a medicinal-tasting amaro at the meal's end. There was a passing fashion among the toughs of the Spanish quarters for an infusion of camomile, which they used to take before retiring in the early hours of the morning, to help them sleep, and once an elderly boss of the *quarteri* offered me a Chivas Regal.

The sugar people put into it with such care may have been tied up with the cult of coffee. Naples was one of Europe's first and biggest importers of sugar. Fernand Braudel in his great work *The Mediterranean* said that in the single year of 1625, when sugar was still barely known in the rest of Europe, Naples imported what he called *the unbelievable quantity* of fifteen hundred tons of it. In the same year Naples also imported five hundred tons of honey. This huge consumption of sugar was recorded half a century after coffee first arrived in Italy from the east. The Venetians first imported coffee in 1580 from Constantinople, where it had arrived thirty years earlier from Egypt. Did Neapolitan sugar consumption jump with the arrival of coffee? Braudel didn't say. *Naples*, he remarked, thinking of the late sixteenth century, *was excessive in every respect ... it was the most astonishing, most fantastically picaresque city in the world.* Since the amount of liquid in a Neapolitan coffee is barely · enough to dissolve the sugar, the thought is inescapable that the coffee is mainly a way of flavouring the sugar and helping its assimilation. And the sugar must be dissolved. In the early days, when I was still into sugar, a *scugnizzo* reprimanded me for bad manners in using the spoon to scoop the undissolved sugar from the bottom of the cup. It was a more venial offence than pouring wine underarm, as Judas did, but an offence nevertheless. A *scugnizzo* is, or was, a Neapolitan street kid, though not in the modern sense of social detritus, abandoned and homeless, but having his own status, prestige even, integrated within the society but not yet tied down, avoiding school but not yet part of any work force. In the nineties, the *scugnizzi* have been mainly recruited as drug couriers, work for which their alertness, streetwise intelligence and their remarkable mobility on Vespas are ideally suited. Their employers call them *muschilli*, little flies, and also appreciate the fact that until the *muschilli* reach the age of fourteen they are entirely immune from prosecution under Italian law.

The seventeenth was a busy century for gourmets in Naples. Ice cream was invented there and the city's Spanish rulers brought chocolate from the new world, and by the 1690s chocolate ice cream was born. Throughout the south the things made with sugar, cakes and pastries and all the other icecreams, *granite*, *semifreddi*, *cassate*, marzipan are still sublime. In Palermo, plump bespectacled Totò of the Sant'Andrea was lately moved to tears as he described the complex intensities of his lifelong love of chocolate. And of the market providors of the borgo of Sant'Antonio Abate in Naples, only the man who sold me cheese rivalled the importance in my life of the little pastrycook on the corner, who was maker as well as purveyor, a wholesaler and supplier of bars and cafés working from a little signless *laboratorio* rather than a shop, as source of information and receiver of confidences, about pastries and other matters.

It occurred to me later that the finicky obsessive play with spoons and powders and flames that coffee and sugar taught may have been part of heroin's charm for young Neapolitans in the getting-to-know-her stage. There's a great deal yet to be written about the arrival of heroin in Italy, which happened while I was there. History's time lag meant heroin reached certain layers of Neapolitan society along with such other manifestations of late capitalism as television and consumer durables, but it worked faster because with heroin there were no controls. Heroin was like a firestorm. There was an aptness in modernity's arriving in Naples through the agency of a delightful drug, in solitude and alienation's coming directly through that intense and fleeting pleasure that enslaved. Neapolitans had always been susceptible to fleeting pleasures.

Heroin wrecked an intricate society of crowded urban spaces and a promiscuous mixing of classes, a culture that made a great deal out of the immaterial, the precarious and the ephemeral, whose highest arts were music and theatre, whose distinctions were rhetorical, erotic, comic, baroque, carnal, metaphysical, a sensibility that was lazily sensual and austerely abstract by turns, choral and instinctive, solitary and systematic. Naples gave the world ice cream, pizza, opera buffa and transvestism as an art form. Naples ravished Virgil, Boccaccio, Stendhal, shocked and disgusted Sade, Ruskin, Sartre. Naples filled the paintings of the visitor Caravaggio and the operas of the visitor Mozart. Naples was the motherland of the polymorphous perverse, and parts of it still recognizably the Greek city of Petronius's *Satyricon* in the dire late twentieth century. Until heroin and the earthquake and all their consequences.

One day a new Braudel will survey the Mediterranean world of the late twentieth century and see and show how heroin changed the patterns of life as sugar had five centuries earlier. The changes wrought by the later white powder that came west from Asia and went on to the Americas were on a similar scale. They also involved a lot of the same places. Heroin started in the south, for all the old reasons of Mediterranean geography, and that's where it destroyed most. One of the people who understood first and registered most acutely what was going on, not the drug business itself but the enabling politics behind it, was Leonardo Sciascia. And Sciascia took the image of the *caffè ristretto*, the very short and very strong black of the south, to express in 1961 through a character in his first novel his intuition of what was going on.

> Maybe all of Italy is becoming a Sicily ... A thought came to me, when I was reading in the papers about the scandals of the regional government: scientists say the palm tree line, that is the climate favourable to the palm tree form of vegetation, is creeping northward at the rate, I think, of five hundred metres every year ... The palm tree line ... I prefer to call it the short black coffee line, the line of the really strong coffee, of scandals: onward and upward through Italy, and it's already past Rome ...

It was a suggestive and prescient image and the notion of the palm tree line gained some currency twenty years later, in the early eighties, among commentators who denounced the civil woes of Italy, the idea of a creeping mafia-ization like a spreading sore, a corruption of manners slowly and inexorably overwhelming Italy. It was, of course, a libel on the palm trees and the coffee of the south.

COLLAPSE OF some kind would've come anyway. Naples in 1978 was, after nearly three millennia, showing her age. The unutterable scenic beauty of the bay and the city hardly bore a closer look. A lot of it was a filthy, pullulating slum standing on the foulest sea in Christendom. Twelve rats for every human, someone had calculated. Its schools, libraries, hospitals, universities, museums, prisons must have been the worst in Europe. Visits to a bank, a post office, the town hall were hallucinatory experiences. The res publica, taken to include health, education, transport, politics, communications, entertainment, sport, personal safety, was a lost cause. By the usual measures of social well-being Naples was a disaster area. Five years earlier there had been an outbreak of cholera. The incidence of hepatitis was the second highest in the world, as I found when I became infected myself. A wave of infant deaths panicked the poorer districts for much of my first year. There was a lot of talk about a mystery illness but there was nothing mysterious about the squalor that bred infection. *The third world begins in Naples*, people used to say, and lot of the statistics were third world.

What Naples still had going for it in the seventies, apart from its decaying heap of incomparable art, was the popular urban life that went back, directly if tenuously, to the city's ancient beginnings. It was unique in Europe and enabled by the very fact that Naples became a backwater at the beginning of the industrial age. In the eighteenth century and into the nineteenth, as Goethe and Stendhal found and vividly testified, Naples was one of the three great capitals of Europe. Stendhal wrote in 1817, *To my eyes it's without compare the most beautiful city in the universe*. It was as big as London and Paris and as splendid. *Paradise and hellfire*, said Gibbon, thinking of Pompeii's fate and Vesuvius still smoking ominously outside the city's perimeter. Marginalized by the shift of power to the north when Italy was unified, Naples went into the economic decline that spared it, at the cost of its decay, the destructive renewals of modernization and development. Urban renewal was fragmentary, sporadic. A wide straight street was ploughed through the port slums late last century after a cholera epidemic. Some land was reclaimed at Santa Lucia. Mussolini later bulldozed another patch below via Toledo in the centre for the Bank of Naples, the police headquarters, the post office in fascist modernist monumental style, the city's only decent new buildings in the last hundred years. Otherwise Naples was left alone. The centre still teemed with people and it still presented in a degraded form a continuity of culture long gone elsewhere.

In a way it seemed enchanted, in those days before the drugs and the killings. That this howling, passional hedonistic life, this art of arranging yourself, was possible in the middle of the modern world. The city's choking traffic and the encroachments of TV felt almost irrelevant. The mad centripetal energy of Naples seemed in the world but not of it. Their shared outsider-excluding language defended Neapolitans from Italy and beyond and gave people a sense of relatedness, of family, that was stronger than their differences of social class. The indolence in practical matters, a shared intense preoccupation with small things, infinitessimal amounts of money, the nuance of a plate of pasta, tiny points of social decorum, marked a society adrift and turned in on itself. Yet the huge expense of passion and energy on the utterly ephemeral gave life a shared imaginative intensity I don't expect to find again. Naples was a theatre, and Neapolitans further offered a newcomer the vast consolation of a people who'd seen it all. They'd learned to live not as the makers of history but as choral onlookers. History in Naples as in Sicily meant two and a half millennia of foreign occupation. The mild moist fug of the climate enhanced a dream-like state in which food, sex, and getting by till tomorrow were the major concerns. I thought I saw the past and it worked. These were the survivors of the ancient world. I was enchanted too. I abandoned my plans and the world to stay in Naples. I thought it'd go on forever. After several thousand years and in the middle of late capitalism, why not ? Like the Neapolitans I'd arrange myself. Three years later it was all gone. The people's Naples had vanished.

When the contrabbandieri of Santa Lucia were still into cigarettes, they kept their fleet of blue drab speedboats moored in the boat harbour of the borgo, under the ancient castel dell'Ovo. The boats were big, formidably fast and manoeuvrable and capacious, boats for collecting Marlbóro outside territorial waters. When they'd done a run the contrabbandieri liked to eat well, and there was a seafood place called da Ettore, which disappeared around the time the fleet of speedboats did and the blue-jumpered daring sailors. It used to stay open to all hours, grilling fish and king prawns and serving *spaghetti con le vongole*. Good food and no nonsense. Sometimes they'd unload the cigarettes in broad daylight, with a line of sentries posted along the waterfront within shouting distance to warn of *'a finanza*. There was no danger of a blitz in the Neapolitan traffic flow. Kids on Vespas would stick a carton of Marlbóro between their legs and rocket across four lanes of traffic and into the impenetrable maze of the Pallonetto. There'd be major skirmishes at times with the financial police, who had their own speedboats and helicopters too, and crowds would line the foreshore above the water to watch the drama. Some contrabbandieri were going to take me out one night on a job, but it fell through and then they were gone. It seemed romantic in the seventies, though the contrabbandieri were already *in Riina's hands*. The other place to eat was in one of the bent lanes that twisted up into the stronghold of the Pallonetto, where you feasted on pasta and *frutti di mare* out on the footpath, using your hands like in the photographs from the last century.

A subtler or a less enraptured observer than I was might have picked up more signals earlier on, might have given more weight to the complaints of the Neapolitans themselves about the degradation of their way of life. Looking back, it's impossible not to see that things were ready to fall apart, that they'd been falling apart for a considerable time and any further tightening of the social screws would lead to a general collapse. A visitor more alive to the interplay of social and economic forces might have seen that criminality was bound to make a qualitative leap from the homely arts of bag snatching, cigarette smuggling, whoring and a mutually acceptable level of protection racketeering to a higher, more industrial plane of activity. The great industry of cigarette contraband had in any case been a partnership between mafia and camorra for four years by the time I arrived, and in the summer of 1979, my first full summer in Naples, Riina and the Cosa Nostra commission were in Naples to renegotiate it. The Neapolitans had been cheating. In the end cigarettes were left to the open market because at Riina's urging Cosa Nostra that year was throwing itself into heroin.

Politics were shifting too in the seventies. A few years earlier the mayor had been Achille Lauro, called the *comandante*, monarchist, demagogue and shipping millionaire, the former cabin boy from Sorrento who'd shipped so many poor Italian migrants to Australia. The Americans who'd arrived in 1944 were still there. Naples had become a cold war bastion, home to the US sixth fleet and the biggest NATO base in southern Europe. Under the American umbrella, Lauro had secured his re-elections as mayor by distributing packets of pasta and shoes. The matching shoe of each pair to be collected after votes were in. The speculators' housing boom in Naples didn't touch the city's heart, unlike the mafia's job on Palermo, but it ruined the suburbs and the buildings were even worse.

When a reforming city administration came to power in 1975, all the communists were able to do was lay bare the social wounds of a city where in the early seventies nearly half the houses lacked a shower or bath and nearly a fifth an indoor toilet. The dreadful gimcrack flats of the speculators' boom in the fifties were already collapsing. Fourteen buildings fell down in three months at the end of 1977 and three thousand people lost their homes. There were almost no qualified administrators. Lauro and the DC had spent the budget filling local government with dustmen and doormen and ushers, their electoral clients. These were away from work most of the time at their real jobs. In hospital with hepatitis, I found the ward's chief paramedic ran a discotheque that was patronized by military personnel from NATO. He used to roar up to the hospital from time to time in a red sports convertible and was fleetingly interested in me as a potential source of new clients. Looking down from a window in the ward, I'd see the kitchen staff driving home with cases of food on the roofs of their baby Fiats. The window itself blew out one night during a spring storm, flooding the ward and showering beds with broken glass. One wing of the hospital, which had been built in the sixties, was out of use and seemed to be falling to pieces. Several camorristi were in the hospital, guarded by carabinieri, and drugs circulated freely. I saw the ward director chasing and grappling with one pyjama'd patient, wrestling for control of a little plastic envelope.

All the positions of economic power in Naples were held by the DC and the efforts of the new left-wing council were blocked. Two thirds of those posts were held by Antonio Gava's people and Gava was an Andreotti man. In the eighties Gava was the real boss of Naples, and he became a minister in two Andreotti governments. People jostled with each other to get to kiss his hand. He was the Salvo Lima of Naples, and in more, it turned out, than manner. As Andreotti's minister for the interior in the late eighties, Gava headed Italy's fight against organized crime, an appointment which was for most Italians an exquisitely insulting signal of how invulnerable Andreotti felt at that time. In the end Gava fell almost as far and hard as his master. He was arrested in September 1994. His first trial was for ordinary corruption, like those of the other Andreotti government ministers from Naples who were also tried and convicted, De Lorenzo and Scotti and Cirino Pomicino. In Gava's corruption trial the most eloquent testimony against him came in the moment when his former bagman remembered a day he'd delivered Gava a third of a million dollars in cash. It was Gava's rake-off from a hospital construction contract, and the court heard how Gava's face darkened in anger when he saw the modest sum, how he growled in that expressive Neapolitan dialect he affected in his dealings with local politicians and crime bosses, *These are crumbs*. Before he was convicted of corruption, Gava also went on trial in Naples for organized crime. There was a mass of detailed evidence against him, and his eighty-one codefendants included crime bosses and killers of the camorra, as well as other former members of the political establishment, a DC deputy minister, a DC senator. I was back in Naples for the opening of Gava's camorra trial at the end of November 1995, but Gava didn't show up. He sent word he'd suffered a stroke and was charged with contempt.

Back in 1978 Gava's golden years had hardly begun. The reformists were paralyzed. The steelworks and the car industry were in crisis and the only other area of the Neapolitan economy not terminally stagnant was crime, but it was modest, traditional crime mainly. Cigarette contraband was the only area of large-scale cooperation with Cosa Nostra. The camorra wasn't organized like the mafia. There were hundreds of neighbourhood crime groups, power might shift overnight, and no hierarchy, no overarching body like the mafia's Cupola coordinated and controlled Neapolitan crime. Then, as the seventies turned into the eighties, in almost perfect synchrony two things happened to change this.

CASTELLAMMARE DI STABIA is the biggest town in that urban spill that runs down the peninsula from Naples to Sorrento around the foot of Vesuvius. It was also the power base of Antonio Gava and his father before him. I was there at dusk on 29 November 1980 when the ground shook and buildings started to collapse on to the streets, crushing parked cars. It was the earthquake. A few miles away whole towns were collapsing. Later that evening I managed to hitch a ride back through the darkness and confusion to Naples, where I spent the cold night in the open under the cannonball-pocked walls of the Angevin castle, along with the huddled masses of the port district and the Spanish quarters, waiting for the end of the world as we knew it. We were lucky. There were no more big shocks. Nearly three thousand people died in the earthquake, but few in Naples. A block of modern flats collapsed, killing those inside. A few more people died of heart attacks or falling masonry. Some days later a handful of destititute old people were crushed in their beds when a wing of the eighteenth-century poorhouse collapsed, in its day the biggest building in Europe. That was all. Naples escaped the hecatomb by a whisker. It was nevertheless the end of the world as we knew it, though it took a few years for this to become clear. The buildings of Naples were a mouthful of rotten teeth that withstood the jolt only because they were packed so tightly together. Cracks snaked across decaying walls all over the city. We slept out for several more nights, until cold and damp and demoralization won out over fear as the aftershocks ceased and people trickled back to their tottering palazzi. When the presidential Maserati rocketed up Toledo on its way to the Irpinia disaster zone a couple of midnights later the street was empty but for me. The Spanish quarters and the other ancient slums of central Naples were quickly caged in amazing geometries of tubular steel, dense webs of scaffolding spanning the alleyways to stop the buildings falling into them. Stairwells were propped up with wooden posts, buildings evacuated, alleys closed off with concrete walls. Inhabitants of the collapsing buildings were shunted out to container parks and holiday flatettes as a temporary emergency measure. They never returned. Many were still living in containers a dozen years later. The others found homes on the dreadful periphery. In the space of days the old centre of Naples lost a big chunk of those people, the most defenceless, who'd most made the city what it so extraordinarily was.

People lost not only their homes. The intricate system of artisan workshops that aerated the old centre, the submerged economy of tiny semi-clandestine businesses employing women and teenagers to work leather, metal, paper, wood, cloth, was choked off by the removal of its workforce and the blocking of the alleys by the steel and concrete buttresses. The only people in Naples making an honest living, if you excluded the public sector employees for the sake, as it were, of argument, were now prevented from doing so. Male and female ladies of the night found it difficult to lure the sailors of the sixth fleet to their cubicles in the Piranesi nightmare the Spanish quarters had become. Pasquale the cook, who ran the Spanish quarters place where I ate in the evenings, was traumatized by the earthquake. None of his wife's scolding could shake him out of his catatonia. He was no longer open in the evenings. The barbers, mechanics, upholsterers and barmen, the apprentice, fully-fledged and retired prostitutes, male and female, the pimps, transexuals, ex-cons, car watchers and car washers, the retailers of counterfeit Rolex and Omega watches and the traffickers in matériel that had fallen off the back of nuclear-powered aircraft carriers, accountants, plumbers, thieves, cooks, waiters and sellers of contraband Marlbóro and Merít, the crowd, in short, with whom I was passing my time in those days, dispersed forever. Heroin was already starting to make the Spanish quarters a waste land at night, and the shootouts that had earlier enlivened dinners at Pasquale's, when I'd be yanked inside by the scruff of my neck and the shutters slammed down until the gunfire ceased, were soon replaced by the more systematic warfare between the drug gangs. I avoided the quarters at night now.

Engineers were sounding every building days after the earthquake and microsurgery by innumerable squads of workmen over the following months saved the city from collapse. It cost tens of billions of dollars. The city administration drew up a reconstruction plan. At some point however you noticed that the work on many buildings was going well beyond the needs of the structural emergency and into the areas of renovation and redecoration. And went on and on. After a few years the rundown old city was looking strangely smart. Empty apartments however remained empty. The evacuated never came back home. Those with least clout went on living in their container parks for ever. Naples was turning into a speculator's dream.

The tarting-up of Naples was the visible face of a gigantic rort. Worse was going on in the towns of Irpinia where the earthquake had its epicentre. Irpinia was also the power base of Ciriaco De Mita, the DC party leader and Italian prime minister in the eighties, and where his brother happened to be in the construction business. Rome poured over fifty billion dollars into Naples and Irpinia as earthquake emergency funds. The money was divvied up, insofar as interests could even be said to be distinguishable, by the politicians and administrators and the construction companies owned by organized crime. In 1985 a young reporter for the Naples daily *Il Mattino* looked into earthquake reconstruction contracts around Gava's power base on the Sorrento peninsula, which had been closer to the earthquake's epicentre than Naples itself and harder hit. The reporter was shot outside his home in Naples. It took ten years for the camorra to be brought to book for the murder. The killing had been *tacitly* ordered by the mayor of one of the towns.

The reforming Naples city council fell, and with it their plan to screen the tendering companies for criminal contamination. The last obstacle to Gava and the camorra was now gone. Three years after the Irpinia disaster the slow earthquake of subsidence stirred again at Pozzuoli, the ancient port city where the sleazier episodes of the *Satyricon* may or may not have been set, now a part of outer Naples, which had been sinking into the sea since Roman times. Another old centre was evacuated, more billions arrived from Rome, an uninhabitable new centre was built nearby. Other major initiatives followed, as year by year daily life in Naples got harder to bear. Dubious firms took over essential services, the underground railway project, the rapid tramway system project, the cable cars, the parking buildings, the World Cup projects. Reconstruction money and drug profits fed into the same stream. In 1993 the Italian government dissolved the Naples city council for reasons of public security. It was the first time such a measure had ever been taken for any city in Italy.

I went away. I came back. I was in the very Neapolitan situation of having glimpsed felicity only to have everything snatched away. What remained was a lacerating sense of loss. Life dragged on, and when I finally decided to up sticks and leave for good at the end of 1992 it was without regrets and after hard-headed calculation. The next year there were far more parliamentarians being investigated for organized crime in the Naples region of Campania than anywhere else in Italy, including Sicily, far more magistrates under criminal investigation for corruption, far more town councils disbanded for criminal activity. The statistics were a small indicator. Only in the killings did Sicily keep a slight edge. In the decade of the eighties there were 2621 homicides in Campania, nearly three hundred less than Sicily's total of 2905 in the same period. No other Italian region came anywhere near, not even Calabria, which was third.

After three weeks of negotiations the chief of the central post office agreed to dispatch my books to Sydney. The builder with the glass eye who lived across the alley took them in on his truck. One dank pre-dawn I walked through the borgo for the last time toward the station. The borgo's black slimy stones cut from volcanic lava were still littered with waste from the day before's market. I'd done a deal of not very rigorous or systematic thinking about what went wrong, and it wasn't just personal. It wasn't personal at all.

THE HEAD decomposing on the front seat and the body found when the car boot was cautiously opened had both belonged to a Roman lawyer. He'd last been seen lunching at the Hotel Royal on the seafront at Santa Lucia, looking out out on the boat harbour with its yachts and contraband fleet and the ancient castel dell'Ovo, and beyond to the bay of Naples, Capri and Vesuvius. The lawyer had been an unsavoury type even in one piece. He must have come to Naples that week in 1982 engaged by Raffaele Cutolo, since it was outside Cutolo's castle on the periphery of Naples that the car was parked. The professor, as Cutolo was called because he'd finished elementary school, was a prisoner at the time, but his New Organized Camorra was the emergent force in Neapolitan organized crime at the start of the eighties. The professor made highly-publicized courtroom appearances from time to time, expensively dressed and slightly overdoing the gold accessories by Cartier, accepting the obeisance of criminals and public figures, declaiming his poetry and issuing veiled threats to politicians and judges. Unlike the grim and obsessively discreet mafiosi, the camorristi enjoyed a little theatre, a little display, for which they were considered buffoons by the Sicilians. Sometimes the professor's veiled threats were contained in the poetry, which was also available in slim volumes.

Cutolo's detention didn't cramp the New Camorra's exponential growth. He'd been in jail since the fifties and that was where he did his recruiting. He'd directed a flourishing cocaine traffic from an insane asylum, in telephone contact with Colombia and Peru. Affairs outside were controlled from the castle-fortress by his unmarried sister,

Rosetta *Ice Eyes* Cutolo. The ice eyes lady was said to be a brilliant accountant and devoted to her brother's interests. When police raided the castle after the failure by a whisker of her plan to blow up the Naples police headquarters, the ice eyes lady got through the police roadblock hidden under a tartan rug on the floor of a car driven by the local priest.

The Naples police headquarters fill a solid structure of six or eight storeys built by the fascists, whose emblem of the axe and rods still adorns its façade, in the city centre. It would have taken some blowing up, but the quantity of explosive was apparently commensurate with the job. That the New Camorra's plan failed by mere hours concerned me, because I was at the time living directly opposite, on the other side of via Medina. The explosion of a bomb in a camorra-owned bank, a few yards down from the police beside a fourteenth-century church, had in the depth of an earlier night already shaken the vast sixteenth-century palazzo where I lived beneath the chambers of the Liberal Party. Once frequented by the philosopher Benedetto Croce, these were now the power base of a rapidly-rising politician named De Lorenzo, whom I used to pass in the courtyard. De Lorenzo was a university professor mapping out a career that would soon turn the ministry of health into a criminal organization, and skim off for himself four million dollars in bribes. Police headquarters over the road were manned by carabinieri in flak jackets with submachineguns, and convoys of screeching Alfas would arrive with terrorists and camorristi, perpetrators of the crimes on that night's news. Around the corner was a grille in the wall, where a knot of stocky women in black would be yelling to husbands, sons, brothers and boyfriends in the cells below. Living with this, you felt involved.

Nobody living in Naples in the early eighties could help feeling involved. Cutolo's New Camorra recruited its forces on the outskirts of Naples, in that network of lawless towns that sprawled amorphously around the city proper. It tapped a huge reserve of youths with neither work prospects nor strong social ties. The organization was new but it functioned in the purest tradition of southern Italian criminal organizations. It looked after its people when the state had abandoned them. The young men who ended in jail for minor crimes had wives and children, since they married young in the south, left without any support. In Poggioreale prison the young men themselves were in dire circumstances. Cutolo protected these kids in jail, looked after their families outside and guaranteed a job on release. In return he got an oath of loyalty to the Nuova Camorra Organizzata. The induction was modelled on the rituals of the camorra's eighteenth-century origins. Giacomo, a plumber's son I'd known in the Spanish quarters, disappeared into the New Camorra. Selling hashish to American sailors of the sixth fleet one night by the waterfront, he'd ended in Poggioreale. Here he had been invited for an audience in the carpeted cell of don Raffaele Cutolo, with whom he took coffee. Cutolo was at that time spending twenty thousand dollars a month on food and related expenses in jail. His fame was almost at its zenith. *The professor had been a real gentleman.* Giacomo's narrative ended here and it would have been tactless to enquire further. I never saw him again.

The New Camorra grew fast and threatened the old camorra families of the city centre. The criminal map of old Naples was divided into zones controlled by family organizations that had coexisted for a long time and carved up the income from contraband, prostitution, counterfeiting consumer goods and extortion rackets. When Cutolo's men started muscling in from the periphery, the old camorra clans formed an alliance they called the New Family to repel the pretenders. I got word of the New Family in 1980 from the horse's mouth, or rather an angelic fifteen-year-old's from one of the families in the Spanish quarters. This was before the violence erupted, before anyone knew what was going to happen. What happened was a prolonged street war that in the first years of the eighties was taking nearly three hundred lives a year. This was a killing rate as high or higher than the mafia's in the Palermo war going on at the same time. In Naples a lot of the victims were in their mid-teens or little older, the new recruits, the foot-soldiers on both sides of a conflict whose ante was being upped week by week. It was a barbaric war of extermination that made Riina's killings look selective and almost refined. It was a time of horror, and the bodies in the streets were not the only horror that transformed Naples in those years.

The other horror was the heroin, directly linked to the camorra war and largely its cause. Unrefined heroin from Asia arrived in Italy with the eighties, and the camorra was Cosa Nostra's partner in its selling. Italy proved a peculiarly vulnerable society to the novelty of heroin. It soon had one of the highest estimated addiction rates in the world and was the only country where the primary cause of AIDS was the use of dirty needles by drug takers. In Naples the camorra distributed hashish, a lot of it free at first, to establish the notion of *la droga* as a cheap and harmless source of pleasure for kids. When heroin arrived it cut a swathe through the city's youth. In 1980 I went to the funeral of one of the first overdose victims, a student of mine, and his death was front page news. The long roll of deaths that followed soon went unnoticed by the press. Kids just disappeared from circulation. The alleys of the Spanish quarters at night were now full of spectral, staggering figures. It had quite a history, what was destroyed. The privileged autonomy of the *scugnizzi* in the street life of Naples, the ferocious energy of the city's teeming plebs. It was inner-directed and self-defeating most of the time, but this youthful proletarian wildness had been formidable whenever it found an object. The fishmonger Masaniello had made the Spanish empire totter at the head of such a crowd. The unarmed starving boys of Naples had driven the German army from their city in 1943. Their heirs, the boys who used to wait up to read the early edition of *Il Mattino* on Toledo after midnight, checking out the crimes and punishments of their elder brothers, were now gone. *I don't know anyone in Naples now*, Oscar Wilde had complained theatrically when he came back to Naples near the end. *All my friends are in jail*. I was starting to feel, as Naples headed into the eighties, that all of my friends were dead.

The old camorra was threatened by Cutolo at the very time it was tapping into the huge new wealth derived from heroin. Cutolo had forbidden the New Camorra to traffic in heroin, having the intelligence to see it would most damage the very social stratum that had empowered him. Later, when Cutolo's NCO found itself overextended and in difficulty as a result of its rapid growth, he may have changed his mind. The New Family, for its part, was drawn by the new money in the eighties drug, cocaine, whose importation Cutolo controlled. Far too much money was now being made by the camorra from both drugs for the profits to be merely reinvested in crime. They had, like the mafia's profits in Sicily, to be ploughed into construction and real estate throughout Italy. Here Gava and the political friends in Rome came in. The camorra wanted to become part of the fabric of national politics and finance, as the mafia had done long before. The stakes were so great that in 1981 Riina's Cosa Nostra tried to broker a settlement of the war between the New Camorra and New Family. Cosa Nostra's ties were to the old camorra of the New Family, several of whose leaders were also made men of Cosa Nostra itself, but the war was inhibiting business. The summit was held on a camorra leader's property on the outskirts of Naples, attended by over a hundred leading mafiosi and camorristi, each of whom arrived in his own car, unnoticed by police, and Riina and his Sicilian delegation were housed in a separate building, on hand to advise and consent. The peacemaking effort failed, and though Cutolo was later defeated, the clans of the New Family won not because of their alliance with Cosa Nostra but through their alliance with the DC.

Cutolo's great moment came in the spring of that year, and by the end of 1981 he seemed to have won acceptance as a major player on the dangerous confines of crime and politics. The failures of the reforming administration in Naples had become paralysis after the earthquake and given a fresh impulse to terrorism. Five months after the earthquake, the Neapolitan column of the Red Brigades in April 1981 kidnapped a powerful DC politician called Ciro Cirillo, killing his driver and bodyguard and wounding his secretary. Cirillo was head of town planning for Campania, president of the earthquake reconstruction committee and a former president of the region. He was also a close friend and ally of Antonio Gava's. The BR wanted to play on popular discontents, and use Cirillo to stop the deportation of people from the city centre, close the great container camp of homeless people, end the requisitioning of houses, interrogate Cirillo as they had Moro about the DC's embarrassing secrets. Three months later, unlike the unfortunate Aldo Moro, Cirillo was released after payment of a big ransom. The political demands were forgotten. Leaders of the DC, Gava's people, had been taken by the secret services to see Cutolo in jail. They'd got him to be the go-between for a deal to buy off the BR. This moment of national squalor was the apex of Cutolo's career.

Cutolo's greatest reward for his mediation was to be big earthquake reconstruction contracts for his firms. Too much became known, however, about the secret prison dealings. There was a public outcry and the DC politicians dragged their feet in repaying Cutolo. To spur them he released a document about a visit he'd had in jail from a DC government minister. It was Scotti, another DC interior minister, another leader of the government's fight against organized crime. This leak made the leaders of the Neapolitan DC realize how dangerously compromised they were with Cutolo, how open to further blackmail. Gava turned to the New Family for help. Within weeks Cutolo's financial director was murdered in hospital, where he was recovering from an earlier attack. Nine months later Cutolo's deputy, military chief and alter ego was blown up in a Rome car bomb explosion. A secret service ID was found in his pocket. The spectacular car bomb killing was intended to underline the finality of Cutolo's elimination. A pentito explained later that Gava's new associates wanted *to demonstrate to Cutolo that he was finished and that once and for all he had to stop blackmailing the politicians and state organizations that had dealt with him in the Cirillo affair.* Immediately, major government reconstruction contracts began flowing to the New Family's companies.

The head on the car seat in 1982 was a response to Cutolo's attempt to blackmail the DC. Before his decapitation the lawyer had been forced to write a note claiming to be the author of the document describing the DC minister's visit to Cutolo in prison. The head was also a portent. A little later that year Antonio Ammaturo, the chief of criminal investigations in the Naples police, was assassinated with his assistant for probing too deeply into the Cirillo kidnapping. His files and most other documents in the case disappeared. The Cirillo affair was still causing death over ten years later. When the parliamentary antimafia commission announced in 1993 that it intended to look into the matter, Cutolo's lawyer, who'd been intimately involved in the deal, told *Il Mattino* that he intended to tell the commission all he knew. Three days later he was assassinated. It happened months before Gava was arrested as a camorrista. The New Camorra's failure to blow up police headquarters marked the beginning of its decline. Cutolo tried to form an alliance with Cosa Nostra in the US, but was blocked by the New Family's ties with Cosa Nostra in Sicily. A hundred other New Camorra members were arrested at the time of the swoop on the castle in 1983, among them a prison chaplain and a nun who savaged the arresting officer during a pre-dawn raid on her convent. She tore off his shirt and severed his finger with her teeth. In the police raids of 1983 and 1984 there were fifteen hundred arrests.

Cutolo was finished, though allowed the special privilege of a wedding in jail. Ice Eyes Rosetta eluded the police for another ten years, but she too was finally taken. The New Family then broke up again into warring clans. This kept the killing at a respectable rate. Between 1980 and 1988 there were over fifteen hundred violent street deaths in the Naples gang wars. As the nineties began the killing figures were up again to hundreds a year Some in the winning families wanted to end heroin trafficking on their own turf. They'd realized rather late what junk had done to their children. There was a prolonged shooting war in the Spanish quarters over this. A group of mothers in the devastated Spanish quarters started to fight the drug camorra on its own ground. By then the camorra was making more money from public works contracts than it ever had from drugs. And anyway, the damage was done.

I WOKE with the earliest light, on the sofa of a friend's smoky attic flat. The flat was atop a huge and decaying sixteenth-century palazzo, whose monumental stone entry arch was at the blind end of a dank alley too narrow for cars to penetrate. The alley had once been a thoroughfare. It was never wide enough for cars, though, and now it was walled off altogether at the far end because the buildings that defined it were about to collapse. It was 1995 and I was back in Naples and it was time to leave again. I had to get a taxi at seven in the piazza, under the even more formidably monumental gateway to the archbishopric. The archbishopric was part of the cathedral complex, whose marble depths held the rich and elaborate frame that held the phials that held the congealed blood of San Gennaro. The fate of the city depended on the regular liquefaction of San Gennaro's blood. Getting to the archbishopric at dawn meant dragging stuff down the countless crumbling and cracked irregular steps. On one of their many wide landings I had lately seen a six-year-old boy already trained in the ways of his world respectfully kissing the hand of a petty boss. At the end of those dim passages running off the landings the corner of my eye would ever catch some door just barely open or clicking shut, some ankle disappearing around a corner, and my ear would pick up the sound of other feet, unseen a couple of turns ahead or behind on the majestic crumbling staircase.

Then across the courtyard, past the scooters and the washing and the rubbish and the improvised sunless gardenette, under the eyes of the Virgin gazing out complacently from her large and handsome recess, brilliantly lit by fluorescent tubes and bright fake flowers massed around her. Then down the dark and slimy alley under the further ever-watchfulness of street-level dwellers, they too staring at all hours out of their airless lightless boxes, over the bottom half of their horizontally divided front doors, like horses from their stalls. And into the handsome space of the largo, where a more public and more modest shrine to the Virgin, high in a corner wall, was being renovated and remodelled the day before by masons and plasterers perched on ladders and watched by some of the same old ladies who gathered in the cathedral twice a year to revile their saint and insult him until his blood liquefied and flowed again, and where at almost any hour of day or night a knot of boys would be scuffling for control of a football.

What woke me was a sound. Not an early stirring of life in the vast tenement below, but a noise gradually defining itself from above as the shape faltered into view. By now I was out on the tiny terrace with its row of dead cactus. It was a helicopter, hovering low in the grey light just before dawn and hugging the roofline and passing very slowly overhead in the direction of Forcella. Even on foot, Forcella was only a minute away down an alley behind the cathedral called *Scassacocchi* because it too was narrow enough to scrape and smash the wheels of a seventeenth-century carriage. Forcella's main artery was a street that ran on from the narrow thoroughfare marked out thousands of years ago by the Greeks and fell steeply into a tiny piazza at the foot of an architectural canyon and then forked. Forcella the casbah of Naples. They were raiding the Giulianos again.

The last time there were raids on the Giulianos and I was around, the family was seriously inconvenienced and so was I. The Giulianos were the strongest camorra family in Naples and for a few years they'd been displaying their domination of the neighbourhood, and by extension the city, more and more flauntingly. They'd set up a system of twenty-four hour floodlighting of the piazzetta. This was at once a staking out of the territory, a blazing intimidation by display and a warning system against incursions by police. Nothing passed unseen by the family, who looked down on the little forked piazza from their hideously renovated and fortified properties. The blaze of light was backed up by an elaborate system of video surveillance and powered at public expense by hooking into the electricity grid. Neither the electricity corporation nor the police had felt up to doing anything about it.

Both the flamboyance and the sense of territory were pure eighties camorra. In the absence of stable political cover on the Sicilian pattern, and a stable structure like Cosa Nostra's Cupola, camorra families were obsessive about control of their home turf and theatrical in the Neapolitan manner about displaying it. The boss in Gava's town of Castellammare, having to report daily to the carabinieri, arrived daily after a procession through the city on the back of a thousand-c.c. motorbike. The bike's rider, and the riders of the identical bikes that preceded, followed and flanked the boss's bike, all wore identical helmets and leather jackets. Others of his escort had previously cleared the route of traffic and pedestrians. In nearby Torre Annunziata, the ruling clan took over a huge old palazzo in the town centre and turned it into a fortress with secret internal tunnels and walled-up windows, protected by armoured doors and window shutters, dozens of closed circuit TV cameras, with armed guards at the entrance and a pack of German shepherd dogs on the roof

When the world's greatest footballer Diego Maradona arrived from Argentina in the mid eighties and a couple of years later Naples won the Italian football championship for the first time ever, the press spoke gravely of a cultural rebirth in Naples and the Giuliano family appropriated Maradona. He spent a fair amount of time partying with the

Giulianos, and it was in their company that he developed the coke habit that brought him down. *I was, am, and will always be an addict*, said the player who was once the greatest, back in Argentina, his career in ruins. *People talk a lot about drugs but not about what drives people to drugs. I took the drug on purpose. I had to get away from Naples.* You knew what he meant. Maradona was photographed often, in earlier and happier days, at Giuliano weddings and other festivities, and was once snapped with a young male of the family inside a huge and costly new bath in the form of a giant scallop shell that the family had bought itself. Both were clothed. When Nunzio Giuliano's seventeen-year-old son died of an overdose, an army of the clan's *guaglioni* marched into the hospital and overpowered the personnel and marched out again with the boy's body for a family wake. A Giuliano and his death were going to be handled as the family saw fit, not the public health authorities. The Giulianos were always good for a little intimidation, a little display.

There had in the end to be an official response to the humiliations the Giulianos were heaping on the representatives of civic order. It came in the form of several police raids on a military scale. Helicopters hovered in the air and directed an army of carabinieri on the ground. Houses were raided. Fugitives were arrested. The floodlights and the surveillance cameras were disconnected. The raid discovered a newly completed private casino and brothel complex hidden in the web of alleys. It was a very secret establishment of several storeys that comprised gambling facilities for the foot soldiers below and luxurious dalliance arrangements for more senior members of the family above. Among the fittings was the scallop shell bath.

The carabinieri found a secret escape route. It started in a hidden trapdoor in the floor of the entrance to the home of a prominent Giuliano and ended, via a rope drop, in the office of a cultural circle operated by an obscure religious order of the catholic church. The Neapolitan curia denied all knowledge of this order and its cultural association. This wasn't the only escape path from the casbah. One of the buildings raided was at the end of an alley that went off the left-hand fork. This building had a stone staircase leading up to the roof above the fifth floor, though access to the roof was barred by an iron gate that was heavily chained and locked. From here the roofs of other buildings, even some distance away, could be quickly reached on foot by anyone who knew the route. The offices of the local administration could be reached this way. The carabinieri must have been particuarly anxious to get to the roof, because they knocked a great hole over the staircase, in the substantial wall by the gate, to reach it. I could see it from the front door of the desolate room I rented on the top floor.

The arrests and the confiscations and the dismantling of the flood-lights and video cameras caused a lot of distress in the neighbourhood. Shortly after the hole appeared, I realized my room had been entered. The pastrycook's wife next door was distressed and evasive and I understood from her replies that it hadn't been the police. Nothing was taken. There was nothing to take. But the room had been searched. It was entered and searched again too. Then the death threats started. They came in two phases, written in pencil on those thick folded foolscap sheets of lined *carta protocollo* with the wide margins down each side and the handsome space at the head of the page: the sheets that were used with costly tax stamps stuck at their head for all manner of bureaucratic grovelling and sold by tobacconists in single sheets. The paper was my own. I'd been using the room as a writing studio in the mornings. I'm not so sure about the pencil. The camorristi may have brought their own pencil. It was certainly blunt, the one used for the messages, which was unlike me, with a soft lead, which was. The night I found the messages the sheets had been lying blank for quite some time. The notes were written in two hands and one was more literate and more reasonable than the other. It was done in cursive script, more or less, as against the other's clumsy printing. Compulsory education has always been a flexible concept in Naples. In a fairly terse, syntactically shaky but reasonably polite manner, the first explained that *unknown persons* were not admitted to the building. The other was more brutal and direct. The other's became the prevailing tone with the second lot of messages. These expressed displeasure that I hadn't yet vacated the premises. *Morirai*, one of them wrote. *You will die*.

It wasn't a lot of fun at any time, passing the caged Alsatian snarling in his straw-strewn dungeon under a naked light bulb, negotiating the lookout woman on the corner, swathed in shawls and seated impassively before an upturned carton displaying a single packet each of contraband Merìt and Marlbòro, both accented on the second syllable, ignoring the glances from behind the corner shop's piles of bread and tins and cheese, brushing past the youths hanging over a scooter under the entrance arch and brazening out the not-quite-closed doors on the intermediate landings. To arrive home with company and find the lock levered open, the front door hanging awry on its hinges and fresh death threats in the reception area really threw in doubt the wisdom of this little luxury. The landlady wasn't pleased when I told her I was leaving. Our agreement had been rigorously informal. I had obviously, she said down the long-distance line, *failed to win my neighbours' confidence.* Didn't I *know* about the rooftop escape route? *Naturally,* she snapped, *people were alarmed.*

PALERMO MADE me see in 1995 what I'd failed to see when I lived in Naples. In Sicily the mafia was always an identifiable entity, for those who cared to know it, and always there'd been a pocket of society immune to its threats and blandishments, a nucleus of resistance and renewal. The camorra had been much less entrenched in the institutions of Naples than the mafia was in Palermo but far more pervasively present in society, in the whole Bourbon culture of friendships and protection on which decrepit old Naples still ran. It was seen with indulgence by the very people employed to repress it. Countless times I'd seen a carabinieri car pull up by a seller of contraband cigarettes and a uniformed officer buy several cartons. The cigarettes were, before the heroin and earthquake days, the camorra's main source of income. I was friends, once, with a whole range of people who in minor ways were part of the camorra network, like old Cchiù Cchiù, the beshawled and toothless crone who sold cigarettes all night on a corner of via Toledo, for whom I'd light fires against the winter cold, or Giacomo, who got drawn into Cutolo's mob, or the elderly boss of the Spanish quarters who shouted me the Chivas Regal. That courtly old boss was one of the last of his kind. As late as the sixties the great Neapolitan actor and dramatist Eduardo De Filippo could still portray his like as a figure of real authority, an arbiter in a world without social justice. There was a certain humanity in the real-life Pascalone 'e Nola, who gave a wad of cash once to a youth who'd made a girl pregnant. *It was a wedding present,* he said. If the boy didn't get married, the cash could be used as a contribution to his funeral expenses. That was how Naples was. At the other end of the scale I found myself taking coffee once in the luxurious house with view of bay of a lawyer-financier later convicted of major operations for the camorra; being told once by a friend of Gava's that *I knew who to approach* in case of need; meeting aristocrats later enmeshed in the reconstruction contract scandals, the World Cup stadium scandals. At either end of the scale, I doubt that I would have known the mafia counterparts in Palermo. I began to see what Orlando had meant when he talked about the greater political maturity of Palermo, a city whose people had had to make hard choices. Naples in 1995 still seemed an utterly disoriented city whose language and gestures remained what they'd been but no longer referred to reality.

A poison was abroad in Naples now. Resentments surfaced quickly. The baroque configuration of the Neapolitan mind was being twisted further into something ugly. Meanwhile you were expected to admire pedestrian zones and open air cafes. The theme park necrosis was taking hold. Sinister forces wanted to embalm the city, create another Venice, a little piece of Tuscany. People were being pushed to the edges, if not out of town. You could see them in the shadows, at the edge of your field of vision. Was it the beauty that blurred my eyes now, or the life gone from the places I'd known? Naples had never seemed more beautiful. I felt like a ghost stalking the streets. *The tourists are coming back!* Twenty years earlier, Naples had been a dying city that belonged to the people who lived there. It was hardly bearable at best, yet there'd been life in the dreadfulness of life. You seldom heard Neapolitan now. The absurd comedy was gone. Naples broke my heart. And yet, as the city always had, it teased, it led you on to dream of more than it would ever deliver, made you remember why you'd thrown away your life to be there and still, for an instant, if you loved it, think it the most marvellous city in the world. In Naples you remembered being happy and never why. Naples, I consoled myself with thinking, would always be more *interesting* than other places. Naples would never bore. When Braudel saw Naples at its nadir in 1983, he reflected that

> Naples has always scandalized, scandalized and seduced ... Italy's lost a lot from not knowing, out of indifference and also fear, how to use the formidable potential of this city, which is really too different, European more than Italian ...

Naples was the only place I'd ever felt at home.

PASOLINI CAME south to Naples and Campania in the late sixties to make his film of Boccaccio's *Decameron*. He came to Naples because *Neapolitans have stayed the same.* The city stayed in his mind, and among his last writings were a series of letters to an imaginary Neapolitan boy. *I prefer the poverty of Neapolitans to the well-being of the Italian republic, I prefer the ignorance of Neapolitans to the schools of the republic ...* In another piece I could no longer trace, in one of the perverse, hallucinated visions he elaborated not long before his murder, he'd spoken of the Neapolitans as a people who had rejected the modern world. He described them as a desert tribe, camped in their black and red piazzas, waiting for the end, choosing to die. Wrong-headed and brilliant as ever, Pasolini didn't know the half of what was coming.

VII

A REALIST IN ROME

RED BANNERS waved in the winter air outside the Pantheon. A band played the *Internationale*. The party leader wept. The coffin arrived from the senate where it had lain in state for days while the president and the former president and the prime minister and former prime ministers and the whole *nomenklatura* and thousands of nameless admirers filed past and paid tearful homage.

Renato Guttuso's in 1987 was Italy's last great communist funeral. Berlinguer's had been vastly bigger, had stopped Rome and the nation. But Berlinguer's had been a political funeral, and the million mourners on the streets had then produced the party's greatest and most evanescent triumph, the dreamt-of *sorpasso* when the communists for the first and last time in history overtook the demochristians and won the largest vote of any party in national elections. Guttuso's, on a wintry day in January a couple of years later, was a funeral for the past, for the people of the left, for the memory of years of struggle, for commitment, passion and death. It was the funeral of a man who'd matured as an artist and militant when he was a resistance leader against the nazis, *military commander for central Rome until the liberation*, as I read on a yellowing central committee document among his papers, and author of a savage series of ink drawings done in hiding on butcher's paper, the *Gott Mit Uns*, Guttuso's horrors of war.

A little embarrassment was unavoidable in 1987. The party was hurtling down that trajectory from the illusory *sorpasso* of 1984 to its autodestruction in the post-wall panic of 1990, and its great artist, painter of the epic canvases of its years of struggle, had too devotedly followed its every twist and turn not to reflect in his expiry something of the current state of play. Unlike all the other artists and intellectuals, Guttuso hadn't left the party in 1956 or 1968 or in any of the other long years of attrition. He'd stayed and he'd been rewarded. He'd served two terms as a communist senator, been hymned by Pablo Neruda and when in the eighties he'd been challenged by his old friend the writer Leonardo Sciascia to choose between Sciascia and Berlinguer on the substance of a conversation among the three on the origins of terror-ism in Italy, Guttuso had chosen Berlinguer and the Party and Sciascia had broken with him. But when Guttuso died Sciascia wept and said *I never stopped loving him.*

The real embarrassment to the memory of communist austerity and struggle was Guttuso's vast wealth, his twenty-year affair with the flamboyant countess Marzotto and some of the friends who'd gathered around him in the wake of Berlinguer's disastrous historic compromise with the right. One of these friends was monsignor Angelini, a sleek and worldly cleric, an intimate of His Holiness and shortly to be raised to the purple. Another was the past and future prime minister Giulio Andreotti. For all these reasons, probably, Alberto Moravia kept his eulogy short and notably light on ideology, and as the politicians stood wrapped in their expensive overcoats he spoke tersely of the *Mediterranean expressionist* from Sicily who'd been his friend. *When an artist dies,* Moravia said, *something of the world dies.* The tall corpulent prime minister Craxi and the slight hunched foreign minister Andreotti both listened impassively and the communist party secretary buried his face in his handkerchief.

Then, to the intense surprise of many, the coffin with Guttuso in it was whisked off to the nearby church of Santa Maria Sopra Minerva, where a second funeral was held. A mass for the dead was celebrated by monsignor Angelini. The perplexed mourners watched the coffin dis-appear into the church and made their personal choices. Prime minis-ter Craxi stayed true to his lay principles and refused *with due respect to the dead* to enter the church. Others of those present, like the past and future prime minister Giulio Andreotti, attended both funerals. Andreotti had been one of the tiny group of people admitted to Guttuso's magnificent apartments in the last months of the painter's life and would now see things through to the end. He was, moreover, a truly devout catholic who went to mass at six every morning of his life. Monsignor Angelini was Andreotti's personal confessor and he'd been another of the tiny group of visitors admitted to the dying painter's presence.

Monsignor Angelini spread himself more widely in his homily for the smaller gathering in the church than Moravia had outside. Reaching for comparisons in remembering Guttuso he evoked among others the names of Leonardo, Michelangelo, Raphael, Caravaggio, Rembrandt and Dürer. If monsignor Angelini went a little over the top in this, he had his reasons. What many of the startled lay mourners outside didn't yet know was that monsignor Angelini had drawn Italy's most famous painter and most famous living communist into the bosom of the catholic church. He had, he announced to the press immediately after Guttuso's death, administered the extreme unction and heard the dying painter's confession. *He died praying to the Madonna and invoking the holy face of Jesus*, he told the media. Even in that moment of loss and mourning, monsignor Angelini must have felt it quite a coup for the mother church. Monsignor Angelini insisted that it wasn't in any case a conversion, but a return to the fold.

Andreotti wrote an article in a national weekly to argue that *it would be crude to see any contradiction* between Guttuso's communist life and his catholic death. He added suavely that *Guttuso's religious production testifies to a faith and a spiritual delicacy that are perhaps more than a prayer*. And monsignor Angelini, for his part, added of Guttuso that *Andreotti ... was his best friend*. Some of Guttuso's other best friends hadn't been present at all during the last months of the painter's life. They hadn't been allowed in. One was Alberto Moravia. Another was Guttuso's lover and model of twenty years, the subject of dozens of paintings and hundreds of drawings and the woman without whom, he'd many times said, *he wouldn't be able to paint*, Marta Vacondio, the countess Marzotto. Marta Marzotto was distraught and enraged.

I'll never forgive them for making me hear Guttuso was dead from the radio.
I'd sworn I'd never leave him alone, that I'd hold his hand to the end ...
They've erased me, kept me away like a plague bearer. I never existed ...

The countess Marzotto had been a daily visitor for twenty years. Three months earlier she'd been stopped from seeing him. Angelini and Andreotti were later to testify before a judge that the dying Guttuso hadn't wanted to see Marta Marzotto. Andreotti had even remarked, perhaps unaware the two were lovers, *I find it quite logical that he shouldn't want to see her any more. She was his model, but now he no longer paints.* The countess said the locks had been changed on the doors at the palazzo del Grillo, so her keys no longer fitted. A strongbox she shared with

Guttuso in a Rome bank she'd found emptied. It'd contained their love letters, jewels, erotic drawings by Guttuso of the countess, gold ingots and paintings by Picasso and Magritte. The value of Guttuso's estate was given variously in the press as something between one hundred and three hundred million dollars. All went to his newly-adopted son. Guttuso's sole heir was his secretary, a young man from Palermo named Fabio Carapezza. The son and heir and former secretary was described in the press as having *black curls and blue eyes like a cherub's in a church.*

———

GUTTUSO WAS born near Palermo in 1912 and made his name as a painter first in the thirties with his charged and solar Sicilian expressionism. He was already a clandestine antifascist, and when the war began he became a communist and fought as a partisan against the nazis. After the war his careers as a painter and as a communist ran together into big cold war epic canvases. These muted over the years, and Guttuso's apotheosis as *the* Italian painter coincided with the ambiguities of the historic compromise in the seventies. Guttuso held the figurative torch high in Italy while abstraction and conceptualism were sweeping the field of international art. He had nothing like the various genius of that other Mediterranean communist Picasso. In the more than three thousand canvases he painted over fifty-five years of tireless facility, he was only prolifically and endlessly himself. But he had a wonderful line, wiry and bounding, especially in the innumerable drawings, and a packed density of form and colour. The great and influential critic Roberto Longhi remarked that Berenson had liked Guttuso's *drawings* because they so embodied Berenson's principle of *ideated sensations of movement*, and added himself that

> the eye doesn't contemplate these drawings but runs over and over them, following the track of their rapid and provocative course ... Guttuso's line doesn't draw, it wounds–it's a sting, a prick, a thorn in the side ...

Pablo Neruda, a poet whose work often read like a literary analogue of Guttuso's art, wrote in 1953

> In your homeland, Guttuso, the moon has the smell
> of white grapes, honey and fallen lemons
> but there is no land
> there is no bread.

Neruda continued, rather feebly, *You give land and bread in your painting.*

His *Poem for Renato Guttuso* got much worse than this before its end, and so did Guttuso's painting. It was the age of militant art under Stalin's umbrella, committed art, and this kind of thing wasn't, in the case of either artist, the whole story. By the seventies Guttuso was a rich man living a very worldly social life and yet was still being hymned, this time by the Spanish poet Rafael Alberti, as

> painter of burning earth
> of stones and scorched harvests
> light that palpitates ceaselessly showing the way of Man.

Nostalgia had a lot to do with Guttuso's appeal. As Italians hurtled into the consumer age, Guttuso reminded them that they were a poor and passionate people with a feel for the simple joys of life. As southern peasants left the land for factories in the north and industrialists socked away their wealth, Guttuso reminded them all that they were close to the earth and the sun and that they would shed blood for what they loved.

This, in a time of transformation and uprooting, was what a lot of people wanted to hear. As Italy changed out of sight, Guttuso's conventionally harsh images reassured them. And a lot of Italians now had money to spend on paintings, and if not paintings, limited edition lithographs. Guttuso, Pasquale had told me at the mill, had owned a series of shops through which he sold his lithographs. It was through this unusual total control of production and distribution that he made a lot of his money. He was an artist for Italy's new industrial age and for his industrial production he had a loyal market at the lower end of the price range in the people of the left.

Rarely was there such a mutually rewarding relation between a party and its artist. Guttuso's loyalty to the PCI, through all its ups and downs and turns and transformations, lasted to the end of his life. The party assiduously promoted its militant and committed artist, and Guttuso responded with great generosity once his name and fortune were made. He made huge donations to the party and lent it prestige and credibility when other artists had abandoned it. He sat on Palermo city council and served two terms as a communist senator in Sicily. People were often struck by Guttuso's affinity for the world of power, his feel for the game of politics. *Guttuso is a man of power. It's the Sicilian in him*, Alberto Moravia sighed around the time Guttuso's reputation and his income really took off. Ever the conceptualizer, ever the explainer and ever loyal to his friends and the party of which he was not himself a member, Moravia added that *his thirst for money is part of his visual thirst. But Guttuso is an artist.* Moravia insisted. *Politics pass, art remains.*

The years passed and Guttuso went from rich to enormously rich. In the beau monde of Rome, ideology was less important than power and the purest expression of power was wealth. The Roman salons were the frontier of radical chic and very different from the Sicily of bombed party offices and murdered union organizers. Guttuso liked aristocratic women, and had done ever since the thirties when he was a poor and deeply seductive young man on the make. The historic compromise of the seventies lent the final sanction to the habitual presence in Guttuso's splendid Roman apartments in the palazzo del Grillo of princes of the church and some of the powerful demochristian politicians closest to the Vatican, such as Giulio Andreotti. Everyone was flattered. Guttuso explained

> *Money is one of the fundamental elements of power. Money gets power. Power gets money. But the power that derives from money is a very bitter thing, because one no longer knows who is a friend and who is an enemy. Power insulates you from the true feelings, even love.*

It sounded like a dreadful intimation of what was coming.

BAGHERIA, WHERE Guttuso was born, is a few miles west of Palermo. He exaggerated his early poverty. It may have been a turn-on for the aristocratic women. He was the son of an agronomist and no worse off as a child than any other member of the austere and cultivated lower middle class in Italy before the first war. His father painted, wrote and played the piano. The fifteen kilometre distance of this small settlement from Palermo was far enough in the old days to be well out of town but still within reach of the city. And Bagheria's situation, on a pleasant hillside just above the promontory that encloses the bay of Palermo on the east, had been delightful enough for the landowning aristocracy to build their villas there. It was rich coastal country planted with citrus orchards and olive groves, part of Palermo's golden bowl, the Conca d'Oro. The stately homes doubled as farmhouses. The first great villa of Bagheria was built in the seventeenth century as a country retreat for prince Butera, and others followed over the next hundred years. The one I wanted to visit was built in 1736. Guttuso had given a big collection of his work to his home town in 1973 and the villa Cattolica had been turned into a museum to house it. On a

Saturday afternoon I stood at a bus stop in Palermo over the road from the steps leading down to the Vucciria market. A woman shopper was already there, going home to Bagheria with her bursting plastic bags. Our desultory words about the buses became more animated as the time passed. An hour later I walked off. It was too late to visit the place before dark. The poor woman was still there with her bags of weekend shopping from the market.

The next morning I was at the same stop. A taxi cruised past. I told the driver I was waiting for a bus, and the driver said the buses didn't run on Sundays The taxi pulled calmly into a cul de sac off the other side of the road. And waited. I continued to stand at the bus stop. I was in no particular hurry. The driver tilted his cap over his eyes and feigned sleep. Gianni had a print of *The Vucciria* at home. Gianni was the taxi driver. He told me this as we worked our way out of town behind the station. Gianni was more than happy with the round trip fare he'd negotiated and the taciturn Sicilian was getting loquacious. It was understood a certain amount of helpfulness was part of the deal. We took a little detour toward the sea. Gianni nodded toward the general dereliction. *Spanò*, he said, with a kind of curt reverence.

Where it used to be. Where they had dinner. The famous fish restaurant.

They? I said.

When the big mafia bosses came over from the States, that's where they had dinner. They say that's where they had dinner. Spanò. I personally wouldn't know. I know nothing.

I was impressed that Gianni was speaking to me about the mafia. Fifteen years earlier people looked blank when you mentioned it.

———

SPANO RANG a bell. A young mafioso who started out as a man of honour in the postwar days remembered eating at Spanò. Tommaso Buscetta, who was even then a rising figure in Cosa Nostra, because *I knew how to talk a little and I had the habit of reasoning*, said twenty-seven years later that he remembered being present at a dinner in a private alcove of Spanò in 1957. The dinner started on October the twelfth of that year. The meal began with *pasta con le sarde* and moved on to grilled fish and by the time the participants had ordered a drop of amaro or limoncello to settle the stomach it had lasted twelve and a half hours. It was perhaps the most important fish dinner in the history of organized crime.

The diners were all Sicilian, but half of them were *oriundi* long resident in the USA. The American delegation was headed by Giuseppe Bonanno, who was Joe Bananas in Brooklyn. When Joe Bananas arrived in Italy he'd been met at Fiumicino airport in Rome with a red carpet and a fervent embrace by the minister for foreign trade, the Sicilian and demochristian Bernardo Mattarella. Like Joe Bananas, Mattarella was a native of Castellammare del Golfo, just out of Palermo. He was the father of Piersanti Mattarella, that president of the Sicilian region who was assassinated in 1980 for wanting to break with Cosa Nostra. He was also the politician who gave the young Vito Ciancimino his start in life with a job in his parliamentary office. The Sicilian delegation was headed by its *capo di tutti i capi* don Giuseppe Genco Russo, successor to the late don Calò Vizzini, who'd expired amid great public lamentation in 1952. Nothing has come down to history of what was said during those twelve and a half hours. The one tiny exception was retailed later by one of Spanò's waiters. *Blessed is he who is far away when a hundred dogs fight over a bone*, murmured Genco Russo at some point during the meal.

The young Tommaso Buscetta must have been moved by the momentousness of the occasion. Few actual men of honour have been such true believers in the notion of a mafia ethic and a mafia culture as Tommaso Buscetta in his long career. This fourteenth child of a poor Palermo family was mafioso in his walk, his posture and his thinking even before he became a made man in 1945 at the age of eighteen. His finger was then pricked, blood was drawn, he passed a burning religious icon from hand to hand. *May my flesh burn like this holy image if ever I betray my vow*. The induction of a man of honour is like something out of *Tom Sawyer*, and Buscetta himself remarked on its foolishness a quarter of a century later. He had his reasons later for diminishing the weight of his early vow, because Buscetta had by then become not quite the first but the most authoritative pentito in the history of Cosa Nostra. It was appropriate that Buscetta should have been present at the long fish dinner at Spanò in October 1957 because it had everything to do with the theorem Buscetta enabled Giovanni Falcone to construct decades later on the unitary structure of Cosa Nostra.

The Grand Hotel et Des Palmes began life as the handsome villa Ingham, became the key hotel of the fin de siècle splendours of Palermo and maintains a certain threadbare and grime-darkened distinction even today. Wagner was painted there by Renoir, while he worked on *Parsifal* in the opulent suite now called after him. A later guest was Raymond Roussel, the French symbolist author of *Locus

Solus and *Impressions de l'Afrique*, who got no closer to Africa than the Grand Hotel et des Palmes. In 1933, after not coming out of Room 224 for forty days, he died there in circumstances that Leonardo Sciascia found mysterious enough to make the subject of his very slimmest slim volume, a book of twenty-eight pages called *Documents Relating to the Death of Raymond Roussel*. After the war the Little Red Room of the Hotel delle Palme was permanently screened off for the use of Lucky Luciano and whoever he was entertaining at the time. It seems to have been Luciano's transatlantic good offices that in 1957 brought together the two groups, the Americans and the Sicilians, for their very intensive four-day encounter in the sala Wagner. From the tenth to the fourteenth of October the two groups were doing serious business and the outing to Spanò on the twelfth was at once a relief and a culmination.

The Americans had come to sell the Sicilians the idea of the Cupola or governing commission, and succeeded. Modern integrated management principles came home to the Sicilian mafia from the United States. The Cupola, on the model of the American commission, became the board of directors that governed Cosa Nostra as a whole. It integrated all the families controlling all the different areas. It decided killings and formalized dealings with the American Cosa Nostra commission on a separate but equal basis. It was under way within months, with the joint-venture elimination of the dangerously psychopathic Albert Anastasia in his New York barber's chair by a Sicilian commando. The Americans were in trouble at home that year with the heroin business. The Sicilians agreed to take over the importing of heroin into the USA, neither side foreseeing the vertiginous profits that heroin would be earning twenty years later. One version of the summit suggestively had Michele Sindona also present. The two sides agreed that henceforth they were autonomous and distinct organizations, ending the informal family traffic across the Atlantic. Though the Sicilian Cupola was temporarily dissolved in the sixties during the government's antimafia activity it has otherwise been Cosa Nostra's governing body ever since. Not even Totò Riina abolished the Cupola. It took the Italian courts thirty years to acknowledge its existence.

WHEN YOU leave Palermo along the waterfront, heading east toward Bagheria, you see piles of rubble on the sand beyond the road and reeking waste on fire, shacks of disparate materials pieced together. There are still people in them at the end of summer, and perhaps all year round. There are other broken-down and boarded-up restaurants and hotels, closed for the season and by the look of them maybe for ever. There are low concrete walls and stands of reeds, used car lots and stands selling watermelon and mussels, fishing boats pulled up on the beach. The road then runs between two rows of mudcoloured houses with heavy wooden shutters on their windows built directly on the narrow street, none of them more than two or three stories high. Behind them loom the big and ugly bleak new boxes. Along the road out of town shops and bars and house doors all have the same dark cavern entrances hung with strips of plastic. The odd greengrocer stands a line of boxes along the narrow footpath, the odd bar has a row of rickety wooden chairs outside, supporting immobile elderly males with cloth caps and grey moustaches, who stare into the traffic passing inches from their face. The sight is quintessentially southern coastal, and quintessentially the season, late summer, early autumn, the violent heat gone from the air, a dusty lethargic golden haze enveloping all. A number of coffin outlets, polished wares stacked like slabs of toffee in the dark, do a subsidiary trade in ugly crucifixes and other appurtenances of mourning.

When the periphery thins out again and you glimpse the sea and a bit of grass and light industry, you start noticing the seaside architecture, the little houses that crop up illegally along the foreshore. Usually two-storied, in whitewashed reinforced concrete and breeze block, with terracotta tile roofs, aluminium window frames and those slatted modern shutters, always in beige, that pull down like venetians and seal the window completely, they often manage to work in a bit of balustrade, several metres of readymade short bulging pillars, always in blinding white. The fancier places may have a plaster nymph or cherub or a plaster David, all of them blurred and softened and melted-looking from the mould and standing, on the fanciest premises, by a little pond or fountain lined with tiles of brilliant swimming pool blue. There may or may not be pots of geraniums, almost certainly a double car port, probably some tiled patio and quite likely an elaborate spiked steel fence around it. Like the older streetscape of mud-coloured houses, these villettas are deeply familiar to anyone who has been around the coastal Mezzogiorno. Their analogues spread in thousands through the violent lawless hinterland of Naples, they spread up and down from Bari on the Adriatic coast. There's an almost uninterrupted line of them down the Tyrrhenian coast of Campania and Calabria. These houses have always fascinated me, partly because the permitted extravagances, certain statues, certain fountains, the white paint and terracotta and the fatly pillared balusters and the concrete gardens, irresistibly stir memories of certain home improvements in Leichhardt or Carlton.

In Italy, being illegal constructions on a single-family scale, they express with a directness unmediated by any architect the dreams and desires and fears of those who build them. You see the fragmented longing for style, the TV image of the good life that comes out in a random assemblage of sites or features that ends up very much like a TV set and whose proliferation is restrained only by the requirements of economy and speed in clandestine building on the one hand and safety on the other. Whence the shutters, the armoured doors, the spiked railings, the walls, the video cameras, the alarms, the spyholes. The coastal constructions are modest enough, being often just holiday homes, for security not to be so visibly the overriding concern. Moving inland into the hills of Sicily, where the villas are bigger, more costly and solid, the new houses look more and more like dreadful fortified bunkers. As they are. There is no grimmer or more palpable expression of the social ethos in Sicily among those who've lately had money to spend. The style isn't without its historical antecedents and continuities, but never as in the late twentieth century have its expressions been so deadly. They are the ultimate expression of fear and mistrust of your neighbours. Thinking this, now and on bus trips inland to Corleone and Racalmuto, I saw the amazing appeal the Australian houses of Glenn Murcutt must have had for the student Vincenzo, sitting so airily and lightly and modestly on the earth, minimal, essential and open to the world around them. From Sicily such houses seem models or dreams of another world, another way of living, and seeing this, I realized as I hadn't earlier the politics of Vincenzo's enthusiasm.

THE BUILDINGS thin for a bit and you see the vast extent along the coast of the famous citrus orchards and their dark green leaves like painted tin, and the wiry silvery olive groves among them. Gianni and I tooled along for a few minutes in the taxi and then we rose into the hills and as the road turned, on a shoulder of the hill, we saw villa Cattolica. It was a handsome, slightly odd, slightly asymmetrical building in that endearing southern way I'd met in the duke of Verdura's villa Niscemi the hot day I lunched with Orlando. It was very high in relation to its floor area, and this combined with its position on a spur made it stick out dramatically like a wedge of pinkish late-baroque cake. The sight was complicated by a tall crane and some high chimneys that seemed to be growing out of it: they belonged to a factory jammed up behind it. The villa itself was once used as a food cannery.

It was closed for *works*. We parked the taxi by the high front gate which was bolted and impenetrable. Following the perimeter wall, we came across an elderly couple with a small child who seemed to live in a large single room, a kind of cave dug into the wall. They told us the villa was closed for *works*. On all else they were vague. Nearby we found a small art gallery selling ceramics, whose dapper owner was more forthcoming. He told us the villa was closed for *works*. Was an end to the works foreseen? *The works of restoration are supposed to be completed by the end of next year*, said the gallery owner. *Supposed*, he repeated with a savage little twirl of his hand. The flow of art lovers past his shop had clearly dried up. I wasn't too happy myself. A fortune on Gianni's taxi for nothing. Were there any other traces of Guttuso left in Bagheria? His family home? *Look*, said the gallery owner.

> *Renato Guttuso left Bagheria a long time ago. He stayed away most of his life. He was famous in Milan, in Rome, not here. He never did a thing for this place. Got out as soon as he could and he only started getting sentimental about the place at the end of his life. The people of Bagheria could not give a STUFF about where Guttuso was born.*

Gianni said, *Let's go and see villa Palagonia.* We went up into the town. The comparison that came first to mind here was the Stalinist housing of eastern Europe. A moment later you reflected that that hideousness had been mitigated in some degree by a sense of public dignity. Destiny required monumental spaces, wide roads between the barracks, heroic scale. This is absent in modern Bagheria, though it must have once been there in the disposition of the noble villas. The lowering cement blocks of Bagheria now hem you in, threatening, greedy, without order or symmetry. From a place first chosen for its light, its vegetation, its view of the sea, all these have been eliminated for those who live in the mafia flats or walk the streets between them.

The statues carved out of soft yellow tufa stone in the middle of the eighteenth century under the direction of the prince of Palagonia stood out once against the blue sky above the walls surrounding his villa and its garden. Those that remain now merge into blocks of flats. The villa of the monsters is choked by the building around it, lost in a modern slum. This is the place that was a must see in the eighteenth century for those on the grand tour, so freakish that its monsters had the fame among the locals of making pregnant women abort. The monsters were the big statues with big heads the prince had carved to his orders and placed on guard at the gates, at the entrance and along the walls surrounding his garden. Many have been vandalized, destroyed, or had their soft shell tufa so worn by time and weather that the figures look as if their bodies are rotten or cankered. All the depredations make it hard to imagine the strong effects these bizarre protoromantic nightmares in stone once had on those who saw them. To a twentieth century eye what remains looks merely playful. Yet Goethe hated this place and the mind of the prince of Palagonia who created it: *he gives freest rein to his passionate appetite for misshapen, tasteless forms, and to credit him with even a spark of imagination would be paying him too much honour.* The man of the *Aufklärung* lists *the elements of Prince Palagonia's folly*.

> *Humans*: beggars male and female, Spaniards male and female, Moors, Turks, hunchbacks, all kinds of deformed people, dwarfs, musicians, Pulcinellas, soldiers in ancient costumes, gods, goddesses, people in Old French costumes, soldiers with ammunition pouches and leggings, mythology with grotesque additions, eg, Achilles and Chiron with Pulcinella. *Animals*: only parts of them, a horse with human hands, a horse's head on a human body, disfigured apes, many dragons and serpents, all kinds of paws on figures of every type, doublings, transposed heads ...

Renato Guttuso's first childhood home was on corso Butera, the main axis of old Bagheria, a few yards from the villa Palagonia, and years later he remembered playing in its abandoned garden, where overgrown and distorted Indian fig plants mixed with the grotesque statues and matched them. He'd been, he later said, much influenced by this mingling of *the fantastic and the real*. Today, everything is lopped, trimmed, hemmed in. Goethe saw *a superb view across the headlands to the sea* from the villa. All he'd see now would be mafia flats. The writer Dacia Maraini, indignant at what'd happened to the enchanted place she'd known as a child after the war, traced the records of the destruction of Bagheria in the fifties and sixties through the council records. It all happened in barely a decade, starting when the council expropriated land surrounding villa Valguarnera to build a primary school. The school could have been elsewhere, but once the developers got a toehold in the parklands around the villas in the town centre, with the collusion of council and administration, roads followed and then the ten-storey blocks of flats. Villa Butera was surrounded and choked in the same way, and all the other eighteenth-century villas and their gardens.

Maraini identified a shadowy engineer called Giammanco who

appeared in the records of nearly every phase in the destruction, at once the council's technical expert who approved projects and the owner of the land to be developed, having strategically befriended some of the aging aristocrats. There were inquiries and court cases after the damage was done, about the laws and regulations that had been broken. Giammanco was acquitted. Maraini, who has aristocratic family connections in Bagheria, is a little sentimental about what it was all like before. So was Fulco di Verdura, the child of the villa Niscemi, who came to spend summers here in his father's villa Serradifalco, and remembered his father meeting the family on horseback, flanked by two toughs on horseback with rifles slung over the shoulders, the *campieri*, the estate guards who followed the family everywhere outside the property. *It didn't help protect us against the mafia*, the duke remarked ingenuously, adding that the Bagheria mafia was *savage and vengeful* and later caused his father a lot of trouble.

It certainly was savage and vengeful. Before the fascist repression and the war, Sicily's still-rural mafia was either that of the large estates of the interior or that of the orchards, the mafia that exploited the citrus cultivators of the coastal strip. Bagheria was the centre of the orchard mafia who terrorized the orchardists through their control of the water supply. In 1888 they murdered the mayor of Bagheria during a religious procession. When Renato Guttuso was seven or eight years old, there were once seventy-seven mafia killings in a single month in Bagheria and one evening he saw a man shot in the back in via Butera by two men with rifles. The child Guttuso was looking down from the balcony of the family house.

> *Everyone instantly knew about it. Nobody had seen a thing. As a child I often heard, as darkness fell in the evening, two rifle shots with a half-second interval between them, followed by total deathly silence.*

Times change, but the orchard mafia still exists, and so does the mafia's control of water supplies all round an island desperately short of water. Many inland communities in Sicily are forced to buy their water from a mafia which therefore has an interest in maintaining and aggravating the shortage. Taking a closer look, I noticed this day in Bagheria that a lot of the beautiful orange and lemon orchards around the town had in fact been abandoned, and many of the trees were dying. The problem in the citrus orchards, however, was no longer water denial but excess production. Now that the Mezzogiorno is integrated into the European community along with the rest of Italy, the community pays citrus producers in Sicily a big compensation to destroy their production in excess of the community quota. The European bureaucrats in Brussels are no better able to handle the mafia than the old market gardeners of the Conca d'Oro. The mafia's business is now destroying imaginary citrus crops, and being paid by Brussels to do so. The year before he was murdered, Giovanni Falcone remarked that even if the entire land surface of Sicily were covered with orange and lemon orchards, the island would still not produce enough to honestly earn the money received from Europe for destroying the excess crops.

Renato Guttuso got out young from Bagheria. The town he left in the thirties was still largely agricultural and not at all the mafia-built slum it became a generation later. But the Bagheria of the orchard mafia was incipiently the Bagheria that was later famous for the Bagheria massacre that was one of the events of Riina's rise to power, and as one of the apices of the area known as the triangle of death for its terrible homicide rate. He kept his distance to the end, despite brief visits and the donation to villa Cattolica, even when he'd bought himself a handsome house in the centre of Palermo. He only came back dead, to be buried among the weeds in the grounds of villa Cattolica, in a hideously kitsch blue marble sarcophagus by the sculptor Manzù, decorated with four gilt doves. Giulio Andreotti was present that day in 1989, at the inauguration of the tomb.

The old communist at the mill, Pasquale, had reminded me how when the PCI put Guttuso up for the Italian senate, as a reward for his loyalty and his financial generosity to the party, they had to find an electorate in another part of Sicily, because Guttuso *wasn't well looked-on in Bagheria*. After his election, his old comrade said, there was a dinner in Palermo, attended by the leading politicians. During the evening Guttuso got fired up and rose to propose a toast. *Down with the mafia!*, he cried, lifting his wine glass. The president of the regional parliament stormed out of the dinner. Guttuso was shattered at his blunder, and ran out after the president, pleading with him to return. He was losing touch. I wondered about this. As the immensely wealthy painter lay dying a few years later, his lung cancer metastasizing in his brain, a prisoner in his palatial Roman apartments, isolated from old friends and his lover by the high prelates and politicians and the adopted son and the adopted son's family from Palermo who perched around his bed like crows, did he, in his moments of lucidity, ever feel he hadn't got so far away after all?

Gianni and I had a pizza down by the villa Cattolica. Downhill from the pizzeria out the back was a gully full of dying lemon trees. *Might as well let them die*, said the proprietor, when I asked about them. *I hope you're going to write something good about Bagheria. All this bad stuff about the mafia. Nobody comes here any more. There's no work in Sicily. Nobody cares.* He launched into the long rhythmically cadenced complaint of the Mezzogiorno. To cut him off I mentioned Guttuso and he brightened. He was an artist himself, having lately taken up sculpture. He showed me some of his pieces. The major work was a portrait bust of the maestro Guttuso himself, larger than life and carved in the same buttery tufa as the prince of Palagonia's monsters. The shape of the head wasn't bad, and the ridgy lines of Guttuso's wavy hair were striking, almost Greek. But something awful had happened to the bridge of his nose. The brow and the nose had been so sculpted away that they'd become concave and for the second time that day I had thoughts of a hideous growth or a flesheating cancer and shuddered. *That's a remarkable likeness,* I said.

Gianni took the motorway back, and ten minutes later put me down in the middle of Palermo. He looked at me hard as we parted. Gianni was sure my parents were Sicilian. In Naples, and later in Sicily, I was often taken for an *oriundo.* The word, like *orient,* comes from the Latin verb meaning *rise,* and all it means is that you were born in the place of which you are *oriundo.* In the south of Italy it takes on the particular sense of a person born in that place and returning home after a long emigration. In the days before football came to be a branch of the media industry, it also meant a footballer from overseas of Italian origin, one who came *home* to play in an Italian team. As far as I know I have no Italian blood, but I was always deeply pleased and touched by the attribution.

———

THE TRIUMPH of Death is a great fifteenth-century fresco from the wall of a Palermo poorhouse hospital, now restored and on display in the palazzo Abatellis. It shows Death on his charger striking down a group of young and beautiful people. A group of kings and prelates are already dead, their corpses heaped in the centre foreground of the painting. The survivors are the poor and the crippled who stare out of the left hand side, behind Death's gaze. The bounding horse Death rides is reductively geometrical, allegorical, skeletal and abstract. Yet it's also full of nostril-flaring energy, a kind of recall to a cruder reality than the rich, the beautiful and the powerful show. Death in this painting is not merely an allegorical skeleton, but a real body in the final stages of fleshly dissolution, with flaps of rotting skin still hanging from his bones. Death has himself died, and the grey horse seems like Picasso's in *Guernica* more a figure of suffering than danger.

The scale of the painting, the sweeping and inescapable grimness of its social message, the overpoweringly didactic intent of it all and the gaunt ugly horse itself inescapably recall the work of Renato Guttuso, and when you see it you can't escape the idea of its influence. The Guttuso famous for the vibrancy of Sicilian sun and earth and sea was always shadowed by another Guttuso, darker and more violent, a painter of negation. His more perceptive critics always insisted on this. *Contrary to appearances*, Sciascia once wrote, *Guttuso is assailed by fear, anguish, suffering and the sense of death ... he 'unlives' even as he deeply lives.*

Guttuso painted his own *Triumph of Death* in 1943, when he was living in hiding through the nazi occupation of Rome, and it had a grey charger in it. His *Crucifixion* of 1941 has a wild-eyed horse in the foreground, and *Battle* of 1943 has two horses, one dead, for only one dead human figure. His horses recurred as images of brute suffering in these years. Picasso was always the painter he looked to, and when he was starting out in those early days of fascism and war he carried a small reproduction of *Guernica* in his wallet like a talisman, an image of art, politics, morality. It was a model he never abandoned. Alberto Moravia remarked on the detritus littering the work of *this painter of Indian figs, olive trees, rocky shores and fishing boats ... a certain almost obsessive unpleasantness*. Even Guttuso's sensuality was like this, Moravia went on:

> Guttuso's women are like his starving dogs and skeletal horses: carcasses with ample flanks and thin legs, sagging breasts and swollen bellies, ready to yield to a fuck that is endured rather than desired.

He described thus a 1959 *Nude* by Guttuso:

> On a blood-coloured blanket, a woman lies thrown on her back, eyes closed, face upside down. Ribs and hips stand out. Massive splayed thighs taper rapidly to narrow shins. The pubic zone is a triangle of dark shadow ... The woman lies on the floor: she has been thrown there ... she lies there, mouth half open and eyes half closed, waiting for another, definitive violence.

The violence of Guttuso's painting, according to Moravia, goes beyond its content and becomes a compositional principle in his big political works.

> The cement of Guttuso's composition is violence. Violence among the figures in the picture and the painter's violence on the figures ...

The violence transmuted into inertness of mind as the political impulse faded over the years. In the last big paintings, when shallowness had closed in, the inertness of the compositions was matched by a crude flatness in the way the figures were rendered. The first work of Guttuso's I saw was one of these, at the end of the seventies, in reproduction, and I loathed it. It must've been the pretentiously allegorical *Spes Contra Spem, Hope Against Hope*, with its room of disconsolate intellectuals, among them Guttuso and Moravia, the nude woman, the balcony, the running child and the glimpse of the sea. The *Walt Disney of Italian Stalinism* was how I saw Guttuso at that time. Other paintings were worse. *La Vucciria* itself was one of them. All the components, the fruit, the vegetables, the fish, that Guttuso so charged with life when he drew them in and for themselves, were diminished in the big canvas, made uniform and marshalled into deadly ranks, elements in a flat pattern broken only by the wooden figure of the standing, staring woman shopper seen from behind. It's very telling, in the old brochure printed for the painting's first presentation, to compare the drama and intensity of the preliminary sketches of the market wares with the deadness of the finished whole. Later he went off the painting himself. In 1980 he said

> The *Vucciria* is a painting I'd been carrying around inside me for years. I come from Bagheria, but I went to high school in Palermo. In the morning I used to go to the market for my lunch, I bought bread and *panelle*. The market stalls fascinated me, their displays of Sicilian fruit and vegetables. I thought of doing a canvas like a great still life, with a path cut through it like a groove and people buying and looking. The idea took over, and there's too much still life in the picture. Too many peppers, too many tomatoes, too many eggs. I'd do it again differently now, but I don't feel up to it. It's hard to go back to a theme you've already dealt with ...

All of Guttuso's best critics saw the split in his work, between the keenness of his eye and the vigour of his hand, and the deadening force of the organizing will, though they hedged about putting it in words. Moravia was clearly holding back when he talked about his friend's work. Roberto Longhi identified Guttuso's masters as Goya, Géricault, Daumier, Delacroix, and after praising Guttuso's wonderful *line*, went on to hint, *A problem might be how often his graphic flights are at a functional tangent with his painting* ...

Though Guttuso left Sicily early to make his way on the continent, he never stopped doing sketches and small oils, in the interstices between his big choral canvases, of Sicilian things, the small things like the fish and the lemons, that had charged his imagination as a hungry Sicilian boy. They may have had a talismanic or a fetishistic value for him too, as touchstones of something he feared losing, emblems of his origins, and painting them may have been a way of staying Sicilian. *The Vucciria* is the work Sicilians know best. There were prints of it everywhere and it was no surprise that Gianni had one at home. There was another framed on the wall of the Horse Shoe, a clamorous, almost Neapolitan, place near the Vucciria itself with terrific cheap workday lunches and excellent caponata. In it Guttuso assembled some of the Sicilian minutiae he had so often handled in sketches and small oils into a large canvas of social statement. The market of the Vucciria was the locus and the symbol, the concentration of this Sicilianness. When Sciascia spoke about the *hungry man's dream* he meant not only the market itself but Guttuso's interpretation of it in the painting. I found Sciascia's note among Guttuso's papers, in the brochure for the first presentation of *La Vucciria* at Vivi Caruso's Palermo gallery in 1974. Guttuso's painting, Sciascia went on to say, wasn't about the abundance it represented, but about its absence, about hunger. Like the Vucciria market itself, *La Vucciria* was *a hungry man's dream*, but Guttuso by then was too far away to make it real.

VIII

A WOMAN'S LIFE

PHOTOS? SAID Letizia Battaglia. It was the third time I'd sidled up to the matter of the photos in twenty-four hours. This time I wasn't going to be shaken off. *They're all put away in boxes,* she mumbled. *It's such a bore to get them out.* I pressed her further, as Pietro urged the tiny white Fiat through the haze-shrouded traffic on a hot Palermo morning. *I HATE my photos!* Letizia Battaglia cried. *They're HORRIBLE.* Her eyes were glinting with pleasure.

In Sydney once I'd heard about a planned exhibition of work by a woman photographer from Sicily. It was going to be held under the auspices of the Italian cultural institute. The cultural institute's director worked from a suite forty-five floors above Circular Quay with a breathtaking two-hundred-and-seventy degree view of the world's greatest harbour. Since the photographer was a woman, a woman moreover from the Mezzogiorno, and seeing that she'd already in 1985 won a very prestigious prize in New York, the Eugene Smith, the institute was thrilled with the idea of promoting Letizia Battaglia as cultural ambassador for Italy. Then shortly before opening time Italy's cultural representatives got a glimpse of some of the black-and-whites, more black than white and more grey than either, that were going on display.

Shattered car windows. Rigid figures in car seats. Eyes staring sightlessly from wrenched back heads. Blood trickling from the corner of an open mouth. Bodies face down in a pool of blood beneath some crumbling wall. Feet in expensive shoes sticking out from one end of a blanket hastily thrown on the footpath, from whose other end a rivulet of sticky blood was flowing. Wailing women on their knees. The legs and feet of bystanders, fencing in the central image. Carabinieri with heavy black moustaches, staring into the middle distance. Chalk outlines on the asphalt. Pine coffins. Police cars with flashing roof lights. Each photo different, each photo the same. Each photo a shock, the accumulative effect devastating. Not taken with art, though with strengths that art might have envied. The perfect reflection of a woman's face in the pool of still-uncongealed dark blood gathered on the near side of a body under a white sheet, nearer still than the half-collapsed umbrella and the fallen cloth cap beside it. A trinity of mourning women by the body, already in black from some earlier death: the old mother twisting a handkerchief, collapsed on a kitchen chair brought out by a neighbour, the reflected sister, the wife on her knees by the body, raising the sheet above the head.

Letizia Battaglia showed the living as well as the dead, in the centre of her native Palermo. Mainly, those who were perversely trying to live in the centre of Palermo, among the ruins of the wartime bombing and the strategic neglect by decades of mafia city administration at the service of mafia developers. A skinny mother, the very image of one of Walker Evans's Appalachian women from the depression, breast-feeding a baby while two other children play naked in the kitchen. A blackening banana skin lies on the floor and one child's face is disfigured by fresh rat bites. A young girl washing dishes in a tub next to an open lavatory. A family standing outside their home, now collapsed to a pile of rubble. Children in a bed. Corpses of three children dead from leaking gas. Toothless old people. A small girl bringing home bread. Small boys playing with guns. A wife with two black eyes. A crone holding the portrait of her disappeared son. The interiors are all the same, the crumbling, damp-blotched walls, the gloom, the oilcloth on the table, the photo of the ancestors on the wall, the sour reek rising from the prints.

The small interior violence of the mainly female domestic images mirrors the larger male violence of the street deaths, but again and again the two overlap. You see it in the female figures curved over the corpses in the gutter, and in the slain prostitute's interior, she and her two slain accomplices, punished for a drug deal, sprawled over an intricately patterned lounge suite, under a poster of a busty nude woman playing suggestively with a football. The pictures of festivities, too, mirror the working day world. The statue of the saint on her carrying frame, the beaten woman on her stretcher. The bloody hyperrealism of the Easter re-enactments and the bodies in the street. The carnival parade in Corleone where the men come masked as mafiosi, carrying shotguns. The fewer images of high society at play similarly match those of the social reality below. The aristocratic receptions in Palermo might be illustrations of *The Leopard*, give or take a few minor anachronisms in the dress, and the faded oval photos of the ancestors are not unlike the others on the walls of slum kitchens. The three beau monde males embracing in Palermo match down to the glinting signet rings another photo's three mafiosi in Trapani. Variety here is less contrast and difference than nuance and interrelationship. It's the same society, the same culture, the same history.

The exhibition was cancelled. Patronage withdrawn. Letizia couldn't now, she claimed, remember anything about it. *Some girl had turned up on her doorstep years ago ...* she remembered vaguely. Southern Italians are people of the here and now, and what might or might not have happened on the other side of the world several years ago was of little interest. The view from the little tin can on wheels was what mattered.

Disgusting! cried Letizia Battaglia as the tiny white Fiat rocketed along a Palermo back street. *Revolting!* She gestured at a few glistening black piles of ruptured plastic bags, their household scraps quietly putrefying in the October morning sun. To someone coming from Naples it was hard to see what was upsetting her. By contrast with the Palermo of the Sicilian novelist Vincenzo Consolo's words a dozen years earlier, written in high summer at the height of the mafia war, it was wonderfully normal.

Palermo is fetid, infected. This fervid July it exhales the sweetish smell of blood and jasmine, the pungent odour of disinfectant and frying oil. The smoke from the rubbish burning at Bellolampo stagnates over the city, like a great dense cloud ... The murdered, tied hand and foot like kids, throats cut, heads severed, gutted, closed in black rubbish bags, in car boots, are already over seventy since the beginning of the year ... Behind these cool walls of tufa the trash from the market and the local inhabitants is piled up, the bones from the butchers' shops. Dogs, cats, children are scavenging through it, rats dancing round it. This is the Palermo destroyed like Beirut by a war that's lasted over forty years, the war of mafia power against the poor ...

But Letizia Battaglia, the happy warrior, was on a mission, and I'd roused myself at six in the morning to follow her. By seven, still stunned despite a couple of double short blacks, I was rubbing my eyes by the newspaper kiosk at the corner of piazza San Domenico when the dusty little car screeched to a halt. Pietro, Letizia's driver and right hand man from city hall and my namesake, was a stocky Palermitan with a carefully short Sicilian moustache and some heavy links of gold chain glinting among the chest hairs. Like Letizia he smoked. With some difficulty I folded myself on to a tiny ledge behind their seats and we were off. She did this every morning.

It was the morning after I finally tracked her down to the little fortress-home she lived and worked in, standing on the corner of two inner-city alleys a few metres, it turned out after lengthy stalking, from my rabbit-warren hotel. *How did you get my number?* had been her first question when I called. I groped my way into a cavernous dim space and made out a sparrow-figure perched behind a desk, sharp eyes under a full and glossy practical fringe of hair. *So what do you want me to talk about?* was the question now, coming warily from behind a lengthily-exhaled cloud of blue smoke. About her life, if she didn't mind. *Lives*, she corrected. Her first life she thought she was ending when she married at sixteen to escape from the prison of her lower-middle-class family and a jealous, possessive father. But marriage was only a continuation, and after twenty years of it, though she'd raised three marvellous daughters, she still felt trapped. At the age of thirty-six she left her husband to make her own life, and this was the real new start. *I don't want anything from you*, she told him. *I'm just leaving. I'll earn my own keep*. And she did. She went to report for *L'Ora*, the time, the Palermo daily that was famous then for its stand against the mafia and mafia interests. *L'Ora* was now defunct. She didn't much like reporting, so she went to Milan and reinvented herself as a photographer. From the start she loved photography. Its strength and immediacy were harder to interfere with than words. She was mad in those days on Diane Arbus. Later she learnt a lot from another tough woman photographer, Mary Ellen Mark. Her life was never only photography, though.

Up north, she met Franco Zecchin in 1974, and brought him back to Palermo in 1975 and they set up as photographers, developing a hard, dark joint style of visual attack in which their work was barely distinguishable. This wasn't I-am-a-camera stuff. This was the camera as weapon, when weapons were hard to find. Neither was it war photography, the fly-by-night toughness of an observer booked on the next plane out. Apart from her two prentice years in Milan, Letizia Battaglia had lived in Palermo all her life. In the twenty years she wielded her camera, Palermo was being strangled, trampled, dismembered by the mafia. After ten years they gave her the Eugene Smith prize in New York, for social photography. In France and America she was famous, though in Italy no publisher had brought out a book of her work, nor ever would.

The Eugene Smith prize must have been a kind of peak, a challenge met, because after that photography had to take its place along with other initiatives. They all, of course, overlapped. If you were antimafia in Palermo in those years when the mafia ruled unchallenged, everything you did flowed into the same reservoir. *Everything related to the mafia*, Letizia said. *Making love, eating, shopping. You didn't go to places where mafia money was.* She got elected to Palermo city council as a green, where she fiercely opposed the demochristian mayor Leoluca Orlando. *Then we realized Orlando was all right. He was in opposition to his own party, a good man. We managed to get him out of the DC and we founded La Rete together, the network.* In 1986 she was one of the founders of a feminist publishing house in Palermo, La Luna, the moon.

Feminism too had a very particular slant to it in Palermo, confronting the grimly all-male Cosa Nostra. If the women of the mafia could break out of their subjugation, the monolith would crack, and it did. Letizia had worked as a photographer with Anna Puglisi and Umberto Santino, who ran the documentation centre in Palermo that was meticulously compiling and analyzing data on Cosa Nostra, its activities, its wealth, its investments, its politics, its culture. The centre was named after Giuseppe Impastato, a young far-leftist in the days when there was a far left, murdered by the mafia. He'd exposed the crimes of Cosa Nostra on a local radio station although he was himself the son of a Palermo mafioso. His fate was to be a paragraph of other news the day in 1978 when Aldo Moro was seized in Rome: Impastato's body was found by a railway line, blown up by explosives to make his death look like a terrorist accident. Now La Luna published the testimony gathered by Puglisi of women who were fighting their way out of the social prison of Cosa Nostra, and one of them was the mafia wife, Giuseppe Impastato's mother. Later, Letizia founded her own publishing house, Edizioni della Battaglia, printing finely crafted and somewhat cryptic pamphlets that mixed poetic text with photography. She gave me an armful of them as I left. Meanwhile, she'd been elected to the regional parliament in 1991 as a member of The Network.

She set up house opposite a brothel in the centre of Palermo, helping or hoping to repopulate the dying heart by the force of her example. Orlando's council now subsidized the costs of people who bought and improved places in the old centre, a stay against the decay and destruction of the mafia decades in city hall. Pippo and Anna Maria of the Sant'Andrea and their two sons and their cats had also given up their spacious building-speculator's flat in the suburbs to live in a miniscule eyrie, a fifth-floor walk-up with a tiny rooftop terrace, just by the university and looking out on a stupendous church dome. The strangely cavernous space in which I'd been talking to Letizia had once been a parking lot for street-vendors' carts in the ruins of a burnt-out eighteenth-century house. The ground floor was about to be turned into a pizzeria when she bought it. Now it was the publishing house. Next floor up was her home, and upstairs from that was her dark room and photography studio. It was so dark downstairs by the end of our talk I'd hardly been able to make her out. She'd been talking about making Palermo liveable, and mentioning her team of men, when I'd startled her by asking to join them next morning. She'd said I could, though.

WAIT TILL you meet my team, she'd said in the dark that late afternoon. *I've got a handpicked team of council workers. We go out at seven every morning. We go to the most degraded parts of the city. We clean up. Dogshit. Syringes. Everything. And we create green spaces. We civilize.* Letizia was no longer in charge of parks and gardens on the council, because her other, grander responsibilities as a member of Sicily's regional parliament didn't permit it. I wondered whether Sicilians still called their regional parliamentarians the ninety thieves. Letizia's first commitment still was the crumbling and degraded heart of her city and she couldn't help feeling that her successor was a little less au fait with the problems, a little less active in seeking their solution. *So they've given me*, she said, *my own intervention squad. Men who share my goals. I've got a truck, a car and driver and a team called Letizia Battaglia's Special Squad.* We were now twisting through some fairly unsavoury minor streets of the centre and abruptly emerged into an open space made by the meeting of several oddly-angled streets.

To call this space a piazza would have been grandiose. Nevertheless a part of it was taken up by low bushy trees planted around arrangements of rocks and gravel. It'd been fenced off by an arrangement of rustic sticks and loops of heavy chain, but these were now trampled in many places. A battered council truck was parked nearby, and standing around leaning on rakes, or sitting on the public bench, smoking or muttering or staring into space, all on the maturely corpulent side, most dressed in worker's blue overalls and few recently shaven, was Letizia's handpicked urban intervention team. None of them moved as the little white Fiat screeched to a halt, but when Letizia sprang out and cried *Breakfast! Coffee! Let's all go to the bar, boys!* the group without seeming to move gathered an almost imperceptible momentum that got it to the nearby bar slash pasticceria in no time at all.

The little park had been an initiative of Letizia's, a piece of consciousness-raising. A small girl had died of a parental beating in one of the nearby slum houses and the dusty gravelled grove had been made her memorial. There was a plaque with her name set into a stone. The plaque was now discoloured and barely legible, the grove dusty, rubbish-strewn, trampled. Letizia was determined to keep it up, not let the tide of squalor submerge it. While Pietro told me about the dead child, Letizia discussed what to do with members of her team. There was some grumbling. When one of the senior men in a cloth cap and half-unbuttoned overall started to protest, Letiza grabbed him and spun him gaily across the gravel in a waltz. A couple of teenage boys stopped their Vespas and stood straddling their scooters openmouthed and motionless in the roadway, watching the couple dance.

Suddenly the dance stopped. Agreement had been reached. Pietro and I were ordered back into the little white car and we shot off. Our next stop was the botanical garden. Two hundred years earlier, Goethe had thought it *the most amazing place in the world*. He'd been overcome by the exotic vegetation, and the play of light and colour and *the impression of that marvellous garden* made him think of Homer. Little this morning recalled Homer. Even Letizia's exuberance was briefly muted here by decrepitude, scrubbiness and sloth. She lacked clout here now. Once she'd had two thousand gardeners and was Orlando's head of *gardens and urban liveability* in Palermo. *We transformed the city*, she said of those days. Then we were off again, to a hospice for social outcasts run by a burly lay Franciscan who had a ruddy face, a big brown beard and laughing eyes. His eyes shone even brighter when Letizia harangued him. He wore a brown habit and a knit cap and we stood in the dusty sunlight as he and Letizia argued about what to do with a junkie with AIDS who was stealing from the others.

Then we rocketed around the back of the Capuchin graveyard to a neobrutalist primary school, a brand new building in a slum where Letizia knew the teachers. A truck had come the week before and dumped tons of gravel in a yard where plants could have grown. Letizia was furious and swore she'd make them cart it off again. Some minutes later, I was dumped amid the morning traffic outside the Teatro

Massimo. Letizia told me she now had to go to work. Her day was just starting. She'd spend a couple of hours on her publishing house, and then be off in mid-morning to one of her committees on the council or the regional parliament. On days when they were in session, she might stay in the chamber till five the next morning. When they weren't, she'd squeeze in some quality time with her daughters and five grandchildren. It was now barely past breakfast time. I'd have to wait if I wanted to see her photos.

LETIZIA'S PHOTOS, she'd told me, led her into politics. *We used to hold exhibitions in the piazza, in schools. Our horrible pictures stirred up anger and revulsion, they made people talk about what the mafia was doing to Palermo, made them want to resist.* Her own interest was less the violence of the men than the lives of women, children, the mad, forced to live with that violence. Politics, power, public life never drew her. *I was a photographer because I had to earn a crust and I used my pictures to fight the mafia. I mixed photos of children crying because their father had been killed with others of children crying because they were hungry. I never wanted to take photos of politicians.* A photojournalist, though, takes what work comes round. Thus it was that one afternoon in 1979, when she was working for *L'Ora*, the paper asked her to take Franco Zecchin's place and cover a political event. The event was also a celebration. Letizia remembered it later as an *apotheosis*. The prime minister, Giulio Andreotti, was coming to Palermo.

Giulio Andreotti was coming to speak at a rally before the election for the European parliament. The DC's candidate was Andreotti's man Salvo Lima. At a minute to seven on the evening of June the seventh, as the Italian national anthem sounded, Andreotti and Lima made a triumphal entrance side by side into the Nazionale cinema in central Palermo. On stage around Andreotti were the potentates of the Sicilian DC. There was Piersanti Mattarella, president of the Sicilian region. Mattarella would be shot six months later, as he left home to go to mass with his family, for wanting to end the DC's understanding with Cosa Nostra. There was Vito Ciancimino, the mayor. Ciancimino would be arrested and convicted as mafioso five years later. There was the secretary of the DC in Sicily, Rosario Nicoletti. He was to kill himself in 1984 after being accused of collusion with Cosa Nostra. There was the DC defence minister Ruffini, nephew of the cardinal primate of Sicily and elected with the votes of the friends. There was the Eurocandidate Lima himself. The made man Lima would be shot in 1992. And there was Nino Salvo, who at the time wasn't widely known outside Sicily. Salvo would be arrested as a mafioso with his cousin and partner Ignazio in 1984. Nino died of a brain tumour during the maxitrial. Ignazio was convicted and was shot in the streets of Palermo in 1992. Until their arrest, the Salvo cousins were mainly known as two of Italy's richest businessmen, and two of the most powerful figures in the Sicilian DC. The group Letizia caught clustered around Andreotti that evening, joined in euphoria, was the crème de la crème of DC power in Sicily at the end of the seventies.

The Salvo cousins took up a lot of *The True History of Italy*. For the Palermo chief prosecutor Gian Carlo Caselli and the magistrates working on the Andreotti case they were the link between Cosa Nostra and the DC. They were the intermediaries, said *The True History*, who'd transmitted to Cosa Nostra the *political desire* of Andreotti that the prefect of Palermo, general Dalla Chiesa, and the journalist Mino Pecorelli be murdered. The Salvos were much talked about in the offices of *L'Ora* when Letizia was around, though Letizia didn't know Nino Salvo when she saw him that evening. She was more interested in getting her shot of Andreotti and Ciancimino laughing and applauding side by side. Ciancimino was already, in 1979, notorious well beyond Palermo as a mafioso, and later, when he'd become the first-ever politician to be convicted as a mafioso, and suddenly nobody ever seemed to have known Vito Ciancimino, Letizia's was the photo people brought out to show that yes they had.

Two hours later that same evening, Letizia was at the monumental Hotel Zagarella, lately built by the Salvos at Santa Flavia near Bagheria, just outside Palermo. She was there to see Nino Salvo greet Andreotti as he arrived on the threshold *surrounded by three hundred members of parliament, senators, city councillors, unionists,* and she snapped the group as they entered together: Salvo, Ruffini, Mattarella, Andreotti, Lima, sleek, trim, pomaded, impeccably dressed. She snapped Andreotti again as he made his way through the fellow guests, eyes invisible behind the glinting lenses, an enigmatic smile still on his lips, and Nino Salvo pressed to his side like a double. The menu for the dinner Salvo's hotel turned on for Andreotti, as *L'Ora*'s report described it the next day, was clearly aspiring to the aristocratic magnificence of the ceremonial meals in *The Leopard*, but sounded more worthy of the monumentally vulgar dinner given by the *Satyricon*'s hugely rich former slave Trimalchio, though without the sexual byplay. Nino Salvo had a lot in common with his fictional Roman antecedent, the huge fortune made in little time, the vast estates in southern Italy. The hotel's director remembered Salvo first showing Andreotti proudly round his newest twelve-million-dollar jewel, paid for, it was later realized, with Italian government development money from the Fund for the Mezzogiorno. The director recalled him flinging open a door for Andreotti with a sweeping gesture. *And here*, he'd said, *is the banquet room for a thousand guests*. The guests on this occasion began with canapés of caviar and smoked salmon, and Russian salad. First course was baked pasticcio of anelletti and lasagne, followed by lobsters and king prawns. Then there were sucking pigs and wild boar, pheasant and milk-fed veal. There were huge fish grilled over charcoal. There were cakes of ricotta and whipped cream, profiteroles and finally a trolley of fresh fruits was wheeled around. A lot of it, and the wines too, would have come from the Salvos' own estates, just like Trimalchio's.

Letizia finished her work, went home and forgot about it all. It'd been just a dreary job and the photos were never even published. She didn't mind. She thought they were awful. Sixteen years later, toward the end of 1993, a squad of carabinieri descended on her studio and took away her archive of negatives. She never dreamt of Andreotti. When she was called in later for questioning, and saw her prints in the hands of Gioacchino Natoli, one of the Andreotti prosecutors, she said to herself *My god Letizia, they're horrendous*. The magistrate wanted to know why they'd never been published. It was probably because they were *so hideous*. And at the time there was nothing special about what they showed. She hadn't recognized Nino Salvo, but she remembered that day and the *climate of apotheosis* that had surrounded Andreotti on his visit to Palermo. To be standing next to him then you'd've had to be a major player. Her evidence was added to Vito Ciancimino's, and the Hotel Zagarella's director's, and the former minister Ruffini's memories of that day. All of them clearly recalled Salvo and Andreotti greeting each other like old friends, and conversing privately amid the crowd. The other witnesses were dead.

Why, then, did Andreotti continue to insist so stubbornly to the magistrates that he'd never known the Salvos, even from the papers, never had dealings of any kind with them, didn't recognize now, when he was asked in 1993, the face in the photo of the man at his side? The refusal to yield an inch on this crucial point, even at the cost of utter disbelief, when to everyone else it was obvious that he must've had dealings with the Salvos during his years in power, and when his most secret private telephone number had been found marked *Giulio* in a Salvo diary, this intransigence, this denial were signs perhaps that he knew like his prosecutors that this was the most dangerous point of all.

The Salvos were at the centre of the power structure, the point where mafia and politics met. The connection was at the heart of *The True History*, and Andreotti must have felt that to give an inch here would be to lose all. So Letizia's *ugly* images of Andreotti and Salvo together became maybe the most important evidence of all in the Palermo trial and she a crucial witness. After a while she got used to the idea. She'd never wanted to photograph politicians, but these prints too were a denunciation of Sicily under the mafia. It seemed a little feeble in the circumstances to insist, as Andreotti did, that he'd thought Salvo, whom he scrupulously called *the person* he'd spent so much time talking to that evening, was the hotel manager.

SAN DOMENICO is the saint to whom a great baroque church of 1640 is dedicated, one of the best known churches in Palermo, huge and splendid even swathed, as it was in the autumn of 1995, by restorers' scaffolding and green net. Coming and going from the Sant'Andrea in the evening, buying my papers there in the morning, looking out with a smoking espresso from a balcony of the rabbit-warren hotel almost opposite, I got to know the rhythms of life in the marble-paved piazza that framed the church, around the eighteenth-century monument to the Virgin on its raised stone base. I used to sit on the steps of the monument to call Australia on my cellular phone. On Sunday mornings there was a market there in old coins, photos and postcards and odds and ends. During the week north Africans sold household wares on the pavement, and at night the piazza became the beat of a group of robust transsexuals and transvestites.

They were a workaday lot, or a workanight lot, dressed without excessive fuss or elegance in a drab tailleur, or an old studded leather jacket thrown on over a very minimal miniskirt and dark stockings that left a substantial margin of depilated thigh exposed between stocking top and miniskirt hem. Stiletto heeled shoes or black and silver platforms in any case threw the lines of muscular calf and sturdy haunch into relief, and that very combination of stiletto-heeled shoe, dark stocking and well fleshed rump more than once reminded me of an endlessly repeated trope in the erotic art of Renato Guttuso. Particularly the later erotic art. The older he got, it seemed, the more often Guttuso returned to that feminine triad of high-heeled shoe, dark stocking, woman's bare rump.

Its acme was the maestro's huge and unfinished last canvas, *In the room the women come and go*, which was now covered in transparent plastic and propped up against a storeroom wall in the villa Cattolica at Bagheria. Guttuso had also and hardly coincidentally been a friend of the photographer Helmut Newton. Newton's special erotic motif, I recalled, was high-class furs and leather, high-heeled shoes, stockings and suspender belts and bare and opalescent female hindquarters, worked and reworked with the same intentness of gaze that Robert Mapplethorpe was later to direct at the African-American penis. *In the room the women come and go*, a work drained of ideology, narrative, symbolism, drama, meaning, was merely a group of female studies, clothed and unclothed, in movement and repose, and one of them was a direct pictorial quote from Helmut Newton. The compliment had been returned. I'd seen somewhere a dizzying interplay of influences, a photo by Newton of the countess Marzotto flanking a large canvas by Guttuso of herself painted nude, apart from a pair of stockings, and from the rear, in an attitude, approximately, of Islamic prayer.

It was thanks to Letizia that I got to see this painting. I'd mentioned to her my failed attempt to get into villa Cattolica and she'd offered to use some parliamentary clout to get us through those massive chained gates. She'd come out too. She'd never been. We'd made an appointment to drive out with Pietro one morning. But one of Letizia's daughters was about to give birth to her sixth grandchild, and as I waited by the newspaper kiosk Pietro drove up flustered in the little white car and explained that Letizia's daughter was in labour and Letizia was needed. We left another morning in a bigger car with a different driver and it started badly. Letizia seemed to have gone off the whole idea and was in a foul mood. The driver was a sullen young man who amplified, in the manner of all Italian functionaries, his boss's mood. It was his job to make sure you got the message and he swung the car around like a weapon, Letizia rigid beside him. *I can't understand*, she said suddenly, *why you're so interested in Guttuso. What is the point of this expedition we're making?* I told her I thought his life and more particularly his death were deeply emblematic of art and politics in postwar Italy. And was he any good as a painter?

This was received in silence. *How are we going to find this place?* Letizia said suddenly again. *Does anyone have any IDEA where we're going?* The driver clearly didn't and started muttering about Bagheria. I explained that it was quite easy, that I'd been there before. The villa Cattolica was on a bend in the secondary coast road as you drove into town. This was ignored by the two in the front seat. Letizia stared ahead and the driver went on babbling disconnected fragments of faulty information. *It's called the triangle of death*, Letizia said abruptly. *Because of all the killings. Bagheria's a vile place.* We were still stuck in the traffic of Palermo and I'd suddenly had enough. Fuck them. *I really appreciate your getting in touch with these people Letizia and offering to go out there but you've clearly got a lot on your mind and a busy day ahead of you and I think perhaps the simplest thing would be for me to go on my own without wasting your time any further–* I still had the unused bus ticket from my first attempt. I opened the car door into the traffic. *IT'S ALL RIGHT*, Letizia said sharply as the car accelerated abruptly. *THEY'RE EXPECTING ME.* She puffed up her feathers. *The director is EAGER to meet me.* We drove the rest of the way in silence. They conspired to ignore my directions and thus spent some time driving around the more hideous parts of modern Bagheria before stumbling on the villa.

Out of the city the sun was flashing off the sea and the leaves of the orange trees. As the director, who was a woman, came to greet us effusively, Letizia's mood suddenly changed. She became vital, passionate, enthusiastic, a devotee of the *real* Guttuso in his early expressionist years and graciously attentive to the details of the director's curriculum vitae. I was transformed into a distinguished critic and art historian from overseas. Every assistance was promised. Noting this change in my status and his boss's temper, the surly driver lost his frown. The local politician in charge of culture was also there, and after her brief display of enthusiasm for what could be seen of the paintings and what could be imagined of the renovated villa, Letizia went into a power huddle with him. The interior was indeed being altered and replastered, though not that day, and the gallery really was in disarray. The paintings were mostly stacked on the floor. I started going through them while Letizia networked in the other room. Then, in the radiance of her *bella figura*, she was off, the driver trotting at her heels. *The Vucciria* wasn't in the collection and I had to postpone satisfying that curiosity. Some of the early paintings were good. After looking at them I peered under its bubble plastic at the enormous *Women come and go*, leaning against a wall.

It was a huge unfinished canvas, over four metres by three, of eight female figures, and Guttuso was working on it up to the moment of his final isolation in 1986. Two of its figures are nude, one dressed, two more in body tights, a couple more in stockings with slips pulled up over their rumps and one in a fur coat and frilly garters. All are wearing vertiginously high stiletto heeled shoes. The faces of five are hidden by their hair, and of the other three, only the standing nude on the right has preliminary facial features sketched in. She's the clue, though,

209

to the others, who are all variants on the manifold splendours of Marta Marzotto's body. A telephone and a bottle of Johnny Walker Black Label were the only other details.

THE GIRLS of piazza San Domenico were hardly up to Helmut Newton fur, and in any case that wasn't their style. At the most a little black leather and even the leather was rigorously utilitarian. It was no joke spending hours in the dark, holding an umbrella in the autumn rain, your bottom resting on a street seller's sodden wooden bench. Transsexual dress and manner maintained, moreover, the rigorous public decorum of Sicily. Hair was well teased up and out, on the whole, not permed or lacquered but a little wild. A hint of wildness never went astray. Makeup tended to be emphatic and a trifle approximate, quickly touched up in poor light between clients I imagined, heavy pancake over traces of stubble and mouth strongly drawn in very dark red. The girls popped in most nights to the Sant'Andrea, nipping down the alley to the tiny ruined piazzetta, or coming straight from where they received their clients in the same old tenement. The kitchen staff always knew how business was doing from the footsteps on the stairs, and business was usually brisk. The girls'd say hello and have a glass of water or something and cast a quick eye over the diners. They were staking out their territory, just in case the Sant'Andrea started getting uppity and started getting ideas about quality. The girls refused to be confined to the nether world.

Sometimes they had a bite and a beer, confusing the tiny Tamil child who sold single roses for the ladies. Did they count or not? More often they came to share a cognac with the kitchen staff when the restaurant was finally empty. One night the girls were, frankly, a little stirred up. Enzuccia, who'd had the operation and was All Woman and all real, including the abundant breasts she made me palpate under her lightweight casual autumn lambswool, to show there was no silicone in them at all, had just come back with Flavia and Fiammetta from the mafia trial in Caltanisetta. She'd been to keep them company and provide a bit of moral support. Flavia and Fiammetta, nevertheless, felt so *ravaged* by their day in the witness box that they hardly knew whether they were up to a full night's work. Not having had the operation, the girls had been brutally presented in court as *homosexuals* under the legal names they'd long since shed, as if they *were* those distant strangers whose names they heard being called out in court, while their real womanly names were recited between inverted commas. So they were still feeling a little fragile and shivery that night after this rough handling, and it was to Enzuccia that I turned to get the story. Enzuccia not only hadn't had to undergo the rigours of cross-examination, but she had that extra self-assurance of knowing she was All Woman. It took more than one night at the Sant'Andrea to get the story from Enzuccia. Apart from the fact that a girl had to work for a living, and Enzuccia turned out to work to an industrial rhythm, she was actually a lot more interested in recounting the history of her coming to consciousness and her self realization as a woman. But I persisted and at last I got the story.

Flavia and Fiammetta had been giving evidence at the trial of the killers of Paolo Borsellino and the five members his police escort who'd died with him. The killing was ordered, like Falcone's, by Totò Riina. One of the accused in the via D'Amelio massacre was Enzo Scarantino, who was charged with having stolen the car that was packed with explosive and parked outside the apartment block. He'd become a pentito and was the principal prosecution witness. The defence had mounted an assault on Scarantino's credibility. He was a liar and an imposter, they said. There was no way Scarantino could have been involved in the attack because there was no way Scarantino could ever have become a man of honour. Scarantino, the defence said, was gay.

They mounted quite a barrage. His wife and the mother of his children was sent up to recite nervously that *she'd always been aware of these tendencies of her husband's*. Flavia and Fiammetta were basically there to confirm the story of Scarantino's relationship with Margot, accent on the second syllable, whose personal tragedy this trial had become. Enzuccia and Fiammetta and Flavia had all lived with Margot in the same tumbledown place handy to their work when they were young girls thirteen years earlier. Margot, who was now thirty-five, had accepted a lift from Scarantino in those days before her operation. *We lived together for nearly two years from that day on. I was in love with him but we never had a total sexual congress. I already felt I was a woman and he acted the man.* Enzuccia knew Margot, whose real name was Michela, pretty well. *She had a twin brother who also later had the operation. They came from a very good family and trained in classical ballet as children,* Enzuccia remembered.

Taking up with Margot, Scarantino had dumped another, who testified in male attire and was introduced in court as *Josephine the Raver*. Josephine told the court, *I loved him and it hurt when he left me for Margot, who later changed sex.* It ended badly for Margot too. *He betrayed me with another woman and he had a child by her.* Margot still saw Scarantino after his marriage, she said. She saw him during his military service in Taranto and later in Palermo too. *He didn't want me to prostitute myself and I never did. He always gave me money. His family were naturally opposed to our relationship and whenever I called Enzo's home they told me to get fucked.* After her operation, Margot headed north to make a new life. Enzuccia told me she lived in Pisa now. She married a *Tuscan small businessman* and everything was just dandy until she was called as a defence witness in the via D'Amelio trial. When her husband read in the papers about her relationship with Scarantino, he walked out on her. Margot had distributed photos of herself to the journalists covering the massacre trial. They were done like VOGUE covers, with the title across the top and Margot with her arms folded over her breasts, hair tumbling over one side of her face or streaming in the wind.

The defence was of course trying to muddy the waters. Everyone knew that in the Mezzogiorno a man who acts the man with a trany in no way compromises his virility. The defence was trying to drag in the red herring of the modern concept of the gay, of men who are sexually drawn to each other, in a region, indeed a country, where everyone knew that the true and only unmanning element was the female. The definitive unmanning was marriage. The cocky unmarried *picciotto* would be transformed almost overnight into a sedentary, overweight and faintly epicene husband and father. Marriage and motherhood were the apotheosis of the southern woman, and she was prepared to put up with a lot to attain it. This meant no fucking around on her part before the wedding and a certain formal submissiveness thereafter.

A husband's fleeting extramarital flings were ideally catered for by Enzuccia and her friends, to the extent that Italy's numerous *femminielle*, to use the Neapolitan name since Naples was the city that raised Italian transexualism to an art form, were unable to match the demand. All through the eighties, Brazilian transsexuals flooded into Italy and headed north to Milan to service the errant husbands of the boom years. A transsexual was less problematic, less challenging for an Italian husband to encounter than another real woman would've been and made the whole thing less like a betrayal of marriage and family. The Brazilians were still coming. Even to Palermo, I discovered one night over a very late drink in one of the few places open after midnight. One such young Brazilian was wearing what appeared to be a nineteen-fifties air hostess's uniform with the insignia removed. She was complaining about her asthma, and said she was flying to Switzerland the next day for treatment. I never saw her again, so maybe she did. Later that night Pippo introduced me to an elegant person named Giulia. Giulia asked me whether I wanted *to meet our mayor*, and seemed a little crestfallen to hear I already had. Pippo later told me Giulia was Orlando's press attaché, and I thought the appointment showed guts and gallantry on Orlando's part.

And now Enzuccia was telling me the story of her life. How she was the ninth of eleven children born just around the corner in the Vucciria. Seven boys and four girls and it wasn't clear where Enzuccia put herself. Her father had been a porter at the Grand Hotel et Des Palmes and her mother had done ironing there in the hotel laundry. There'd been conflict with her mother, though her brothers had been very understanding and lent her a lot of support in the early years. *You're just jealous of me, you cow!* Enza had yelled at her mother. *You're jealous of my youth, my looks, my freedom. I'm everything you wanted to be and never were!* Life at home was no idyll. Enza's story got a bit confused when she was recounting the times her brother, who was a junkie, had fought with their mother and smashed the place up and cut her and the police had come. Recollections merged. I wasn't sure if this was the same brother at different moments or different brothers in the different stories. Enza's first real step to freedom, the second and culminating one having been getting operated on and becoming All Woman, had been going out to work for the first time at the age of fourteen. Right there in the piazza San Domenico. It was a big step. After that she never looked back. *You'll never guess who my first customer was,* Enzuccia said, her eyes glowing fondly at the memory. *Who?* I said. *My brother,* she said.

By now Enza had put on a certain middle-aged embonpoint and as much as anything she liked playing with her little nieces when they came to visit her in her little flat, before she went off to give head of an evening. She had a faintly maternal air with Fulvia and Fiammetta too, though they were no chickens either. Yet they lacked Enzuccia's solid self assurance, which came perhaps from knowing she was a real woman. Flavia verged on the twitchy, and Fiammetta was given to wild though charming shrieks of laughter through her wildly but charmingly teased hair. Enza owned not only the flat she lived in but another four or five, dotted around Palermo. *You'll be able to retire soon,* I said. *Live off the rent.* Enza looked at me. *Retire?* she said. *I don't rent them anyhow. I just keep them.* I asked her, *You wouldn't rent one to me?* and got a very cool response. Not that we didn't get on. She reached down between her breasts and gave me her business card. *ENZUCCIA* was printed in big smudgy gothic, and in smaller letters underneath *for a touch of class.* In the bottom corner was her mobile phone number. *If you're ever at a loose end in the afternoon*, she said. *Feeling a bit down. Give us a call and come on over.* I slipped the card into my pocket and said I sure would. The hotel chambermaid gave me a dark look when she found it next day.

THE VIA D'Amelio trial exposed the puritanism of Cosa Nostra, which believed in traditional family values. *The only woman really important for a mafioso is and must be the mother of his sons. The others 'are all whores'*, observed Giovanni Falcone.

> If a man of honour happens to make the wrong marriage, too bad, because marriage isn't an essential thing in his life. If he's married the wrong woman, he can keep her. Just make sure he conforms to the key family values and sees that mother and children are respected and properly looked after. Otherwise he can do what he likes, discreetly.

The husband went out and refined heroin or collected money or confected bombs or carried messages and the wife stayed home and did the housework and brought up the children and had a hot meal waiting when father came home after a hard day's work killing people. She went to mass. Above all she kept her eyes and ears and mouth shut. In return, her husband did not conspicuously fuck around. At the upper levels marriage bonds had likely been joined for dynastic reasons, but in any case Cosa Nostra did not believe in divorce for unhappy couples. Only death did them part, though it did that often enough. Tommaso Buscetta's problem had been his intense and irregular sex life. However much Cosa Nostra had needed him in times of gravest crisis, Buscetta was still, from the organization's point of view, too passionate a man. He lacked discipline, control, they felt in the Cupola. The interesting thing about that judgement was that events fully vindicated it. It was a deeply emotional sense that the Corleonesi had betrayed a mafia ethic he passionately believed in that made Buscetta tell everything he knew to Giovanni Falcone. As well, of course, as the fact that Riina had had a dozen of Buscetta's near relatives killed in rapid succession, because they were Buscetta's near relatives. Buscetta was never a pentito, but, as he saw it, the spokesman for a mafia culture that had been annihilated by the barbarism of the Corleonesi.

The difficulty of being a mafia wife was summed up in the sad fate of Vincenzina Bagarella and the intertwined story of her brother Pino Marchese. She was the wife of Leoluca Bagarella, who was Riina's brother-in-law and, for the two years between Riina's arrest in 1993 and his own, the effective head of Cosa Nostra. Vincenzina Marchese was married to Bagarella in April 1992, in a quiet and tender moment a month after the assassination of Salvo Lima and a month before the massacre of Giovanni Falcone and his wife and three of his escort. The marriage was ill-viewed from the start by the women of Corleone because the bride was from Palermo, and from the bleak hill town of Corleone Palermo was seen as a seething pit of corruption. Bagarella's spinster sisters sat doing their embroidery in the Riina house and denouncing the bride as a *city whore*, in the words recorded by the carabinieri. Riina himself opposed the marriage on more concrete grounds. Vincenzina was from a Palermo family he'd used and destroyed. After the marriage Riina used to say Vincenzina's brother Pino Marchese was *in his heart*, which should have been a warning.

Pino had driven the getaway car in the bungled 1981 Christmas massacre in Bagheria and as a clumsy teenage *picciotto* had left his bloody fingerprints on it. They'd been identified by the professor of forensic medicine at Palermo university. The professor had rejected a suggestion that he modify his evidence and had to be killed. For Riina, Pino had in 1989 smashed in the skull of his own sleeping boss in the Ucciardone with a cast iron frying pan. When Riina then let him rot in jail, Pino became a pentito. He told the magistrates why Salvo Lima had been killed. Lima had been given *very strict orders to fix the maxitrial. They'd told him, 'stick to your promise or we'll kill you and your family'.*

Even Pino's love life had been destroyed by Cosa Nostra, which brought its family values to bear on a matter that didn't even involve him directly. The father of the girl Pino wanted to marry had divorced his wife to live with another woman, and this would have made Pino's marriage dishonourable. The stain could be removed if Pino killed her father before he married the girl, his brother-in-law Bagarella and his own brother said, adding that they'd do it themselves if he didn't. For Pino, *the only way ... was to break off the engagement with the girl I loved, pretending I no longer cared for her. This decision naturally was very painful and my relationship with my brother and with Bagarella were no longer the same.*

Viewed from the start with suspicion and hostility by her husband's family, Vincenzina must've been in an unbearable position when her brother turned less than six months into her marriage. Hidden from the world, trapped by their life of hiding inside an elegant city flat, silent, invisible, alone, hated as a traitor's sister, Vincenzina must've felt crushed. Riina's arrest and her husband's growing power would have intensified the pressures. And when Bagarella himself was seized in

1995, the police who burst into the apartment found a saucepan of tripe simmering on the stove, fifty designer shirts in Bagarella's wardrobe, Vincenzina's clothes and a bunch of fresh flowers in front of a photo of Vincenzina. But no Vincenzina. They found that Bagarella was wearing her wedding ring around his neck and in a jewel box in the flat they found a note scribbled on exercise paper. *All forgiven my dears, my husband deserves a statue of gold. Hugs and kisses for everyone. Luca, the fault's all mine, forgive me ... I didn't want ... kisses ... kisses ...* Vincenzina was dead, and this was her suicide note. She'd hanged herself in the flat, pentiti said later. They'd dressed and combed her body and walked it out of the apartment block into central Palermo, where it disappeared. The magistrates thought for a long time that Bagarella had killed her. Vincenzina had no choice. Such was family life in Cosa Nostra. From the look of a wedding-day photo, where she was pale, unhappy, puffy-eyed, she knew what she was getting into when she married the ambitious killer, always at Riina's shoulder, eager to take his place.

Giovanni Falcone and Paolo Borsellino felt for the travails of the pentiti they dealt with, respected mafia values and understood that turning against Cosa Nostra was not mere expediency. The men of honour had begun to turn in the eighties because the primitive and ferocious mafia ethic was breaking down. Ordinary life began to offer, even in Sicily, something more than the rewards of blind clan loyalty. The colossal wealth brought by the drug trade brought no improvement to the lives of those who risked their necks for it. The furtive enjoyment of a fast car or a gold Rolex or expensive clothes was cold comfort in a life of hiding, sexual misery, mistrust, the constant fear of betrayal and death. The old mafia reward hadn't been wealth but power. *Giving orders is better than fucking* was an often-heard mafia saying. Francesco Marino Mannoia told the magistrate Roberto Scarpinato, *A lot of people think you join Cosa Nostra for the money ... You know why I became a man of honour? Because before in Palermo I was Mr Nobody. Afterward, wherever I went people bowed their heads. No money could have got me that.* The choice, wrote the sociologist Renate Siebert, who came from the Frankfurt school, was now between eros and thanatos, the contrary impulses of love and death, and in the long self-explainings of such complex and intelligent pentiti as Buscetta and Antonio Calderone what struck you were the claims of feeling. It was one thing to be a member of Cosa Nostra, as only a man could, and another to be a woman who shared the deadly ethos and the anguish but not the limited autonomy of the man. Outside the mafia, women like Letizia Battaglia might repudiate the old subordinate roles they inherited. For a woman inside that world it was a lot harder.

It was Shobha who told me about Rita Atria. The morning I met Shobha she was sitting in the sun in the village of Scopello and the sun flashed off her dense long golden hair as it did off the sea in the bay of Castellammare below us. Shobha had a fat black leatherbound diary with thousands of names and addresses and telephone numbers in it. It had fallen in the sea at some point. Now it was dry again but most of the numbers were illegible. We made an appointment to meet in the bar Roney a few days later. The bar Roney was one of the key meeting places of Palermo, and a place to observe the interplay of senile aristocracy, mafia of the second level, the business level, and wannabes. Shobha, by weird chance, was one of Letizia's marvellous daughters, and she too turned out to be a photographer. She'd been in India, where she'd taken a Hindu name and the Hindu religion. She'd been in Cuba, and done reportage on Che Guevara's children and Fidel's rebel daughter. She'd caught rows and rows of Palermo aristocrats and pinned them up as photo butterflies. She did stories on the mafia and that was how she met Piera Aiello. People didn't normally meet Piera Aiello because she was in hiding, under witness protection. Piera Aiello was Rita Atria's sister-in-law.

THE ATRIAS were a mafia family from Partanna, where a war was going on between two clans. The father Vito had been killed in 1984. His son Nicola grew up and dealt in drugs and said he'd avenge his father's death. Nicola had a sister Rita, ten years younger, who adored him. He used to play with her when she was little and later, when their father had been killed and Nicola got involved in men's business and their mother forbade Rita to see him, they used to meet secretly in another town. Nicola had a girlfriend, Piera, whose family weren't mafia. She was a tough girl, though, and a tough woman later. *My name is Piera Aiello and my life can be soon told. At fourteen I got engaged, married at eighteen, I was a mother at twenty-one and a widow at twenty-three.* Piera was ten years older than Rita and remembered Nicola cuddling the little girl when she was six years old. Later Piera wanted to leave Nicola and his mafia life. *But I hadn't taken the honour of the Atrias into account. They forced me to marry him.* She was working, though, on getting Nicola to turn when he too was shot down in front of her, in the bar slash pizzeria she ran in town. *I loved Nicola, he was the father of my daughter ... my daughter mustn't ever be ashamed of being an Atria or of being Sicilian.* Piera

217

went to the magistrates. She was going to speak. *The women of the mafiosi always know everything. If they speak, it'll be the ruin of Cosa Nostra ... I was on the point of convincing Nicola to collaborate ... a woman can take her own man where she wants. Even if the man's a superboss.* A few months later, seventeen-year-old Rita decided to speak too. Together Rita and Piera Atria drew Paolo Borsellino a map of mafia power in Partanna.

For Rita's mother the choice was a tragedy. Having lost her husband and her son, she was now losing her daughter to the perfidious influence, she believed, of her daughter-in-law. She called them *infami*, took legal action against Borsellino's office for kidnapping Rita. In her desperation she threatened Rita with *what happened to her brother.* Piera and Rita were taken to a hiding place in Rome. *She was a young girl very attached to her mother, a mother who'd never accepted the choice she'd made,* Piera remembered. *There were angry telephone calls, furious rows that left her in a dreadful state.* But it was better than the terrible fear that had surrounded her in Partanna. Rita had kept a diary there.

> Four in the afternoon. When I was outside just now hanging out the washing I saw Claudio Cantalicio go by in his car. It isn't the first time I've seen him ... Claudio lowered his head but the other person moved over to get a look at me ... Better to be in a cage of hungry lions than face the Accardos' hatred. I can go off into the smallest hiding hole in the world and hide there for ever, but if they want to they'll find me there and kill me ... One in the morning and I can't sleep ... I'm terribly afraid ... this evening at about eleven thirty-five I heard someone knock at the door ... they went on knocking insistently ... It was Andrea d'Anna ... I know he always carries a gun ... This evening he wasn't drunk, he was able to do what they've ordered him to do, kill me and my mother ... I told my mother everything was OK, I invented some excuse to calm her down but I'm afraid tomorrow they'll kill me.

Piera Aiello's and Rita Atria's new life in Rome at first was almost fun, almost normal. They went sightseeing and dancing together and met other young people. But they had to keep changing house and their minders forbade them for security reasons to make lasting friendships. Rita was allowed to see a young seaman called Gabriele, but she herself was afraid. She wasn't afraid of Gabriele but of his family, and what would happen when his mother discovered who she really was. Paolo Borsellino was their one link with life back home. Borsellino had a peculiar gift of intimacy, of friendship, and he stayed close to Rita and Piera long after their usefulness was exhausted and didn't leave them. His sister remembered that

Paolo used to talk about Rita with his own daughters because he thought of her as one of them and because he wanted to get a better understanding of the psychology of such a young girl. He used to call her *a picciridda* [the little girl, in Sicilian] and she was like his own daughter ... he was deeply attached to her.

Borsellino used to tease Rita and she used to call him Uncle Paolo. Apart from Piera, he was all the family she now had. She used to think, in Rome, about becoming a woman. She puzzled about it in her diary.

> I'd be a woman if I were really a woman. What little thing is it that makes the difference between me and a woman? Maybe that I haven't yet tried the pleasures of the flesh? I didn't realize how important that was. If that's the only difference, then take me out in a public place and lay me out on a bed and only then you'll understand how old I am. I'm younger than you can know, but I'll give you such immense pleasures that your spirit will enjoy them more than you can ever dream. If there exists an adjective greater than that woman, well, that adjective will be mine.

She wrote this in 1992, in the last months of her life. On July 26, at the age of seventeen and a week after Paolo Borsellino and his escort were blown up in via D'Amelio, Rita threw herself from the balcony of her safe house in Rome. *There's no one left to protect me*, she wrote. She also wrote in her diary

> Before you fight the mafia you have to examine your own conscience and then, after you've defeated the mafia inside yourself, you can fight the mafia that exists among your friends, the mafia is us and our wrong way of behaving.

For a young girl who'd grown up in a mafia family in a mafia town, it was too much to ask of herself that terrible summer. There were no men at Rita's funeral in Partanna, apart from the local priest, and no relatives. *My mother must on no account come to my funeral or see me after my death*, she'd written. Her mother didn't want to come. She shut herself in her house as the little procession passed and pressed a pillow over her face. There were a few friends from school, a few teachers, a message of condolence from the magistrates of the district. Antimafia women came from Palermo, and they were the ones who carried Rita's light wood coffin. The old priest, sweating in the summer heat, gave a blessing outside but refused her a church funeral because as a suicide she was a sinner. He called her *a flower uprooted by a violent cyclone*, chose psalms with a heavy emphasis on sin and referred vaguely in his homily to human wickedness. A year later, when the corrupt industrialist and suicide Raoul Gardini was given a solemn funeral in Ravenna cathedral, Paolo Borsellino's family remembered this discrimination and recalled bitterly in a statement to the press that *the priest of her town refused her a funeral ... our grateful thought goes to Rita Atria, dead, like Paolo Borsellino, for love of truth and justice.*

Rita was buried, as she'd wished, away from her father and next to her brother. A photo was fixed to the stone and *TRUTH LIVES*, words chosen by Piera, engraved on it. On the Day of the Dead three months later Rita's mother came and smashed the headstone with a hammer and obliterated photo and words. *Nobody had the right to put that picture there. Rita should be somewhere else.* For months after Rita's death, her mother had been catatonic, spoon fed by nuns. She managed, in the end, by legal action, to get Rita's body moved to the family tomb. Piera Aiello never lost her nerve.

> Now and then I go back to Partanna, sure I do. I go to visit the cemetery and pray on Rita's tomb. I go with bodyguards, so people can see me, everyone sees me but no one can come near. They can only look and I walk with my head high, like a lady.

This was how Piera looked to one of the women of Partanna when she came back, and how she was remembered:

> In one of the cars Piera Aiello was sitting in the back seat, alone even though she was protected by a lot of bodyguards. She was subdued but smiling shyly, sad at times, not at all overcome, hidden behind her mirror shades. I saw an infinite loneliness in her, a lot more tragic than I ever imagined all those years ago, when we used to go and have a cold beer in the hot summer evenings at her bar at Montevago, the only one that stayed open late. She used to stand behind the bar, silent but uneasy, gentle but suspicious, overwhelmed by her husband's boisterousness ...

The woman had a message for Piera. *Remember, you're not alone.* One woman who'd been particularly angry about Rita's *sinner's burial* was Rosaria Schifani, and she said the same. *Rita a sinner? What sin? The sin of speaking out? ... we'll never leave a woman alone again.* Rosaria Schifani knew something about speaking out, and being left alone. She was twenty-three years old and two months earlier her husband Vito had been murdered with Giovanni Falcone and Francesca Morvillo and two colleagues in the massacre on the airport freeway at Capaci. There was a fine photo of her by Letizia, fragile and resolute, wide mouth, heavy-lidded eye, high cheek bone, half her face hidden in shadow. The photo reminded me of Antonello da Messina's great portrait of the *Annunziata* in the gallery at palazzo Abatellis. Both high-cheeked faces half in shadow, both staring directly at the viewer, the fingers of the Annunziata's right hand extended, softly commanding attention. But the gaze of both was at the same time somehow inward and unreachable.

The funeral for Falcone and his wife Francesca Morvillo and the three of his escort was held on a rainy day in May 1992 in the church of San Domenico. The horror of those deaths and the sense of a terrible loss, a betrayal by the state, charged the funeral with a peculiar intensity, which was screwed to its highest when Rosaria Schifano stood and spoke to the authorities of Italy who'd rushed south to render homage. People have never forgotten the moment the young widow of a Sicilian policeman, a delicate and implacable young woman in black, ordered the country's leaders *to their knees*. She spoke about her dead husband, more to herself than the mourners crowding the church. *He was so beautiful*, she said. *He had such beautiful legs*. She spoke some further words she'd prepared with a priest's help. In the emotion of the moment they came out loud and clear but in fragments.

My Vito Schifani
the state, the state
why are mafiosi still inside the state
I pardon you
but get down on your knees
but they don't want to change
they don't change
too much blood
there's no love here
there's no love here
there's no love here
there's no love here at all.

IX

FRIENDS

IF YOU head west along the coast from Palermo, past the airport of Punta Raisi and if you skirt the bay of Castellammare, that same wide bay Pasquale's mill looks down on, after cutting inland past a promontory that is now an untrafficked wildlife reserve, you see the ancient town of Erice. It stands almost hidden above you, high over the sea and the coastal flatlands, contained inside a perfect equilateral triangle at the top of a rocky citadel surrounded by trees. You can feel the temperature dropping in the minutes it takes to wind up the steep sides of the rock, to a place where Phoenicians, Greeks and Romans all maintained a temple to the goddess of fertility. She was Astarte, the whore of Babylon, then Aphrodite, Venus. What you find now is the medieval town, grey, intact, silent in its carlessness, and despite its fame and beauty, its difference and the stream of visitors, closed, stony, withdrawn like all Sicilian hilltop towns; dead and sinister too in this case, living off its past. And starting almost at the foot of this steep outcrop, and extending west along a curved tongue of land that tapers into the sea, is Trapani.

Trapani is as old as Erice, about three thousand years. Almost forever it was an entrepôt on the Mediterranean sea routes of the Phoenicians and those who followed them. It was part of that chain of toeholds the Phoenicians wedged into the coast of western Sicily. After the Romans destroyed the Carthaginian fleet and took the city in the third century BCE, it went into a long, slow decline. It was brought out of that decline by the Arabs, and the meandering alleyways of Trapani's old centre are a survival of the Islamic city the Arabs built in the early ninth century. To the city's industries of work in gold and coral the Arabs added maritime commerce, and Trapani continued to grow long after the Normans arrived in 1077. The Arabs also brought their cookery, and a thousand years later Saracen food is still strongly present in Trapani. The north African couscous is entrenched in Trapani though hardly known in Sicily outside the city. The steamed semolina, with vegetables cooked in the steaming broth, is usually eaten in north Africa with lamb or chicken, grilled separately or cooked in the broth, but Trapani *cuscussu* is made with fish.

Which was why, on another fine autumn Sunday when the Sant'Andrea was closed, Pippo and I were making the leisurely sweep down through Castellammare and Erice to Trapani. This time we were on a mission. We were coming to Trapani to borrow some couscous plates. At Scopello, down on a rocky inlet, we saw the remains of the *tonnara*, the tuna fishing station which had been busy from the beginning of the thirteenth century until a few years ago. The coast was dotted with these abandoned tuna works, which have suffered the decay of the Mediterranean and been replaced by Japanese factory ships working around the globe. For centuries the annual tuna kill in spring, the *mattanza*, had been a great Sicilian industry and a savage ritual. When the schools of great tuna entered the Mediterranean each spring to breed, as they swam eastward past the coast of Sicily they were met by groups of open fishing boats whose crews might've been resting on their oars for days, miles offshore, waiting to sight a school, waiting with their huge assemblage of nets, a series of floating corrals into which they would drive the big fish.

The marquis of Villabianca, who was rowed out four miles off Palermo to witness a *mattanza* on 26 May 1757, described the floating complex of nets as

> the walls, the columns and the beams that form an atrium of nets under the sea and what would be a marvellous palatial house on land ... This maritime house consists of four chambers. The first of these is called the Square Chamber, because of its square shape ... Through its door, which is the main entrance to the *tonnara*, the tuna enter, and they are happy to make their entry there, being unaware of the insidious art by which Man receives them in this ingenious edifice ... This chamber leads into the second, which they call the Small Chamber ... There follows the third chamber toward the east, whose entrance is called Clear, because it is made with a

long mesh, and then the fourth and last and final one called the Chamber of Death ... where the solemn festive sacrifice is made.

When the tuna are finally trapped in the Chamber of Death,

> ... the fishermen, who all do the killing in the livery of the owner of the *tonnara*, raise the nets of the said fatal chamber by means of pulleys to the surface of the water, then throw themselves like so many starving wolves on the fish that have been brought up and hurl sharp spears and harpoons at them and with these they massacre them and take their lives.

On a summer morning in the early seventies of this century, Dominique Fernandez saw the last-ever *mattanza* of a big *tonnara* on the furthest southern cape of Sicily. As the huge fish thrashed around in the bloody water, he noted that the harpoonists' faces were utterly impassive.

> No blood frenzy, no dance of death. Not even a shadow of anger, of vendetta against those tuna they had waited for for three days, slumped over their oars, under the pitiless sun that had ruined their skin and made even the straw of their hats transparent ... no sign of joy, of human enthusiasm on their faces, closed to every emotion by poverty and apathy.

Watching the last *mattanza* from the shore through a pair of binoculars and counting the fish was a Neapolitan prince. He'd always spent nine months of each year idle in Naples, coming south only for the *mattanza* off which he lived. Now he was extrapolating from the size of the last catch to learn how much longer he would be at leisure.

The memory of Sicily is in its names. The chief, the fisher foreman who chose the place and coordinated and ordered the *mattanza* of the tuna and swordfish, was always called in Sicily by his Arabic name. He was the *rais*, in Arabic the commander. The Palermo prosecutor Lo Forte described Riina's prolonged massacre of his rivals a *mattanza*. And the room in Palermo at piazza Sant'Erasmo where the mafia boss Filippo Marchese interrogated, tortured, strangled and dissolved his victims in acid was known as the Chamber of Death. The pentito who revealed this place of horrors was one of fourteen children of a fisherman who hadn't been able to feed them from the depleted seas of Sicily. Growing up into petty crime to survive, he had run foul of his local mafia. They gave him the choice of leaving Palermo, working for them, or death. He had to work in the Chamber of Death and row partly-dissolved body parts into Palermo harbour and drop them overboard in weighted plastic bags. Vincenzo Sinagra the fisherman's son never quite made it as a mafioso. He angered his boss because his face showed horror at the murders he witnessed. After his arrest, he learnt Italian through the old school books of Borsellino's children. He'd only spoken Sicilian before.

The Zingarello park was a speck on the map, but the survival of each of its palms and great carob trees and its fragrant Mediterranean *macchia*, its brilliant flowering of irises, narcissi and violets in spring, had been won by environmentalists some years earlier, after a long tussle in a region where building speculation was the ground on which mafia and politics sealed their pact. The Sicilian earth was made to be concreted over, if big money could be made doing it. There was no money in greenery. Pippo was very proud of these arid-looking slopes and he had a right to be.

After traipsing around in the chill air of Erice and peering down from the promontory, we rolled back down toward the sea and Trapani. We were heading for Angelo and Clara's. I knew very little about these two, only that they were friends and that in some way they were the inspiration behind Anna Maria's and Pippo's Sant'Andrea restaurant. Angelo and Clara had opened a restaurant in Trapani that served abundant portions of robust and strongly flavoured local cooking. The Trybynis became famous among knowledgeable eaters. Informed Palermitans would take a day driving down to Trapani, eating at the Trybynis and driving back again. *Their kind of food*, Anna Maria said, *people love it or they hate it. It's too overpowering for a lot of people. I love it*, she added. About the time the Trybynis achieved its singular renown, Angelo and Clara realized that a love of cooking and eating didn't necessarily translate into cooking day in and day out for large numbers of total strangers. They were people with diverse interests and complicated political and artistic pasts. They had a family of assorted children that each had brought from a previous relationship. Clara was a singer and Angelo had been heavily into far left politics and alternative jewellery and was now a primary producer. And as the Trybynis reached its brilliant zenith, they'd lost interest.

They'd closed down the restaurant in town and withdrawn to their farmhouse on the outskirts. There was an orchard and an olive grove attached to the farm and Angelo's main interest now was harvesting his olives and pressing them nearby. He produced a very fine, very high quality olive oil. He and Clara hadn't lost interest in cooking or eating, or even, quite, in sharing it with others. Really determined diners, who knew how to get in touch with them beforehand and trace a path to their farmhouse through the network of local roads, following the cryptic little handpainted markers Pippo now pointed out to me at certain crossroads, were allowed, strictly by prior arrangement and only ever in very small numbers, to come out and sit at a little table away from the family's and eat some of whatever Angelo and Clara had decided to cook for themselves and their kids and visiting relatives and friends.

As we drove up unannounced this first Sunday, though, I knew none of this. Angelo and Clara were just these friends who'd run some kind of restaurant and had a set of couscous bowls. Pippo needed the couscous bowls because Anna Maria and he were planning an Arab evening at the Sant'Andrea. Their idea of making a go of their own new restaurant in Palermo wasn't just business or even merely gastronomy. The Sant'Andrea was a cultural undertaking. The Sant'Andrea was to be an exercise in consciousness-raising. Clearly, no consciousnesses were going to be raised if the food didn't impress. The cuisine was intrinsic to the politics of the place. The Arab evening was going to be a set meal of maghrebin dishes and music. The cooking would be overseen by Nabil, on whom the honour of himself, his family, Tunisia, the maghreb, the Arab world and Islam itself would thus in some degree depend. Nabil was in a state. He'd been spending a lot of the day time in a long-distance telephonic huddle with his mother in a Tunisian fishing village, checking on details of her home cooking. One of the things to be served was a couscous and the Sant'Andrea had no couscous bowls. Fish couscous was a Trapani dish and a Trapani family dish at that, strictly home cooking. It wasn't something you were likely to find in restaurants, though you might at Angelo and Clara's. The roads were getting narrower and the buildings left behind when we swung down an unsealed lane and in through a gate in a high white wall. There was a yard with autumn leaves and a couple of cars and a tree and a snaking garden hose and a low whitewashed house. As the little car pulled up, a huge female polar bear loomed over it, or what looked like one. It was Lola the *maremmana*, a kind of Tuscan sheepdog, and she was followed by a skinny tan whippetlike dog swinging a tail like a scythe in a lopsided arc.

Pippo fended off Lola's tongue and struggled out of the Fiat. We'd been seen through the window and the door was now wrenched open by an outdoor-looking type in his forties. He had glasses and kinky golden hair pulled back into a rough pony tail and stubble on his chin. This was Angelo. Lola was excluded without acrimony after a short tussle and we squeezed inside. The front door led straight into a big smoky well-lit room as wide as the house. It had a tiled floor and a central passage leading down the back. An overpowering aroma of garlic came from down the passage and filled the space, stronger than any garlic I have smelt before or since, dizzying and mixed with herbs and cigarette smoke and slow-cooked wine. Half of the big room was filled by an immensely long table, maybe several pushed together. Sitting along it were a dozen or fifteen people of both sexes and aged between puberty and ninety. They had empty well-used-looking plates in front of them and the benign and slightly comatose look of people who'd eaten well. Then a cloud of steam billowed from a doorway in the passage, the odour of garlic and herbs swelled to new heights and a huge bowl of food entered the room. It was borne by a large-eyed woman also in her forties, with short brown hair, a rather narrow face and a wide mouth with a cigarette hanging from its lower lip. She looked amused and enigmatic. This was Clara.

A second huge bowl followed and then two great oven dishes were plonked at intervals along the board. There were some vague introductions and Pippo and I were inserted at the table. Wine was poured, new plates were brought. Nobody had any idea who I was or any foreknowledge of our coming but Pippo was a friend of theirs and I was a friend of Pippo's and it was eating time. I was starving but the others, whatever they'd eaten before, now gazed with appreciation but no hunger at the food. The huge china bowls contained strings of little Italian sausages of coarsely chopped pork meat set in an abundance of a dark greenish-grey sauteed leaf vegetable. *Friarielli!* I cried, though they weren't.

People ate *friarielli* only in Naples. They were the commonest Neapolitan green, a coarse weedy fibrous-stalked and slightly furry-leaved plant with yellow flowers that grew overnight and sold in bunches for next to nothing. They had to be eaten quickly, or leprous yellow patches appeared in the leaves with black spots at their centre. Most of the coarse stringy stalk had to be discarded. Friarielli must've been a humble relation of the vast broccoli family. *We feed this stuff to cattle up north*, said a Milanese friend who came to visit. *Friarielli*, which only have a name in Neapolitan, had a sharp distinctive sweetish bitterness none of the others shared. *Friarielli* were to other green leaf vegetables what the bitter dark green weed *rucchetta* is to any kind of salad lettuce, dark, unbland and deeply memorable. Ruchetta is known by Neapolitans from the shape of its narrow leaves as *little cunt*. Away from Naples, I missed this stuff as much as mozzarella made from buffalo milk. Neapolitans ate *friarielli*, sauteed with garlic and olive oil and chilli, and served rather dry, particularly with sausages like the ones now before us, but fine and pungent with any kind of beef or pork. In Apulia and other parts of the south they ate a lot of rape greens, the tender sauteed tips of the plant, as in *orecchiette con cime di rape*, which are Apulia's *little ears* of fresh pasta pressed into that shape by the thumb against the fingers. To one who knows and loves *friarielli*, rape is a sickly and insipid thing. At the market in Trani I asked if they ever had *friarielli. We got a box once*, they said, *but nobody liked them*. Only Neapolitans knew how, as Donne said, *to feed on that, which to disus'd tasts seemes tough*. It applied to more than food. So I was really asking for information from Clara, who had sat down next to me. She knew *friarielli*, which was impressive, and these weren't they. She did tell me what the greens were, a local name in Sicilian, but I immediately forgot.

There were enormous country chickens in the oven dishes. These had been done *alla cacciatora* with potatoes added, and were the main source of the garlic herb and wine aroma which still had my head reeling. It was a serve yourself situation and I reached for a modest portion of bird, only to find that these giant country fowls had been rough-hewn into pieces no single person could think of devouring. It seemed to be an entire articulated pterodactyl I was dragging on to my plate and that was the smallest piece I could see in the dish. I tried to push it back and set off a rockslide of fragrant potatoes. *You'll need a spoon for the juice*, people said helpfully. *How are you going to get the juice without a spoon?* Someone passed me an industrial-grade ladle and I got the juice. I was abashed by the setting, overcome by this mythic family board. Beside Angelo and Clara there was the mother of each. Angelo's was white-haired, frail and anxious, drifting out of range. Clara's was dark-haired and dynamic in a very smart grey silk dress with vertical cream stripes. She was smoking even more than Clara. There was a couple, one of whom was a sibling of either Angelo or Clara and there was a sister and her husband who was an engineer in Naples.

Then there was a cluster of breathtakingly beautiful adolescents who were variously Angelo's and Clara's and their siblings' and in-laws' and some of whom had frizzy crowns of pale gold hair and looked like Piero della Francesca's angels and whose sex I was unable to determine. I was far too flustered to remember anyone's name except Lola's. Every so often the room darkened and a huge face filled the front window and it was Lola on her hind legs looking in. Or she would knock on the door with her paw. Once the door burst open and Lola and her sidekick rushed in. A peach tree brushed its laden branch against a side window. Backlit by the afternoon sun, the kids' hair looked like golden aureoles. Smoke rose lazily from Clara's cigarette. Some of the visitors left. Then we snapped out of somnolence for ice cream. Jasmine ice-cream. *Trapani*, Clara told me with her ironical smile, *is the only place in the world where they make jasmine ice cream*. She told me how to make it too, but I can no longer remember how many jasmine flowers have to be soaked overnight in every litre of water. Jasmine ice cream was highly perfumed and *interesting* and we all laughed when we tasted it.

ICE CREAM is one of the delights of the Mezzogiorno, one of the triumphs of its culture, yet restaurants never offer it these days. I wondered whether the Trybynis had served ice cream, whether Trapani was an outpost of civilization in this respect, guardian of half a millenium's pleasure. It'd have made sense, since we were in Arab country and it was surely the Arabs who'd brought ices and sherberts to the south. That jasmine could only be Arabian. Such was my idle thought. The essential components of ice cream were ice and sugar, and sugar cane arrived in Sicily with the Arabs. The ice was always there, or rather snow, oddly, in that almost African island of mild short winters and scorching summers. Sciasca remembered it from his childhood before the war and before refrigeration in Racalmuto.

> You used to hear the cry, *Snow from Cammarata, snow from Cammarata* as soon as the June heat became suffocating. Cammarata is a mountain town, very high up, and the snow that was gathered there arrived in Racalmuto on carts between two layers of salt and straw. Salt and straw were used to insulate and preserve the snow. And at home too it was covered in straw to make it last longer. It was used to cool the wine and water and make granitas. A handful of snow was splashed with blackcurrant or gooseberry syrup, that kids particularly loved. You used to hold it in the hollow of your hand and swallow it quickly before it melted. At home there were even special bottles with an inside compartment you put the snow in, so you could drink cool wine at the height of summer. When the ice factory was built in the thirties, the kids missed the snow from Cammarata but they loved ... the blocks of ice sliding along the conveyor belt. And for a penny they gave you a bit of grated ice with syrup.

These were the simple pleasures of a poor town in the interior. In Palermo and Naples the snow from the volcano mountains, Etna and Vesuvius, was used to develop a variety of rich and subtle and exquisite pleasures. The tradition lasted unbroken. The Scimmia, the Monkey, in piazza Carità on via Toledo, where I used to go on Sunday evenings with the people of the Spanish quarters and Montesanto, had been making and selling ice creams for three hundred years. The camorra of the hinterland, apparently, got in early on the act and according to Addison the essayist, who visited in 1700, was running a protection racket on ice supplies in Naples. The same thing happened in Sicily. The Palermo council was making money out of snow sales not long after, and when the friends got a grip on the business in 1820, the Austrian troops, who happened to be occupying Sicily at the time, were ordered to Etna to *seize the snow* and told to shoot if challenged. Sicily was exporting snow and the trade was subject to piracy.

I discovered this from a posthumous work of Elizabeth David, which was published around the time I met Angelo and Clara. From being an amateur cook and writer, Elizabeth David had gone on, in the nearly forty years between the writing of *Italian Food*, and her death in 1992, to being a professional cook and a professional writer, and then an historian and cultural critic of food. Her two last books weren't of recipes at all, but a study of bread and the not quite completed *Harvest of the Cold Months*, published in 1995. David observed that

> The Sicilians, like the Neapolitans, had from the early days shown an extraordinary aptitude for the confection of ices. The people of the island as a whole had very quickly taken to eating ices in great profusion and wonderful variety. Along with sugar confectionary of all kinds, candied and fresh fruit, cakes and sweetmeats, the Sicilians devoured ices on every festive occasion. During his brief reign as King of Sicily (1713-20), Victor Amadeus of Savoy had made fun of the Palermo government as the 'ice cream parliament'. Eating ice-cream, he said, seemed to be the members' most noticeable occupation during sessions.

I'd always believed the Neapolitans invented ice cream. Sensuous, ephemeral, useless, exquisite, it was a quintessentially Neapolitan thing to invent. I hunted through Elizabeth David for an answer on the origins. She was cautious.

> That eventually Neapolitan ices, as also those of Sicily, were based on oriental sherberts can hardly be doubted. By implication, the assumption would be that sherberts came to Sicily and Naples by way of the Arabs and the Spanish. But did they? And if so, when?

David had found a scruffy little undated pamphlet printed in Naples, almost certainly in the seventeenth century, that included ice cream among its sherbert recipes, and she cited a report from the end of the seventeenth century that

> in the city of Naples a great quantity of sorbette is consumed, they
> are the consistency of sugar and snow and every Neapolitan, it
> would appear, is born knowing how they are made.

Since other letters and reports from the beginning of the century
implied that these were then unknown, ice cream in Naples seemed to
have grown out of a seventeenth-century trade in sherbert between the
Turkish empire and western Europe. The scruffy booklet gave recipes
for water-based and milk-based ice creams, and one of the flavours was
jasmine flowers. Trapani might be the last place on earth to make jasmine ice cream, but it wasn't the first. Other popular flavours in seventeenth-century Naples were apricots, muscatel grapes, strawberries,
bitter cherries, muscat pears, pistachios, chestnut and chocolate. Vanilla
had also arrived from Spain's colony Peru. About half of those flavours
were still going strong, with many new ones, at the Scimmia three centuries later. I found many of the same in Palermo, where people often
ate them between the halves of a sweet brioche.

I looked in vain through Elizabeth David's last work for a discussion
of *cassata*. *Cassata* had been gnawing at me, and I could've used some
authoritative views. The nearest I'd come to argument with Pippo had
been about *cassata* and not politics. Pippo described it as *of course* typically baroque. I knew what he was talking about, that concentrated
richness, that excess of the Spanish seventeenth century, in the packed
density of the candied fruit and the unbearable sweetness of the icing
over the ricotta. But after a long day of being told things, I reacted to
that *of course* and replied that to me it was clearly Saracen. Neither of us
was able to take the discussion forward, and it left me curious.

Cassata, and this was the start of the difficulty, was two things. For
many years I'd believed Sicilian cassata was only an ice cream. It was a
surprise to find in Sicily it was also a cake, and that the cake likely antedated the ice cream. Though they had things in common, the cake and
the icecream were different. What they had in common was the diced
candied fruit. The cake was a rich cream of ricotta and sugar with candied fruit and little pellets of chocolate in it, flavoured with vanilla and
a slosh of maraschino liqueur and held together by sponge cake under
a shell of hard green icing. The ice cream was rich white ice cream
made with masses of egg yolks and frozen around a filling of whipped
cream imbedded with diced candied fruit and chopped praline
almonds. In some vague sense the ice cream was a frozen equivalent of
the cake, but they weren't the same. The cassata question had always

absorbed me, and it was a disappointment to find Elizabeth David ignored this great ice cream in her work. It confirmed a sense born of reading *Italian Food* that she nursed a secret antipathy for Sicily and its food and maybe never went there or ate there at all. The ice cream cassata was surely eaten by houris in paradise, whereas the cake cassata for me was always claggily earthbound, so sweet it set your teeth on edge, soft, heavy, obscurely repellent, too much, baroque in all the worst ways. David might have looked at this because this contrast epitomized what made ice cream sublime, what coldness did to sweetness.

Etymologically cassata was a dilemma. In the fourteenth century Latin of central Italy cassata was *panis cum caseo commixtus, bread mixed with cheese*, which might become sponge cake, *pan di Spagna* in Italian, and creamy ricotta cheese. There were variants going back to the twelfth century, *casata* and *casiata* as a dish of cheese and eggs. This made sense but presented morphological problems in the Mezzogiorno. It also clashed with the theory that the name was Arabic in origin, from the word *qas'a* or *qas'at*, meaning a *big deep bowl*, which would be the one lined with pieces of spongecake to hold the ricotta cream. After the fleeting contretemps with Pippo, I was bound to prefer the Arabic.

RICOTTA WAS the central element in the other great Sicilian sweet, *cannoli*. There was no problem with origins here. *Canna* was cane, as in sugar cane and also the barrel of a gun. The mafia's *lupara a canna mozzata* was a sawn-off shotgun. The *cannolo* was a crisp pastry tube filled with a ricotta cream, looking like a larger version of the brandy snaps I remembered from children's parties in Toorak. The shell was made by wrapping the hot soft pastry around a broomstick. It hardened into a cylinder as it cooled. The raw pastry for cannoli shells was wrapped around metal tubes and fried into cylinders. The ricotta cream allowed all sorts of variants, but it too was usually studded with tiny pieces of candied fruit and little pellets of chocolate. The cream might be vanilla or chocolate or chocolate at one end of the tube and vanilla at the other. The late Waverley Root claimed that cannoli were very ancient, not just pre-Saracen but pre-Christian too. For Waverley Root cannoli were phallic and

> thought to antedate Saracen times and even Christian times. According to this theory, the shape of cannoli reproduces that of those mysterious prehistoric stone steles of magical or religious

import called menhirs, which were probably fertility symbols. In any case, cannoli seem to have been served originally at weddings; the guests who ate them were participating in a ceremony designed to insure fruitfulness to the new family. Later, cannoli became associated with Easter – a feast of rebirth – but nowadays, though the Easter association has not wholly disappeared, they are eaten all year round by persons most of whom are quite unconscious of the mystical past of this sweet.

Not quite all the year round, it seemed. When Stefania, the longhaired sociology student who worked at the Sant'Andrea, had brought me the first cannolo of autumn a little while earlier, I'd asked her whether she ever ate them in summer. *Oh yeah*, she replied without reflection. *They're not so good in the summer, but you can get them.* The seasonal nature of the cannolo had been at issue in a Sicilian court case I remembered from five or ten years earlier. A man was charged with raping a thirteen-year-old girl, in Palermo I seemed to recall. Maybe she'd been twelve, maybe fourteen. The man, in his early twenties, was the lover of the girl's mother and according to the prosecutors the mother was an accessory to the crime. The young girl had shown some bravery and enterprise in going to the carabinieri on her own to denounce the man.

In the girl's story, it had been a hot August evening and her mother had been sitting round eating and drinking with her lover and several other young men, also, perhaps, her lovers. I imagined one of those interiors that figured in Letizia's photographs of domestic violence and ruin. Eyes, at some point in the evening, began to be cast covetously at the barely pubescent daughter asleep or half-asleep or feigning sleep in the room. The mother then, according to her daughter, offered her child as a prize to that one of the men who could eat the most cannoli. The mother's own lover had won. Maybe the contest had been rigged. The girl was had on the spot. Various circumstances confirmed the girl's story and the mother's lover was jailed. He appealed the sentence, though, and the crux of the appeal when it was heard was that the girl's story couldn't be true. It didn't hold up. She'd said cannoli and the rape was supposed to have happened on a hot August night and everyone knew, the defence lawyer said triumphantly, that in Sicily cannoli were a winter sweet. The ricotta went off in the heat and anyway they were much too heavy. The judges agreed. They didn't disbelieve the girl, they said kindly, but she'd clearly been far too upset and confused to give reliable evidence. The mother's lover was acquitted.

If cannoli tenuously represented life and fertility in Sicily, the other sweets, of the Day of the Dead, were unmistakeable. It was a festive time in Palermo, a time of presents for the children, and the city streets were crowded till late with families milling around the stalls that were set up so that in places you couldn't move. Anna Maria had put little marzipan fruits that evening on each of the Sant'Andrea's tables. Sciascia had described the scene in *Open Doors*, one of his last stories.

mannikins of sugar and marzipan brightened the pastry shop windows ... the *things of the dead*, the mannikins and the marzipan fruit that the children hunt for round the house on the morning of the second of November ...

And Giovanni Falcone underlined what they meant.

The culture of death doesn't belong only to the mafia. All of Sicily is impregnated with it. The day of the dead is a great holiday with us. We offer sweets called heads of the dead, made of sugar hard as stone. Solitude, pessimism, death are the themes of our literature from Pirandello to Sciascia ...

ACROSS THE table Angelo was talking about his olive harvest. He talked about costs and labour and quantities and qualities and sales. He sounded like a man who wasn't used to employing workers and paying wages and keeping accounts and was rather enjoying it for that reason. He dwelt on the unexpected ways of his seasonal labourers. They all wanted to be paid in kind instead of money. They wanted oil from the press. It was so good that after supplying their own families they could sell it at a handsome profit. So did the German wholesaler he was selling his entire production to. Angelo's oil was so fine the German could mix it with a great deal of inferior oil and still market the blend as first grade cold pressed extra virgin olive oil. *The oil we produce has an acidity of point one per cent*, said Angelo. *Anything up to one per cent acidity still counts as extra virgin.* Ten times the acidity. The criteria weren't subtle. It seemed a pity to drown his production in a wash of lesser stuff.

A boutique oil, I yelled. The place was going to my head. *Get a fancy bottle and a distributor and you're in business.* Angelo glanced across for an instant. Business was not something he really wanted to be in. Playing farmers was altogether different. He'd inherited the farm a few years earlier. Before that, and before he met Clara and started the restaurant with her, a new start for each of them after a major breakup, his life had described a very Italian trajectory, for someone his age. Angelo talked about growing up in Salemi. Salemi was a hilltop town, inland from

Trapani but closely linked to it, in the strategic middle of western Sicily. It had a castle and was another of those very ancient settlements that was given its character and importance by the Arabs, as well as its name, Salem, *health and safety*. Later it was a refuge for the Jews driven out of Spain, and the site of a great Jesuit college. Salemi was strategically placed for the mafia too. It was the home town of the two cousins who became the most powerful men in postwar Sicily and two of the richest in Italy. I mentioned the Salvos.

God yes, Angelo said. *Town like that everyone knew everyone else. Played with their children when we were kids, went to their houses. Matter of fact*, he added indifferently, *Angela was my girlfriend. We had a little thing going there for a while when we were kids. Nothing really serious. We were hardly in our teens.*

Angela? I said. *Not the one who got married and—*

Right, said Angelo. He'd been looking at me obliquely, wondering whether I'd pick it up. *Nino's daughter. The wedding present. The silver tray.* I'd heard a few things about the Salvos. Now Angelo told me their story.

JUST AFTER the war, when the cousins Nino and Ignazio Salvo were young men, two members of a well-known local family, they were mentioned in a carabinieri report on the 1946 election campaign as mafiosi. Another report by the commander of carabinieri at Salemi in 1965 described each of the cousins as *a member of the mafia and son of a mafioso*. They were in fact the sons of mafia bosses. In 1971 colonel Dalla Chiesa, when he commanded the Palermo carabinieri, was asking questions about them. Others defended them and it was a number of years before anyone outside Salemi remembered the Salvos' origins and connections. To do so would've been dangerous, useless and rather tasteless. By the late seventies the Salvos had become, fairly discreetly, the most powerful people in Sicily and among the richest in Italy. For thirty years or so, the Salvos were on a roll.

When Rome had created the largely autonomous region of Sicily to dampen the separatist fires of the forties, the new regional assembly had to decide the question of tax collection. They discussed the matter for two years and in 1952 finally decided by a one-vote majority to perpetuate a curious tradition that went back to the Bourbon Kingdom of the Two Sicilies. They handed the job over to private tax collectors. The young Nino Salvo had married the daughter of a local tax collector and got into the new business. He formed a company called Satris with his cousin and in ten years it had tied up the tax collection agencies for almost all of Sicily. Instead of the normal three and a half per cent fee on money collected, the Satris monopoly got ten per cent. It also got permission to hand over the money collected after a delay of several months. The Salvos used these months, and the tax revenue of Sicily, the liquidity of a small state, to build their empire. By the age of thirty they were operating out of Palermo and hugely rich.

The Salvos became, on a huge scale, landowners, developers, hoteliers, winemakers. Angelo reproached me once for liking Torre Vecchia because it was a Salvo wine. At the same time the Salvos moved from controlling the Salemi town council to controlling the Trapani province DC. Challenges to their tax monopoly were regularly defeated in the regional assembly. The Salvos' power was inseparable from the DC's. The cousins were *one of the gravest factors of mafia interference in Trapani province, where they control the local DC*, reported the parliamentary antimafia commission in 1976. Not that this stopped them, or anything else. They kept a twenty-six metre yacht in Palermo harbour, mainly for having parties on. A frequent guest, I'd read in *The True History*, was Claudio Vitalone, the former minister now on trial with Andreotti for the Pecorelli murder. The *Alicia* was hung with paintings by Van Gogh and Matisse. Alicia had been the Roman name for Salemi.

Things started going wrong for the Salvos in the early eighties. They had the misfortune to come to the attention of Giovanni Falcone, who was just then being drawn into a concern with the mafia because that was where all the cases he was assigned led him. In May of 1982 they were stunned by the arrival of fifty inspectors from the financial police who searched their Palermo homes and their offices. Thirty cartons of documents were taken away. The Salvos thought the orders had come from Rome, and at the beginning of July Nino Salvo emerged from the shadows to issue a warning to the DC in Rome. He gave an interview to *L'Espresso*, Italy's influential weekly. *Can [the DC] allow the systematic persecution of those members of the business community that have always been closest to it?* In the first week of August the Italian government fell: it was a rapid and mysterious crisis, a kind of warning, and five days later an identical government was set back up. The Salvos and their empire remained intact, although Falcone had meanwhile made some interesting discoveries about business and politics in Sicily.

He'd discovered that the Hotel Zagarella the Salvos had built in the seventies on the outskirts of Palermo, which was invariably described in Italy as *pharaonic* and was that same hotel where Giulio Andreotti would arrive for the DC's friendship festival five years later, had cost fifteen million dollars to build, fifty or more in nineties money. Of the fifteen million, the Salvos had ponied up six hundred thousand, just over a thirtieth. The rest had been paid by the Italian government through the Cassa per il Mezzogiorno, the Italian government's southern development fund. Remembering a little wedding bash for eighteen hundred guests that a Sicilian parliamentarian had thrown at the Zagarella the year before, the colonel leading the police inspection checked the accounts. The prominent parliamentarian hadn't paid a lira. The Zagarella was popular not only with demochristian politicians. It was also a place for mafia weddings and mafia meetings. The Salvos' reprieve lasted only a couple of years. In July 1983 Rocco Chinnici and Giovanni Falcone signed an arrest warrent for Riina and the Cosa Nostra Cupola for the murder of general Dalla Chiesa. Three weeks later a car bomb blew Chinnici to pieces, and his driver and two bodyguards and the doorman of his apartment building. His wife saw the killing through the window. Falcone however continued to be interested in the Salvo cousins.

Tommaso Buscetta began to tell Falcone about the workings of Cosa Nostra in 1984. He remained carefully silent for nearly another decade about the politicians, but he said enough about the Salvos in 1984 for the cousins to be arrested finally and tried in the Palermo maxitrial. A big part of the indictment was a reconstruction of the Salvos' career. The Salvos and Vito Ciancimino were the only political figures among the four hundred and seventy-five mafiosi on trial, but the question of the *third level* of the mafia was raised openly and formally for the first time. The third level was the political level. Nino Salvo died of lung cancer just before the trial opened. Ignazio was convicted, and was under house arrest, still a very rich man, when Riina's killers shot him in September 1992.

WHEN ANGELA Salvo, Nino's daughter, got married in September 1976, she was twenty years old and she'd left the likes of her pubescent crush Angelo far, far behind. The formal reception was of a legendary magnificence even for the Salvos, and the guests were the richest and most powerful people in Sicily. The display of huge and costly wedding gifts filled four rooms. Salvo Lima gave the couple a big silver tureen. The most valued gift of all, whether or not it was the most costly, had a table to itself in the central room, and the wedding guests filed up with a certain reverence to admire a huge silver tray and the card expressing the best wishes of the prime minister Giulio Andreotti. A Palermo photographer who was hired to film and photograph the marriage and the reception filmed the wedding presents meticulously, but the bride's father when he later received the pictures also bought up all the negatives of everything filmed that day.

It was hardly surprizing then that the officer, later murdered, who arrested Nino Salvo in 1984 should have found under the letter G of the little address book in Salvo's pocket the name *Giulio* followed by the now foreign minister's most private and secret personal telephone number. The only surprise was the stubbornness with which Giulio Andreotti denied ever giving his secret number to Salvo and denied making Salvo's daughter a wedding present of a huge silver tray. These denials came in the context of a larger denial, that he'd ever met Nino Salvo or his cousin Ignazio Salvo. *I have never seen or known the cousins Ignazio and Antonino Salvo or anyone belonging to that family*. It was the same as when he'd been shown Letizia's photograph, the one showing himself with Nino Salvo and the DC potentates at the Salvos' Hotel Zagarella, when Andreotti identified everyone except *the person on the left, who your honours tell me is Nino Salvo; I do not recognize him and have never seen him ... He certainly wasn't sitting at* my *table*. He denied even having seen Salvo's photos in the papers at the time of his arrest in 1984. *Maybe these photographs were published only in the Sicilian papers*. At this point the prosecuting magistrates described Andreotti with some exasperation as *appearing to be one of the worst informed citizens in the history of Italy*. Neither had Andreotti seen, you supposed, Forattini's cruel cartoon in *La Repubblica* which showed him crucified on Golgotha between the two Salvo cousins.

One last time, Andreotti was asked how it was possible, when so many in his close political entourage had said they knew the Salvos, that *only he* hadn't known them at all. *It is not only possible*, Andreotti had replied. *It is so*. Andreotti's denials, concluded the investigating magistrates in *The True History*, were *incomprehensible and absurd, disproved not only by the most elementary logic, political and other, but by concrete evidence*. The only way of making sense of the stonewalling, they decided, was

the hypothesis, at this point more than legitimate, that Senator Andreotti was forced to deny this acquaintance because to admit it meant conceding the validity of the charge of *mafia-type association*, since the Salvos' status as men of honour has been recognized by verdicts pronounced in mafia trials.

While Clara took Pippo out to the kitchen to see the couscous bowls, the kids went outside with a basket to pick some fruit. There was a moment's alarm when Clara's mother went to give Lola some chicken bones. *I didn't know they'd hurt her,* she said without taking her cigarette from her mouth. We sipped our marsala. Angelo lit a cigarette. I was thinking a couple of things. One was, how foolish Andreotti sounded in his stubborn blanket denials. The other was, this man who said he knew so little of Sicily, that he found it foreign and hostile ground, was sounding awfully like a mafioso under interrogation. The mafia response to the law was always to deny everything. Deny totally. However false it sounds. Don't open a chink. Let the other do the work. Throw in a few stupid explanations to show your contempt for the questioner and the institutions he represents. Give nothing away. I'd have expected *the finest political mind in Europe* to articulate something a little more plausible.

Angelo shot two dragon blasts of smoke from his nostrils and reminded me of what was at stake for Andreotti. The charge that the Salvos had asked Cosa Nostra to kill Pecorelli because they in turn had been asked by Andreotti to get rid of him. The charge that it was in the surviving Salvo's house that Andreotti sealed his pact with Cosa Nostra's new chief Riina. The overarching thesis that the Salvos were the necessary link between the DC and Cosa Nostra, mediating between Andreotti and the bosses. So that when the pact was broken in 1992 by Andreotti's failure to deliver a supreme court acquittal in the maxitrial, the murders that year of Lima and Salvo were as close as Cosa Nostra could get to settling with Andreotti himself. For Andreotti, to admit any link at all with the Salvos might be the beginning of the end. Better deny the obvious than run this risk. The kids came in with some mandarins. Lola followed and nobody seemed to notice. The pungent smell of peeled mandarins cut through the stale smoke.

THE OPULENCE of Angela Salvo's wedding, whose photographic record had disappeared, foreshadowed the Salvos' obscene banquet for Andreotti at the Hotel Zagarella, whose opening moment Letizia Battaglia's photos had accidentally immortalized. The Salvos' habits of conspicuous consumption were further described in *The True History of Italy* by another witness revolted by their ostentation of power. This witness spoke severely of parties and outings that recalled *The Great*

Gatsby, Scott Fitzgerald's novel of the New York twenties, easy money, jazz and prohibited booze, as much as they did the high life of Rome under Nero, as represented in the *Satyricon* of Petronius. It made sense. The fabulously rich former gangster Gatsby was modelled by Fitzgerald on the fabulously rich former slave Trimalchio. Gatsby's gaudy story is told in the novel by his prim and uptight but fascinated young neighbour, and this was rather how the lawyer Alfonso Conte came across in the pages of *The True History*. He wasn't otherwise identified, and he sounded so disapproving in his evidence that I wondered how he'd ever come to be mixing socially with the Salvos in the first place. So prissy, indeed, that it took me a long time to remember that I'd known avvocato Alfonso Conte. I'd been to his house. I knew one or two things about him.

When I was struggling to keep afloat in Naples at the end of the seventies, I'd given private lessons in English, as few and as expensive as I could make them. I charged so shamelessly much that people imagined I must be rather good. For a brief golden time I was the most fashionable private English teacher in the city, fought over by women in mink, and thus made my entrance into the salons of *Napoli bene*. One day a message was delivered summoning me to the presence of a certain avv. Alfonso Conte. The doorman passed it on rather more ceremoniously than he usually treated my affairs and he was distressed by my fuck-you response to its imperiousness. *You haven't been to see the avvocato*, he said anxiously a day or so later. Another minion had been around and the doorman seemed to be in a cold sweat. I finally made my way up to a gorgeous home carved into the hill over the bay of Naples and took coffee over a very deep pile white carpet with the avvocato's blonde wife and teenage son. The son's English needed urgent attention over the approaching summer, and I was expected to cross the water several mornings a week, to where the avvocato's huge yacht would be anchored off Capri for the season, and give the son some injections of English before breakfast. Quite how the rest of my life would be moulded to this requirement was of little interest. *You could stay on Capri*, said the avvocato's wife vaguely. *Or you could go back to Naples*. Then the avvocato himself arrived, distinguished under wavy grey hair, in silk shirt and moccasins, like a slightly over-the-hill TV actor. The matter was clinched. By the time the summer heat descended I badly needed the money and even more I was curious. Reading in *L'Espresso* about some murky affair, I'd incidentally learnt of the avvocato Conte's rapid rise to immense wealth and his equally rapid rise inside the communist party. The stateroom of the yacht was said to be strewn with red silk cushions embroidered with little hammers and sickles in gold thread. Or to have been so strewn until the PCI expelled the avvocato for unworthiness. When I rang to finalize the summer details however, his wife had forgotten who I was. The son, his English, I persisted. *We sent him to England*, she said and hung up.

The Contes were busy people, I thought philosophically and passed a lean summer. They sure were. Many years later I read in the parliamentary antimafia commission's report of avvocato Conte's conviction for crimes relating to the Fabbrocini bank, owned by the camorra family of the same name, the bank whose Naples office had been bombed in my street. He'd later been in trouble again for fraud and other crimes, other banks, other camorra financial operations. And now *The True History* revealed that at the same time, in the late seventies, the Conte couple were leading an intense social life in Sicily, where they were mixing with the Salvo cousins and Andreotti's man Claudio Vitalone. Like his former political master, Vitalone in 1994 was denying ever having known the Salvos. One witness in *The True History* who remembered how often Vitalone had been seen aboard the Salvos' yacht burst out laughing when he heard this, and told the magistrates how Palermo society *fought with knives* for invitations to the Salvos' parties.

In particular Alfonso Conte offered the magistrates of *The True History* a memory of a very Gatsbian party in Palermo in the villa of his business partner, a party he thought maybe took place in the late summer of 1979, the summer I'd been meant to be fixing his son's English on the yacht at Capri. There were a hundred or so guests, and the Contes and many others were put up by their host in the Hotel Villa Igiea. Conte's partner had flown Vitalone and his wife from Rome for the party in a private jet, along with Salvo Lima. Other guests were the Salvo cousins and whoever was mayor of Palermo that year, and Aristide Gunnella, an already-notorious government minister later convicted as a mafioso. Conte emphasized to the magistrates that after this party he personally had broken with that social world because *I was particularly disgusted by the exessive display of wealth and power that one noticed on these convivial occasions*. Conte's sensibility was offended at this party by the sight of *the long avenue leading to the villa illuminated by various persons holding burning torches and dressed in traditional Sicilian costumes*. All through the dinner Conte noticed Vitalone deep in conversation with the Salvo cousins and with Salvo Lima. All evening Nino Salvo kept summoning this or that powerful figure to his side and going into a conversational huddle. At another moment Conte heard Lima and

Gunnella deciding together who to make the next mayor of Palermo. The next day some of the guests, including the Contes, the Vitalones and the Salvo cousins, were taken on a scenic tour of the beauties of Palermo in a motorcade of a dozen Mercedes Benz limos, before returning to lunch by the villa's swimming pool. *It was like the visit of a head of state.* After that the avvocato Conte had to go back to Naples, for work.

THEY'RE CRUDE people, Angelo said suddenly. *Brutal and primitive and petty. Outsiders forget this. When you live on the territory you never forget.* He told me how they'd burnt his house down a few years earlier. The house we were sitting in had only recently been rebuilt and repainted.

> *I had a very good gun dog, a bitch. She had a litter and this guy from Trapani wanted to buy a couple of the pups. I told him I was sorry, they were all bespoken. A while later the pups went missing, stolen. We knew who it was. In town one day Clara and I saw the guy in a bar. Clara bawled him out in front of a crowd of people. She can be terrible when she gets going, scathing, sarcastic. It was a burning humiliation for a man of honour.*

I could imagine how Clara might be when she got going with her low hoarse voice. A couple of weeks later their house was set on fire. Luckily they were out that night.

Angelo was still living in Salemi when an earthquake struck the Belice valley below Salemi in 1968. It was the earthquake that destroyed the palace of Lampedusa's childhood in Santa Margherita di Belice, the original of Donnafugata in *The Leopard*. It killed five hundred villagers and left ninety thousand homeless. The Italian government reacted to that emergency as it was to react twelve years later after the much bigger Irpinia earthquake near Naples. It showered money on the disaster zone. Paul Ginsborg describes what happened to the money in his *History of Contemporary Italy*.

> Nine years later, 60,000 people in the valley were still living in the Nissen huts which had been erected immediately after the earthquake. Huge and surreal infrastructures had been built in the valley – roads that led nowhere, flyovers used only by flocks of sheep, pedestrian walkways with no pedestrians ... not a single new house had been assigned by the authorities to any of the villagers. The money voted by Parliament had not been spent, or it had been misspent or simply embezzled.

243

At the prompting of a local priest, children of homeless families wrote in 1976 to parliamentarians, and Ginsborg reproduces a young girl's letter to *the veteran Christian Democrat leader* Andreotti. With his reply Andreotti sent the girl a doll.

Travelling anywhere through the interior of Sicily you recognized the landscape Ginsborg describes. The Belice earthquake locally intensified what's always gone on all over Sicily. Huge amounts of government money have always been channeled into private interests like the Hotel Zagarella and the development of Palermo, or into huge and pointless public works projects whose only real reason for existing was to provide contracts for companies owned by the friends. Sciascia's favourite instance was the usually deserted Messina-Catania freeway. There was plenty of money to spend. Its special status as an autonomous region let Sicily keep all the taxes the Salvos collected and guaranteed a generous flow of finance from Rome as part of the 1948 package. The government's Cassa per il Mezzogiorno chipped in huge sums of development money as well. What Angelo remembered was that the aftermath of the Belice earthquake was when the Salvo cousins made their spectacular leap into power, from being very rich and very influential tax collectors and businessmen into a super rich political power that attracted demochristian ministers from Rome to political rallies in Salemi. The flyovers for sheep were theirs.

Angelo himself got out. He went to study architecture in Palermo and later moved to the continent and enrolled in the university at Florence. He plunged into the swirling currents of student activism, the more and more extreme attempts to find an alternative to the DC's suffocating power and the PCI's cautious immobilism. He brushed with those groups that were passing into clandestinity and terrorist action. It all passed. The left failed and the demochristian regime was left to collapse years later on its own. Angelo never finished his degree. He made a living as an artisan, working and selling metal jewellery. After a long relationship he broke up with the mother of his daughter and returned to Sicily. Clara in Trapani had children from another relationship that had lately ended. Not long after they linked up they started the Trybynis together. Angelo's father died and he inherited the little farm.

The arson at the farmhouse had a sequel after the 1994 elections, Angelo said. The previous year Berlusconi swept to an ephemeral power as the head of the first new government after the collapse of the demochristian regime. *New*, of course, was a relative term in a society as old as Sicily, and there were old interests for the politicians to look after. There were interests the DC had looked after pretty well for half a century that now needed fresh political allies, fresh cover. It wasn't until after Angelo and I spoke that autumn Sunday in 1995 that the president of Palermo province, a man called Musotto, was arrested at dawn as a mafioso, but when it happened I was struck by the fact that he was a leading member in Sicily of Berlusconi's political group. And it wasn't until some months later that it clearly emerged that Giovanni Brusca, the boss who seemed to be Cosa Nostra's new *capo di tutti capi* after Riina's arrest in 1993 and Bagarella's in 1995, had been issuing instructions to the families to vote Berlusconi. You didn't need to know, however, given the evident strength of Berlusconi's people in Sicily. Even in 1996, when Berlusconi was soundly defeated by the moderate left group and Italy got its first really new government since the war, the Berlusconians won in Sicily. In 1996 Sicily was the only region in Italy where the Berlusconians did win.

But in 1994, in his hour of triumph, Berlusconi had suffered a tiny but stinging reverse in Trapani. The various forces of the left had been able to unite on a platform and a candidate and Angelo had been active in a campaign that was effective enough to win the election in Trapani, to everyone's surprise. The Berlusconians were greatly displeased. A friend of Angelo's who'd been foolish enough to approach the Berlusconi headquarters on election night was badly beaten. Shortly after that there was a fire in the Trybynis. A passerby saw smoke coming from the restaurant and gave the alarm in time. A week or so later there was another and more damaging blaze.

———

ANGELO WENT away after 1968, and while he was being a student in Palermo and Florence his home province of Trapani was flourishing. In the nineteen eighties the town of Trapani, with a population of eighty thousand, held in its banks forty per cent of Sicily's bank deposits. Trapani had a lot of banks. Six regional banks, twenty-eight provincial banks and two hundred-odd savings banks and finance companies were in Trapani. There'd been a magistrate in Trapani in the early eighties, one of only two, called Giangiacomo Ciaccio Montalto, who thought the money they held had to do with tons of heroin being shipped from Trapani to America. The mayor of Trapani, however, denied the existence of the mafia there and the sub-prefect protested against the criminalization of *this serious and hardworking city*. In late 1982 Ciaccio Montalto had traced heroin shipments from

Trapani to Montreal via Paris worth a third of a billion dollars. He was working closely with a magistrate in northern Italy, Carlo Palermo, who was following the international traffic in drugs and arms from another angle. In January 1983, five months after the murder of Dalla Chiesa in Palermo, Ciaccio Montalto was shot outside his house at night. *He had the feeling a vacuum was being created around him*, said his wife. He'd also had the feeling his only colleague was working for the mafia.

In the northern investigation, Carlo Palermo had made some very embarrassing discoveries about the financing of prime minister Craxi's socialist party but was blocked by parliament from continuing. Craxi had lately voted against forcing Andreotti's resignation over the Sindona business, and now Andreotti's people had voted to save Craxi. Carlo Palermo then got a transfer to Trapani to take the place of the murdered Ciaccio Montalto, a job for which there was little competition. In April 1985 Palermo's car was blown up by a huge bomb, but he wasn't killed because a passing car took the force of the blast and those killed were a mother and her six-year-old twin children. A few days after the attempt on Palermo's life, the police officer Saverio Montalbano discovered the largest heroin refinery in Europe near Alcamo in Trapani province. It'd only been in operation two months. It was a joint venture of Totò Riina and Bernardo Brusca, father of Giovanni, and they were ropable, in a pentito's later testimony. Montalbano also made some interesting discoveries about Trapani's political-criminal masonic network and was in general so effective that he was charged with *improper use of a public vehicle*, demoted and transferred. A protesting judge wrote that *one couldn't help maintaining there was outside interest in getting rid of such a formidable investigator*.

In 1988 judge Alberto Giacomelli was murdered in Trapani. Two weeks later the activist Mauro Rostagno, who'd started a drug rehabilitation community in Trapani and broadcast against the mafia on a local TV channel, was murdered. In 1989 the Trapani judge Costa was arrested. He was the colleague whom Ciaccio Montalto had unwisely realized, a week before being murdered, was working with the mafia. Judge Costa's house was full of weaponry and cash. To the passing visitor, Trapani seemed an utterly sleepy silent place, with its low white houses in the blinding sun and the wide straight road that ran down to the promontory and ended at the blinding sea.

CLARA WAS curious at the thought I might be going to write something. It was doubtful, I said. How could you make Sicily intelligible? Even just to explain what was going on with the mafia and the politicians— *At least you're not an American,* Clara said thoughtfully, more to herself than me. She dragged on her cigarette. *We've already had an American. Couple of years ago. Don't talk to me about Americans.* Clara went on,

> *This American woman turned up in Trapani. An Italo-American woman. Her ancestors emigrated from somewhere round Trapani and she was looking for her roots. Like, digging up her past. The world she never knew and stuff. She'd got some letter of introduction to a friend of mine, and since I've got a certain interest in the local history and culture she was handed on to me.*
>
> *Turned out we were in the same boat. Both single mothers bringing up kids on our own. At the time that was the case. Or had recently been. A kind of fellow feeling grew up between us, sharing experiences and problems. Women alone. She hung round and we talked. She liked the restaurant a lot. She spent more time here than she planned and more than I expected too but finally she moved on to other parts of Sicily. She was writing kind of like a travel book. She finally went back to America and a year or so later a copy of this book arrived in the mail. We couldn't read it at all. The whole thing was in English. But we could see there was a whole lot about us, much more than we were led to expect. A whole chapter for instance called Clara's Restaurant.*

Clara gave a slight shudder and ground out her cigarette. She looked at me grimly.

> *Apparently it was quite a success. Ten days ago I got a phone call from a travel agent in Palermo. He had a coachload of American ladies and they all wanted to come and eat at Clara's Restaurant. I told him it was closed and he said they were coming anyway. They wanted to see me. So this mob of American women in polyester trousers arrived in a great coach and I had to give them lunch. They followed me around. They wanted to see everything that was in the book. They all wanted to TOUCH me. And there's more of them coming next summer.*

She poured us each a little more marsala and relaxed. *So that's what Americans are like. They're so ... You wouldn't be writing anything like that, after all.* She looked at me.

Of course not, I said. *I'm trying to make sense of the Andreotti trial. All quite rebarbative.*

So what's your problem? said Clara. *Have some marsala. Have a mandarin.*

X

A LOVER DENIED

MARTA MARZOTTO was still one of the best known women in Italy but she took time to track down nevertheless in the autumn of 1995. She was always on the move. Rome, Venice, Cortina. France, Africa, America. She'd even been to Australia. And when she was in Milan you had to be careful. *Don't ring too early for the love of God*, her scared-sounding manservant said urgently when I did get through to her house. *She gets angry.* When we did finally get to speak long distance, the countess wasn't angry at all but she was very impatient. *Make it snappy, whatever you want*, she said. *I'm off to a funeral in three minutes. One of my earliest lovers.*

I'm sorry, I said. *Really sorry to hear that.*

Darling of course we'll have lunch together, the countess then crooned. I hesitated.

Perhaps ... I said.

What? Well TELL THEM to send a car for you, the countess snapped loudly. *It's absurd.*

Tonal shifts suggested I wasn't the only person she was speaking to. I hoped I was picking up the right bits. I offered to ring later, after the funeral. *No no no*, she said. *Come right on up to Milan. Only not today because there's the funeral and not tomorrow because I've got my fashion showing and before the weekend because then I'm off to Venice. Whenever you like. And we'll have a NICE LONG CHAT.* Then she added peremptorily in another register, *Put it down over there.* So I got on a plane in Palermo and we took off past the stony treacherous peaks of Punta Raisi and climbed steeply over the cobalt sea. A couple of hours later I was puttering sedately toward the centre of Milan through a placid and leafy suburb with curved tram tracks running down the empty road. I'd never done such a thing before, flown from one end of Italy to the other, and no amount of foreknowledge could have muffled the jolt. The crowds and the clarity and the drama and the ruins of the south were gone. When I got near the centre of Milan, I saw a wasteland of abandoned public works begun by the vanished socialists. One of the holes was probably where the fountain had been, the beautiful old fountain dismantled and trucked off for restoration work when prime minister Craxi's brother-in-law was mayor of Milan. It'd lately been sighted, apparently, restored and reconstructed in the garden of the exiled Craxi's Tunisian villa. The countess was at home and in the middle of a telephone conversation.

Dreadful, said the countess, shaking her head over something she'd just heard on the phone. *Too too awful*. She put down the receiver and tucked her bare feet up on to the sofa, under her green silk peignoir. She looked at me. *They want me back you know*, she said. *Oh yes. They miss me badly and they'd give anything to have me back. But I'll never return. Never. Ever*. I'd been surprised to find her now living in Milan, and had wondered why she had left Rome, and why she seemed to be casting anathemas on the capital. *When your HUSBAND betrays you*, she intoned solemnly, *you EXPECT that. You accept it. That's normal, that's life*. She paused. *But when your LOVER cheats on you, no, no, that's too much. The humiliation, the pain— No. There can be no going back*. That shut me up. I was expected to know and I'd no idea who the lover was she was talking about. I'd no idea even how things stood with the count Umberto, though I presumed they were separated. I thought they separated after the Guttuso drama. I nodded slowly.

Marta Marzotto en déshabillé was a very handsome woman. She needed no cosmetic arts. She had silvery blonde hair and a strong, open nordic face. She was instantly recognizable from the hundreds of paintings and thousands of sketches, the tens of thousands of photographs. I couldn't believe it when I heard later she was sixty-five. *He hasn't got a penny*, said the countess, reverting to an earlier conversation. She had a touch telephone with a line in one hand and a cellular in the other and was stabbing out a number with her fingernail. *And now he's not even getting money from the TV. It's terrible. They've dumped him from the show*. I wasn't quite sure where this was going or why I was being told about it. The countess had a way of flying several different conversational kites at once, even when you were the only person she was talking to. Sometimes their lines got tangled. Maybe she wasn't talking to me. *Nonsense*, cried the countess, jabbing at the buttons on her touch phone with a nail of the hand that wasn't holding her cellular. *That show aims to shock. It's a freak show. A court of miracles. I've been a guest myself. It's meant to be unpleasant. So why can't they have a guest with AIDS?* Calls were coming in on the two phones as fast as they were going out. She called her lawyers to get some documents Guttuso had left, documents she said would show me his real state of mind toward the end. Then a friend rang. She and Marta had been out together the night before.

—*Well, you know darling at OUR AGE*— The other phone rang. The countess listened for a minute. *Well send me the copy.* Lawyers were quick in Milan, I thought. *Ivory Coast, mmm. And he's got a driver's licence? And how's her cooking? And they're absolutely trustworthy? I MEAN darling that I've got THINGS at home ...* She'd been saying *coppia*, not *copia*, couple not *copy*. It was a servant problem. Then she got down to setting the record straight.

———————

THE PALAZZO del Grillo in Rome stands next to a thirteenth-century tower of the same name, not far from the Colosseum, by the site of the imperial forum. It's an opulently decorated rococò building of the eighteenth century, with a splendid main staircase, and has its own internal garden with a fountain and statues of nymphs. In 1964 a chunk of it was for sale, and by 1964, the time of *La Dolce Vita* and the height of the first Italian boom, Renato Guttuso was the most sought-after painter in Italy. As speculators' blocks spread like a cancer over Italy, he reminded its occupants of the poor and passionate world they had lost. And he looked around for something gracious for himself. For the first time ever he had real money to spend and he was looking for a better house. Through his communist party connections he'd got to know a powerful financier who was then head of the Banca Commerciale Italiana. From him Guttuso learnt of two apartments for sale in the palazzo del Grillo, and through him he got a loan to buy the vast and luxurious new studio and home. It helped that the seller was a friend of his wife, Mimise Dotti. She was a wealthy northern Italian woman, extraordinarily beautiful when Guttuso first met her in 1937, when she was still married to a count with Vatican ties.

The first floor apartment became the huge and opulent studio, from which by lift or a spiral staircase you ascended to the living quarters on the second floor. The first floor studio soon became also a salon for the beautiful people and the powerful people. The second floor was strictly private. You reached the studio though an upper courtyard and a terrace garden. In 1980 Guttuso painted an oil of this garden that he called *The Evening Visit*. He said his idea was *a picture of a visit to my studio at dusk. I was unable to bring the visitor into focus, until I had ... a vision: a tiger.* He added that *looking back, the tiger soon became something more, a visitor who comes bringing me her beauty but ... also her ferocity.* It seemed an invitation to identify in the tiger a beautiful and ferocious woman who by the time of this painting had been visiting Guttuso in his studio for a decade, Marta Vacondio, the countess Marzotto.

La Marzotto is unmistakeable in the images of Guttuso's prolific last twenty years. Hundreds of them. Clothed, nude and partly clad, often only in stockings and suspender belt. Wearing net stockings. Awake, asleep and half awake, in movement and repose. Sitting, standing, lying and on all fours, seen from in front, behind, above, and much more often below, culminating in the vast unfinished canvas of multiple images, dominated by a huge-haunched yet wolflike standing nude Marta in very high heels, that lay wrapped in bubble plastic and stacked against a wall in the villa Cattolica.

At some moments in life you need somebody to shake you up, Guttuso said years after he met Marta, *and it happened to me when I was getting on for sixty ... I like women who are erotically mature, erotically open and without taboos. I don't like really young women.* Although Marta Marzotto was knocking forty when she first arrived as the evening tiger, and had five children, she was still twenty years younger than the maestro, while Mimise was seven years older. The countess had started life in northern Italy as a railway labourer's daughter. In the hard days of the war her father rounded out his labourer's wage by delivering coal in winter with a handcart. Little Marta used to do the rounds with him, perched on top of the coal sacks. *That way you can see the world from high up,* her father said. She used to hunt for frogs in the ditches and sell them for food, frogs being a popular dish in the Po valley. Her mother worked in one of the factories of the Marzotto textile empire, and also in the ricefields in the season, and when Marta was eleven she helped in the ricefields too. When she was fifteen she started getting up at four in the morning and going to town by train to work as a dressmaker's apprentice, coming home after dark to the railway shack where she and her brother and her parents all slept in the same room. *Like something out of Dickens,* she said years later. *But that was Italy and that was me.* She was a tall skinny blonde with a freckled face and fabulous long legs, and when a model was sick one day Marta took her place. She was an immediate success, never looked back. In 1954 she married Umberto, count Marzotto, and entered Italy's biggest textile dynasty, and for the next thirteen years, until the birth of her fifth child and the fateful meeting with Guttuso, she was a wife and mother and a great cook in the rich sleek Italy of the provinces.

When Guttuso first met her in Milan at a friend's house in 1967, Marta Marzotto was pregnant with her fifth child and admiring one of his paintings. She wasn't yet Rome's leading society hostess and fun person. Her intellectual slash artistic salon on the piazza di Spagna started by chance four years later. By then Marta was ceaselessly busy on the beautiful people scene. The guest list of the famous at her legendary evenings was endless. There were Francesco Rosi and Lina Wertmüller, the film directors, Moravia the writer, Pasolini who was both, Andy Warhol who was everything, and the architect and Venice biennale director Paolo Portoghesi, with his trademark black beaver hat. Rival hostesses and students of the salon as an art form said Marta's was too mixed, too inclusive, too much fun to qualify as great. *What do you mean, salon*, she replied, *they're just friends.* Later in the seventies politicians started coming, people like Giulio Andreotti, and industrialists like Agnelli of Fiat and De Benedetti of Olivetti. Maybe it was the arrival of the suits that made her suddenly tire of the whole thing after a decade. She sold up and moved to a grander house nearby and her life entered a more formal mode. Meanwhile Guttuso's wife Mimise's health was failing by the seventies, and she knew about Renato and Marta. Mimise was thinking of suicide.

The palazzo del Grillo had split by then into two separate realms. Mimise Dotti never left the second floor and Marta Marzotto never went above the first. Guttuso's secretary carefully eliminated all mention of Marta Marzotto from the newspapers, letters, invitations and photographs that reached Mimise on the second floor, and the domestic staff were trained to filter out all news of the countess. This divided world of the adored and failing wife on the second floor and the carnal, worldly mistress on the first was further split by Guttuso's division of the visitors to the lower realm into the Sunday friends and the others. The prelates, the politicians and the intellectuals, the power figures who would surround him at the end, all came to visit on Sundays. Sundays were for serious conversation and exalted networking. The working-day friends who came in the afternoon to play cards and gossip and drink whisky and bring women and girl friends, these came every other day. The household ran on duplicity like this for a decade and a half. The countess became Guttuso's muse and model as well as his lover. He still, though, loved his aging wife on the second floor. And Marta Marzotto meanwhile continued her ceaseless social round as *stakhanovist of high society* and an influential hostess. Italians have invented a word for the kind of person the countess consummately was, and still is, *presenzialista*. Marta Marzotto was present at every opening, at every party, every festival. She was on every chat show and in the pages of every newspaper, of every glossy. She's published her memoirs and a book called *The Success of Excess*. Even now, in her sixties, she's tirelessly there, and endlessly reported.

The one major crisis of jealousy was the time of Marta's affair in 1977 and 1978 with the modish far-left party leader Lucio Magri. Since Magri had left the PCI and later rejoined, the affair also had a political dimension that particularly gnawed at Guttuso. The jealous painter did a striking series of big *Allegories* on the countess's very public betrayal in 1979, in which the countess is always nude and Guttuso's rival always has a monkey's head. In one of them the couple is shown embracing naked on the Roman rooftops among rats and owls, their genitals thrust toward the viewer. Below, an older naked male hides his face, flanked by Michelangelo's *Night*. The day after the opening of the exhibition that included this series of savagely carnal *Allegories*, the social page was removed from the copy of the Roman daily *Il Messaggero* that was delivered upstairs to Mimise. The years passed. In 1984 Mimise had a first stroke. The year after, the chain-smoker Guttuso showed the first signs of the lung cancer that would kill him. Though his wife was increasingly frail, it was Guttuso who seemed to have the most cause for worry as he tried to keep knowledge of his spreading cancer from Mimise. Then in 1986, quite unexpectedly, Mimise had a second stroke at the beginning of October and died.

Marta Marzotto spoke to Guttuso on the phone. Ill with cancer, he was devastated by his wife's death. *Come on over Marta, come*, he said. *I'm in such pain that I'm grinding my teeth so hard I hurt myself*. It was the last time they spoke together. Monsignor Angelini came on the line. *Do come, countess*, the prelate said. She did go to the palazzo del Grillo, but when she went the doorkeeper wouldn't let her up. When she rang her calls weren't passed to Guttuso. She wrote and her letters were never answered. A little over three months later, Marta Marzotto heard on the radio that Guttuso was dead, and she wept in anger as well as sorrow.

What happened in the apartments of the palazzo del Grillo in those months, between Mimise Dotti's death on the fifth of October and

Renato Guttuso's just after midnight on the following eighteenth of January, not even the investigating magistrates were able to decide in the end. The magistrates themselves were bitterly divided. There were some great surprises and some grave accusations. Marta Marzotto wasn't the only person who'd been unable to see Guttuso in late 1986. Vivi Caruso, his old friend the gallery-owner in Palermo, remembered the big retrospective that was being organized that year by the Fondation Maeght in France. When the director of the foundation and the show's curator had come to Rome to discuss it, Vivi Caruso said, *I rang palazzo del Grillo and asked the manservant to tell him they'd arrived. I can't tell him, he said. But why, I said, is he too ill? No, he said, I just can't tell him.*

Days after Guttuso's death, another close friend, a famous psychiatrist who'd known him for fifty years, said he too had been prevented from seeing the painter. *I was greatly disturbed by this.* Giampiero Dotti, an international financier who was nephew of Mimise and close to both, had seen Guttuso four times, and had the impression that a cordon sanitaire was being thrown around the ever frailer painter. Dotti wrote that every other time he'd been to visit the doorkeeper had told him *I have orders not to let anyone up*, and that every time he'd rung the manservant had answered, *The maestro doesn't wish to be disturbed.* When Marta Marzotto had gone to the safe deposit box in a Roman bank to which she and Guttuso had each held the keys and found it empty, Fabio Carapezza was already Guttuso's son and heir. He'd been adopted in a lightning legal procedure that was begun eight days after Mimise's death and completed in less than two weeks. Dotti was startled when he heard. He'd been at the palazzo del Grillo the day the adoption request was made, and nobody had mentioned it.

Young Fabio Carapezza, a junior public servant and son of Palermo friends, was now worth maybe a hundred million dollars. Maybe double that. *Who can say how much it's all worth*, sighed Guttuso's old lawyer, who was now Carapezza's. Days after the painter's death, Marta Marzotto's cry of outrage was followed by more detailed charges from other quarters. Dotti said he was worried about the future of the Renato and Mimise Guttuso Foundation, which the painter and his wife had established a year earlier. The Dotti country estate in northern Italy, summer home and studio for decades, was supposed to become a museum of the painter's work. Dotti was determined the Foundation *wouldn't be sabotaged by people interested solely in the material side of this sorry affair.* The Foundation was stalled because the gift first had to be acknowledged by the Italian president and Dotti believed, he wrote, that *Fabio Carapezza, with his recent and powerful friends, had applied pressure to slow this down.* The *recent and powerful friends* could only be monsignor Angelini and the Hon. Giulio Andreotti.

Dotti's anger and suspicion had been aroused when he found Carapezza had given forty paintings Guttuso had earmarked for the foundation to the Museum of Modern Art in Rome instead. The Carapezzas weren't talking. *Precious one,* Ginevra Carapezza, Fabio's mother, had earlier crooned at Dotti on the phone, *legally we can't be touched.* When Dotti had asked her after the funeral what'd happened to a list he'd seen Guttuso make of things he wanted to leave people after his death, Ginevra Carapezza had said, *My precious, you know what your uncle was like. He'd write something one day and tear it up the next.* It was neither Marta Marzotto nor Giampiero Dotti, however, who brought in the magistrates. It was a hanger-on of the art scene who'd managed to get past the doorkeeper at palazzo del Grillo and sneak into Guttuso's apartment, where he saw, he told the magistrates, the painter *lying with a dead, empty, absent gaze.* The magistrates were legally required to investigate.

The big Guttuso retrospective for the Fondation Maeght had been due to open in St Paul de Vence in the south of France in the coming spring. In mid 1986 its curator and Guttuso and others had selected the paintings in his studio. *We chose fifty or more paintings. There were thousands of drawings around. I remember Renato said there were no worries with the drawings, we could have paved the road from Rome to Milan with them.* The paintings chosen were photographed and preparation of the catalogue was under way. Guttuso was very excited. He'd refused a group show at the Grand Palais in Paris for this one-man retrospective. Then at the end of summer the curator suddenly found he was no longer able to speak to Guttuso. The manservant wouldn't put him on the phone, the doorkeeper wouldn't let him up. *We made a last try on November the nineteenth,* he said. But they weren't allowed in. The lawyers took over. The curator spoke out because Ginevra Carapezza was saying there were practically no pictures left in Guttuso's studio. The curator said

> *In his last days I felt he was living for that exhibition at St Paul de Vence. It was inhuman of the Carapezzas not to let him hold it ... Sure there were paintings in the studio. And not just little drawings but canvases two metres by three. One day they'll turn up again ...*

Among those who remembered over a hundred canvases in Guttuso's cluttered studio, and thousands of drawings, was the governor of the Bank of Italy. After three weeks of *dignified silence* Fabio Carapezza Guttuso sued Dotti, a couple of daily papers and *persons unknown.* His lawyer explained it was the only way *to stifle a vulgar polemic created around an affair that was crystal-clear as spring water.* It was hard to avoid vulgar polemic the way things were unfolding. Angelini's deathbed conversion of Italy's communist painter hadn't passed unnoticed. A satirical paper came out with a banner headline *GOD EXISTS* and in slightly smaller letters *AND HE WANTS HIS SHARE OF THE LOOT.* The authors of this effort were taken to task for bad taste and disrespect in communist and catholic papers. Antonello Trombadori, the communist leader who'd spent a lot of time by the deathbed, announced that he'd *smash the face in* of anyone who doubted the maestro's conversion in extremis. This Trombadori was the same communist who'd proclaimed *Moro is dead* in the corridors of parliament while Moro was fighting for his life. It was too much for the journalist Giorgio Bocca, who wrote that it showed the historic compromise had been rather more than a passing political stratagem. Bocca was disgusted by *this display of sleazy vulgarity: the old hacks of stalinism and clerofascism gathered around the deathbed.* He saw Guttuso's conversion as very Italian.

> We're all drenched in catholicism. We sin and then we confess ... We went to bed fascists and woke up democrats. We're all mamma's boys supplied with insurance and counterinsurance, like those middle class families during the Resistance who used to send one son up to the mountains with the communists and another down to the family firm to negotiate with the Germans.

Bocca then turned his attention to Guttuso himself, whom the past and future demochristian prime minister Fanfani, the one who'd had two and a half million dollars from Sindona, had just described on TV as *one of the fathers of the democratic Republic.* A remarkable tribute, Bocca thought, to someone who'd remained a Stalinist sectarian all his life.

> As an individual Guttuso could live as he pleased, loving the proletariat *viscerally*, as he used to say, but very much at home in the villas of the haute bourgeoisie of Varese; being *for* the most radical communism but using capitalist cunning to accumulate a great fortune. But to call him an example, a master of democratic culture, takes some barefaced cheek ... He pretended not to understand that he was always favoured by the Soviets not for the good paintings of his youth or the *pompier* over-production of his maturity—that horrible *Funeral of Togliatti* —but for his betrayal as an intellectual.

Others were shocked by the treatment of Marta Marzotto. Alberto Moravia, another old friend who'd been kept at bay, said

It isn't logical to behave like that toward a woman one's been deeply in love with, as he was without a doubt. For me the really obscure point of the whole affair is not the conversion and it isn't the inheritance. It's Marta's story.

The film director Lina Wertmüller agreed.

This whole business of conversions and inheritances and monsignori and adoptions is murky. There's something sixteenth-century about it ... During my life I've seen so many love affairs with my own eyes and Renato's and Marta's was one of the strongest ... Sure, Guttuso was terrified of death, and maybe he didn't want to be seen any more by anyone in the condition he was, not even Marta. But not even a last phone call?

Marta Marzotto needed a bit of support. The count Marzotto, discreetly understanding for years, was now appalled by the publicity and the scandal and was trying to prevent her using the name Marzotto any longer. He wanted a separation. Marta, through her lawyer, blamed the media, which she said had *spared neither the living nor the dead*. She was really quite alone. Nearly all the beautiful people who'd lounged on the white divans of her salon in piazza di Spagna had all disappeared *like snow in the sun*, as a woman friend put it. She'd been cast as the seductress, the spoiler, the scarlet woman. It was the old story.

THE WIFE of the Uruguayan ambassador to the Hague was shown in, very smart in a houndstooth tailleur. She'd been part of Marta's circle when her husband was ambassador in Rome. Now she brought news from Rome to the court in exile in Milan. Or she would, when the countess got off the phones. So the ambassadress and I made muted small talk, so as not to rudely listen in. We kept our voices down, to leave the countess undisturbed and because we were both trying to overhear what she said.

Well INTERRUPT him then. My god, these girls today— The countess at moments sounded a little like the Red Queen in *Alice*. The ambassadress and I spoke in whispers of the trial. Andreotti had been such an intelligent man, streets ahead of all the others. Very witty at dinner parties. We agreed that Italian politics were a nightmare for outsiders. You never knew where anyone stood. *Andreotti gave Renato a solid gold Rolex. It was engraved with someone else's name. Renato gave it to my son. He's still got it.* The countess was shouting over the buzz and squeak of somebody on the phone. The ambassadress's time in Rome had been *the years of lead* and at the Uruguayan embassy in Rome nobody had been able to understand the Red Brigades at all. So the ambassadress had done the political reports herself. In Uruguay they'd had the Tupamaros, and she knew a thing or two about terrorism. I imagined her finely manicured hands flying over a keyboard late at night. Terrorist cells. Kneecappings. Abductions. People's courts. Executions. Interrogation techniques.

That GARBAGE of Andreotti's in the paper. About Renato turning over in his grave. His dear dear friend. It was quite SICKENING. He was NEVER a friend of Renato's. Did you see the Corriere? She flailed around on the divan. The manservant, an elderly and stately Sri Lankan in a striped jacket, brought in an armful of fax paper to the countess, at least a dozen yards. It was the Ivory Coast couple's references. Every page was emblazoned with a coat of arms. *Angelini is a HORRENDOUS individual. He got made a cardinal after he looked after the pope that time he was shot. The others didn't want him at all.* The countess's manservant returned with a silver tray with a silver teapot and a gold rimmed cup. The countess wasn't having anything. Neither was the ambassadress. I sipped alone. The countess was now on the phone to an art gallery in Palermo, the same one, I realized, where Sciascia had presented *La Vucciria.* She was getting on to Vivi Caruso. *Friends of Renato's, Leonardo's, it's a whole CULTURE.* After a couple of peremptory requests she got through. *And who was it kept me out, that time I arrived at the palazzo del Grillo with the police? What? Yes I know it was Angelini. BUT WHO WAS BEHIND ANGELINI?* I craned forward, but before the answer came the countess was distracted by a call on the other line. There was a problem with the photos of her fashion showing. She'd lately taken up fashion designing and her clothes were being distributed by a chain of department stores. A trifle down market, to be frank about it.

MARTA'S WORLD. MAD MARTA. FOR THE WOMAN WHO WANTS EVERYTHING AND WANTS IT NOW.

She'd been going to use a portrait of her by Guttuso as her trademark label, when Fabio Carapezza demanded a million dollars in reproduction rights. *He could have ruined the launch. I had to yield.* It wasn't the first time Guttuso's images of Marta Marzotto had been suppressed. After the retrospective at the Fondation Maeght had fallen through and Guttuso was dead, Fabio Carapezza had taken legal action to stop an Italian weekly reproducing the paintings that would've been shown. The magazine had got hold of the pictures taken for the catalogue in Guttuso's studio. They were almost all of the countess. The retrospective would have been a hymn to Marta Marzotto's body. How did Carapezza become part of the household?

I introduced him myself. It was all my idea to hire him as secretary. I said to
Renato, he's such an affectionate boy and he can keep all your affairs in order.
He was trying for a public service career, but he kept failing to get in. Finally
Andreotti intervened and he got through.

Marta Marzotto was graciously dredging things up, but you could see she'd no driving interest in them now. Not in the money, never had. She'd said that forthrightly at the time. So had Giampiero Dotti. Neither had wanted any of Guttuso's fortune for themselves. Nearly a decade had passed now and the countess had moved on to a new life. Death and the past were clearly not her thing. From time to time her interest would shine again briefly on some detail of iniquity, but on the whole you felt she'd seen so much in her time that even these held her attention only briefly. The empty strongbox even amused her. Renato Guttuso had hoarded his treasure there. It wasn't only the love letters and the erotic paintings. I had to understand, she said, that Renato had been very poor for a very long time. They both held keys, but the countess had opened the box for the first and only time ten days after after the death of Mimise. The countess went to retrieve their love letters and the erotic drawings. She found it emptied of everything. The jewels, the gold ingots, the paintings by Picasso and Balthus and Magritte were gone. It was a big strongbox, a metre by three. Earlier, she'd been surprized to learn from the ailing Guttuso that his long-serving business advisor and accountant had been replaced by a young man Guttuso didn't know. The countess discovered, after the painter's death, that the old advisor had been sacked by Carapezza.

The rapidity of Carapezza's adoption still impressed her, years later. Guttuso, she insisted, was seriously ill, often catatonic and in deep mourning. The lung cancer had metastasized to his brain, and moments of mental clarity alternated with lengthening periods of blankness or confusion. An adoption request in Italy, as anywhere, had to be supported by copious documentation, birth certificates, formal declarations and so on, and in Italy the bureaucracy which supplied this was monumentally slow-moving. Usually it took an age for the machinery of public offices to crank out a response to the simplest request for certification. Then there was the adoption process itself. The whole thing, in Carapezza's case, had taken a couple of weeks.

UNDER INVESTIGATION by the magistrates on suspicion of having taken advantage of a sick man, Carapezza announced he would produce Guttuso's secret will and clarify things once and for all. Since a secret will by Italian law had to be published immediately on its maker's death, by the lawyer in whose presence it'd been written, witnessed and sealed, this announcement itself raised a few questions. And when it was opened, the secret will resolved nothing. The five-line document, prepared by a solicitor called to the palazzo del Grillo and signed by the dying painter, simply annulled all previous wills and left his estate to his legal heir. There was no mention of Carapezza as his heir, which was odd. If the adoption were invalid the heirs were Dotti and his brother. Not that they wanted anything. Or might the heir have been Guttuso's extramatrimonial son? Marta Marzotto had suddenly thrown everyone into even greater confusion by mentioning for the first time an unacknowledged *secret* natural son. Suddenly everyone was talking about Guttuso's real son but nobody could trace him.

In mid January Carapezza called the undertakers to arrange the funeral and three days later Guttuso was dead. A leading Sicilian judge later observed of Guttuso's final disposition,

> It's a non-will. Renato Guttuso chose not to leave a will. He called the solicitor only to cancel his previous wills. A typically Sicilian way of solving a problem by washing his hands of it.

The central question remained. Had Guttuso been in possession of his faculties in the time he was incommunicado? Or had the cancer of the lungs and liver, its metastasis in his brain, the effects of chemotherapy, the shock of his wife's death and the *rivers* of whisky drunk compromised his mental powers? Carapezza's lawyers proposed to present a number of distinguished witnesses to Guttuso's last days who would testify to Guttuso's lucidity of mind. The first name on the lawyers' list was Giulio Andreotti's.

Marta Marzotto told me about what happened to the *Gott mit uns*. This was a series of drawings that more than anything else had made the young Guttuso's name. Hiding in Rome in the early forties, the resistance fighter Guttuso had done a series of crude but powerful Goyaesque ink drawings on the horrors of the nazi war. The drawings were done on cheap butcher's paper that had turned yellow and brittle with time. Guttuso had confided to the countess that a number of these now hugely valuable sheets had disappeared from the palazzo del Grillo. It was in this context that she started to speak now of *the thief*.

This was one of the four servants, two married couples, who'd run the show with Carapezza at the palazzo del Grillo. *They fix everything now*, sighed the sick Guttuso to Giampiero Dotti, possibly meaning also Carapezza's parents, who'd lately come from Palermo and installed themselves in his palazzo del Grillo apartments. Someone in Guttuso's employ was in touch with the forgery industry that had grown up around Guttuso's work. Real works were vanishing and fakes were appearing on the market. The painter had been enraged once by the forgeries, ripping up fakes in art galleries, but now he was tired. He asked Marta to do something about it, and with great vigour she did. A police operation was planned on the galleries and printers she'd identified, but someone in Guttuso's house tipped the forgers off. Marta urged Guttuso to sack the person she suspected. The painter said, *There are so many wolves around. One goes, others arrive.*

Aldo Torroni was the doorkeeper of the palazzo del Grillo. Usually he was downstairs in his little lodge, waving up the visitors he'd known for years, famous and otherwise, the regulars of Guttuso's circle, while the servants busied themselves upstairs in the painter's apartments. Marta Marzotto, for instance, had been coming every morning at a quarter to ten for the last nineteen years, and staying till one. The whole household was at Mimise Dotti Guttuso's funeral, just after her death on 6 October 1986, and in the movement of mourners the good Aldo heard one of the servants say distinctly, *If we can keep Marzotto away for just two days, then it's done.* He was puzzled by this, and even more puzzled when the next day he was ordered to keep out all those friends of Guttuso's he'd been nodding to daily, weekly for the last twenty years. He was perturbed enough to ask advice from the administrator of the palazzo del Grillo, who said *Ask the maestro for a written statement.* That way he'd know who should now be admitted and who not. The advice seemed good, and the doorkeeper asked upstairs for *a written statement.* He was promised one, but it never came. When Marta Marzotto rang one day, asking yet again what was going on, the good Aldo blurted out, referring to the soap of millionaire family intrigue that was all the rage then, *Compared with us, countess, Dynasty's a joke.*

Two months after the painter's death, the *distinguished witnesses* were testifying for Carapezza to the magistrates, and all agreed that Guttuso had been *lucid to the end.* The press reported that Giulio Andreotti, *one of the few to be admitted to palazzo del Grillo even in the last months of the artist's life,* was busy trying to form a new government, but on the fifteenth of March *found time, despite his efforts to resolve the crisis of government, to testify ... that Guttuso had been lucid to the end.* The communist leader Antonello Trombadori denounced *keyhole history* and issued veiled threats against *those who wanted to take the soap opera road.* He too testified that Guttuso was *lucid to the end.* Some witnesses even described Guttuso as *lucidissimo* to the end. These were the *Sunday friends* who'd seen Guttuso only intermittently and briefly, said Dotti's lawyer. Marta Marzotto had herself by now run up fifteen hours of testimony to the magistrates. She thought Guttuso had been lucid part of the time and not all the time, because that was the effect of his afflictions. Another old family friend remembered Guttuso's confusion, memory lapses, the way he'd say the same thing six or seven times, even before the death of his wife.

Giampiero Dotti said the only useful testimony now would be from medical experts, and asked that proper medical evidence be given. Dotti was sueing to have Fabio Carapezza's adoption annulled. Carapezza's lawyers submitted he had no right to, since he wasn't claiming the inheritance. A new police raid prompted by Marta Marzotto caught printers in the act of running off a fake Guttuso lithograph, and fake Picassos, fake De Chiricos, fake Chagalls and fake Miròs. The natural son had meanwhile been found, and claimed legal recognition as Guttuso's son. In April 1987 the investigating magistrates who'd led the adoption inquiry protested against the intention to wind it up and one of them resigned. After what *La Repubblica* called *a silent but stubborn trial of strength* inside the prosecutor's office in Rome, the case was reopened. Carapezza sued the weekly *L'Espresso* for an article called *The Colour of Money*. It included Dotti's description of the four visits he'd been able to make to Guttuso in the last months.

> These visits were always preceded by laborious and humiliating contacts with Fabio, since nobody answered the telephone at palazzo del Grillo ... during these visits, which always took place in the presence of the Carapezzas, the atmosphere was very strange. Renato seemed happy to see me but confused and as if afraid. He often said that Mimise was at home [she was dead] ... Every time I passed on greetings from his friends to Renato, he was moved to tears and in many cases said he wanted to see them as soon as possible. Several times ... Renato asked me to contact Jean Louis Prat of the Fondation Maeght for him, about his exhibition ... Until the third of December 1986 I had never heard the slightest reference to this sudden adoption ...

Carapezza also tried to block legal recognition of Guttuso's natural son, and to this end Trombadori weighed in with the information that the son's mother had slept around a lot. To her further discredit she was described as having been ravishingly beautiful and uninterested in Guttuso's art. Three months later the son's application was nevertheless declared admissible, which meant it would likely succeed. Two days after that Carapezza was exonerated by another court of the suspicion that he'd kept Guttuso isolated from the world and taken advantage of the artist's physical and mental frailty to get himself adopted. Citing Giulio Andreotti, monsignor Angelini, Antonello Trombadori and the other Sunday friends, the magistrate, one of those who'd wanted to close down the inquiry months earlier, decided that Renato Guttuso had been *lucid to the end*. Carapezza was confirmed as sole heir. Giampiero Dotti and Marta Marzotto were now put under investigation themselves, for slander. Marta also found herself under investigation by the financial police over the sale of the house of her salon on piazza di Spagna. The magistrate spoke of Marta's and Renato's twenty-year relationship as *not only artistic but also intimate* and judged her *amply rewarded for the full range of her services rendered*.

I'm speechless, Marta said when she heard. She'd had no part in starting the law suit. She'd done her best to keep her mouth shut. *SERVICES RENDERED? I wasn't Guttuso's servant. Or his employee ... I feel I've been attacked, attacked as a person. And I'm simply furious*. She'd wanted nothing out of the whole affair except vindication as a woman and what she'd got was a threatened libel suit, a police investigation of her property dealings and separation from her husband. Dotti was scathing too.

> *Why weren't my witnesses called? The people who saw Renato every day, who'd been his real friends forever? Even if they weren't distinguished and Roman and weren't tied to politics ... Renato Guttuso's mental lucidity was decided by witnesses and not by medical or scientific proof.*

He was particularly hard on Angelini — *please don't call him Monsignore* — and the *curial cynicism of this enigmatic character*. I remembered this when Angelini's evidence was made public two years after he'd testified. He was still Monsignore and his elevation to the purple, described as imminent two and a half years earlier, seemed to be taking an unconscionable time. The magistrate must have got his idea of the countess from Angelini, who'd said

> Marta Marzotto was amply endowed by Guttuso with money, paintings ... such paintings were systematically sold off by Marzotto, who in such manner maintained herself, effecting various expenditures ... The countess was always polite to me ... during his life Guttuso wished to break off his relation with the countess. It was not possible for him due to blackmail in the press. The grave illness and the full consciousness which he soon perceived of a not far distant eclipse of his life gave him the courage ... to recover his

equilibrium and return to being another self.

Nothing ever ended cleanly, especially in Italy. The story dragged on, the court cases multiplied and were never concluded. Would the maestro's tomb be opened to make a DNA test possible and definitively establish the identity of the natural son? The maestro's remains had been transported in 1989 to Bagheria and entombed in a hideous cylindrical sarcophagus of mauve marble by the sculptor Manzù, surrounded by a shallow moat and adorned with four gilt pigeons, the Stalinist peace doves probably, that the maestro used to draw so prolifically during the cold war years, and set among the weeds in the grounds of villa Cattolica. The natural son by now had disappeared from view as rapidly and silently as he'd emerged into the public gaze. What had made him lose interest in the estate, I wondered, which he'd said he wanted for his young daughters? Three years after Guttuso's death, Carapezza's libel suit against Dotti was still under way. Dotti, having lost the first round of his battle to have Carapezza's adoption annulled, because not wanting the money he was judged *unqualified to raise the problem*, pointed out that he'd always been denied access to the adoption documents. The Carapezza adoption file seemed to have disappeared.

The Guttuso Foundation, the only alternative to Carapezza's total control of the Guttuso inheritance, was by now on the verge of extinction. Only Dotti was struggling to keep it alive. Without funds or plans, the other members of the board had voted to dissolve it. The foundation that Renato and Mimise had established together was meant to be housed on the handsome Dotti estate, where Guttuso had had his summer studio, near the northern Italian city of Varese. The death blow was a proposal to open a Guttuso Room in the Varese art gallery. This idea came from the mayor of Varese, a close friend of Giulio Andreotti and a member of his faction in the DC, and a bishop who was also a close friend of prime minister Andreotti's. Andreotti himself seemed to have engineered this coup de grace between speeches at the Bagheria commemoration. The mayor of Varese, who was there for the ceremony in January 1990, confided happily to the press that *Andreotti is a kind of advisor to Carapezza*. The country estate too was now all Carapezza's. After that I lost track.

THE CARAPEZZA adoption file turned out not to have been the only thing that had disappeared inside the justice building in Rome.

Someone had anonymously forwarded to the investigating magistrates, a couple of months after the painter's death, a letter from Guttuso addressed to Marta Marzotto. The letter took more than eight years to reach its destination. It lay for most of that time in a closed file on the shelves of the prosecutor's office in Rome. Marta Marzotto discovered its existence by chance in November 1994. *I wept in pain and anger when I read it,* she said. The letter was written on a single page of fifteen shaky lines in Guttuso's hand.

Dearest Martina.

I hope to get this letter to you through the good Aldo, even though I know it's going to be difficult. I'm very sick and I'd like to have you near me and I can't understand why you haven't come back yet.

The crows surround me and my lucid moments are getting rarer and rarer. They won't let me use the telephone ... I'm sorry to tell you these things, but if you were with me I might even be able to get better.

I'm always waiting to see you come in through the door, why don't you come my soul. Come. Come, I'm waiting for you anxiously, I hug you and kiss you.

Your

Renato

PS At least call me on the phone.

Marta Marzotto was silent for a moment now. She tucked her bare feet under her on the white divan. Even the telephones had stopped ringing now. She was convinced it'd been the good Aldo who'd sent the letter on. *And now he's vanished. I can't find him anywhere.* Even the ambassadress lost her composure for an instant. Her mouth dropped open. *The doorkeeper has disappeared?* breathed the ambassadress. The countess nodded. *The good Aldo has vanished. Without trace.*

The ambassadress looked at me in silence. I wondered what went on in the justice building in Rome, that cases, files, documents could disappear like this. I was about to turn my attention to the murder of Mino Pecorelli, the journalist who was shot dead in the street in Rome as he delved into scandals involving Andreotti. That investigation too had been swallowed up in the darkness of the Rome *procura* for years and years. Marta Marzotto would have had a pretty good idea, I thought. She'd remarked, coming out from one of her interminable interrogations about Guttuso, that she was *starting to feel quite at home in the justice building.* Even Marta Marzotto, though, was probably as surprized as I was when a few months after our meeting, in the Italian spring of 1996, one of its leading judges was arrested on very serious, not to say massive, corruption charges involving the Berlusconi financial empire, and that other senior judges in that office were under investigation. But now the countess was working the phones again.

I've just had a call from Licio Gelli, she announced. *Spoke to him this morning. You ought to speak to him. Like to? HE could tell you things. Want his number?* She knew she was being naughty, and laughed. It was like being invited to have a cup of tea and a chat with Heinrich Himmler, whom Gelli also rather resembled. Maybe the young Gelli had known Himmler, when he was starting out. He'd fought for Franco in Spain, fought for Mussolini under the republic of Salò. He'd known a lot of movers and shakers over the years. The countess was daring me. This was a test. *Yes,* I said faintly. The countess started rummaging in her folder of telephone numbers. *That man is SO CLEVER,* she said. *Not only has he got his passport back. He's got a two-car police escort everywhere he goes. With sirens. He has INFLUENCE. The Vatican,* she added distractedly, *has put him up for the Nobel Prize. Where did I put that damn number? For Literature. They're putting pressure on the South American embassies. He could tell you a lot.* I was sure he could. I'd also heard something about Gelli's creative writing, I suddenly remembered, a long time ago. In the early eighties, Tullio Pironti in Naples, the publisher of *The True History of Italy*, had wanted to publish Gelli's memoirs. *The Venerable* was in the news back then. It was in 1981, when he'd just inadvertently brought down the Italian government. A raid on his villa discovered the membership list, or a membership list, of the secret and illegal P2 masonic lodge, one of whose purposes may have been to lay the ground for a right-wing dictatorship in Italy. The raid was Sindona's fault, part of the fallout from the failure of his secret blackmailing expedition to Sicily in the summer of 1979. Gelli's financial advisor and Cosa Nostra's, as well as the Vatican's, had lost them all billions. After his arrest in Switzerland, where he'd fled in a wig and false moustache like Sindona's, Gelli made a helicopter prison escape to hiding in south America.

I could tell you about Sindona, said Marta Marzotto, reading my thoughts. *I know everything. I could tell you about them all.* The membership list of the P2 included the names of five past and present government ministers and thirty-eight members of parliament; fourteen judges; eleven police chiefs; ten bank presidents; two hundred high officers in the armed forces, carabinieri and the financial police and most of the heads of the secret services. It also included the owner and the editor of the *Corriere della Sera*; a businessman of obscure origins and sudden wealth called Silvio Berlusconi, who a dozen years later would be prime minister and later still one of three former Italian prime ministers simultaneously facing quite different criminal charges; and the very chat show compere who'd just banished the talking head with AIDS.

The list did not include the name of Giulio Andreotti. This absence gave rise to a number of theories. The minimalist position was that the members' register was simply incomplete and the real one held elsewhere. The maximalist was that Gelli himself was merely a front and that the real venerable grand master of the Propaganda 2 lodge, the real orchestrator of its plans for the coup it amusingly called *democratic renaissance*, was the little man his admirers called *the god Giulio* and others *Beelzebub*. There was no evidence for these speculations. It was just that for many years in Italy people found it hard to conceive of any signifcant dealings that weren't secret, or of any secret dealings that weren't orchestrated by Andreotti. Nobody had ever been able to decide whether Gelli was a power in himself, or just a go-between, a blackmailer, an agent for others, and the P2 list epitomized the dilemma. Gelli had a lot of friends in South America.

Goodness yes, said the ambassadress. *Huge cattle properties in Uruguay.* At a certain point she and her husband the ambassador in Rome had felt unable to accept further invitations from Gelli or his associate Umberto Ortolani, who owned maybe even more of Uruguay than Gelli did. *They'd become too, how to put it, too compromised?* Gelli later negotiated his return from Brazil to Switzerland, whence he was duly extradited to Italy, but only to face financial charges. A few days after I called on the countess, the supreme court confirmed his conviction as one of the people responsible for the bomb which killed sixteen people on the Naples Milan express train eleven years earlier. Gelli was settled back in Italy but the terms of his Swiss extradition kept him out of jail. Andreotti admitted once bumping into Gelli while visiting the Argentine dictator Juan Peròn at the Casa Rosada in Buenos Aires. Before that, he said, he'd known Gelli only as the managing director of the Permaflex mattress factory in Frosinone. *I thought to myself*, Andreotti said on a chat show just before his trial opened in Palermo, *I thought, 'there's someone who looks just like the managing director of the Permaflex mattress company in Frosinone'*. Others said it was Gelli who introduced Andreotti to Peron. Andreotti told the talk-show host he thought Gelli was an influential figure in South America. *Not in Italy, though. Definitely not in Italy.*

It was in Italy, however, that Gelli arranged the banker Roberto

Calvi's payment of many millions of dollars to Bettino Craxi, shortly before he became prime minister. Craxi was now holed up in Tunisia, out of range of his three Italian prison sentences which, were they ever to be served, would have kept him behind bars for a quarter of a century. Calvi, who'd succeeded his early mentor Sindona as the mafia's and the Vatican's banker and international financier of choice, was found hanging under Blackfriars bridge in London in 1982, his body disposed according to masonic rites. He'd caused the world's biggest banking collapse since the war. A Palermo boss of Cosa Nostra then living in London was mentioned in connection with Calvi's death. Calvi's widow insisted Andreotti was head of the P2. Soon after I left Marta Marzotto, magistrates at Vico Equense near Naples questioned Gelli about his part in an international traffic they had accidentally uncovered in arms, gold, plutonium and diamonds. He told them,

I devote several days a week to conversations with people who ask for my advice from Italy and abroad. Advice of a general nature, nothing against the law, no favours and no recommendations. Just advice, because I like human relations.

Maybe I could ask Gelli about his human relations. Another possibility was on the cards, given that the Venerable was now aiming at the Nobel. *Poetry*. I remembered now that when Tullio Pironti failed to get a political memoir out of Gelli, he was offered instead a slim volume of verse. But the countess was distracted again before she found the number.

Heavens, said Marta Marzotto suddenly. It was almost lunch time. Would I like to share a salad? She told the ambassadress to show me round while she whipped under a shower and slipped into something even more comfortable. I'd been casting the odd glance around the countess's bower all morning, mainly at the Guttusos. The biggest one was on the wall facing me. It was the *Night of Gibellina*, a grim dark crudely painted scene of bonfire, ruin and despair that remembered the Belice valley earthquake in Sicily in 1968. It was Guttuso in his earlier peasant tragedy social mode, an instance of people suffering the kind of double violence Moravia had identified, in this case the earthquake's as well as the painter's. I felt I'd seen it before, maybe in reproduction or in another variant. It didn't seem entirely at home in this rococò bower of bliss. There were some small Guttusos too, and one in which Marta Marzotto was recognizable, but under the brisk guidance of the ambassadress I didn't get to linger on them. We were in a low-ceilinged attic with its old beams exposed, crammed with knickknackery and extravagance and altogether pleasing as a whole. In one corner was the countess's collection of big gaudy goblets in coloured Murano glass and a lot of gilt.

A long kind of empire-inspired sofa, upholstered in lolly-pink silk, ran the entire length of a wall of the adjoining room, and its huge undulant back, upholstered in the same silk and studded around the edge, almost reached the ceiling and took up most of the wall. It was a wild thronelike fantasy that might have come from a stage set for *Cinderella*. *What a lot of trouble we had getting that up here*, said the ambassadress, eyeing the pink silk bulges. Between these two rooms was a large area of wall that was entirely covered with small drawings in ink and coloured wash. Each was under its own glass panel. Even from a distance I could see they had the vigorous Guttuso line, the shapely blocking, the poised energies, the elegant tension between form and movement that so rarely seemed to survive the construction of his larger canvases. I moved toward them. The ambassadress moved faster. *The erotic drawings*, she said tersely. *Very amusing*.

The erotic drawings! Were these the nineteen that had been taken from the strongbox, the one to which only Marta Marzotto and Fabio Carapezza had the keys? Had she got them back? Had she got her letters back? As the ambassadress discreetly but firmly pushed me into the other room, I glimpsed the countess nude on all fours and what was either a serpent or a giant phallus waving behind her. The drawings looked animated, vigorous, charming. It was my opinion that Marta Marzotto had done a great deal for Renato Guttuso's painting. I hoped to sidle back later, but as things turned out I never had a chance. In the other room was a life size German plaster statue from the last century, of a gipsy woman in a rocking chair suckling a child. It was shoved into a corner. The countess had kept barking her shin on it.

Marta Marzotto now reappeared, fresh and radiant. Another friend arrived, a wan woman who seemed to be in jewellery. She had no appetite, but Marta hustled her up to the table with the rest of us. It'd be just a casual bite, she said. Scraps, mainly. The manservant in the striped jacket came and went. He brought meaty moist prosciutto crudo pieces and a dark rucchetta salad. Rich venetian ox tail stew and slices of fried polenta. *I like it best like that*, said Marta Marzotto, heaping our plates. Slices off a huge pink mortadella. *You must have some of this*, said Marta. *It's a present from Pavarotti*. The mortadella looked not unlike its donor, minus beard and teeth. There was a subtle chicken and lemon casserole. The most beautiful gorgonzola I'd ever seen. Entire, hacked open and voluptuously spilling out its creamy blue guts.

The countess offered wine from an unlabelled bottle. A fine fruity white wine that was drunk even less than the food was eaten. We ate with massive, weighty cutlery made for real hands, and drank from Marta's fantastical coloured goblets of Murano glass. A gloriously insubstantial coffee semifreddo. *Have some more*, said the countess generously, shovelling semifreddo on to my plate. *It's warming up.*

I'm trying to diet Marta, whined the lady of the jewels. *And you do this to me.*

Marta Marzotto and the ambassadress were talking about their travels. I was eating. *My children all adore Australia*, said the countess kindly. *Love it. Go there all the time. And New Zealand. I do too. I've been to Adelaide.* She paused. *Ugly little town. My children are direct descendants of Frederick Barbarossa.*

We love Sydney, said the ambassadress. *So many friends. Love going back. We love Australian films.*

Adored The Piano, said Marta Marzotto tonelessly.

Bad Boy Bubby, said the ambassadress with a sudden force that startled the others. *A very unusual film. About this boy kept in a room all his life—* She started to run through *Bad Boy Bubby*. The countess looked bored. When the ambassadress mentioned cockroach eating, the countess's eyes narrowed and she poured a little wine. When the ambassadress got on to the suffocation of the parents wrapped in cling wrap, the countess rattled her heavy cutlery. *I'm going to Argentina*, said Marta Marzotto suddenly. *To stay in the Casa Rosada. Menem keeps asking and asking and finally I've just got to go. After Venice. After Kenya.*

Isn't Menem a sweetie? said the ambassadress. *We love him. What do you think of HER? Such a publicity seeker. All that performance about leaving him and moving out of the Casa Rosada. A president's wife—*

Want to see my new clothes? asked Marta Marzotto suddenly. *I've just had a showing.* She jumped up suddenly and ran from the room. She came back pushing a chrome clothes trolley on coasters, packed with autumn ready-to-wear in synthetic fabrics. The ambassadress sprang from the table and rifled through them. She pulled on a quilted parka, turned up its collar and strutted and struck catwalk poses in front of Marta's antique mirror.

My sister-in-law might like these, I said, looking at some dresses. *I could get her a present.*

Get you a discount if you buy in Milan, said the countess. *At the main store.*

You could export to Australia, I said. *Italian fashion—*

Tariff barriers, snapped the countess quickly. *Prohibitive duties. No way*

271

I could run a profit. She paused. *Besides, they've got THEIR OWN UGLY LITTLE FASHIONS over there.* She ordered coffee. The stately Sri Lankan sailed from the room without acknowledging her. *I can't get him to listen. Takes no notice of me at all. He's always like this before he goes home.*

His mind's elsewhere, explained the ambassadress from Uruguay. *He's living in another world.*

I hope the Ivory Coast couple won't be like that, said the countess. Then we had real coffee, as good as you might expect in Milan. I sipped it and looked at this strong woman, this survivor, and imagined Guttuso, or rather Sciascia's imagining of him. *He wanted to keep everyone happy ... In spite of his virility, he was very fragile psychologically.* As for the aftermath,

It's a story out of Pirandello. That's the only Sicilian thing about it.
There are so many different truths that you can't piece the thing together.

You know what I think? Pasquale had said back at the mill. *They just sat round the table and divvied the money up between them. The communist party and the Vatican.*

And the son? I asked. *What about the adopted son?*

Naturally they had to keep the friends in Palermo happy.

XI

A MAZE MAKER

BRONZE ARCHANGELS looking over my shoulder, I sat one muggy day in Palermo on the cool white steps at the base of piazza San Domenico's monument to the Virgin and worried at Sciascia's words about the painting of *La Vucciria*, or rather the Vucciria market itself, the *hungry man's dream* just out of sight below me. Sciascia had mentioned *certain sweet and savoury dishes that contain everything, where the savoury merges into the sweet and the sweet into the savoury*. With their suggestion of a gorgeous fantasy anchored in a palpable sensuous reality, something out of the *Arabian Nights*, the words were wildly romantic and at the same time domestic, familiar. What was Sciascia talking about? Then I remembered *caponata*.

The *caponata* I first knew had been a cheap cold dish eaten at night at a trestle table amid the traffic at Porta Capuana in Naples, a change from steamed mussels. Anchovy and chopped octopus tentacle and black Gaeta olives, with a bit of salad and some broth slopped over a flat and rocklike hard biscuit. Elizabeth David described this accurately as *a primitive fisherman's and sailor's dish*. She called it *caponata alla marinara*. It was only when craning over a neighbouring table once, under the fluorescent lights of the Horse Shoe, through the flying bread and the slamming plates and the wine-splashed paper cloths, that I realized caponata in Palermo was something very different. It was the colour that struck me first. The colour of darkness. A heap of cubes of that unmistakeably luminescent dark, dark purply-reddish goldy richness, glimmerings from a baroque canvas, that comes from eggplant, black olives, tomato and olive oil densely cooked together, long and gently. The colour of southern Italian cooking. Caponata was one of the world's great sweet and sour dishes, sweet, sour and savoury.

The eggplant was the heart of caponata. The celery hearts were the most striking component: essential and surprising. Pieces of each were fried separately in olive oil until they were a fine golden colour and then added to a sauce made by cooking tomato, sugar and vinegar with a golden chopped onion in oil and adding Sicilian olives, capers and *bottarga*, which was tuna roe dried into a block and sliced or shaved or grated for use. This, however, was only the beginning of the full blown caponata. I doubted whether any prized bottarga was grated into the one the Horse Shoe served up daily in great quantities for next to nothing. The Horse Shoe's was delicious, but essentially a vegetable dish. I used to eat it with their boiled beef. Elizabeth David had a perfunctory version from a French cook book of 1913 which got it from the German ambassador's cook in Rome. She presented it with a very English putdown. *An interesting dish ... Try it in half quantities.* A Palermitan wrote that *he who has not eaten a caponatina of eggplant has never reached the antechamber of the terrestrial paradise.* He described its taste as

a composite flavour comparable to no other, but which recalls nostalgically exotic lands and seas, whose mingled aromas evoke the chief characteristic of Sicilian cuisine, the field on which all the other cuisines give battle to each other.

What the writer meant was made clear by Ada Boni in her *Talismano della Felicità*. After adding the golden eggplant and celery heart pieces to the sweet and sour sauce of tomato, capers and olives, she added severely, *you will have already prepared separately some baby octopuses and possibly a small lobster ... You may also add if desired some slices of swordfish cooked in a little oil.* After the baby octopuses, the lobster and the swordfish slices were added to the pot, the St Bernard sauce had to be prepared. This contained almonds, anchovies, orange juice, and grated chocolate among more mundane ingredients, and had to be spread over the caponata after it had cooled completely and was arranged on a dish in the form of a cupola. All that then remained was to garnish the caponata with pieces of hard boiled egg, shrimps and lobster claws. It was caponata, I decided, that Sciascia had in mind. A lot of the ingredients were displayed in Guttuso's painting of *The Vucciria*.

You could tell from the comment that what really interested Sciascia in all this wasn't the abundance but its absence, not the food but the hunger, just as he said elsewhere that Guttuso *unlived even as he lived*, that the painter's blazing vitality was veined by negation and death. Guttuso remarked himself about Sicily's heterogeneous richness that in Sicily, *you can find dramas, pastorals, idylls, politics, gastronomy, geography, history, literature ... in the end you can find anything and everything, but you can't find truth ...* It was like Lampedusa on the short life truth had in Sicily, how it was always being seized on and twisted into something else by interested parties. It was less a problem for a painter dealing in images than a writer who dealt in words. Truth was a function of language, like its opposite. *Lying really is a cursed vice*, Montaigne had said. *It's only words that link us together and make us human.* Sciascia's terse, stripped down stories found their own truth in the absence of certainty, the impossibility of knowing, and I wondered what Sicily that came from, and what it had to do with *The True History*'s hope of shedding light. *The best word is the one not spoken* was a mafia saying much quoted by Giovanni Falcone. How close was Sciascia to his own forger priest, the one in *The Council of Egypt* who'd said *History's all an imposture. History doesn't exist?*

THE TRUTH for Sciascia started where he'd always lived, in the bleak interior town of Racalmuto in the hills above Agrigento. He wrote about what he knew. He started slowly and modestly as a writer, not working at it full time until he was forty-eight, but even as his fame grew, first in Italy and then spreading abroad, Sciascia stayed where he'd always lived, in Racalmuto. He was the grandson of a *caruso*, a miner in the nearby sulphur mines, and the son of a mine company clerk. After the war he became a primary school teacher in Racalmuto, where he felt unease at instructing children faint with hunger in the achievements of the Italian renaissance. Racalmuto was a mafia town, and nearby Agrigento on the coast, after Palermo and Trapani, was the biggest mafia centre in Sicily. Sciascia wrote about what he knew.

> In every town and every neighbourhood, the mafia bosses and their associates were as well known as the carabinieri and their commanders. The politicians they *brought along* – recommended to the electorate – were also well known ... and so were their systems of illegally making money ... Far from hiding, the bosses made a show of themselves. They never pronounced nor accepted the word mafia and liked to use the word friendship instead. They were sceptical and pessimistic about their fellow-men, society and

its institutions. The institutions for their part denied the existence in Sicily of a vast and efficient criminal network called the mafia ...

Racalmuto is another Sicilian town whose name has an Arab origin. The name of Sciascia's town in Arabic meant *the dead village* or *the ruined homestead*. It should have been a warning. I wanted to see, though, the town Sciascia stuck in all his life and wrote about, directly and indirectly, so much. It had no special notoriety in the history of art or crime that I knew of, was neither large nor small. A Leonardo Sciascia Foundation was set up there after Sciascia died, but I'd heard it soon expired from lack of funds. Except as Sciascia's town, I'd never heard Racalmuto mentioned at all. It'd be a Sicilian experience.

A swarm of schoolkids and students were heading home from Palermo for the weekend, each with a fluorescent Invicta backpack, and I had an ugly scuffle for a seat on the bus. The rather few other passengers buying tickets and waiting around amid these teeming contemporary adolescents were instantly recognizable from early Sciascia. There were youngish housewives and white-haired women in black, elderly men in cloth caps with leathery faces, the odd priest and carabiniere. Most of the minor figures from Sciascia's first mafia novel *The Day of the Owl* were heading inland that day, including, by the look of them, the barber, the police informer, the very young widow and the tree pruner. There were no killers I could identify. Even in the fifties, when cars were still a notable luxury, killers didn't use public transport.

The bus left Palermo at the beginning of a hot afternoon. By the time it'd wound up, through orchards and vineyards at first, whose leaves were reddening and falling, into the arid hilly vastness of the Sicilian interior, dropped its load of homegoing students bit by bit at little towns along the way, stopped for flocks of skinny sheep and their pedestrian shepherds, passed various strange and uncompleted concrete roadworks, the roads getting ever steeper and narrower and more twisted, the landscape dryer and rockier, and finally, after struggling through a funeral crowd outside a grey baroque church, dropped its last few students and me on the stony outcrop with a mass of terraced dun-coloured tiled-roofed houses crouching on it which turned out to be Racalmuto, it was nearly dark. Sciascia spoke once of the two faces of Racalmuto, the mild and sunny slopes below the town on the seaward side, planted with vineyards and olive and almond groves, and the harsh and sulphurous inland side. In the spiralling approach to the hilltop, both sides looked pretty bleak in the fading light.

It was suddenly chill and at moments a faint drizzle condensed out of the darkening air. I was still dressed for the warmth of Palermo and shivered. Most of the town was above me and everything around was closed and shuttered. The bus would go back at dawn, and having arranged to be collected then at the edge of town I set off to find a place to sleep and see what I could before dark of the town where Sciascia had spent his life. I set off along one of the narrow sightless streets that curved along the side of the hill like an old sheep track. It was hemmed in by houses on each side, their doors opening directly into the traffic. The doors would've opened directly into the traffic, if there were any traffic and the doors ever opened. They were all now tight shut, and heavy wooden shutters were drawn across the windows. Sometimes through the slats I thought I glimpsed a glimmer from a low-watt electric bulb. Here and there was a pane of glass covered inside by lace through which an inhabitant might or might not have been peering. All the doors and shutters were thickly painted in the same milk-chocolate brown that is the only colour you see painted on wood in these towns. Was it taste, or was the milk chocolate paint cheaper than the dark green used on shutters in the cities? There was nobody in the streets. There were no cars. There were no shops.

Then there was some traffic. A funeral procession was shuffling toward me down the narrow street. It must have been the big funeral we passed in the bus. Since my year in Trani, when every grey winter afternoon the funeral processions passed under the window, all but the very poorest accompanied by a band playing an off-key dead march as a chill wet wind blew in over the Adriatic, I have tried to keep out of the way of funeral processions in small southern Italian towns. The funerals in winter are almost as grim as the weddings in spring. The lugubrious tide was washing closer now, filling the street. With the air of someone who'd just remembered leaving a saucepan of milk on the stove, I doubled back and up the nearest uphill alley to the next sheep track.

This street was identical to the first, narrow, shuttered, empty and getting darker. Some way along was a cavernous bar where I had a coffee, which failed to warm. I remembered the always boiling coffees that puncutate Sciascia's stories. The barman didn't know of any hotels or pensioni around. He was sunk in some morose thoughts of his own so I didn't ask what was more urgently on my mind, which was where the centre was, some people, movement, life. You couldn't see where they led, these narrow streets curving level along the contours of the hill, interrupted here and there by interminable flights of of broad stone steps, ascending in dizzying recessions of almost touching parallel lines, like some creation of an obsessed child with a pencil and ruler, something to run up endlessly in a dream, and each, as someone says somewhere in Sciascia, *surmounted by an ugly baroque church.*

I continued along this lifeless street, blind, closed, dark and empty, while the thought gnawed at me that maybe the next parallel was full of people, animation, light and places to eat and stay. There was no way of knowing, and I'd glimpsed enough of this town to intuit that I could walk these streets to exhaustion without finding the nexus of life I was looking for, round and round the stony outcrop. Perhaps these horizontal streets weren't in fact parallels, like altitude lines on a map but a single spiral, one immensely long street winding through the deserted town from top to bottom, like the thread in a screw. Then in the shadows I saw another hearse, another glimpse of polished mahogany, another silent crowd shuffling toward me. Or was it the same funeral procession, dogging me up and down the narrow parallels or winding round and round Racalmuto on its way to the graveyard? I turned and ran some way up the nearest flight of steps.

Outside a garage in a little piazza made where the hillside bulged a bit a greasy mechanic was fiddling with a Fiat. A rush of grateful relief came for this normality. I asked if he could direct me to an hotel. *There was none*, he told me amiably. *Not in Racalmuto. A pensione? However simple? Not in Racalmuto.* With a brittle laugh I enquired how a town of well over ten thousand people could be without a single place to stay. *There used to be a hotel*, he reminisced in a wondering singsong, *years and years ago. Then it closed.* Although he seemed not entirely at ease with the concept of a centre, he gave me some suggestions for getting to where the middle of Racalmuto might be and I set off again. By now, my one thought was to get out. Forget Sciascia's house. Forget colour. It was getting colder. There was no bus till dawn. Heading off along a street the mechanic had recommended, I saw a light in the distance, livid neon. It was a shop window. Approaching eagerly, I saw it was a butchery and was closed. A single irregular sign read FRESH MEAT. Turning, I saw a lone figure, a man in a cloth cap and a slate-coloured jacket walking slowly toward me. As I approached, he changed his route almost imperceptibly and averted his eyes, though mine were fixed on him. Clearly he didn't want any trouble. Didn't want to get involved in anything that might— *Mi scusi*, I said loudly. There was nobody else around. He had to stop.

To my joy, he told me what I wanted to hear. There was a railway line. There was a station. I might be able to leave this place. To get there, he told me, I had to go back along the way I'd come. And start going up the steps. *And then–* I asked. *Just keep climbing*, he said. *Just keep on going till you get there.* He was silent for a moment, looking into some inner space. *You'll get there in the end,* he decided. I retraced my steps, turned right and started climbing. My heart was insanely light. It buoyed me and carried me up the hill. Taking deep lungfuls of chill night air, I danced up the deserted steps, toward an ugly baroque church lowering indistinctly on the brow. The flight didn't end at the church, but continued on up, slightly displaced to its side, and this time the upward vista was dizzying. Up I sailed. Wherever a baroque church provoked a kink or a break in the upward flight and brought on uncertainty, a youth seated on a stone marker was there to wave me on. At last the buildings gave way to open ground and I saw a railway line.

The woman in the station had a small child with a large ball beside her in the ticket office and they were helpfulness itself. There was a local train down to Agrigento in an hour and a half. Forty-five minutes after that a train left Agrigento for Palermo. I could be back in Palermo by eleven. The iron grille stopped me from embracing her, but we had quite a chat as she thumbed through schedules for the fares and the times and wrote the tickets out laboriously by hand. Not many people made this journey it seemed. I settled on to the wooden bench of the graffito-covered waiting room. On that bench, thinking about the huddled defensive secretiveness of the Sicilian hilltop towns of the interior, I recalled something I'd read some years before, at the Istituto Orientale in Naples.

The Orientale, now a university, had been founded in the eighteenth century by the Jesuits as a college for training Chinese acolytes and was known, in those heady days of the great plan to Christianize China, as the Chinese college. The French philosopher Montesquieu observed the firework display that was part of the opening celebrations and said he thought the educational effort might've been more usefully directed at Chinese business people. There was a painting in the rector's office of the founding father with two ostensibly Chinese boys who looked strangely like Neapolitan *scugnizzi*. Teaching English there to students of Arabic and Chinese, I used a text once on Islamic architecture, knowing nothing about this, and was struck by its exposition of the interiority of Islamic design in cities and buildings. Unlike European architects who were much concerned with a building's external appearance, Arab architects ignored or minimized the outside and turned wholly inward to the harmonies of interior space and interior decoration. The same was true of Arab town plans, with their bewildering maze, for those who didn't know them, of irregular streets, blind alleys, hidden almost private courtyards on to which a cluster of houses linked by family or trade would open. What I was starting to discover was how much Racalmuto, like many other old Sicilian town centres, kept to the patterns laid out by the Arab planners a thousand years ago, patterns that persisted through the monumental design imposed by later rulers, even though the mosques and nearly all the Arab buildings themselves had long ago disappeared.

It was as if this town embodied the hidden secrets and the vertiginous symmetries or asymmetries in the architecture of Sciascia's own labyrinthine stories. Many readers of his books had remarked that unlike the investigative thrillers they seemed to be, which started from a problem and arrived at a solution, Sciascia started from a problem that looked susceptible of rational solution and moved carefully and logically to a conclusion of total unknowing and enveloping dread. Was it the same funeral in the same street, or different funerals in different streets, or the same funeral in different streets, or ... The naturalistic Sciascia owed to his master Borges that sense of an annihilating metaphysics hidden in experience, that narrative shock you got when experience was thrown on to another plane of reality altogether. And if Sciascia's great enabling influence was Borges, *perhaps the key text in Borges' life and work*, as Robert Irwin wrote, was the great secular book of Arab literature *The Thousand and One Nights*.

> Borges found in the *Nights* precisely what he was hoping to find – *doppelgängers*, self-reflexiveness, labyrinthine structures and paradoxes, and especially paradoxes of circularity and infinity.

Borges had mentioned an almost apocryphal moment in the *Nights*,

> when Queen Scheherazade, through a magical mistake on the part of her copyist, started to tell the story of *The Thousand and One Nights*, with the risk of again arriving at the night upon which she will relate it, and so on to infinity.

Something odd was going on here. The oddness was that all this literary filtering and indirection from Arabic to English to Spanish to Italian came back to the old Arabic starting point. Through the *Arabian Nights*, Borges was making it possible for Sciascia to make stories out of an Arabic reality he lived in all his life in the closed and secret hilltop warren of Racalmuto, *the dead village*. Sciascia's very name was Arabic, meaning head veil, and until Italian unification had been written Xaxa. These closed and enigmatic alleys bodied forth what Sciascia found in Borges. Or Borges codified the physical and social world of inland Sicily. And not only Racalmuto, but all of Sicily and in the end Italy itself.

There were more concrete reasons for that grim silence too. Between Sciascia's birth in 1921 and his death in 1989 Racalmuto's population fell by more than three thousand, a quarter, most of them gone in the last forty years. Some of those closed and lightless houses were simply abandoned. The thousands were lost to emigration in the hard times as the sulphur mines closed one by one: the crisis came after the war, when the young Sciascia was teaching hungry children in a local school. The mine work itself had been a horror. Children sent down sometimes as young as ten, buggered as their induction to the bottom of a hierarchy of naked labourers slaving in the scorching air-less underground passages. Sciascia's grandfather, whom he worshipped, had been one of these. At the age of nine he'd taken his father's place in the mine and stayed there all his life. He taught himself to read and write in the evenings after work in the mine. He was a mine foreman by the end, who never did deals with the mafia. His son, Sciascia's father, worked as a mine clerk, which meant that the child Sciascia wore shoes to school, unlike the children of the miners and peasants. Guttuso painted the bare forked *carusi* of the sulphur mines, an image of the oppressed that was already out of date.

Sciascia's childhood and adolescence were the years of fascism, and as he told it later it was fascism that shaped and drove his noncon-formism. His father had put on a black shirt to keep his job. *My grand-father would never have done that.* They were the years of mean compro-mise and little humiliations. Pirandello had left earnest instructions when he died that he be buried naked, appalled at the thought the regime might display his corpse in the fascist hierarch's fig he wore in life. About the mafia Sciascia's feelings were more complex. Fascism had been imposed from outside, from the continent. It was less easy in Racalmuto to separate yourself from an expression of your own cul-ture.

> Take this Sicilian reality I live in: a lot of things that make it up I dis-approve of and condemn, but I see them with pain and *from inside* ...
> It hurts when I denounce the mafia because a residue of mafia feel-ing stays alive in me, as it does in any Sicilian. So struggling against the mafia I struggle against myself. It's like a split, a laceration.

The Day of the Owl was in 1961 the first Italian novel to take the mafia as its subject, and Sciascia was always proud of this. It was immediate-ly successful and for years now, suitably expurgated of the odd coarse-ness in the dialogue, has been taught in Italian schools as a classic. Remarking on the rather long time it had taken him to complete a novel of barely a hundred pages, Sciascia wrote that most of that time had been spent cutting. He added that the cutting was directed less at honing and refining the narrative art than at

> fending off the possible intolerances of those who might consider themselves more or less directly attacked by my representation. Because in Italy, as is well known, you're not allowed to play round ... so imagine what might happen if instead of playing round one wants to be serious. The United States of America can have in their novels and films imbecile generals, corrupt judges and crooked cops. Even England, France ... Italy's never had them, hasn't now and never will. That's how it is ... I don't feel enough of a hero to provoke charges of slander and libel, not deliberately. So when I realized that my imagination hadn't taken sufficiently into account the limits imposed by the laws of the state, and even more than the laws, the susceptibilities of those who enforce them, I set myself to cut, cut, cut ... a few characters have disappeared, a few others have retreated into anonymity, a few sequences have gone. The story may even have been improved. Certainly, however, I haven't written it in that complete freedom a writer (and I call myself a writer only because I happen to write) should always enjoy.

The usual legal disclaimer follows. Thus are new art forms born. The Sciascian art of the word not spoken, the missing fact, the eliminated detail, the unstated relation, sleight of hand, banality knitted into something that constricts and chokes, started from the legal need to strip away politically sensitive detail from a flatly realistic scene of life in a Sicilian town. This is the kind of problem writers used to have in the countries of really existing socialism, to which the cold war Italy of limited sovereignty had more in common culturally than the Italians or their friends liked to admit.

That the three most famous Italian writers of this time, the friends and exact contemporaries Calvino, Pasolini and Sciascia, all in their early twenties at the war's end, all moved rapidly from a confidently realistic fiction to oblique, enigmatic and allegorical forms is worth pondering. It made for formal interest in their work at the expense of life. There is something pinched and limited in the solutions each found, a withering of promise. The most variously and openly productive, the most careless in the good sense, was Pasolini with his poetry, novels, films, journalism, and Pasolini was hounded all his life until his murder by hundreds of court cases for obscenity, blasphemy, immorality. Art was never untrammeled in postwar Italy.

The best fiction writer of postwar Italy was wholly forgotten and ignored well before the nineties. Giorgio Bassani's cluster of novels and novellas and stories, which he called *The Novel of Ferrara*, has a sensuous and subtle economy, a fulness of dramatic life and a depth of art that none of the other three come near. Bassani was somewhat older, and the difference was crucial, since his subject emerged from the unmentioned loss and devastation of the war and the annihilation of Ferrara's Jewish culture. He wrote about exclusion, desire, betrayal, memory. To read Bassani is to see why the others aren't novelists. It's telling that it was Bassani who recognized *The Leopard* as a masterpiece after the manuscript had been rejected in Lampedusa's life by the influential and progressive Sicilian writer Vittorini.

The Day of the Owl tells the spare and simple story of a mafia killing, later three mafia killings, in a Sicilian town and their investigation by the local police and carabinieri. A small building contractor is murdered in the town piazza for having resisted mafia protection offers. A witness and an informer are later eliminated. The captain of carabinieri is a bright young northerner, in whom some thought they recognized the young Dalla Chiesa, who by cunning entraps the killers and more dangerously ensnares in the process the powerful old mafia boss of the district, or maybe the *capo di tutti i capi* of all Sicily, who looks and sounds a lot like don Calò Vizzini. The game of entrapment is the story's real spark, the germ of Sciascia's future art. The rest is economical, generic, sometimes witty. It opens on a bus leaving a country town piazza early on a cold morning, the driver and conductor and the peasant women with their produce, the seller of hot *panelle* and the two shots in the grey light and the boarding passenger in the dark suit who falls back off the step. The ashen faces of driver and conductor, bound to be witnesses, the *panelle* man, *shuffling crabwise off toward the church door*. Even as the carabinieri arrive, the passengers vanish.

> In apparent indolence, turning back as if trying to gauge the right distance from which to admire the bell-tower, they moved off toward the margins of the piazza and after a final glance, slipped away.

Nobody's seen a thing. The captain's investigation is intercut with conversations, some in Rome and others over the telephone, in which the speakers aren't always identified. This is the story's other level and it corresponds to what *The True History* calls the third level of mafia activity, the political one. The conversations variously involve nameless mafiosi in Rome, a nameless minister and his parliamentary factotum, the nameless commander of carabinieri, a nameless member of parliament. Other politicians are named, and you're left uncertain whether the compromising words are theirs. The young captain's investigation connects the killers and the mafia boss, and the conversations trace the links between the mafia boss don Mariano through the great chain of political being to the minister. Clearly, this was where Sciascia did his airbrushing.

Young captain Bellodi works away at the case, unaware of what his superiors are saying about him, or then again, perhaps not. For the minister, Bellodi is

> one who sees mafia in everything, one of those northerners with their head full of prejudices who start seeing mafia everywhere the moment they get off the ferry ... he's said things that'd make your hair stand on end: that the mafia exists, that it's a powerful organization, that it controls everything: sheep, market produce, public works and Greek vases.

The captain is duly reproved by his nameless superior for insisting that the mafia exists.

> ... is it possible to conceive of the existence of a criminal association so vast and well-organized, so secret and powerful that it dominates not only half of Sicily but the United States of America as well? And with a chief here in Sicily, visited by journalists and then presented in the papers, poor man, in the darkest tones ... has there ever been a trial in which it has emerged that a criminal organization called the mafia existed, and that the order and execution of any crime could be attributed to it with certainty? Has any document ever been found, any testimony, any proof of any kind that proves a connection between any criminal act and the so-called mafia?

The parliamentarian frets as

> the chain gets longer and longer, long enough for me to get caught up in it, and the minister and the heavenly father himself. A disaster, my dear friend, a disaster ...

while Bellodi, aware of the boss's social power if not yet of the protection he enjoys, reflects as his investigation begins to stall, that it's

> useless trying to catch out someone like him in breaking the law. There'll never be sufficient proof, the silence of the honest and the dishonest will always protect him ... get them on tax evasion, like they do in America ... you'd have to raid the banks, get expert hands on the accounts books, usually double accounting, of the big and little firms, look into property values ...

The crux of the story is the confrontation between the cunning old boss and the bright young carabiniere captain, in the discovery of a reciprocal *respect*, essential Sicilian concept, which momentarily disconcerts captain Bellodi. The mafioso don Mariano lists the degrees of being in his all-male mafioso hierarchy of humanity.

> *Real men, half-men, little men, the ones who get fucked over and the quackers, total nobodies, ... You, even if you nail me like Christ to these documents, are a man.*
>
> *And so are you*, said the captain with some emotion. And in the unease he soon felt at this exchange of military salutes with a mafia boss, he recalled, to justify himself, having shaken the hands of the minister Mancuso and the Hon. Livigni ... over whom don Mariano had the advantage of being a real man. Beyond law and morality, he was an unredeemed mass of human energy, a mass of solitude, a blind and tragic will. And as a blind man reconstructs the dark and shapeless world of objects in his mind, so did don Mariano reconstruct the world of feelings, laws, human relations. And what other notion of the world could he have, if around him the voice of the law had always been stifled by force and the wind of events had only changed the colour of the words on an immobile and putrid reality.

The fatalism of the last lines is very like that historical fatalism expressed three years earlier in Tomasi di Lampedusa's *The Leopard*, a book Sciascia had sharply criticized for its fatalistic vision of an unchanging Sicily. Sciascia's is a deeply sympathetic portrait of the mafioso in rural Sicily as a principle of order, however imperfect, and a helpless victim of outside forces.

Sciascia's picture of the mafia as an essentially rural force was losing actuality even in 1961. By the end of the fifties, the mafia's centre of gravity had shifted to the cities and Cosa Nostra was heavily into construction and real estate. This was four years after the 1957 summit at the hotel Delle Palme when the Cupola was formed and the Sicilians took over the international drug traffic. The acuteness, frankness, daring and the sheer novelty of the way Sciascia linked the political complicities reaching from a murder in rural Sicily to the government in Rome obscured the affectionate nostalgia in his portrait of the old killer. The folk wisdom offered by Sciascia's capo, and the captain's response, are picturesque and almost reassuring.

> The truth is at the bottom of a well. You look in a well and you see the sun or the moon, but if you jump in there's no longer the sun or the moon, there's the truth ...

You've helped a lot of men find truth at the bottom of a well ...

———————

THE MAFIOSO opens up to the young carabiniere because he's treated for once with intelligence and respect. This was a value that survived the move to the cities, and something Giovanni Falcone would've appreciated in Sciascia, and maybe learnt from. Thirty years later Falcone explained the phenomenon of the pentiti, and why it was he who'd gained the confidence of mafiosi in crisis.

> ... why have these men of honour shown trust in me? Because, I believe, they know what respect I have for their torments, that I don't deceive them ... I've tried to enter into their human drama and before going on to the real interrogation, I've always tried to understand each one's personal problems and place them in a precise context.

Within the mafia the overriding imperative for each man of honour was to tell the truth. Falcone explained that when a mass of complex activities were all conducted by word of mouth, this was a matter of organizational necessity. Embodied in mafia culture, it became something more, as Falcone recognized.

> The categorical imperative of the mafiosi, *tell the truth*, has become a key principle in my own personal ethic ... however strange it might seem, the mafia has taught me a lesson in morality ... Knowing mafiosi has deeply influenced my way of relating to others and even my beliefs.

Falcone went on to say that his experience of the mafia-state made him realize how much more functional and efficient it was than the Italian state he was representing. All this was close to the empathy and respect that pass between the young captain and the old boss in the novel, and to Sciascia's recognition in himself of the mafia mindset. The Sicilian writer and the Sicilian magistrate were both able to interiorize mafia values and identify with men of honour. This, though unspoken in anything I was later able to elicit from the magistrates I met who were now working on the mafia in Palermo, was what Falcone and the anti-mafia pool and its successor magistrates found really valuable in Sciascia and why they continued to revere him as a master. It was knowing the mafia's part in Sicilian history, being aware they were themselves a part of that history and culture. A sense of relatedness, empathy and, yes, respect.

It wasn't any special knowledge Sciascia had of what Cosa Nostra was and how it worked. As he sat with Guttuso on Palermo city council in the seventies, then in the eighties sat in parliament in Rome and later still Strasbourg, Sciascia developed a brilliantly inward knowledge of Italy's mafioso politics, as he showed in his essay on Moro's death. He didn't show any particular sense after the sixties and his first two novels, *The Day of the Owl* and *To Each His Own*, of the social reality of Cosa Nostra and how it was changing. The more Sciascia became known as an authority on Sicily and the mafia, the more out of touch he became with what the mafia was becoming in that time of rapid change.

He wasn't particularly alive to the momentousness of the maxitrial, and the blow Falcone and Borsellino struck at Cosa Nostra at a time when Cosa Nostra was incomparably more rich and powerful and cruel than it'd ever been in history. Thinking more of the past, and Mussolini's fascist repression of the mafia, than of the present, he rather misread its significance. Alexander Stille rightly calls the maxitrial indictment, largely written by Falcone, *a truly magisterial document: a great historical saga with the sweep of a Tolstoyan novel.* It opens

> This is the trial of the mafia organization named Cosa Nostra, a highly dangerous criminal association which through violence and intimidation has sown and continues to sow death and terror ...

Like *The True History of Italy*, the corresponding document for the Andreotti trial, the maxitrial document published in Italy as *Mafia* transfixes the reader by its wealth of detail and the power of its organizing intelligence. Fourteen years before the maxitrial opened, when Sciascia wrote the afterword to *The Context* in 1971, he was able to say quite correctly that imaginative writers were the only people to have really examined the criminal and political realities of modern Italy. Seven years later he returned to the theme in his essay on *The Moro Affair* and he was still right. Seven years on, however, the real history was being recorded by people involved in making it, the magistrates of Italy. In the nineteen-eighties Sciascia was at the apex of his prestige and authority as a writer and intellectual, but he'd lost that central awareness he'd once had.

Shortly before the maxitrial began, Leoluca Orlando was elected mayor of Palermo. As a demochristian politician trying to break the city's long habit of cohabitation and connivance with Cosa Nostra, Orlando like Falcone and Borsellino had many political enemies. It wasn't surprizing that in the middle of the maxitrial, at the beginning of 1987, Borsellino and Orlando and by implication Falcone should have found themselves, not for the first time, under heavy attack in the media. What surprized and disoriented people was that the attack was led by Leonardo Sciascia. In one of his pieces for the *Corriere della Sera*, reviewing a book on the mafia under fascism, he'd drawn a parallel between Mussolini's repression and the suddenly effective antimafia effort of the eighties. Borsellino by name and Orlando by unmistakeable allusion were accused of using the antimafia stance to promote their own careers. The attack was soon out of Sciascia's hands. It was seized on by antiantimafia interests who used the cover of his great prestige to pump it into one of those controversies that were so often made to serve dubious politics in Italy, a duststorm.

Sciascia's article led directly to Falcone's defeat at the end of 1987 in the election of a new Palermo chief prosecutor. A magistrate was chosen whose last case as criminal prosecutor had been in northern Italy in 1949. Some magistrates cited Sciascia's piece and the controversy to justify voting against Falcone. *That was when they began to kill him*, said Paolo Borsellino after Falcone died. Meanwhile a lot of very dubious people not hitherto known as readers found that they *agreed with Sciascia*. Orlando and Borsellino kept their own counsel. *Sciascia is the Italian language*, Orlando told a reporter wanting a soundbite. *I have the greatest respect for the Italian language*. Borsellino merely said how much he admired Sciascia the writer. It was the time of Riina's secret order to kill them.

Sciascia never retracted his words. He became increasingly intolerant of *imbeciles*, *cretins* and anyone, always *in bad faith*, who disagreed with him. He showed a certain odd self-identification with Voltaire and some reluctance to admit in those confused and violent years that he might not know the answers to questions about mafia and politics. Earlier he'd sometimes seemed like an Italian Orwell, a careful, scrupulous truth teller who valued his integrity more highly than his art, and the sick and pessimistic Sciascia of the last years also recalled the blackness of the dying Orwell. Sciascia's deepening gloom was sometimes lit by flashes of arrogance, meannness or perversity. He didn't seem to realize how much people had come to value his thought or what damage he did. He didn't seem to realize how dangerous a gift a nonconformist reputation was. He later admitted privately to Borsellino that the accusation of careerism was based on misinformation. The day after Sciascia's attack on the *antimafia professionals* appeared, Falcone and Orlando flew to Moscow together. Orlando quoted a Sicilian proverb about how when it rained all the snails put out their horns, and Falcone laughed. When Sciascia was dying, Orlando visited him to make peace. *I'm finished*, Sciascia whispered. *But so are you, mayor.* Orlando told him, *Don't you worry about me*, and he was right. Orlando was a survivor.

Racalmuto closed for Sciascia's funeral in 1989 and maybe seven thousand people crowded outside the church, more than half the town. His coffin was carried by some he'd taught as children. The old *carusi* from the sulphur mines rang the bells and the funeral notice posted on the town's walls by the labourers who'd occupied the feudal estates fifty years earlier remembered Sciascia tersely as *a friend of the oppressed*. His publishers Einaudi and Sellerio were there; and the Mezzogiorno's film directors Lina Wertmüller and Francesco Rosi, and the writer Gesualdo Bufalino, a Sciascia discovery, who remarked that *maybe his true religion was doubt*. Orlando came, and a number of politicians from the three major parties, including the socialist leader and former prime minister Bettino Craxi, the former minister Giacomo Mancini and the demochristian minister Calogero Mannino. Craxi found time to say, as he elbowed his way with his bodyguards to his armour-plated car, that *Sciascia was a man who loved the truth, who searched for it and wrote it. He was a free mind who opposed above all fanaticism and intolerance.*

Sciascia would've liked the compliment, but I wondered what he would have thought of its source. I sat in the waiting room at Racalmuto and my eye fell on one of the extensive pencilled remarks on its painted wall. *CRACI IS COKSUKER*. In the eighties, a lot of people thought that was why the then prime minister had built himself a lavish villa on the beach in Tunisia, but instead it was foresight. Tunisia has no extradition treaty with Italy and three years after Sciascia's funeral Craxi had skipped abroad just ahead of his first arrest warrant, and he'd been living in Tunisia ever since, mounting up sentences for corruption of twenty-five-odd years in all and a court order to repay at least fifty million dollars of the money he'd pocketed in office. The former minister Mannino was in jail now on charges of mafia membership and the former minister Mancini was about to be convicted of the same thing in Calabria. It'd been an equivocal funeral homage for the truth-seeker.

Railway users in Racalmuto turned out to be highly opinionated, though terrible spellers. One ancient inscription read *ANDREOTI IS MAFIA BOSS*. There were imprecations against the antimafia Network, the DC, the Pope, the Vatican and Palermo. *THE MAYOR OF RACALMUTO MAFIA* read another. Judgements extended to economics: *THE ITALIAN LIRA MAKES ME SIK.* The most striking phrase wasn't pencilled but done with a housepainting brush in big brown letters. *DON'T BETRAY US NITTO SANTAPAOLA.* Santapaola was a very important figure in Cosa Nostra, the most powerful boss of the Catania mafia, at least until his arrest. Was the exhortation not to talk, not to repent, or did it predate the arrest and refer to some internecine conflict, maybe the reason Santapaola's wife had been murdered at home by gunmen? As areas of influence went, it was a puzzling message to find in Racalmuto. I was brooding on it when the train arrived. After a wait in the warm drizzle of a dark and deserted Agrigento, I headed north to Palermo and made it to the Sant'Andrea in time for a grilled fish at nearly midnight.

NO ARTIST made art of the mafia before Sciascia and nobody has so far followed him. His own first master had been Pirandello and the first book Sciascia ever wrote was on *Pirandello and Sicily*, on the metaphysician of uncertain identity, the social mask, appearance and reality. They were almost neighbours, Sciascia and Pirandello. Agrigento where I was changing trains just down the hill on the sea was Pirandello's town. Even in Pirandello's time it was a great mafia centre but you'd never know it from Pirandello's work, however well you saw his themes belonged, once you did know, to the world of the mafia.

As for Sciascia himself, after his first novels on the mafia and politics, he turned more and more to working in a genre he'd practically invented, probing into the documents of old real life mysteries, reconstructing and interpreting events of the past. If the turning point in his writing seemed to be marked by the pamphlet on the Moro affair, that was hardly an accident. At the start of the essay he'd remarked on the frightening way the whole business seemed to have been anticipated in his fiction, making him seem almost responsible for what'd then happened in life. This wasn't just an opening cleverness, as his work after that showed. To make it even clearer he explained a few years later,

> Since Moro's death I no longer feel free to imagine things. This is one of the reasons I prefer to reconstruct things that have already happened. I'm afraid to say things that might happen.

XII

MIDNIGHT IN SICILY

THE TWENTY-SIXTH of September was a very hot late summer day in Palermo. The air was full of heat and dust and reflections of the blinding sun. Outside the high steel fence that protected the bunker courtroom, reached at the end of a rustic alley cut below the level of the main road, having passed the soldiers in camouflage standing by a truck with their submachine guns ready, having shown their documents to these and been fed down the path to the steel fence and the gate, three hundred and twenty-eight accredited members of the international media sweated and jostled in a narrow space as the sun inched higher and the light became blinding and they wondered whether the trial would ever start. An Italian journalist was trying to explain in halting English to a Japanese TV reporter just who Andreotti was and why he was on trial. The Japanese had no idea. Most people had no idea, but they knew the word mafia and clung to it. The word created a fleeting sense of community and solidarity as we all jostled for precedence and pretended not to jostle. It was the word everyone knew. We were here for the mafia. Our various publics wanted to know about the mafia. Perhaps our publics didn't, or not all that much, but they'd like to see a mafioso for a moment on the evening news. They'd see at any rate the event, the guards, the machine guns, the dogs, the fence, the helicopters, the TV crews, the crowd. Giorgio Bocca was feeding sound bites to a series of TV cameras, and when he'd finished and they'd turned away we spoke and made an appointment for the Villa Igiea that evening. Then we turned our attention once again to the narrow gate in the high steel fence.

Somewhere outside of this crowd, somewhere out of the choked city centre, in some as yet unidentified shed on the outskirts of the city, was Giovanni Brusca. Riina had been taken and Bagarella had been taken but still there was Brusca. He was the man who'd pressed the detonator under the olive tree that'd exploded under Falcone's caravan of armourplated cars on the way from the airport to Palermo. Brusca was the man who'd had a child kidnapped and strangled and dissolved in acid because the child was the son of a pentito. Brusca, when he wanted to know something, asked questions with a chain saw. Brusca was known now to have in his as yet unlocated shed on the outskirts of Palermo a missile launcher, and it was thought he might be aiming it now at the bunker courtroom. Fortunately for the good humour and serenity of the cosmopolitan group now chatting and jostling and pretending not to jostle outside the gate, the fact was not yet widely known.

After nine and already sweltering, the soldiers and the police and the carabinieri braced themselves and opened the narrow gate to the members of the media who were authorized to enter and who'd converged distractedly on the heat and dust of Palermo from different parts of the world and were now slowly filtered into the bunker through documentary scrutiny and three separate sets of electronic controls, pushing and pretending not to push, their documents in many languages scrutinized, their names checked off lists at the gate, their bags opened and passed through metal detectors, slowly, interminably, along to another checkpoint, fed in through a kind of decompression chamber, peered at through bulletproof glass, heaving at the massive door, fed into a sloping corridor and into the *aula bunker*, bigger than a football field, with kilometres of polished wooden benches, thousands of mikes like drooping silver poppies, a dais for the judges that could've handled a rock concert, and at the back, lining the interminable and slightly curved walls, the dozens and dozens of green-barred empty mafia cages that still bore the scars and smears and stains of the maxitrial. In the gallery above the cages were a handful of ordinary Palermitans and the TV cameras and the photographers. The media were allowed now on to the benches that had once been the lawyers', the hundreds of lawyers of the maxitrial. A little cord separated the first three rows that were now the lawyers'.

On the left of a central dividing corridor was the Palermo chief prosecutor Gian Carlo Caselli, slender in a dark suit, carrying his mane of snowy hair like a banner of righteousness, Falcone's and Borsellino's successor, by now one of the best known names and the most seen coiffures in Italy. Beside him were Gioacchino Natoli, Guido Lo Forte and Roberto Scarpinato the three prosecutors, the three who'd assembled the mass of memories and accusations that was *The True History of Italy*. Beyond them, beyond another little chasm between rows, was Leoluca Orlando sitting with the lawyers of the city of Palermo, dark faced, dark haired, dark suited. I sat near the front and near the middle. I looked around the air-conditioned vastness of the courtroom. THE LAW IS EQUAL FOR ALL said the letters on the judges' empty bench. I took in the prosecutors and Orlando, the carabinieri standing in pairs, the mob of unshaven bodyguards lounging around the prosecutors in jeans and vests. I wondered when the judge would appear, the little man they said was inflexible, incorruptible, the *iron toga*, Ingargiola. I rang Australia on my cellular phone. Then I noticed, last, the little knot of people just in front of me. The little unnoticed figure between two lawyers. There was something almost familiar in that figure. I hadn't seen him come in.

Hunched and immobile between those costly lawyers, big head still thick with hair, triangular ears projecting horizontally, the tiny seventy-six-year-old body was collapsed in on itself, drained of power, and the hump a kind of bulwark. It was good luck in the Mezzogiorno to touch a hunchback's hump, and from my front row seat I could have leaned over the intervening bench and reached it, that hump. Ingargiola had entered flanked by his deputies and the prosecution was well into the elaborate and lengthy expression of its opposition to the live TV broadcasting of the trial then starting, when, for the first time since proceedings began, the stony figure moved. Only a little. Lizard-like. Crunching sweets inside that lipless mouth They sounded like breaking stones. Toying with a pen in those *diaphanous* hands. Then the head swivelled almost imperceptibly to his right, as if feeling the weight of the gaze I was unable to lift, and through the glittering lenses, for an instant our gazes locked. *Clever and cunning and with friendships beyond all imagining*, the pentito Marino Mannoia had said. The little hairs on my spine stood on end. This was Life Senator Andreotti. This, dressed in a dreadful little double breasted suit the colour of the uniform worn by employees of the Italian state railway, with under the jacket on this sweltering day a heavy grey long-sleeved cardigan like a priest's, was Beelzebub.

ANDREOTTI HAD arrived in Palermo the evening before. He'd flown down from Rome on an ordinary Alitalia flight, because, as he'd said, *it would have been inopportune to use the aeroplane I had a right to as former prime minister.* He'd packed with his pyjamas the works of Saint Teresa of Lisieux, the catholic visionary who'd seen her name written across the heavens. He'd brought *The Way*, by Escrivà, who'd founded Opus Dei, and I wondered on learning that whether this mightn't have been a little hint to His Holiness. Coming south for his trial, Andreotti had consoled himself with a passage from this book.

> Tongues have loosened and you have suffered insults that have wounded you the more because you did not expect them. Your reaction must be to pardon and even to ask for pardon and draw profit from the experience to detach yourself from creatures.

He'd toyed aloud with the idea of reading it in court before his accusers, wondering what the effect might be. It was inevitable, as he flew south, that Andreotti should have reminisced about Sicily, the island he'd first visited as a catholic student leader in 1942 and where he'd spent at most, he'd said, a total of twenty days in his whole life. *A lot of things are dangerous in Sicily*, he'd said, He was talking about the baffling social rituals, the humid heat and the dust and the hand kissing and the food.

> *I found myself with my stomach full of marvellous but terrible food, the pasta con le sarde, the cassata, and not only did I not understand a thing there but I was ill too. I wonder whether there's a connection between food like this and the growth of the mafia.*

He talked about the art too, and the abandoned museums of Sicily.

> *And yet it's a region so rich in art, perhaps that's the very reason they don't take too much care of it. I often thought I'd like to make a tour, a proper tour of Sicily. Just as well I didn't. I'd be in jail by now for sure.*

As politicians will, Andreotti had started running through names on the flight toward Palermo, people he'd known in Sicily, Sicilians he'd known elsewhere, names that might have reflected well on his own. He'd touched only briefly on Sciascia, *we chatted a few times*, because Sciascia was rebarbative even with his friends, but he'd let himself flow more freely on Guttuso. *How amazed he'd be today to know his old friend Giulio is the chief of the mafia ... I was a great friend of Renato Guttuso. I met him soon after the war ...* He'd remembered the Sunday friends,

> *all communists except me and monsignor Angelini. We never talked about*

politics. We were great friends. Guttuso especially. He often came to my place, he was a family friend. I remember he so insisted he wanted to paint my portrait. But I didn't want to seem over-keen and I kept putting him off ...

The old fox was establishing his credentials, his friendships. I recalled Montaigne. *Who can we trust when he speaks about himself? ... Truth for us today isn't what is, but what others can be brought to believe...*

Andreotti had been playing for pathos with some effect, and calling in his credits where he could. Andreotti had been alluding at the airport to the fact that he might well be dead before his years in court were over. He'd been spending a lot of time at prayer in the better-known churches of Rome. There'd been a flurry of pretrial chat show appearances, in which brave, stoic, tiny hunched Giulio Andreotti *displayed flashes of his old wit*. The publicity had had some startling spinoffs. Colonel Gheddafi was touched enough by what he heard to offer the next day to pay Andreotti's legal costs, which might have been unwise. You wondered whether he knew what he was letting himself in for, and whether the offer extended to the costs of the Pecorelli murder trial that was also about to open in Perugia and would be running concurrently with the mafia trial in Palermo. The life senator hadn't mentioned the Pecorelli trial on the plane south. He hadn't mentioned it at all. The Pecorelli trial was certainly related to the mafia trial but it lacked the political colouring, the historical patina, the cast of thousands. The Pecorelli trial was unpleasantly specific and circumscribed in its circumstances and logic. There'd been one clear beneficiary from Pecorelli's death. There was less to reminisce engagingly about.

The Gheddafi offer could hardly be seen as a major publicity plus in a country where many well remembered the string of the colonel's exiled political opponents found with their throats cut in cheap pensioni up and down the peninsula fifteen years earlier, and all the ambiguities of Italy's foreign policy in the Andreotti years. The Kissinger withdrawal a couple of weeks earlier had been a definite minus. There'd been hints, in the weeks before the trial, that Henry Kissinger would be testifying for the defence in Palermo. Shortly before the trial opened the senior partner of Kissinger Associates had been in Rome and had greeted Andreotti, but there'd been a rather loud silence after their meeting on the question of testimony. Nixon's Metternich knew a no-win situation when he saw one. A further unpleasantness for Andreotti had been the humiliation of booking Room 102 at the Villa Igiea, with sea view and private terrace, and then being whisked off on landing *for security reasons* to the Delle Palme which was definitely not the hotel it had once been. *I do not understand*, he'd hissed in the foyer of the Delle Palme, *why they have made me change hotels.*

Giorgio Bocca was there, though, at the Villa Igiea, and we sat and talked on the evening of the trial's first day amid the faded relics of art nouveau. The Villa Igiea dated, like Fulco di Verdura, from 1900, a beautiful people year in Palermo, when the rich and the royal came in their yachts. Old photos on the wall of the Villa Igiea showed Edward VII, Rilke, the King of Siam and ladies in furs and big hats. There was none of John Gambino or his girlfriend Mixie Ritz. Bocca was smilingly pessimistic about everything. About the trial, about the mafia, especially about Sicily. He came from the far north of Italy, at its cold and mountainous extremity of Cuneo, he'd fought in the snow with the partisans as a boy. He was one of Calvino's, Sciascia's, Pasolini's generation, and in books and articles of commentary he'd charted the course of the Italian republic's first fifty years.

Sciascia, he said at the mention of that name. *He really did know about the mafia. When I was down here going around for my book I asked him for some introductions. When I went to see these people they were all local mafia bosses.* Bocca was openly and simply a northerner in seeing the mafia as an alien growth of the south, and something that contaminated everything. Falcone, he said, had had the mafia mentality. Falcone and Sciascia had both said this about themselves. *Falcone made pentiti call him Judge, he insisted on respect. In Milan they wouldn't give a damn what you called them, they'd just get on with their work.* Nothing about the trial surprised him or stirred him or gave him hope. Andreotti always kept bad company, he said. Had a taste for the very worst. Bocca dwelt on the grimness of mafia lives, the losing families locked in their jerry built flats with armoured doors and shutters always closed, scared to go out. And it would, he insisted, be always so. Personally, he preferred the camorristi of Naples. *At least they know how to enjoy themselves.*

He'd been the same with Paolo Borsellino in 1992, when Borsellino had given him a brilliant, terse summary of the state of play for Bocca's book on the Mezzogiorno, the book he then went and called *Inferno.* *Haven't we got good reasons for pessimism?* he'd asked, and Borsellino had given him an emphatic *No*, recalling the Sicily he'd grown up in, the new consciousness he saw abroad in young Sicilians. *Progress is slow, I agree. But no mayor of Palermo before Orlando had ever pronounced the word mafia, and Orlando's spoken it.* Bocca had grumbled in his book that now people pronounced the word far too much. From Borsellino's house, the judge had given Bocca a lift to the Villa Igiea in his armourplated car, and had stopped a moment at the reception desk to make a phone call. Bocca went to dinner that night with another journalist, who stopped in the pizzeria to speak with someone Bocca didn't know. When he rejoined Bocca, he told him the other worked for the secret services, and had said, *Bocca was seen with Borsellino today. What's he doing here?* The news could only have come from one of the three impeccable tail-coated doormen at the grand hotel Villa Igiea. *One of them was a police informer and maybe the mafia's.* A month or so after the meeting Borsellino was blown up. For the second time that day, I shivered as I walked out into the damp and salty seafront warmth of the night.

THE TRIAL'S first day arrived first at a ruling against live television transmissions of the proceedings, which was a point for the prosecution, and then an adjournment for the judges to consider the defence application to move the trial from Palermo. The defence seemed less concerned about where the trial *was* held, as long as it was out of Palermo. Franco Coppi, Andreotti's Roman advocate, delivered a tightly argued and subtly modulated speech of an hour and more without notes, strong and elegant, and led the courtroom spellbound through the intricate and compelling architecture of vast Latinate periods constructed to persuade the judges that as minister and head of government during the time of his alleged mafia crimes, Andreotti should be tried in Rome, or in Perugia where he was being tried in the related case of the murder of Mino Pecorelli. For the prosecution, the clerkly Guido Lo Forte insisted that on the contrary the crimes of which Andreotti was accused were commited in Palermo, where Cosa Nostra had its seat, and that therefore he should be tried in Palermo. A trial in Rome would presumably have meant starting again from scratch, given Italy's complicated territorial divisions, under a different prosecution team as well as a different judge. I wasn't able to find anyone to clarify this point, so unthinkable was a transfer considered. Nor was I ever able to find out why the Pecorelli murder trial was being heard in Perugia, which seemed to have nothing to do with the ordering, planning or execution of the killing. It was going to take the court a couple of weeks to rule on Palermo as the trial site.

So there was some time to follow other matters, and one trail I'd been wanting to follow for years led not into the recent past of Palermo and Rome but back down the western coast of Sicily a bit beyond Trapani, and two and a half thousand years into the island's past. The Greek historian Thucydides wrote in the fifth century BCE that, in Thomas Hobbes's seventeenth-century translation the Phoenecians inhabited the coast of Sicily on all sides, having taken possession of certain promontories and little islands adjacent, for trade's sake with the Sicilians. But after that many Grecians were come in by sea, the Phoenecians abandoned most of their former habitations, and uniting themselves, dwelt in Motya and Soloeis and Panormus... because also from thence lay the shortest cut over unto Carthage. These were the barbarians, and thus they inhabited Sicily.

The island of Mozia still lies on *the shortest cut over unto Carthage* from Panormus. The ferry from Palermo to Tunis passes Mozia as it follows the western coast of Sicily from Trapani to Marsala and beyond, heading south to Africa. Mozia's hidden on the seaward side by another, larger island. Mozia itself is tiny, forty-five hectares, though it was once the biggest Phoenician settlement in Sicily and the oldest. Seven centuries BCE the Carthaginians surrounded the island with a mile and a half of fortified walls with towers and gates. It was their key base in Sicily in their endless war with the Greeks for control of the trade routes of the western Mediterranean.

Three centuries later, just after Thucydides wrote, the Carthaginians attacked and destroyed the Greek city of Selinunte in the Belice valley further south. What remained of Selinunte has now been reduced by earthquakes over the centuries to a pile of stones. The great panels from its temple, carved with scenes from the Greek myths, are now in the museum at Palermo. Twelve years later the Greeks struck back, besieged Motya and finally destroyed the settlement after a great naval clash. Warfare made a technological leap here with the first use of catapults. The Carthaginians soon returned, but moved their base to a place they massively fortified, which later became Marsala, a few miles south on the Sicilian mainland. Motya never regained its former importance, and as Motya the little island was soon forgotten.

It wasn't until late last century that the island mentioned by Thucydides was identified as San Pantaleo, where the Whitaker family, one of those English families like the Woodhouses and the Inghams that got rich in Sicily from the export of marsala, had built a handsome villa. Giuseppe Whitaker started excavating his island's remains, uncovering the dry dock carved out of the stone and the ship repair yards, the walls, the towers, the gate that opened on the paved road that once led north to the mainland and was now under water. Pottery kilns were found, houses, a temple, a cemetery and the *tophet* where the Phoenicians ritually sacrificed small children to their god Baal. A small museum was made in the villa Whitaker to house the finds. In 1995 the museum also held a statue, much more recently uncovered from the rubble on the island. It was found in 1979, lying on its back, without head or arms or feet. The arms and feet were never found, but the head turned up nearby and fitted perfectly. The statue was marble, Greek and for fifteen years I'd wanted to see it. I seized my chance when the moment came to return the couscous bowls to Angelo and Clara.

The day was grey and the area around Trapani and Marsala utterly flat. We passed huge salt pans, and little hills of discoloured salt. The windmills, mostly abandoned, that now dotted the landscape weren't the only thing that recalled the North Sea, now that the green and sunny look of the earlier visit was gone. A mean, nagging wind whistled in off the sea and heaped clouds tumbled overhead. Everything now looked grey. A small breakwater jutted toward Mozia's trees and the pink villa partly hidden among them. The water was quite shallow and a couple of stone markers showed where horses could be ridden over at low tide. Nailed to the side of a shed was a notice saying the day's last boat had gone.

We moped as the wind whipped up shimmies and scuds of waves. There was nobody else in sight. The water's surface looked solid, like hammered metal. The sun through the boiling clouds turned the sky and sea pewter and silver, dark and dazzling together. Then our luck changed. A small boat was crossing shortly on an errand. We'd have half an hour on the island, maybe an hour. We chugged across. It was high tide and the wind was sheeting water over Mozia's little wooden jetty, where a couple of big dogs were ducking the spray and wagging their tails and barking up a frenzy at our approach. The island sprouted a lot of big scarred Indian figs in its dry sandy ground, and someone had hoisted a child's swing under one of the pines. Further on there were vines and olive trees. The bent and ruddy caretaker, a caretaker's caretaker, cheerful as you might expect someone to be who lived in such a place and had just had a proper Sunday lunch, took us round the back. The dogs came too, doing festive somersaults. The mean, sawing wind had suddenly dropped and the air was warm and still.

The museum of villa Whitaker held the results of Giuseppe Whitaker's amateur archeological potterings from the beginning of the century, and later findings of scientific excavation. Funeral steles and terracotta masks from the *tophet*, weapons and tools in bronze and iron, rare traces of history's cancelled Phoenicians, were grouped around dusty old glass cases of coloured beads. *Elements of a Punic necklace,* said the faded copperplate on one curling card, *recomposed by Miss Delia Whitaker.* I spent some dutiful minutes on all of these, later. The moment the caretaker opened up I headed for the statue of the Boy of Mozia. It took about two seconds to confirm a feeling I'd nursed for fifteen years, based on a newspaper description and some photos in an archeological review. Instinct had been right. This was one of the greatest surviving works of Greek sculpture. I was standing in front of a thing of unutterable beauty. This was one of the world's great art works. Skipping lunch left me suddenly weak and shaky. I stood back for a moment and leant on a case of Miss Whitaker's Punic necklaces.

GREAT ART is always an enigma. Nothing could be so unknown, so deeply and probably forever unknowable as the questions now enclosed by this statue. The Youth of Mozia was carved early in the fifth century BCE. This was one of European history's more significant centuries, the time of Athens and democracy, tragedy and sculpture. The Athenian democracy had defeated the invading Persian empire from the east in 480 BCE and in the same year, maybe on the very same day, the Greeks in Sicily had defeated the invading Carthaginians in the west near Panormus, or Palermo. The Carthaginians were forced back on their coastal strongholds of Motya, Panormus and Solunto, near Bagheria. Trade, contact, influence continued between the Greeks and the Phoenicians in Sicily, as the Greek vases found in the tombs of Mozia showed. Greeks lived and worked with the Carthaginians on Motya. Less than a hundred years later Mozia too would be wiped out by the Greeks.

The Persians sacked Athens and destroyed the Acropolis in 480 BCE, before they were defeated and driven back. Among the rubble of their destruction another headless marble statue of a boy was unearthed in 1865. Twenty-three years later its head was found. The forearms, both feet and the lower part of the right leg were missing, but the marble statue was otherwise intact and eighty-six centimetres high. The statue, now in the Acropolis museum in Athens, was new at the time of the Persian attack and may have been by the sculptor Kritios. The nude boy was a victor in the games. He was one of those works on which the history of art pivots, one of those works after which nothing is ever the same again. In Reinhard Lullies' description of the figure

> The boy ... stands calmly and confidently. The right leg is bent at the knee, the right thigh thrust forward, the shank placed slightly to the side and to the back, so that the displacement of the weight on to the left leg is also expressed in the upper part of the body and the

relation between the axes is shifted a little. The upper arms were drawn back, the left rather more than the right; the forearms were slightly raised from the elbow. The head is turned to the right. The eyes, which were inlaid with coloured material, gazed ahead self-confidently. The hair lies on the head in fine waves running from the crown of the head, and is taken up over a circlet. The down on the nape of the neck is arranged in alternating curls and straight wisps. The modelling of the body is extremely lively ...

The boy marked the moment when Greek sculpture became alive, when the frontal, rigid, upright smiling archaic *kouros* had become an observed living figure, not an idea of the young male but a real young athlete, distributing his weight and flexing his muscles as a living creature does. It was the moment of realism. The statue's nudity was realistic too. The statues of the fifth century showed athletes and warriors, and its gods as athletes and warriors, as they were in life in a society where the rituals of sport were supplanting those of war. The nude male's beauty was realistic and ideal at once.

The armless boy of Mozia departed more radically still from the at-attention stance of the statues of a few years earlier. His head was turned distinctly to the left, his left hand planted firmly on his hip. The right arm was raised high at the shoulder and must have carried a spear or a victor's wreath. Weight was thrust on to the tensed and straight left leg, leaving the right relaxed and half bent. His chest was thrust forward and the left cheek of his bum, the side taking his weight, jutted out prominently under his resting hand. Though the arm was missing, the thumb and two fingers of his left hand remained, pressing into the flesh of his hip. The whole body was slightly twisted around its vertical axis and the effect was of a lazy uncompleted movement quite unlike the Kritios boy's eager directness. It was quite different too from the exultance in the bodies of the two stupendous bronze warriors fished from the sea off Calabria seven years before the Mozia boy was found, two warriors who may have been contemporary with him. The Mozia body was splendid, muscular, shapely, but it didn't have the warrior's or the athlete's ideal tension.

The face was obliterated in the extremities of nose, mouth and chin and around the right cheek bone, but as you stared it seemed oddly intact and distinctive and undamaged by this blurring of its features. It wasn't unlike the Kritios boy's, artistically of that period, with a trace of the archaic stasis, but the oblique gaze made it more distinctly focused and more beautiful. The mouth seemed to have been rather large. Three rows of tight curls ran across his forehead, above his ears and lay longer on the back of his neck. The rest of the head was more or less smooth, and this and the presence of two bronze plates, and holes for three more, showed that it must have been set with a wreath or crown, some kind of head covering. He was a metre and eighty-one tall without his feet, larger than life.

The relaxed and sensual stance, the almost Hellenistic softness and subtlety of the modelling under that austerely beautiful head, was only part of the story. The uniqueness of the boy of Mozia, his baffling anomaly in the history of Greek art, was that he was clothed. He was wearing a long soft light sleeveless dress fastened, millennia ago, by a tight wide band around his chest, just under his arms, maybe some kind of bronze plate, and thereunder flowing loosely and lightly almost to the ground. The tunic was rendered as an ultralight fabric, I imagined a cotton, that puckered together in long narrow folds that became, in the sculpture, countless sinuous nearly vertical grooves. It was sleeveless but otherwise rather like a garment a friend of mine had worn on a trip up the Nile one summer, hot weather wear, floating and aerating with the slightest movement, clinging as if wet where the body pressed against it.

Its lightness and grace were modelled with incomparable fineness, but the most remarkable effect was the sensuousness of the cloth clinging to the bum and groin, the utter antithesis of that open vigorous nonsensual nudity of nearly every other extant Greek sculpture of a young male. The modelling of the hand pressing through the thin cloth into the flesh at the hip, the emphasis of the round buttock flattening the folds of the fabric where it protruded, the prominence given the genitals by the sense of the fabric flowing over them, revealing and not revealing, made them the focus of an erotic attention quite absent in the nudes. Modelling, posture, the teasing play of the gossamer fabric, were extraordinarily sensual, an erotically charged body under a strong and nearly archaic face. Nothing else remotely like this body would come out of Greece for hundreds of years, and when it did the tension, the strength that were also present here had been lost. Dario, who was studying art history at school, was baffled. He thought it was late, Hellenistic, until I pointed out the form of the head and, more persuasively, cited the authorities. His bafflement over style and dating concealed a deeper bafflement at this rendering of the male as erotic object.

This great and almost unknown work, not a whit less amazing than the bronzes of Riace, had been placed, in this little museum the size of a two-car garage, in a kind of fairground booth made out of unfinished packing-case pine boards nailed together to make a little waist-high platform on which the statue had been placed on a sheet of tin, and closed in by raw wooden walls at the back and each side and a roof just above the head. For the sake of a little finish, a scalloped fringe in burgundy cloth had been nailed along the front of the roof and a rope on stands covered with burgundy velvet had been placed in front. The statue was in deep shade and except from the front, totally hidden by its wooden box. The caretaker was chuffed when I asked about the box. *The roof was leaking*, he said, *and we wanted to put the statue somewhere nice, somewhere appropriate* ... He was beaming that his thought and care were so appreciated. With the caretaker's permisssion I stepped over the velvet rope and hoisted myself on to the dusty tin. I could see details but it was impossible, without ripping down the box, to see the boy in the round from a distance. You could only make mental elaborations and remember photos from the time of the discovery.

What did it represent, this anomalous Greek masterpiece imprisoned in its little booth? How had it come to Mozia? Nobody knew. The boy seemed too young to be a priestly figure, too languid to be an athlete or a warrior. The marble he was made of had come from Anatolia in Turkey and time had turned it pale gold. The alternatives seemed to be that the statue had been war booty taken by the Carthagians, maybe from Selinunte when they destroyed it, or that it had been commissioned from a Greek sculptor by a Carthaginian. That the amazing tunic was the Carthaginians' style of dress made the latter more likely. I had a fleeting vision of a sleek Phoenician businessman who'd known what he liked and had money to spend on art. A sculptor who'd entered into the spirit of the commission. Who'd found, even, that it drew from him resources of skill and daring he hadn't known he possessed until he was freed of the usual constraints ... The little historical fancy evaporated. It dispelled none of the enigma. It was hard to believe the truth about the sculpture would ever be known. And now the boatmen wanted to leave, so the dogs escorted us dancing back to the jetty.

In Palermo I returned later to the archeological museum whose best treasures were the carved panels from the temple at Selinunte, the city not far from Mozia the Carthaginians had destroyed. I was wondering whether the boy might have been carried off from there. The weather-ravaged panels were still wonderful, especially the carving of Actaeon savaged by his own dogs as he turned into a deer, but offered no stylistic clue. There was a statue in the same hall, a small one, that I'd forgotten, and this set me firm against the idea the Mozia boy could have come from the same place. This was another fifth-century ephebe, but a bronze one, pretty crudely proportioned, almost a caricature, not without a certain bug-eyed charm, though the head was far too big. The youth of Mozia belonged to no known world.

A bunch of barely pubescent schoolkids in rainbow leisurewear were trailing dreamily around with their teachers. It was a very warm day. But the little man in the tweed jacket from the museum staff made up for all of them in his bustling enthusiasm. He swamped the question and answer format by providing his own responses to every query. When the kids spoke he cut them short. It was the little bronze Ephebe of Selinunte that raised him to his greatest eloquence. He hymned the glories of the male nude in art, underlining its essentially ideal nature. The kids were taking a languid full frontal view, but he ushered the girls and boys to the rear. *Look at those buttocks, children. See that modelling. There is no vulgarity in those buttocks.* The contemplative silence was broken only by the muted explosions of bursting bubblegum.

The finest sculpture in the Palermo museum was another bronze up on the first floor, the bronze ram of Syracuse, lying down but lifting its forepaw and turning its head with a bleat, caught in the instant before standing, a marvel of animal intensity from the third century BCE. The sitting ram, and a scrawny one to Australian eyes, was given great presence and dignity by the attentiveness of its rendering. It had the strength of realism you often found in animals in art, things done out of delight in their life and not invested with ideal values as human figures were, and lions. Lions, being symbolic and rarely seen by the artists who sculpted them, were usually duds. The ram had been one of two, guarding the port in Syracuse. Goethe had admired the pair of them. The other was destroyed by a cannonball hit in the revolution of 1848.

HEADING NORTH back toward Trapani and Palermo along the road from Marsala, we passed a military airport called Birgi. We were just north of Mozia now, near where the Phoenician road had once joined it to the mainland. All you could see of the airport was a lot of flat grassy ground, a few trees, some asphalted drives joining clusters of green painted military buildings of one or two storeys inside a barbed wire perimeter fence. Pippo remarked that that was where he'd done his military service in the late sixties. Two years' military service was still compulsory for young Italian males. We drove on. Then I whipped around. Had he said Birgi? He had.

... a dark coloured armour-plated Alfa Romeo arrived, with tinted windows. In it were both the Salvo cousins and the Hon. Giulio Andreotti. The car belonged to the Salvos ... I'd often seen one or the other of them using it. I heard Andreotti had come from Trapani, where he'd arrived on a private plane rented by the Salvos ...

This was on page 107 of *The True History of Italy*. Francesco Marino Mannoia had stayed in the garden during the meeting with the mafia bosses after Sicilian regional president Piersanti Mattarella's murder in 1980. *I clearly heard shouting coming from inside*. This was the meeting where Stefano Bontate had shouted at Andreotti, *In Sicily we're in charge and if you don't want to totally wipe out the DC you do what we say*. Andreotti denied ever coming to Sicily by private plane, but others, like a businessman friend who ran an airline called Air Capitol and the Air Capitol pilot both said he often had. A public servant remembered being sent by Lima to pick up Andreotti from such a flight. The Salvos had private planes. Nino Salvo had used one to bring Tommaso Buscetta and his family to Palermo at Christmas that same year, for his last attempt to mediate between the warring Cosa Nostra families, the mediation Buscetta had seen was hopeless. The Caltagirone brothers had a plane too, talked-about businessmen involved in the Italcasse scandal and friends of Andreotti's.

Air traffic was controlled by the military and the civilian offices were out of sight of the landing strip and waiting zone and often the military didn't tell the civilians what was going on. The magistrates found the arrival records were full of errors and omissions, or destroyed. There was no fixed police presence at Birgi. It was easy, if you had friends, to land at the airport and leave unseen and unrecorded. The civilian airport director and two of the air force people who'd kept the records had all been members of those strange masonic lodges in Trapani that Saverio Montalbano, the police officer who was disciplined and transferred for being too effective an antimafia investigator, had been looking into, mafia lodges. The Salvos were powerful people in Trapani, and Andreotti had been Italy's defence minister for years and years. He had a little influence in the defence area.

It was like the secret kiss in 1987. *How*, Andreotti's defence had asked, *could Andreotti elude his own minders?*

Senator Andreotti is under escort twenty-four hours a day by a carabinieri patrol and a permanent police guard is stationed on the landing of his apartment building ... One or two members of his escort follow him outside Rome, including overseas. And moreover, wherever he goes Senator Andreotti, whether in government or not, is greeted and escorted by local security authorities, often double, both carabinieri and police ...

This was on page 185 of *The True History*. The defence demanded that the records be examined. They were. After wading through a sea of documents from carabinieri and police, the magistrates found that until 1982, Andreotti's chief minders had been unsupervised and free to organize the escort outside Rome as they wished. They didn't have to relay details of Andreotti's movements to their office. The chief minders had always been personally selected by Andreotti himself, and received money and privileges from him. There'd often been last-minute changes in the escort personnel on these trips, when one of Andreotti's preferred men would take the place of a scheduled guard and the change was never recorded. Andreotti had often dismissed his guards and disappeared. They'd never bothered anyway to note who Andreotti met, and many of Andreotti's trips and meetings in and out of Italy had left no trace in the records of his escorts.

When the investigating magistrate had interviewed Andreotti's chief minder from 1974 to 1988, he'd brought along records of Andreotti's trips to Sicily in the period of the alleged secret meetings with Cosa Nostra. *Realizing they'd be needed, he'd prepared them himself.* Pressed by the magistrates, however, he'd then admitted that he hadn't done all of them. For Andreotti's Sicilian visits in question he'd been given records ready made up by Andreotti's other chief minder. The magistrates confronted the two minders together. The second broke down, and begging for understanding, admitted he'd in turn been given the records by Andreotti's secretary. It was to refresh the memory of the other minders in case they'd remembered differently. Andreotti had done a similar thing in the Pecorelli murder inquiry. He'd tried through a go-between to *refresh the memory* of a crucial witness, *reminding* him that he'd had certain cheques from others, not from Andreotti. The green airport under the grey sky was silent and deserted now. There was no movement, there were no planes. It was sitting on its secrets.

───────

A LIFE-OR-DEATH situation. A medical emergency. A fit, a seizure, a crisis of some kind inside the justice building. In the stifling heat of Palermo in the dog days, at the height of the Sicilian summer, public offices have skeleton staffs and everyone else is by the sea. Ferragosto is the still point of the Italian year. Everything stopped, everything collapses in the middle of August under the weight of the summer. Palermo's nearness to the Sahara makes itself felt and ferragosto was not a moment of maximum concentration. *Someone would be taken ill. Someone else would call an ambulance.* Roberto Scarpinato was inside the Palermo justice building in the summer of 1995. He was one of the few in Palermo with things on their mind in the middle of last August. Things other than sun and sea and lunch. Scarpinato was putting together the last of the hundred thousand pages that made up the criminal indictment of life senator Giulio Andreotti, the final additions to *The True History of Italy*. The trial was five weeks off.

The steel gates would open. The sweating soldiers with machine guns would wave the ambulance in. The ambulance would get as close as possible to Scarpinato's office. Room 50 on the second floor. Roberto Scarpinato was forty-four years old, the youngest of the three *pubblici ministeri.* Andreotti's prosecutors. He'd be presenting the case against Andreotti with Gioacchino Natoli and Guido Lo Forte. For three years they'd worked to assemble it with the the Palermo chief prosecutor Gian Carlo Caselli, who was now the leader of Italy's judicial war on Cosa Nostra. For years Scarpinato had made a particular study of the mafia's relations with the world of politics and had been called the ideologue of the prosecution team.

The ambulance would be packed with plastic explosive It would be detonated by remote control. It would take out Caselli and Scarpinato. It was Cosa Nostra's planned answer to Caselli, worked out by Riina's brother-in-law and successor, the Corleonese Leoluca Bagarella. The Cupola thought Scarpinato was *too aggressive.* It was headed off when word of the planned massacre came through the pentiti. The ambulance never arrived and the plastic explosive was never detonated. The Andreotti trial started on schedule. A couple of weeks into the trial, just before the decision was announced on whether it would continue in Palermo, I visited Scarpinato in his crowded little Room No 50 in the justice building, hemmed in by industrial-size computers and photocopiers and filing cabinets, files and folders heaped everywhere. Even before he spoke, Scarpinato's crumpled mop of already-grey curls and the pouchy, seen-it-all eyes told you a lot. Unlike the silver-haired Caselli, with his impeccable dress and slender whipcord figure, who manages to play football surrounded by guards, the chain-smoking Scarpinato had a heavy, sedentary, and deeply melancholy air about him. The justice building itself in Palermo looked like a central

American seat of government. A blinding ash grey monolith, set well back from the palm trees of the piazza, a disposition that demonstrated acute strategic foresight on the part of its fascist-period architects, and ringed by a massive steel fence about three metres high. Peering through the black rectangular bars, you could see, beyond the parked cars, the tiny figures of soldiers in camouflage and berets. They stood with machine guns ready and legs wide apart, like toy figures planted on the waste of dazzling steps.

On the wall of Room No 50 was a framed enlargement of the much-reproduced and ever affecting black-and-white news photo of Falcone and Borsellino sharing a joke. Under the photo was the caption *TO MAKE THAT SMILE LIVE FOREVER*. Scarpinato, like the other magistrates in the Palermo pool, worked for years with Falcone and Borsellino. He's a Sicilian from Caltanisetta, where Totò Riina was even then on trial for the murder of Falcone, and a magistrate by family tradition as well as personal conviction, what Italians called a son of art. In the fifties, Scarpinato's father was the judge who sent don Giuseppe Genco Russo, the boss of bosses of that time, chairman of the board at the transatlantic conference in the sala Wagner of the hotel Delle Palme in 1957 and genial host at the Spanò fish dinner, the successor to don Calò Vizzini, to internal exile. Moving a mafia boss out of his home territory was the ultimate sanction in those days, and did a lot to help Cosa Nostra extend its activities to other parts of Italy.

When the Andreotti trial resumed a couple of days later, Scarpinato and I happened to arrive outside the bunker at the same instant. Two bullet-proofed Alfas screamed down from the opposite end of the driveway, very fast and a few inches apart. They stopped abruptly, still a few inches apart, skidding on gravel and dust. Three doors of the second car flew open before it had even stopped and there were three unshaven crouching figures in vests pointing these giant pistols at me. Holding them in both hands. It was a make my day situation. Scarpinato slouched out of the first car and shambled toward the lawyers' steel door with his bursting old leather briefcase of documents and he didn't even look up. He'd been living like that for years. It had been a couple of years ago, he told me, while he was gathering evidence on Andreotti, that a telecom technician had visited Scarpinato's apartment block in Palermo and left behind a little telecom toolbag. The man was noticed, however. Checks were made, and there turned out to be no such telecom technician. And the little technical toolkit, checked just in time, turned out not to contain tools. Such were the uses of a bodyguard. Scarpinato was protected around the clock by a team of eight men. It was striking that even inside the bunker courtroom, where everyone present had passed these endless checks, documentary, physical, electronic, Scarpinato was shadowed at every step by two or three bodyguards. He was the member of the prosecution group *held to be most at risk*.

The afternoon our arrivals coincided at the bunker, everyone was a little jumpy. The minister for the interior had just confirmed that there were indeed good reasons for believing that Brusca's strik group had missiles and a military missile launcher. The Ucciardone bunker courtroom and the justice building were held to be the most likely targets, for fairly obvious reasons. Scarpinato himself was a lot less alarmed about the physical danger than the political dangers magistrates in Italy were then facing. The pursuit of justice in Italy had always been subject to grave political interference, until the collapse of the old regime in Italy in 1992 had let magistrates work unhampered for three years on Italy's massive and institutionalized illegalities. Antonio Di Pietro's corruption investigations in Milan had made him the national hero of a country that still seemed alarmingly eager to find heroes and scapegoats. The fall of the old order and shock at the murders of Falcone and Borsellino had given a similar impetus to the Palermo magistrates who were fighting the crimes of the mafia. For three years the magistrates of both cities had felt the surge of consensus behind them as they'd probed into the dark areas of Italy's recent past.

As they worked, said Scarpinato, magistrates in both cities had become aware that they were looking at what he described as *systemic criminality*, based on the mafia in the south and corruption in the north, something so deeply rooted in the society and so widespread that the judicial system couldn't cope with it, couldn't *metabolize* it, in another Scarpinato phrase. And as they'd moved further into the grey areas of complicity, the magistrates of Milan and Palermo found consensus drained away. *Outlaw Italy* was a pyramid. At the apex were those who ordered the murder of the state's representatives and at its base were sleazebag businessmen, corrupt local politicians, tax evaders and bylaw breakers. The problem was political, and the solution could only be political. For the northern crimes of bribery and corruption some form of amnesty might have been eventually conceivable. *But for the killers of Cosa Nostra there can be no armistice.* Palermo was the ultimate goal of those who were determined to stop the reform process, and it wasn't negotiable. In Palermo there could be no compromise. Scarpinato pointed out that *Cosa Nostra has been part of a wider criminal system that has written some of the most bloody and tragic pages in the history of our country*. Ten thousand deaths between 1983 and 1993. You lost track.

He was also talking about a string of aborted coups d'état, about the activities of the secret P2 lodge and the deviant secret services, about the connections of both of these with right-wing terrorism, left-wing terrorism, organized crime and the Vatican. Palermo, said Scarpinato, perhaps unconsciously echoing Leonardo Sciascia, was an extreme metaphor for Italy. If the Palermo magistrates were ever to piece together the whole picture of Cosa Nostra's activities, the consequences for Italy would be felt far outside the confines of the legal system. Which was why the magistrates working on the Andreotti case felt so exposed to hidden dangers. And yet, he insisted, the fate of democracy in Italy depended on the outcome of their work. *A democracy that left killers and mass murderers unpunished would be a democracy without truth or justice, a deformed democracy condemned sooner or later to relive its terrible past.*

The magistrates had been attacked for years, even by Sciascia, for being careless of human rights in their paper storms of arrest warrants. Scarpinato insisted he didn't mean the law should limit the human rights of mafiosi, but that it should recognize the difference between kinds of crime. *You can't fight an organization responsible for systematic massacres with a law designed to punish housebreaking and crimes of passion.* Crimes of passion was a nice Sicilian touch, I thought. *It's like trying to perform microsurgery on the brain with the instruments used for appendicitis,* he offered instead. *You need lasers, not forceps. Or the patient dies.* The example he gave me was this. The Italian government had abolished the legal sanction of prison that would oblige a person to give evidence in court against the mafia. The sanction, along with witness protection measures, was absolutely necessary, Scarpinato said. *A witness against the mafia is not an ordinary witness. A witness against the mafia is under sentence of death for the rest of his life.* Another issue was the limit on the length of time an accused criminal could be held in prison before conviction. This was a real guarantee of individual rights, and not a principle Italian justice should forgo, but the scrupulousness of the procedure in principle and its susceptibility to manipulation in fact had made the time limit on preventive custody a prime escape route for the mafia. Years of brave and meticulous investigation had been annulled on this ground, and professional killers freed. It had become a cavil much used by the egregious Corrado Carnevale, the supreme court judge now suspended and under investigation for his own ties to the mafia.

Scarpinato made it clear from the start that he wouldn't talk about the trial under way or about politics. He was equally reticent about his private life, and given the portentousness of what we touched on, I didn't press him. I wanted, though, to know what it was like, practically and intimately, to live such a public and such a lonely life, victim designate of a criminal organization of unprecedented power and cruelty, more a prisoner than anyone he convicted, as the old order regrouped and the tide of public solidarity receded. A woman friend told me he was separated from his magistrate wife, that he now lived alone, when not travelling the world in search of evidence, in a flat with an empty fridge *and without any trace of a woman*. He reads vastly, she told me, literature of all kinds, listens endlessly to music and when he gets the time he writes. What does he write, I wanted to know. *His thoughts. His thoughts about life.*

If you pressed Scarpinato too hard, if you spoke too tendentiously about the situation the Palermo magistrates were in, he snapped back with a flash of professional pride. He reminded you that organized crime had become an wholly international phenomenon and that it had become imbedded in the political life of a number of other countries beside Italy. He refused to name them. He said Italian magistrates had developed techniques of investigation whose sophistication and effectiveness were unmatched elsewhere. Warming up, he mentioned France. He noted how every inquiry into signs of major corruption and institutionalized criminality in France had been promptly stifled. He mentioned eastern Europe and Cosa Nostra's other international links. He spoke of the incredible rapidity with which criminal money could be passed thorough the international banking system. *We have to wait months for approval to examine a single bank account.* He added that one longstanding proposal had been the establishment of a central financial data bank which would have recorded every banking transaction in Italy the moment it was made. It was perfectly feasible. It would've been an amazing help. It had never been approved.

WEEKS LATER I went back to the Palermo justice building to speak with Gian Carlo Caselli. The long summer had suddenly broken and turned to winter overnight. Snow dusted the spiky peaks around Palermo, the sky was streaked and livid and gusts of rain swept the desolate space before the justice building as daylight faded. Two days earlier, the leading Italian newsweekly had announced *fear had come back to Palermo. A major terror attack was imminent. Probably with heat-seeking missiles.* They were talking about Giovanni Brusca and his missile launcher again. Brusca had had some narrow escapes, but he'd always got away and taken his missile launcher with him. In one villa the police squad had burst in to find Brusca just gone and an open copy of Giovanni Falcone's book on Cosa Nostra by the bed.

A group of armed soldiers nervously circled me at the gates, eyeing my bag, and the police officer in charge insultingly described me to his subordinates as *this person* while they checked me out. A morose functionary was waiting by the electronic controls. He led me across the dark, immense and now deserted marble hall to the lift. Outside Caselli's office, a dozen piratical bodyguards lounging on pews stiffened like rottweilers at our approach. The door to Caselli's antechamber, under its wood veneer, was like a bank vault's. Caselli was from Turin and earlier was deeply involved in the suppression of BR terrorism in Italy. When he'd applied for transfer to Palermo three years ago, this possibly suicidal move was decided by a sense of duty. He was taking up the baton of his murdered colleagues and friends Falcone and Borsellino. It'd been Caselli who'd led the magistrates for Falcone in January 1988, with his passionate championing before the vote that denied Falcone the chief investigator's post in Palermo. It had been Falcone's cruellest defeat, at the hands of his own jealous and obscurely motivated colleagues. Caselli arrived to work in Palermo some months later, on the fifteenth of January 1993. *It was a momentous day*, they joked in the prosecutor's office Caselli now headed, because that same day police seized Totò Riina. Since then Caselli had been living, as he'd known before coming south, under constant threat of assassination, probably never more in danger than at the time of the Andreotti trial's opening. Like the others, he'd serenely renounced personal freedom and family life, *to do what one can*. It was a choice they'd all willingly made. It was the paradox of Italy that this gravely compromised state, in the murky interregnum of jostling forces between the first republic and whatever might follow, still produced intellectuals who readily accepted to die for it. It wasn't a choice any peacetime Australian had yet been asked to make.

With Caselli was the dapper Guido Lo Forte in an off-duty jumper. If Scarpinato was the world weary bohemian of the Andreotti prosecution, Lo Forte had the air of a clever and amiable seminarian. I'd last seen him swathed in a black gown with ruff and tassels, leading the case against Andreotti and bearing with infinite courtesy the endless quibbles and interruptions of the defence. *Do you realize the first objection came twenty seconds into the prosecution case?* he asked me now. Lo Forte's imperturbable mask had momentarily slipped at the end of that wearing day in the bunker when a radio reporter's mike picked up a string of ripe

Sicilian obscenities muttered to Scarpinato and Natoli. *He wasn't going to take it up the fucking ass any fucking longer*, had been the appproximate sense. And at the next hearing the prosecution had startled the court by choosing silence, leaving unfinished its outline of the case that Andreotti was in effect a Cosa Nostra member. *The interruptions made it impossible to demonstrate the logic of the evidence*, Lo Forte said. Caselli grimly insisted it was *not a polemical move, it was a purely technical matter*, even when I remarked that it was without precedent in Italian legal history.

Caselli's reaction, he told me, to the menace of a ministerial inspection of the Palermo office, which was the just-announced political threat then hanging over them, had been *surprise and curiosity. We have absolutely no idea what the reasons might be.* Caselli was utterly reticent about the political climate in which the trial was opening, a trial he insisted repeatedly and publicly was not itself political. *The purpose of the trial is to ascertain the facts, irrespective of the importance of those involved. The trial is not political. It is not a vendetta and it is not a beatification.* Nobody, I noticed, was mentioning Andreotti except myself. I felt doltish and indiscreet. It was hard, though, to resist observing that the very fact Caselli felt it necessary to reaffirm so often the basic principles of civil law had itself a certain political point. Coming down from Piedmont, Caselli had been conscious of entering a culture whose subtleties were often hard to grasp, and that he couldn't hope to emulate Falcone's inwardness with the shades of the mafia mindset. But a great complementarity had evolved, Lo Forte put in now, with the Sicilian magistrates, an outsider-insider synergy of organization and psychology that had led to the arrest and trial since Caselli's arrival of hundreds of mafiosi at all levels of the Cosa Nostra hierarchy.

With a sudden hooked smile, Lo Forte remarked that *Sicily was often too complicated even for Sicilians to understand*, and didn't seem particularly perturbed by the thought. He added, as if something big had hit him as we lounged on these low soft chairs behind armoured doors, that *it's as though in Sicily there were so many different truths* ... He was Sicilian himself, and his sharp, beaming, seminarian's glint showed that this was a joke. The northerner Caselli shifted in his chair and his eyes flashed signals. Caselli showed no taste for metaphysical web spinning. Maybe he was wondering what it had to do with the matter in hand. Everyone became serious, though, when Lo Forte spoke of Sciascia's corrosive Sicilian scepticism, that fatalism that had led him to attack Borsellino, Orlando and by implication Falcone as antimafia careerists eight years earlier. Lo Forte repeated more thoughtfully now that *the difficulty is to find one truth when there are so many and maybe none.* He started to talk about Borges and I'd have liked to pursue this, but Caselli had clearly had enough of literary criticism. Scepticism laid traps in Sicily. Caselli added though that he gave his children Sciascia's books to read, *so they'd understand.*

When I mentioned Scarpinato's remarks on the international activities of the mafia, Caselli leaned forward in his chair. *The mafia*, he said, speaking slowly and weighting his words, *Cosa Nostra, the Sicilian mafia.*

It kills in Palermo. It invests in Milan. In Frankfurt. In London. New York. Maybe in Sydney. Cosa Nostra is a machine for producing power and money. Wherever and however it can. It would be a disaster to think of the mafia as just a Sicilian problem, or even as just an Italian problem. The immense wealth of Cosa Nostra is ever more massively present in the economy. Polluting legitimate interests. Nationally and internationally. Cosa Nostra's historical roots are in Sicily, the heart and the brain probably still are. But its activities and interests are now entrenched in the world economy. It's because the economic stakes are so high that the mafia inevitably contaminates politics. Where the mafia is, human rights, freedom, democracy are in danger.

Outside it was already dark as I trailed across the rain puddles. I remembered what Sciascia had said. *Sicily is a metaphor for the modern world.* A soldier barked at me to use the other gate. And unlike the magistrates I'd left inside, I was free to go where I wished.

A FEW nights later, not long before I left Palermo, I invited Letizia and Shobha to dinner at the Sant'Andrea, where they'd never been. We met in the lobby of the Delle Palme, waiting for a German writer, a woman who'd been with Shobha to Corleone, to do a joint piece for the German *Playboy*. At the Sant'Andrea Saverio Montalbano joined us, now a deputy police chief of Palermo, the man who'd discovered the biggest heroin refinery in Europe and been demoted for probing into Trapani's mafia lodges. I was curious to meet the intrepid police officer, and looked out eagerly when the Alfa driven by his bodyguard screeched into the tiny piazza. He was welcomed by a kick in the shins, but it was just Anna Maria trying to keep out Miele, the abandoned Persian cat who'd adopted the Sant'Andrea and taken to sinking his claws into the soft thighs of women diners when he wanted their fish. I'd vaguely had the younger Al Pacino in mind, Serpico in a leather jacket, but Saverio Montalbano turned out to be a very slight, balding intellectual-looking man with a mild and refined manner.

Shobha tossed her golden mane and recounted how they'd seen a little bent old black-clad widow that day in the Corleone supermarket, wearing a solid gold Rolex studded with diamonds. She said she'd photographed some gipsy children in the cemetery, dancing naked on Luciano Liggio's grave. *They had no pants on?* asked Letizia, rather shocked. *Just underpants*, said Shobha. A man came up from another table and told Letizia how much he admired her. Petra the German and I talked about how hard it was to make the mafia intelligible, how much you needed to know and how little you could say. I told Letizia that Naples was dying and she said she wanted to come to Australia. I thought maybe she could hold that exhibition. She wanted to take photos there. *Not in the cities. I want to go to the more remote parts.* Saverio Montalbano was talking about his small boys. *They respect me, you know*, he was saying with emphasis. *My kids respect me.*

Letizia's talk about coming to Australia reminded me that Roberto Scarpinato had told me he'd been to Sydney once, in the eighties. He'd gone there with Falcone, when they were looking into Cosa Nostra's investments. *What had he found there?* I'd asked. Scarpinato had given a funny, wild, incredulous little laugh.

Australia was wide open, he'd said.

I hung round the Sant'Andrea after the others left, having a last drink with the Bissos and the kitchen staff. By the time we closed up, and I crossed the deserted piazza in the direction of the hotel, it was already midnight.

IN THE deep sea of Sicily, things go on changing and things go on staying the same. At the end of 1995 I came up for air, though like Cola Pesce I might've stayed underwater forever. The Andreotti mafia trial in Palermo inched forward through 1996. Nearly a year from its opening, three significant witnesses had been heard, the pentiti Tommaso Buscetta, Gaspare Mutolo and the one-time Palermo doctor, man of honour and DC politician Gioacchino Pennino. One of the assisting judges was hurt in a traffic accident early in 1996 and for a moment the trial risked aborting. A string of minor pentiti insisted, though only by hearsay, on Cosa Nostra's reliance on Andreotti as its link with the supreme court judge Corrado Carnevale, who liquidated their convictions, and its fury when this confidence was betrayed in 1992. Appeals in the Andreotti trials would surely take *The True History of Italy* well into the third millenium before we'd know whether the court agreed it was all true, too.

Unlike the Palermo mafia trial, vast in its elaboration of a whole system of political power, the Perugia murder charge against Andreotti and his factotum Vitalone was precisely focused and highly documented, and was moving briskly toward a conclusion. The accused was now seventy-seven and ever more likely to have run his mortal race ere the Palermo judges decided, but a murder rap loomed. Between the start of the mafia trial in Palermo and the start of the murder trial in Perugia, His Holiness Pope John Paul II found time in the Vatican to clasp Andreotti's hands fervently between his own in a photo opportunity the media described as *almost an embrace*. The former prime minister seemed heartened by the Holy Father's attention, but a student challenged the Pope from the pulpit of Saint Peter's over this, and it was the first time a pope had been challenged in his own church in seven hundred years.

The most ominous sign for Andreotti was the conviction in April 1996 of Bruno Contrada as mafioso and his ten-year prison sentence. Contrada was still a figure with very powerful friends, a former head of the Palermo investigative police and later third in charge of one of the Italian secret services, and his conviction after a two-year trial was a major victory for Gian Carlo Caselli and his team in the first political mafia trial. Contrada was always deeply distrusted by Giovanni Falcone, who'd seen him as one of *the highly refined minds* behind the failed bomb attack in 1989. His conviction meant the court and its judge Francesco Ingargiola, the same presiding over the Andreotti trial, accepted the evidence of the mafia pentiti, who among other things testified that Riina owed his long avoidance of capture to Contrada.

The political context too had changed and not changed a year later. In spring the election of a mildly reforming Italian government with a strong popular mandate looked like the real beginning of a bipolar parliamentary system in Italy, and this government's leaders immediately promised an end to political interference in the administration of justice and full support for the antimafia magistrates in Palermo and the anticorruption magistrates in Milan. One of the new ministers was Antonio Di Pietro, the former magistrate who'd set off the political cataclysm in 1992, and one of the government parties the post-communists. Berlusconi, to whom Sicily alone of all the regions had given a majority, was now facing his own corruption charges, while the other leaders of his empire were simultaneously entangled in charges of corrupting the Rome magistracy, and of involvement with the mafia. The Rome justice building, where such strange things had happened to the Pecorelli murder enquiry and the Guttuso adoption enquiry, among countless other cases, was finally under investigation itself.

Cosa Nostra in 1996 had more to worry about than which politicians to back. The arrest of Giovanni Brusca in May left only two leaders of the Corleone group and its allies at large, Pietro Aglieri and Bernardo Provenzano, and it seemed that the long wave of hideous violence might now be nearly over, or at least in abeyance after twenty years. This was not, Gian Carlo Caselli warned in June, a reason for believing Cosa Nostra less active, less powerful, less internationally dangerous, or that other great areas of mafia activity weren't still intact. The international network of organized crime alliances was becoming ever more close-knit.

In 1996 after a decade of inattention, there were Guttuso retrospectives in London and Ferrara. The *New York Review* briefly praised Leonardo Sciascia as the exponent of a *brilliant and haunting* crime fiction in which *what matters is not so much the crime as the danger of knowing anything about it*. Leoluca Orlando was still mayor of Palermo, though sliding in popularity, and Marta Marzotto's instant fashions were moving briskly off the supermarket racks. Letizia Battaglia was seeing a lot of her newest granddaughter and Licio Gelli continued to advise those who were around to listen. Early in the year many magistrates applied for transfer from the stress-wracked Palermo prosecutor's office, but Gian Carlo Caselli, Guido Lo Forte and Roberto Scarpinato kept plugging away. In Palermo the Sant'Andrea was crowded every night.

SOME PLAYERS

AMBROSOLI Giorgio: Milan lawyer, appointed by Italian government to oversee liquidation of Banca Privata Italiana: murdered July 1979

ANDREOTTI Giulio: DC politician & life senator: first entered Italian government in 1947, twenty times minister & seven times prime minister until 1992: on trial for mafia & Pecorelli murder

BADALAMENTI Gaetano: Palermo mafia boss, expelled from Cupola early in Riina's rise to power & escaped to Brazil in 1979: in prison in US since 1987

BONTATE Stefano: Palermo mafia boss & member of Cupola from 1970: leading opponent of Riina's rise to power: killed April 1981

BORSELLINO Paolo: magistrate in Palermo prosecutor's office, leading member of antimafia pool in 1980s & close colleague of Giovanni Falcone: deputy chief prosecutor in Palermo from 1991: killed July 1992

BUSCETTA Tommaso [Masino]: leading mafioso of Palermo group defeated by Riina & Corleonesi: arrested in Brazil 1983: decided to collaborate with Falcone 1984 after murder of most of his family: most important mafioso pentito

CALO` Pippo: mafia boss, ally of Riina, the Cupola's financial expert: based in Rome for many years: arrested March 1985, convicted in maxitrial & still in prison: witness at Andreotti murder trial

CAPONNETTO Antonino: Florentine magistrate, became Palermo chief prosecutor after murder of Rocco Chinnici in 1983: created Palermo antimafia pool, enabling the maxitrial of 1985: retired 1987

CARNEVALE Corrado: Sicilian supreme court judge: overturned many mafia convictions on technicalities: suspended & under investigation for mafia links

CASELLI Gian Carlo: from Torino, in Palermo as chief prosecutor since January 1993: close friend & colleague of Falcone

CHINNICI Rocco: Palermo chief prosecutor after 1979: campaigned against mafia's cultural prestige in Sicily, initiated major investigations into drug traffic, indicted Cupola for Dalla Chiesa murder: killed July 1983

CRAXI Bettino: former socialist party leader, prime minister 1983 - 1987, now facing twenty-four years' imprisonment for corruption: in Tunisia

CUTOLO Raffaele: Naples camorrista, founder & head of Nuova Camorra Organizzata, in prison for many decades, mediated release of kidnapped DC politician Ciro Cirillo in 1981

DALLA CHIESA Carlo Alberto: carabinieri general: served twice in Sicily, defeated leftwing terrorism in seventies: made prefect of Palermo: killed with wife September 1982

DI MAGGIO Baldassare [Baldo]: mafioso pentito, former member of Brusca family & driver to Totò Riina: enabled police to arrest Riina & claims to have witnessed 1987 kiss between Riina & Andreotti

FALCONE Giovanni: leading Palermo antimafia magistrate, prepared maxi-trial indictment in 1985, transferred to Rome justice ministry 1991, killed in May 1992 with wife & three of escort

GAVA Antonio: Naples DC politician, minister of interior in eighties: convicted of corruption 1996: on trial as camorrista 1995-6

GELLI Licio: presumed head of secret P2 lodge uncovered in 1981: financier & influence peddler: convicted of rightwing terrorism 1996: linked to mafia & Vatican

LIGGIO Luciano: former estate guard from Corleone, murdered predecessor in 1953 to become head of Corleone mafia clan & later head of Cosa Nostra & mentor of Salvatore Riina: arrested 1974, died in prison

LIMA Salvo: Palermo DC politician & member of Cosa Nostra, successively mayor of Palermo, government minister, member of European parliament: head of Andreotti faction of DC in Sicily: killed March 1992

LUCIANO Lucky: born Salvatore Lucania at Lercara Friddi in Sicily, emigrated to US in 1919, head of US Cosa Nostra in thirties & forties, thought to have assisted allied invasion of Sicily 1943, freed & repatriated to Italy 1946: died Naples 1962

MORO Aldo: DC politician from Bari: prime minister: ideologue of understanding with PCI: kidnapped & murdered by Red Brigades 1978

PECORELLI Mino: journalist, former member of Italian secret services, owner & writer of Rome political newletter OP: murdered March 1979

RIINA Salvatore [Totò]: head of Corleone mafia clan since mid-seventies & head of Cosa Nostra from early eighties: operated in hiding in Palermo from 1969 until arrest in January 1993: now serving various life sentences

SALVO Ignazio: wealthy Sicilian businessman & DC politician: arrested as mafioso November 1984: convicted in maxitrial: killed September 1992

SALVO Nino: wealthy Sicilian businessman & DC politician, cousin & partner of Ignazio Salvo: arrested as mafioso November 1984: died of brain tumour 1986

SINDONA Michele: Sicilian banker, financier, mafioso: poisoned 1986

TERRANOVA Cesare: Sicilian magistrate, prosecutor of mafia in seventies: after serving in Italian parliament returned to Palermo as chief prosecutor: killed September 1979

VITALONE Claudio: former Rome magistrate, member of Andreotti entourage, DC senator & minister: on trial in Perugia with Andreotti, accused of organizing Mino Pecorelli murder for Andreotti

VIZZINI Calogero: mafia boss of Villalba, boss of bosses of Sicilian mafia at time of allied invasion in 1943: made honorary colonel in US army: died 1952.

SOURCES

THE RAW documents are in Italian and are the most enthralling of all. In published form there are Caselli et al. *La Vera Storia d'Italia*, for the Andreotti trial, and Falcone et al. [ed. Stajano], *Mafia*, for the *mafia* maxitrial, and the parliamentary reports in Commissione parlamentare antimafia, *Mafia e politica* and Commissione parlamentare antimafia, *Camorra e politica*, and in Tranfaglia [ed.], *Mafia, politica e affari 1943 - 1991*.

Three indispensable books, however, are in English. Paul Ginsborg's *A History of Contemporary Italy. Politics and Society 1943 - 1988* is a lucid synthesis of the social and political context of the crimes discussed here, sparely and movingly written. Alexander Stille's *Excellent Cadavers. The Mafia and the Death of the First Italian Republic* for the first time makes intelligible the nightmare complexity of mafia history and antimafia history over the last twenty years: It recounts meticulously Falcone's and Borsellino's process of discovery of Cosa Nostra and its history, dealing rather less fully with the political relationship that began to come to light after their murders. The late Claire Sterling's *Octopus*, aka *The Mafia*, is now like Ginsborg's *History* slightly out of date in its information and also slightly heightened in its colour but formidably accurate and detailed, particularly useful on the American connection, and unputdownable.

Leonardo Sciascia's books come and go in English. *The Day of the Owl* and *Equal Danger* [*Il Giorno della Civetta* and *Il Contesto*] were published together by Paladin [HarperCollins] in 1987 but seem to be out of print. *The Moro Affair* and *One Way or Another* [*L'Affaire Moro* and *Todo Modo*] were published by Carcanet in the UK in 1987 and may be still around.

Ada Boni's *Talismano della Felicità* is the indispensable Italian cook book and Elizabeth David warns against denatured English versions of it. Her own *Italian Food* remains a necessary document of the anglo experience of Italian eating and a book you'd want, anyway, to read.

Otherwise I've scavenged freely, using the books below, as Montaigne says somewhere, not to form my ideas but to prop up the opinions I'd already formed.

Aa. vv., *Renato Guttuso dagli esordi al Gott mit uns 1924 - 1944,* Palermo 1987
Abulafia, David, *Frederick II. A Medieval Emperor* [1988], London 1992

Andreotti, Giulio, *Cosa Loro. Mai visti da vicino*, Milano 1995

Arlacchi, Pino, *Il processo*, Milano 1995

Arlacchi, Pino, *La mafia imprenditrice. L'etica mafiosa e lo spirito del capitalismo*, Bologna 1983

Arlacchi, Pino, *Gli uomini del disonore. La mafia siciliana nella vita del grande pentito Antonino Calderone*, Milano 1992

Barthes, Roland, *Wilhelm von Gloeden*, Napoli 1978

Barzini, Luigi, *From Caesar to the Mafia*, London 1971

Barzini, Luigi, *The Italians*, London 1964

Bassani, Giorgio, *Il Romanzo di Ferrara*, Milano 1981

Benton, Barbara, *Ellis Island*, New York 1985

Biagi, Enzo, *Il boss è solo*, Milano 1986

Boardman, John et al., *The Oxford History of the Classical World*, Oxford 1986

Bocca, Giorgio, *L'Inferno. Profondo sud, male oscuro*, Milano 1992

Bolzoni, Attilio & D'Avanzo, Giuseppe, *La giustizia è cosa nostra. Il caso Carnevale tra delitti e impunità*, Milano 1995

Boni, Ada, *Il talismano della felicità* [c. 1932], Roma 1995

Borges, Jorge Luis, *Ficciones* [1956], London 1993

Borges, Jorge Luis, *Tutte le opere* [vol.I], Milano 1984

Borsellino, Paolo [ed. Cimino. Marta & D'Onofrio, Gettina], *...sai, Lucia*, Palermo 1994

Braudel, Fernand, *The Mediterranean and the Mediterranean World in the Age of Philip II* [1949, 1966], London, 1972

Bufalino, Gesualdo & Zago, Nunzio [eds], *Cento Sicilie. Testimonianze per un ritratto*, Firenze 1993

Buongiorno, Pino, *Totò Riina. La sua storia*, Milano 1993

Caldarola, Giuseppe [ed.], *Autobiografia di Cosa Nostra*, Roma 1994

Calvesi, Maurizio & Lo Cascio, Dora Favatella, *Museo Guttuso*, Palermo 1991

Calvi, Fabrizio, *La vita quotidiana della mafia dal 1950 a oggi*, Milano 1986

Calvino, Italo, *Fiabe Italiane* [1956], Torino 1989

Calvino, Italo, *Saggi* [vol. I], Milano 1995

Caselli, Gian Carlo et al., "La giustizia e i suoi nemici", *MicroMega* 4/95

Caselli, Gian Carlo et al., *La Vera Storia d'Italia*, Napoli 1995

Cavallero, Felice [ed.], *Mafia. Album di cosa nostra*, Milano 1992

Chroniques siciliennes. Photographies de Letizia Battaglia et Franco Zecchin, Paris 1989

Cipri, Daniele & Maresco, Franco, *Lo Zio di Brooklyn*, Milano 1995

Coletti, Alessandro, *Mafie. Storia della criminalità organizzata nel Mezzogiorno*, Torino 1995

Commissione parlamentare antimafia, *Camorra e politica. Relazione approvata dalla Commissione il 21 dicembre 1993*, Roma & Bari 1994

Commissione parlamentare antimafia, *Mafia e politica. Relazione del 6 aprile 1993*, Roma & Bari 1993

Cornwell, Rupert, *God's Banker. An Account of the Life and Death of Roberto Calvi*, London 1983

Corrao, Francesca Maria [ed.], *Poeti Arabi di Sicilia*, Milano 1987

Cortelazzo, Manlio & Zolli, Paolo, *Dizionario etimologico della lingua italiana* [5 vols], Bologna 1979 - 1988

Costantini, Costanzo, *Ritratto di Renato Guttuso*, Roma 1985

Costantini, Costanzo, *Il caso Guttuso tra scandalo e mistero*, Roma 1987

Craft, Robert, *Stravinsky. Chronicle of a Friendship. Revised & Expanded Edition*, Nashville & London 1994

Croce, Benedetto, *Storie e leggende napoletane* [1919], Milano 1990

Dalla Chiesa, Nando, *Delitto imperfetto*. Milano 1984

Dalla Chiesa, Nando, *Il giudice ragazzino. Storia di Rosario Livatino assassinato dalla mafia sotto il regime della corruzione*, Torino 1992

Dalla Chiesa, Nando, *Storie di boss ministri tribunali giornali intellettuali cittadini*, Torino 1990

David, Elizabeth, *Italian Food* [1954], rev. ed., London 1989

David, Elizabeth, *Harvest of the Cold Months. The Social History of Ice and Ices*, London 1995

Deaglio, Enrico, *Raccolto Rosso*, Milano 1993

De Filippo, Eduardo, *Cantata dei giorni dispari* [vol. III], Torino 1995

Di Lello, Giuseppe, *Giudici. Cinquant'anni di processi di mafia*, Palermo 1994

Falcone, Giovanni & Padovani, Marcelle, *Cose di Cosa Nostra* , Milano 1991

Falcone, Giovanni et al. [ed. Stajano, Corrado], *Mafia. L'atto di accusa dei giudici di Palermo*, Roma 1992

Fava, Claudio, *Cinque delitti imperfetti. Impastato, Giuliano, Insalaco, Rostagno, Falcone*, Milano 1994

Fernandez, Dominique, *La Zattera della Gorgone. Passeggiate in Sicilia. Fotografie di Ferrante Ferranti*, Palermo 1992

Fiandaca, Giovanni & Costantino, Rosario [eds.], *La mafia, le mafie. Tra vecchi e nuovi paradigmi*, Roma & Bari 1994

Finley, M.I., *Ancient Sicily*, London 1964

Fitzgerald, F. Scott, *The Great Gatsby* [1925] in *The Bodley Head Scott Fitzgerald* [Vol. 1], London 1958

Franchetti, Leopoldo, *Condizioni politiche e amministrative della Sicilia* [1877], Roma 1993

Galasso, Alfredo, *La mafia politica*, Milano 1993

Gambetta, Diego, *La mafia siciliana*, Torino 1992

Gibbon, Edward, *The History of the Decline and Fall of the Roman Empire* [1776 - 1788] [3 vols.], London 1994

Gilmour, David, *The Last Leopard. A life of Giuseppe Tomasi di Lampedusa*, London 1988

Ginsborg, Paul, *A History of Contemporary Italy. Society and politics 1943 - 1988*, London 1990

Goethe, Johann Wolfgang von, *Italian Journey. The Collected Works* [vol. 6] [1816 & 1817], Princeton 1994

Green, Peter, *Alexander to Actium. The Hellenistic Age*, London 1990

Hess, Henner, *Mafia. Le origini e la struttura*, Roma & Bari 1973

Irwin, Robert, *The Arabian Nights. A companion*, London 1994

La Duca, Rosario, *I veleni di Palermo*, Palermo 1988

Lampedusa, Giuseppe Tomasi di, *Il Gattopardo* [1957 Ms, X ed.], Milano 1992

Lampedusa, Giuseppe Tomasi di, *Opere*, Milano 1995

Lewis, Norman, *The Honoured Society* [1964], London, 1984

Lewis, Norman, *Naples '44* [1978], New York 1994

Longhi, Roberto, *Caravaggio* [1952, 1968], Roma 1982

Lullies, Reinhard & Hirmer, Max, *Greek Sculpture* [rev. ed.], London 1960

Lupo. Salvatore, *Storia della mafia*, Roma 1993

Maraini, Dacia, *Bagheria*, Milano 1993

Marchese, Pasquale, *L'invenzione della forchetta*, Soveria Mannelli 1989

Minna, Rosario, *La mafia in cassazione*, Firenze 1995

Montaigne, Michel de [ed. Rat, Maurice], *Essais* [1580], Paris 1962

Montale. Eugenio, *Satura. 1962 - 1970*, Milano 1971

Moravia, Alberto, *Renato Guttuso*, Palermo 1962

The New Shorter Oxford English Dictionary [2 vols], Oxford 1993

Orioles, Riccardo et al. [eds.], *30 anni. Mafia e politica 1965 - 1995. I Siciliani* III/28, Catania 1995

Orlando, Leoluca, *Palermo*, Milano 1990

Ovid [tr. Peter Green], *The Erotic Poems*, Harmondsworth 1982

The Oxford English Dictionary [Compact Edition, 2 vols], Oxford 1971

Pasolini, Pier Paolo, *Lettere Luterane*, Torino 1976

Pasolini, Pier Paolo, *Scritti Corsari*, Milano 1975

Patroni Griffi, Giuseppe, *Scende giù per Toledo*, Milano 1981

Penny, Nicholas, *The Materials of Sculpture*, New Haven & London 1993

Petronius [tr. Branham, Bracht & Kinney, Daniel], *Satyrica*, Berkeley 1996

Pezzino, Paolo, *Mafia: industria della violenza. Scritti e documenti inediti sulla mafia dalle origini ai giorni nostri*, Firenze 1995

Polo, Marco [ed. Pizzorusso, Valeria Bertolucci]: *Milione. Versione toscana del trecento* [1975], Milano 1982

Putnam, Robert D., *Making Democracy Work. Civic Traditions in Modern Italy*, Princeton 1993

Ramondino, Fabrizia, *Althénopis*, Torino 1981

Ramondino, Fabrizia & Müller Andreas Friedrich, *Dadapolis. Caleidoscopio napoletano*. Torino 1989

Rea, Ermanno, *Mistero napoletano. Vita e passione di una comunista negli anni della guerra fredda*, Torino 1995

Renda, Francesco, *Storia della Sicilia dal 1860 al 1970* [3 vols], Palermo 1984 - 1987

La Repubblica [ed. Scalfari, Eugenio], *passim*, Roma, 1975 - 1996

Root, Waverley, *The Food of Italy*, New York 1971

Rossi-Doria, Manlio, *Scritti sul Mezzogiorno*, Torino 1982

Ruggieri Tricoli, Maria Clara, *La Villa Niscemi*, Palermo 1989

Runciman, Steven, *The Sicilian Vespers. A history of the Mediterranean world in the later thirteenth century* [1958], Cambridge 1992

Russo, Enzo, *Uomo di rispetto*, Milano 1988

Sales, Isaia, *La camorra, le camorre* [1988], Roma 1993

Santino, Umberto, *La mafia interpretata. Dilemmi, stereotipi, paradigmi*, Soveria Mannelli 1995

Santino, Umberto, *La borghesia mafiosa*, Palermo 1994

Santino, Umberto & La Fiura, Giovanni, *L'impresa mafiosa*, Milano 1990

Santino, Umberto & La Fiura, Giovanni, *Dietro la droga. Economie di sopravvivenza, imprese criminali, azioni di guerra, progetti di sviluppo*, Torino 1993

Santino, Umberto, *Sicilia 102. Caduti nella lotta contro la mafia e per la democrazia dal 1893 al 1994*, Palermo 1995

Sciascia, Leonardo, *La palma va a nord*, N.P. 1982

Sciascia, Leonardo, *L'affaire Moro*, Palermo 1978

Sciascia, Leonardo & Padovani, Marcelle, *La Sicilia Come Metafora*, Milano 1979

Sciascia, Leonardo, *Opere 1956 - 1971*, Milano 1987

Sciascia, Leonardo, *Opere 1971 - 1983*, Milano 1989

Sciascia, Leonardo, *Opere 1984 - 1989*, Milano 1991

Siciliano, Enzo, *Vita di Pasolini*, Milano 1978

Siebert, Renate, *La mafia, la morte e il ricordo*, Soveria Mannelli 1995

Siebert, Renate, *Le donne, la mafia*, Milano 1994

Stajano, Corrado, *Un eroe borghese. Il caso dell'avvocato Giorgio Ambrosoli assassinato dalla mafia politica*, Torino 1991

Stajano, Corrado, *Africo*, Torino 1979

Stendhal, *Voyages en Italie* [1827 & 1829], Paris 1973

Sterling, Claire, *Octopus. The Long Reach of the International Sicilian Mafia*, New York 1990 [British ed. *The Mafia*, London 1990]

Stille, Alexander, *Excellent Cadavers. The mafia and the death of the first Italian republic*, New York 1995

Stille, Alexander, "The Fall of Caesar", *The New Yorker*, 11 September 1995

Theocritus [tr. Wells, Robert], *The Idylls of Theocritus*, Manchester 1988

Thucydides [tr. Hobbes, Thos.], *The Peloponnesian War* [411 BCE, 1628], Chicago 1989

Touring Club Italiano, *Sicilia* [VI ed.], Milano 1989

Tranfaglia, Nicola [ed.], *Mafia, politica e affari nell'Italia repubblicana*, Roma & Bari 1992

Tranfaglia, Nicola [ed.], *Cirillo, Ligato e Lima. Tre storie di mafia e politica*, Roma & Bari 1994

Vasile, Vincenzo [ed.], *L'affare Cirillo. L'atto di accusa del giudice Carlo Alemi*, Roma 1989

Verdura, Fulco di, *Estati Felici* [1976], Palermo 1994

Vidal, Gore, *United States. Essays 1952 - 1992*, New York 1993

Violante, Luciano, *Non è la piovra. Dodici tesi sulle mafie italiane*, Torino 1994